CU-G

'/p @ £70—   £35—

FINANCE AND MODERNIZATION

Dedicated to Gerald D. Feldman

Finance and Modernization

A Transnational and Transcontinental Perspective for the
Nineteenth and Twentieth Centuries

Edited by
GERALD D. FELDMAN[†] and PETER HERTNER

Co-Edited by
MONIKA POHLE FRASER and IAIN L. FRASER

ASHGATE

Published by
Ashgate Publishing Limited
Wey Court East
Union Road
Farnham
Surrey, GU9 7PT
England

Ashgate Publishing Company
Suite 420
101 Cherry Street
Burlington
VT 05401-4405
USA

www.ashgate.com

British Library Cataloguing in Publication Data
Finance and modernization: a transnational and transcontinental perspective for the 19th and
    20th centuries. – (Studies in banking and financial history)
    1. Banks and banking – Europe – History – 19th century – Congresses 2. Banks and banking
    – Europe – History – 20th century – Congresses 3. Banks and banking – Asia – History – 19th
    century – Congresses 4. Banks and banking – Asia – History – 20th century – Congresses
    I. Feldman, Gerald D. II. Hertner, Peter III. European Association for Banking History
    332.1'094'09034

Library of Congress Cataloging-in-Publication Data
Finance and modernization: a transnational and transcontinental perspective for the 19th and
20th centuries / edited by Gerald D. Feldman and Peter Hertner.
    p. cm. – (Studies in banking and financial history)
    Includes bibliographical references and index.
    ISBN 978-0-7546-6271-6 (alk. paper)
    1. Banks and banking–Europe–History–19th century. 2.Banks and banking–
Europe–History–20th century. 3. Banks and banking–Asia–History–19th century.
4. Banks and banking–Asia–History–20th century. I. Feldman, Gerald D. II.
Hertner, Peter. III. European Association for Banking and Financial History.

HG2974.F563 2008
332.1094'09034–dc22

                                                                    2007044793

ISBN 978-0-7546-6271-6

Printed and bound in Great Britain by
MPG Books Ltd, Bodmin, Cornwall.

Contents

List of Figures

List of Tables

Notes on Contributors

Oskar Broberg is Research Fellow in the Department of Economic History at the School of Business, Economics and Law in Gothenburg, Sweden. His research interests include various aspects of business history during the nineteenth and twentieth centuries. His dissertation dealt with the incorporation process during the Swedish industrial breakthrough and its consequences for the modernization of the financial system. He is currently working on the structural transformation of the Swedish dairy industry in the late twentieth century and the emergence of the organic-farming movement.

Margarita Dritsas is Professor of European Economic and Social History at the School of Humanities, Hellenic Open University, Greece. Her recent publications are *Τράπεζα Εργασίας 1975–2000, Η Τράπεζα με τις Ανοικτές Πόρτες (The Ergasias Bank 1975–2000. 'The Bank with Open Doors'*), Dionikos (Athens, 2006); 'Banking, Politics and Corporate Culture' in *Archives and Corporate Culture*, edited by Gabriele Teichmann and Charlotte Natmeßnig (EABH, Frankfurt, 2006); 'From Travellers' Accounts to Travel Books and Guide Books: The formation of a Greek tourism market in the 19th century', in *Tourismos*, vol. 1, 1, 2006, pp. 27–52; *The Commercial Bank of Greece 1907–2007: A Hundred Years of History* (Athens, 2007).

Peter Eigner is associate professor at the University of Vienna, Department of Economic and Social History. He is the author of articles and books on Austrian economic and social history (eighteenth to twentieth centuries). His main interests lie in the economic (banking and industrial) development of the Habsburg Monarchy and in the urbanization process of Vienna. His publications include (with Franz Eder et al.) *Wien im 20. Jahrhundert. Wirtschaft – Bevölkerung – Konsum* (2003) and *Österreichische Wirtschafts- und Sozialgeschichte im 19. und 20. Jahrhundert* (1999).

Gerald D. Feldman passed away in November 2007. He taught history at the University of California in Berkeley from 1963, where he was the Director of the Institute of European Studies until 2006. Gerald Feldman wrote a history of the Austrian Banks in the National Socialist period, and, in 2001, he published Allianz and the German Insurance Business, 1933–1945 (Munich 2001, English edition Cambridge 2001). Gerald Feldman published widely on German economic history, e.g. the chapter on 'The Deutsche Bank from World War to World Economic Crises 1914–1933', in Lothar Gall, Gerald D. Feldman, Harold James, Carl-Ludwig Holtfrerich, Hans E. Büschgen, Die Deutsche Bank 1870–1995 (Munich 1995, English edition London 1995), and a biography of the German industrialist Hugo Stinnes (Munich 1998). He was actively involved with the EABH e.V. since its foundation, as Chairman of its Academic Advisory Council and Bureau Member.

Peter Hertner is professor emeritus of economic and social history at Martin-Luther-Universität Halle-Wittenberg at Halle (Germany). Before going to Halle he taught at the European University Institute, Florence (Italy) and the Technische Hochschule Darmstadt in Darmstadt (Germany). His current main interests are Italian economic history (nineteenth and twentieth centuries) as well as the history of banking and of multinational companies in Germany and Western Europe, particularly in the electricity sector.

Hartmut Kiehling (Dipl.Kfm. and Dr.rer.pol., both University of Munich) is associate professor of finance at the German University in Cairo, since 2005. He became Vice-Director at Deutsche Bundesbank in 1983 and head of German stock-market research at Bayerische Vereinsbank in 1988. He was Division Manager Investments for Swiss Life Germany (1991) and MBA director of Ingolstadt School of Management (2000). His publications include: *Stock-Market Psychology and Behavioral Finance, Vahlen* (in German, 2001); *Stock-Market Crashes in History*, dtv (in German, 1992, 2nd ed. 2000); 'Nonlinear and Chaotic Dynamics and its Application to Historical Financial Markets', *Historical Social Research* 21 (1996); 'Financial Markets losing their Function during German Hyperinflation 1914–1923' (in German), *Economic History Yearbook 1998/ 1*; 'Efficiency of Early German Stock Market, 1835–1848' (in English), *Economic History Yearbook 2006/ 1*.

Frank H.H. King is professor emeritus in the University of Hong Kong and Distinguished Honorary Fellow in that institution's Centre of Asian Studies. He holds a senior doctorate, D. Litt., from Oxford. A former economist with the World Bank, King also taught economics in the American University (Washington, D.C.), the University of Kansas, Oxford University, and the University of Hong Kong. Among his publications are a four-volume history of *The Hongkong and Shanghai Banking Corporation* (Cambridge, 1987–91), *Money and Monetary Policy in China, 1845–95* (Harvard, 1965), and various studies including essays on corporate culture, the Hong Kong monetary system, the Pekin Syndicate, Sir Robert Hart and the Boxer Indemnity, a biography of Robert Montgomery Martin, and a guide to China-coast newspapers, 1822–1911.

Rainer Liedtke (MA Warwick; D.Phil Oxon) is Privatdozent in Modern History at the University of Gießen and specializes in Comparative European History, the History of Modern Greece and Jewish History. He has recently published *N.M. Rothschild & Sons. Kommunikation im europäischen Bankenwesen des 19. Jahrhunderts*, Köln (Böhlau) 2006.

Abhik Ray B.A. (Hons.), Calcutta University, PGDBM, Deputy General Manager, State Bank of India, History Cell, Kolkata, is a regular contributor of articles on the history of Indian banking and Kolkata's business history. He is the author of *The Evolution of the State Bank of India*, Volume 3, *The Era of the Imperial Bank of India, 1921–1955* (New Delhi, Sage Publications, 2003), and the forthcoming publication *The Evolution of the State Bank of India*, Volume 4, 1955–1980 (Portfolio Penguin).

Ray is also intimately associated with the setting up of India's only banking museum, in Kolkata.

Aurel Schubert holds a Ph.D. in Economics from the University of South Carolina (USA) and a Master's degree in Business Administration from the University of Economics and Business Administration in Vienna. He is Director of Statistics of the Oesterreichische Nationalbank, a member of several Austrian and European statistical bodies, lecturer at the Diplomatic Academy Vienna, at the University of Applied Sciences Wiener Neustadt, the Summer Programme of the University of Vienna, and the Deutsche Vereinigung für Finanzanalyse und Asset Management. His publications include *The Credit-Anstalt Crisis of 1931* (Cambridge University Press), as well as over 30 articles on central banking, monetary policy and monetary history.

Dieter Stiefel (Mag. Dr rer.soc.oec., Dr phil.) studied commercial sciences at the Wirtschaftsuniversität Wien and history at the University of Vienna. From 1973 to 1992 he was University Assistant, then Lecturer, at the Wirtschaftsuniversität Wien, and has since 1993 been University Professor at the Institute for Economic and Social History of the University of Vienna and jointly at its Institute for Economics. He is the author of numerous articles and books on Austrian and international economic, social and political history of the twentieth century.

Alice Teichova is Emeritus Professor of Economic History of the University of East Anglia, Norwich, and Honorary Fellow of Girton College, Cambridge. Her research interests are in economic, social and political history of Central and Eastern Europe in the nineteenth and twentieth centuries. Recently, with Mikuláš Teich, she published *Zwischen der kleinen und grossen Welt - Ein gemeinsames Leben im 20. Jahrhundert* (Vienna-Cologne-Weimar, 2005) and 'Banking and Industry in Central-East Europe in the first decades of the 20th century', in Oliver Rathkolb, Theodor Venus and Ulrike Zimmerl (eds), *150 Jahre österreichische Bankgeschichte im Zentrum Europas* (Vienna, 2005).

Douwe C.J. van der Werf studied economics at the University of Tilburg, the Netherlands, where he obtained his doctorate in 1988. The author's publications in the field of nineteenth- and twentieth-century banking history include *De Bond, de banken en de beurzen (1903–1974)* and *Banken, bankiers en hun fusies* (1998), a volume about the mergers of the four biggest Dutch commercial banks in 1964. The author is researching the development of the Nederlandsche Middenstandsbank (1850–1989), a universal bank. He currently works at ING Group Historical Archives.

Fritz Weber teaches Economic, Social and Cultural History at the University of Commerce, Vienna, and the Universities of Vienna and Salzburg. His most recent publications include (together with D. Stiefel) '*Drei zu Zwei'. Probleme und Folgen der Währungsumstellung Schilling – Reichsmark beim 'Anschluß' 1938*, in: K. Bachinger et al., *Auf Heller und Cent. Beiträge zur Finanz- und Währungsgeschichte*, Wien 2001, and *Große Hoffnungen und k(l)eine Erfolge. Zur Vorgeschichte der österreichischen*

Finanzkrise von 1931, in: O. Rathkolb et al. (eds), *Bank Austria Creditanstalt. 150 Jahre österreichische Bankengeschichte im Zentrum Europas*, Wien 2005. Et al., *Ökonomie der Arisierung*, Wien-München 2004; */Susanne Kirchner (eds), Die ersten zehn Jahre. Der wirtschafts- und gesellschaftspolitische Diskurs in der Besatzungszeit*, Wien 2005.

Introduction

This volume presents the revised papers given at a conference of the European Association for Banking and Financial History in Vienna in May 2005 to celebrate the 150th anniversary of the Österreichische Creditananstalt. It was hosted by the Bank Austria Creditanstalt, which is the successor institution to the Österreichische Creditanstalt. The theme of the conference and of this volume, 'Finance and Modernisation', seemed particularly appropriate for this occasion since it centres on a set of historical developments and problems typified in important ways by the long history of the Österreichische Creditanstalt and its successor organizations but that also opens the way to compare and contrast experiences throughout Central and Western Europe and on other continents.

Since the findings of the conference are summarized and discussed by Alice Teichova at the conclusion of this volume, we will refrain from discussing the papers themselves and limit this introduction to a few general remarks about the general themes that run across the studies presented here.

It is obvious that banks are at the crossroads of capitalist economies. In a very elementary way, they may be said to serve as intermediaries between those who have money to invest and those who are seeking credit for their economic activities. They are also major transmitters of information and seek profit from their knowledge. As economies become industrialized and modernized, banks change their roles. They become bigger because of the size of demand as is reflected in the growth of their customers, and they become more involved in industrial and commercial matters. They also become more diversified and serve a variety of markets. Hence the differing roles and functions of private banks, savings banks, cooperatives, merchant banks and big deposit banks. The banks of Central and Eastern Europe were especially important in the development of universal banks, that is, banks that mixed investment and commercial banking. In fact, in the case of the Creditanstalt, a bank could also serve as an industrial concern, not only providing credit to industrial and commercial enterprises, but actually running enterprises itself. In any case, what the history of the development of financial institutions demonstrates is that it is a story of continuous innovation. Banks adapt to the needs of an industrializing economy but, at the same time, industrialization influences the manner in which banking systems grow and the structures which they adopt.

The structure of this volume has been determined by the above-mentioned interests and priorities. For obvious reasons, we begin with studies of the Austrian banks, their development and their crises. Part II, however, deals with case studies of important aspects of financial activity – German stock markets, railroad investment, and information networks. This is followed by a section on country studies of banking modernization in Sweden, the Netherlands and Greece. Finally, we conclude with two papers, one on banking in China and the other on banking in India, certainly both of intrinsic interest and of importance in a era of globalization. Professor Teichova, one of the great scholars in the field, concludes with reflections on the individual contributions and the general problems addressed in this book.

We wish to express our gratitude to Bank Austria Creditanstalt, Ferdinand Lacina, Bank Austria Creditanstalt staff and European Association for Banking History staff.

Gerald D. Feldman and Peter Hertner

PART I
Banking in Austria and Vienna

'The Bankers' View': Austria's Economic and Political Development and the Role of the Banks

Dieter Stiefel

A main topic in business history is the different view of politicians and businessmen, including bankers. Generally, bankers complain about the irrationality of politics and the limited understanding of economic necessities. But in the last 150 years state influence in Austrian banking was strong and sometimes even dominant. What were the attitudes and the reactions of bankers during this long and eventful period of Austrian history? What was their response to the challenges of prosperity and crisis, to political turmoil and war, to reconstruction, liberalization and globalization? Given the difficulty for a historian to see the world with the eyes of a banker, we have to make some assumptions.

Economic Conditions

A fundamental condition for successful business is the prosperity of the whole economy. This includes rising income, wealth and saving and the participation of the public in the possibilities of the financial market, including the stock market. It also includes investment, credit and the ability of debtors to pay back their loans.

Political Conditions

The other foundation of successful banking is political stability and a reasonable economic policy which not only supports economic activities but understands the logic and necessities of business.

Competitive Status

Finally a banker wants to hold a good position in his market and also in the eyes of his competitors, depending on his goals and strategic planning. This includes innovation, product development and regional expansion.

These three conditions should be the yardstick for Austria's history in the following phases:

- The Period until World War I 1855–1918
- The Interwar Years 1918–1938
- The Time of National Socialism and World War II 1938–1945
- The Reconstruction Period 1945–1955
- The Period from the 1950s to the Present

The Period until World War I (1855–1918)

Economic Conditions

In this first phase, the territory that later became Austria was part of a completely different economic area. The Austrian Empire (Cisleithania) consisted of islands of modernization amidst a sea of underdevelopment. Felix Butschek estimates that a third of the population – notably the territories in the Balkans and Galicia – made almost no contribution to economic growth.[1] The proto-industrial conditions in the territory today occupied by the Austrian Republic and in the then Bohemia were not bad initially, but by mid-century those areas had lost their connection with the leading industrial countries. Only from the *Gründerzeit* (1866–73) onwards did the central territories reach industrial growth rates, which they managed, despite some slumps, to keep until the outbreak of World War I. The motor of economic growth was the construction of railways, but also the emergence of large-scale industry and partly, still, the agricultural sector. Overall, Austria-Hungary of 1913 was largely agricultural, but with important pockets of industrialization (see Tables 1.1 and 1.2).

Table 1.1   GDP per capita, in 1990 international dollars (borderlines of 1990)

	1820	1913
Austria	1,295	3,488
Czechoslovakia	849	2,096
Hungary	—	2,098
Germany	1,112	3,833
UK	1,756	5,032
USA	1,287	5,307

---

1   F. Butschek, *Statistische Reihen zur österreichischen Wirtschaftsgeschichte. Die österreichische Wirtschaft seit der Industriellen Revolution* (Vienna, 1996), p. 1.

Table 1.2   GDP per capita, average annual growth, in 1990 international dollars

	1820–1870	1870–1913
Austria	0.9	2.0
Czechoslovakia	0.7	1.9
Hungary	—	1.5
Germany	1.4	2.3
UK	1.7	1.3
USA	1.8	2.7

Source: A. Maddison, Monitoring the World Economy 1820–1992 (OECD, Paris, 1995), p. 23.

Political Conditions

The political conditions in the Empire were unlikely to meet with a banker's enthusiasm. It is true that there were positive events, such as the reforms of 1848, the freedom of trade in the 1860s, the construction of railways and the foundation of big banks; however, the influence of a conservative aristocracy and power politics did not necessarily have positive effects on economic development. The lost Austro-Italian war in 1859 and Austria's defeat against Prussia in 1866 reduced the political weight of the Empire and also had repercussions for its economy. The oscillation between liberal approaches, all of which failed, and conservative setbacks prevented the continuity of economic policy. Additional factors were the crisis of the national budget which followed the lost wars, and the *Ausgleich*, the economically sensitive 'compromise' with Hungary. Monetary policy was not a stable basis as a result of long adherence to silver currency and the oscillation between inflation and deflation. Finally, the greatest atavism for banking policy was the nationalities' conflict. Although Vienna's big banks were ultimately a vital link in financial transactions, in Czech territories and in Hungary it was partly better to work with national banks. Some banks, such as the Živnostenská banka, built their business activity precisely on this nationalistic basis. The Empire's economic policy had not been able to create a perfectly homogeneous economic area. The size of the Empire was therefore mystifying: the country was divided into several, at times very different, markets. It was a country full of both obstacles and opportunities.

Competitive Status

The first half of the nineteenth century was the era of private bankers. In 1847 there were 92 private banks in Vienna, among which could be found such well-known names as Rothschild or Geymüller. Their business consisted mainly of government bonds or loans to the aristocracy. Individually, however, they also took an active part in the financing of industry and in the beginnings of railway construction. Their only competitor was the Austrian National Bank, founded in 1816, practically the state's banker, which also ran the Escompte- und Lombardgesellschaft and from 1855 created a section for agricultural loans. From 1867, following the compromise with Hungary, this became the Austro-Hungarian National Bank and by then boasted 18 branches. In 1853, the Niederösterreichische Escompte Gesellschaft was added, which mainly granted loans to the upper class. For the simple financial need of small tradesmen, peasants, workers and employees, savings banks and cooperative banks were created (Raiffeisen, Volksbanken).[2]

This banking structure, however, did not at all meet the requirements of inchoate industrialization. Above all, railway construction required capital resources of unprecedented magnitude. As also in other countries, the needs were met by issuing shares, which in Austria were always oversubscribed. But its speculative character was apparent, and at the first sign of crisis the shares were sold off again. Private banks could not and would not implement supporting measures and so the state had to intervene, until it ultimately became majority shareholder and continued railway construction on its own. In 1854, in connection with a budget crisis caused by the Crimean war, the railway had to be privatized again (Railway Concession Law 1854). With this, the need for an efficient banking system became explicit. So in 1855 the state took the initiative and, following the French model of the Crédit Mobilier (1853), it founded the Creditanstalt. Its responsibility was the promotion of industry and of railway construction. Its share capital of 100 million Austrian guldens was higher than that of the National Bank or the Crédit Mobilier and at the time of the foundation it was ten times oversubscribed. With the emergence of joint-stock banks (*Aktienbanken*), the era of private bankers was over. These either receded into niches, or they understood the signs of the time and became major shareholders of the new banking system, as the House of Rothschild did. The Creditanstalt first dedicated itself to its national task and took part in the measures implemented in support of railway shares, which brought losses. Subsequently, however, it succeeded in freeing itself from the state's influence and by 1867 had consolidated itself. The Creditanstalt was now active exclusively in the private sector, but it did not remain isolated. Amongst the most famous others were:

    1859 Banca Commerciale Triestina
    1863 Boden-Creditanstalt
    1863 Anglo-Österreichische Bank
    1869 Wiener Bankverein
    1869 Živnostenská banka
    1881 Länderbank

Foreign capital was also involved in many new foundations, notably the Anglo-Österreichische Bank and the Länderbank (France). During the *Gründerzeit* (1867–73), big banks, which had been founded partly for specific business sectors, became universal banks, with the exception of the Boden-Creditanstalt. The *Gründerzeit*, which brought about Austria's industrial success, was a highly speculative phase that ended with the crisis of 1873. It was also accompanied by the foundation of numerous banks, many of which, however, did not survive the crisis.

---

2   H. Matis and F. Weber, 'Kaisertum Österreich – Donaumonarchie', in H. Pohl (ed.), *Europäische Bankengeschichte* (Frankfurt, 1993), p. 316.

Number of banks in Cisleithania, (joint-stock and private)

1873   141
1885   42

As a reaction to the crisis of 1873, Austria's banking policy grew rather conservative. In addition to the business of government bonds, it had experienced a limited regional expansion since the 1890s. In 1896, Vienna's ten biggest banks had 34 branches, whose number grew to 127 branches by 1913, of which 25 were situated within the territory composing modern-day Austria. However, the main focus was in Cisleithania; in Hungary there were three branches, with a further eight abroad, yet hardly a single one in the Balkans. The banks of Vienna, therefore, had not conquered the whole economic area of the Empire; rather, they had concentrated on the industrially most advanced regions. The second characteristic of the time was the emergence of industrial groups in connection with the lucrative transformation of business into a joint-stock company (*Aktiengesellschaft*). This happened either because of failure, in which case loans were converted into equity capital, or of success, when growth in size of a business made the new form of company preferable. In any case, the bank issued shares and took a substantial part of them into its own portfolio, often out of necessity. Rudolf Hilferding defined this link with shares and loans 'Finanzkapitalismus'.[3] Until World War I, therefore, banks built industrial groups around themselves: if in 1890 the Creditanstalt boasted just two allied companies, in 1913 this number had risen dramatically to 102.

From a banker's perspective, World War I was a disturbing factor for business. On the one hand, the war interrupted Austria's relations with the most important Western-European financial markets, notably France and Great Britain. A banking system is by definition internationally oriented, and political limitations obviously brought about difficulties. On the other hand, the abundance of liquid capital in the economy during the war was responsible for the decreasing importance of banks. A particularly predominant new business activity was the eight war loans granted in the Austro-Hungarian Empire.

---

3   R. Hilferding, *Das Finanzkapital. Eine Studie über die jüngste Entwicklung des Kapitalismus* (Vienna, 1910).

The Interwar Years (1918–1938)

Economic Conditions (see Tables 1.3–1.5)

Table 1.3   GDP per capita, in 1990 international dollars

	1913	1950
Austria	3,488	3,731
Germany	3,833	3,881
USA	5,307	9,561

Table 1.4   GDP per capita, average annual growth, in 1990 international dollars

	1913–50
Austria	0.18
Germany	0.17
USA	1.61

Table 1.5   Austria GDP, 1913 = 100

1929	105.1	best year of the First Republic
1933	81.5	low point of the world economic crisis
1937	90.9	last year of the First Republic
1941	121.3	peak of war production
1945	50.0	first year of the Second Republic
1950	106.6	end of the reconstruction period

Source: Maddison, *Monitoring the World Economy*, p. 148.

The two World Wars and their consequences were a catastrophe for the Austrian economy. For over 30 years the GDP stagnated; 1913 value was reached again in 1929, but sank by 22 per cent in the world economic crisis; it returned to its previous level in 1937 and again in 1950, after the highs and lows of the war economy. Whereas in the USA GDP per capita almost doubled, in Germany and Austria it remained at the same level. This crisis scenario also characterizes the interwar years. The year 1918 saw first the disintegration of the Habsburg Empire and a time of economic disorientation: an oscillation between collaboration with the other successor states and its orientation to the German Reich. The first post-war years were also marked by enduring inflation. The Austrian crown had already lost two thirds of its value during the war and it kept falling until in 1922 it was 1/15,000 of its value of 1913. After the League of Nations rehabilitation measure in 1922 and the introduction of the Schilling in 1925, the economy recovered until 1929, when people could again hope for a normalization of conditions. Then the world economic crisis hit the country, which even after 1933 was still slowly recovering.[4] In 1937, therefore, people looked admiringly in the direction of the Reich, as its economy was already booming thanks to the armament industry; in Austria there was still 25 per cent unemployment.[5]

Political Conditions

Still more problematic than the economic developments were political ones. From the perspective of the Vienna banks it was unreasonable to disrupt arbitrarily the large market of the Austro-Hungarian Empire. The political slogan 'Away from Vienna' and the numerous intergovernmental obstacles which were now created could only lead to a loss of welfare for the regions involved. Politics no longer showed any consideration for economic rationality. As a rule, holdings, subsidiaries and offices of Austrian banks passed into national ownership and the board of directors had to be filled with local forces. One could get around it through trust agreements or the construction of firms on neutral foreign territory, but the sectionalism and the nationalistic regulations were at any rate an economic difficulty.

On the other hand, banks were not exactly patriotic members of the new Austrian Republic. Although they were based in Vienna, which was still an economic, cultural and social centre in Central Europe, they could not fully identify with the Austrian Republic, because bankers were less satisfied with political developments in Austria. Political leadership in the Empire consisted essentially of the upper middle class and aristocracy. Although their policy was not always met with general approval, they still enjoyed social respect. With the Austrian Republic, the aristocracy disappeared almost completely from the political scene. Now that the right to vote was universal and equal, and extended to both men and women, the time of mass parties finally began. Their leaders were professional politicians who were mainly the parties' own officers; and banks – perhaps correctly – did not have much confidence in them. This friction became evident almost immediately with the battle against inflation, and banks certainly felt better when the rehabilitation of the currency was assigned to the League of Nations commissioner, who controlled the Austrian budget from 1922 to 1928. As he was subordinate to the League of Nations' Financial Committee, whose members were bankers and in which the Bank of England played a leading role, they knew Austrian economic policy to be in the right hands. The main goal was thus the stability of the currency and a balanced budget, and also a more extensive retreat of the state from the economy.

---

4   D. Stiefel, *Die große Krise in einem kleinen Land. Österreichische Finanz- und Wirtschaftspolitik 1929–1938* (Vienna, 1988), pp. 153–211.

5   D. Stiefel, *Arbeitslosigkeit. Soziale, politische und wirtschaftliche Auswirkungen – am Beispiel Österreichs 1918–1938* (Berlin, 1979), p. 132.

The reason for this is that in the early post-war years a coalition of the Christian Social Party with the Socialist Party had issued social legislation which was now felt to be extremely burdensome. From 1919 working hours were reduced, transfer payments – e.g. in support of the unemployed – guaranteed, and employees granted more decisional power through workers' councils, the chamber of labour and the trade unions' right to collective bargaining. The financial resources were social security payments and taxes. During the interwar period, this led employers to unanimous complaint regarding overly high taxes and social burdens which they felt were an obstacle to economic growth. In addition, the number of employees in the banks had ballooned during the time of inflation. Business activity with the now foreign countries which had previously been part of the Monarchy became increasingly difficult. The inflation period also meant more complicated arithmetical operations which were mainly still done by hand, and led to a numerical increase in the workforce, which was now more difficult and more expensive to reduce as a result of the new regulations concerning employees. In Vienna's ten biggest banks the number of employees increased from 5,500 in 1913 to 16,000 in 1923. This latent problem became particularly acute during the world economic crisis, when a reduction of workforce and wages to rehabilitate the banking system was difficult to implement. It was therefore understandable that bankers welcomed the dictatorship of the corporate state as now they could implement the measures they considered necessary. The 'Bank Relief Decree' of March 1933 and the 'Bank Pension Decree' in the August of the same year were 'Emergency Decrees' of the authoritarian government and thus had no regard for the principles of collective agreements when they brought about the much-needed reduction of staff costs.[6]

Competitive Status

Banking activities may never have been easy, but they can rarely have been as difficult as they were in Austria between the wars. A primary difficulty was the economic impact of the war and of the inflation period; it is hard to say which caused the greater damage. During the post-war inflation, speculation with foreign currency and shares and in the commodity market seemed to be the only lucrative business, and banks participated throughout. This phase ended with the unfortunate speculation with the French franc in 1924. With the stabilization of the currency the veil of money was thrown back and the Austrian economy was faced with its losses. The opening balance sheet of 1925 showed that Vienna's big banks had lost between 70 per cent and 90 per cent in comparison with capital and new issues in 1914.[7] Even if we accept a certain margin of error, it is certain that banks began their business activity now with a weaker financial basis: as a reaction some resorted to foreign capital, which would have also guaranteed independence from Austrian politics. In Vienna's ten largest banks the foreign quota in the share capital increased from 10 per

---

6   D. Stiefel, *Finanzdiplomatie und Weltwirtschaftskrise. Die Krise der Credit-Anstalt für Handel und Gewerbe 1931* (Frankfurt, 1989), p. 214.

7   E. März, *Österreichische Bankenpolitik in der Zeit der großen Wende, 1913–1923. Am Beispiel der Creditanstalt für Handel und Gewerbe* (Vienna, 1981), p. 458.

cent in 1913 to 30 per cent in 1923. Two banks, Anglobank and Länderbank, passed completely into foreign ownership. Some also resorted to loans from abroad, usually short-term ones. These short-term liabilities that Vienna's big banks had towards foreign institutions amounted to 240 million schillings in 1924 and increased to one billion schillings by the beginning of 1931. Thus, in the 1920s, Viennese banks were perfectly aware of having become international banks based in Vienna.

This international orientation of Vienna's banks paralleled their own business activity. As a result of the peace treaty of Saint Germain and the nationalistic legislation in the successor states, banks had to either give up or re-define their position in these countries. Of the 143 branches of Vienna's ten big banks in the year 1918, only nine survived in 1924. But Vienna ultimately remained a central link in great financial transactions.[8] Western capital often feared direct investments in these countries and preferred the mediation of Vienna's banks, which had long been part and parcel of the international financial system. Thus Vienna's banks spread their provision of finance for industry in Central, Eastern, and South-Eastern Europe. In later years, this strategy was criticized; however, if we put ourselves in the position of an Austrian banker at the beginning of the 1920s, we can see that limiting one's business activity to the territory of the Austrian Republic alone would have been utterly preposterous. The preservation of a Central-European position, albeit under deteriorated circumstances, was the expression of an economic rationality.[9]

However, the economic upswing in the 1920s was in most regions only moderate, and problems increased. Only with substantial economic growth could the weakening which resulted from war and inflation be compensated; but this did not happen. It is an open question whether and to what degree wrong management strategies are to be blamed for this increasingly problematic situation. At any rate, the number of banks in Austria can already be seen to decrease in the 1920s, often as a consequence of absorption into bigger banks (see Table 1.6).

Table 1.6   Number of banks in Austria, joint-stock banks and private banks

1919	180
1923	358
1927	192
1935	150

Source: März, *Bankpolitik*.

---

8   D. Stiefel, 'Austrian Banks at the Zenith of Power and Influence', in H. Matis (ed.), *The Economic Development of Austria since 1870. An Elgar Reference Collection* (Aldershot, 1994), reprinted in *German Yearbook on Business History* (Cologne, 1986).

9   D. Stiefel, 'For better, for worse: the Credit-Anstalt and its Customers in 1931', in A. Teichova et al. (eds), *Universal Banking in the Twentieth Century. Finance, Industry and the State in North and Central Europe* (London, 1994).

The most dramatic case was the Boden-Credit-Anstalt, which encountered difficulties in 1929 and was promptly absorbed by the Creditanstalt. This merger increased the size of the Creditanstalt by about 50 per cent. But these were only the clouds before the storm of the 1931 bank crisis.[10] In May 1931, the Creditanstalt also had to admit losses which threatened its own existence. A first rehabilitation measure implemented by the government quickly vanished into thin air, generating a rush to the banks and a flight of capital which led to a monetary crisis. The Creditanstalt was now at the mercy of national and international politics. It had been the first big bank to encounter difficulties during the world economic crisis, and foreign creditors were accordingly inflexible in their requirements. Foreign creditors were certain of the support of Great Britain and France as well as about their influence on the League of Nations and the Bank of England. It was under this impression that the Austrian government was led to assume full liability for the debts of the Creditanstalt. This, however, was, in the face of the state's financial problems, a mere illusion. As soon as the bank crisis reached the foreign creditors' countries too, it became clear that the Creditanstalt crisis was not an isolated case, and its creditors saw themselves having to make considerable concessions. The rehabilitation of the Creditanstalt, which lasted until 1936, was carried out with substantial losses for both foreign creditors and the Austrian state. Through the absorption of most losses the Austrian state had thus become the owner of the Creditanstalt against its own will. In 1934, as the remaining big banks also encountered difficulties, the Austrian National Bank conducted the ultimate reorganization of Vienna's banking system. The Niederösterreichische Escomptegesellschaft was liquidated, the Creditanstalt absorbed a substantial part of its business activity, and the Wiener Bankverein was merged with the Creditanstalt. Thus, the banking scene in Vienna consisted of only one big bank, given that the Merkurbank, which was under German influence, and the Länderbank, a French branch, only had limited business activity. At the same time, the flight of capital and losses had caused the number of foreign loans to Austrian banks to drop dramatically, and the banks' deposits and holdings abroad were drawn upon to pay their debts to foreign creditors. One can therefore speak of an 'Austrification' of the Austrian banking system; the international position of Vienna as a financial centre had been almost entirely lost.

The Time of National Socialism and World War II (1938–1945)

Economic Conditions (see Table 1.7)

In Austrian historiography the interwar years end notably with the *Anschluss*, Austria's annexation to the Reich in March 1938. From an economic perspective, the *Anschluss* was initially an enormous success. Unemployment disappeared after six months, investments grew, and thus GDP grew by 13 per cent from 1938 to 1939. The economic optimism was shaken by the outbreak of the war. From now

---

10 A. Schubert, *The Credit-Anstalt Crisis of 1931* (Cambridge, 1991); Stiefel, *Finanzdiplomatie und Weltwirtschaftskrise.*

Table 1.7   GDP, 1990 international Geary-Khamis dollar

	per capita	total in millions
1937	3,177	21,458
1938	3,583	24,197
1939	4,123	27,431
1940	3,985	26,723
1941	4,245	28,635
1942	4,009	27,195
1943	4,092	27,856
1944	4,180	28,564
1945	1,736	11,803

Source: Maddison, *Monitoring the World Economy*, The World Economy: Historical Statistics, p. 181.

on, the renewal of the Austrian economy was put aside and existing resources were exploited to their limits for the war industry. The growth brought about by the war reached its climax in 1941, and, with extreme efforts, a second time in 1944. In 1945 the GDP dropped by over 50 per cent.

Political Conditions

Nationalism was hostile towards the internationalism of the banking world and considered the field of finance as an 'accumulation of capital' rather than 'productive capital'. Even when the Third Reich as an industrial state had to rely upon the productive efficiency of a banking system, the latter was still looked upon with suspicion and absolute loyalty was requested. Austrian bankers thus faced an unprecedented degree of politicization of their business field. The dictatorship of the corporate state, too, had already contributed to a politicization of the economy, but this could not be compared to what befell it now. Above all, political persecution and Aryanization were counterproductive in economic terms. They brought about a loss of staff members and of customers, and were unwise from a business management standpoint. The political cleansing concerned mainly state representatives and Jews. If such measures were implemented with special rigour in the financial field, this was because that field in particular was suspected to include many Jews. With the *Anschluss*, therefore, Nazis and people of proven loyalty were appointed to the leading positions of banks. World War II saw limitations and regulations of the banking activity to an even higher degree than World War I. A substantial part of the staff was removed from their position to serve in the army, and many things, such as the forceful subscription of war loans, were decreed by the authorities. In addition, the Reich's dubious economic policy to finance armament and war could only be looked at with anxiety by bankers. It is therefore difficult to put oneself in the position of a 'Nazi banker'. He had to act on the assumption that politics had priority over the economy and that, after the revolutionary and military phase and the Reich's victory, a financial consolidation had to be built at the expense of the subjugated countries. One certainly could not speak of 'reasonable economic conditions'.

Competitive Status

After the *Anschluss*, the situation of Austrian banks changed abruptly. As a result of the political persecution and Aryanization, numerous private banks were closed – which could, however, still be seen as a structural adjustment, albeit at the expense of a minority. The number of joint-stock and mortgage banks (*Aktienbanken, Hypothekenbanken*) remained almost unchanged, that of savings banks (*Sparkassen*) and credit cooperatives for agriculture (*Raiffeisenkassen*) decreased by 10 per cent, that of credit cooperatives for trade (*Volksbanken*) by two thirds and that of individual bankers by six sevenths.[11] But above all the remaining big banks were absorbed by their German business rivals. After long political disputes, the Länderbank came under the influence of the Dresdner Bank, and the Creditanstalt under that of the Deutsche Bank. In addition, they had to cede their industrial holdings to German public or private corporations of the armament industry. Along with other forms of 'unfriendly take-over,' a substantial part of the Austrian economy passed into German hands (see Table 1.8).

Table 1.8   The Germanization of Austria's economy, 1938–1944

Branch	German share of Austrian joint-stock companies (in %)	
	1938	1944
Banks	8	83
Insurances	6	51
Oil	0	92
Mining and Metallurgy	25	72
Electrical Industry	19	72
Chemical Industry	4	71
Industry total	9	57

Source: O. Klambauer, Zur Frage des deutschen Eigentums in Österreich, in *Jahrbuch für Zeitgeschichte*, 1978, p. 148.

As a related phenomenon, a replacement of the leading positions in the Austrian economic sphere had already taken place in 1938–39. In the six leading banks and the fourteen big insurance companies about two thirds of the directors and of the members of the supervisory board were replaced.

From an economic perspective, however, the *Anschluss* and the Reich's military expansion seemed to offer a fascinating opportunity. 'A businessman follows the flag', said Eduard Hilgard, *Reichsgruppenleiter* for the insurance branch and a

---

11 S. Janas, 'Die Konzentration im österreichischen Bankwesen', in *Bankarchiv*, vol. 10, 1968.

member of the executive board of the insurance company Allianz.[12] After Vienna lost its importance as a financial centre, it was still hoped that German capital would help it achieve a leading position again in Eastern and Southern Europe. Vienna hoped to become the 'Hamburg of the East', and the military successes of the war years seemed to justify this ambition. In the light of the expectations of the current German parent companies, it seemed natural that Vienna's banks should regain control of their ancestral markets. Politics was now readily used as an instrument for economic expansion. The Reich's economic plan foresaw a hierarchy even in economic relations, and Vienna was at its centre. This plan, however, ultimately failed, with considerable losses – something that could not be attributed only to the military defeat, as it had already become manifest that market-economy relations could not be built exclusively on subjugation. The hope that Vienna's banks could recapture their old position in South-Eastern Europe with the use of force was a speculation based on the victory of Nazi Germany. By 1942 at the latest, it had become clear that this hope would be dashed.[13]

The Reconstruction Period (1945–1955)

Economic Conditions

As a result of the war economy, of the destructions and dismantling, the Austrian economy collapsed. Without foreign help there would have been an unprecedented catastrophe. The major wants were food and energy supplies. In the winter of 1946–47 Vienna was still threatened by famine. The country was divided into four zones of occupation and was isolated from the international scene. The reconstruction during the first post-war years, therefore, saw only a slow advance.[14] It was only with the Marshall Plan (European Recovery Programme) that a rapid economic growth began, which was, however, accompanied by high inflation. From 1945 until 1955 Austria received foreign help amounting to US $1,585.1 million, of which 956.4 million came from the ERP. In 1949 the GDP reached the 1937 value again, and in 1953 that of 1941. Real GDP had altogether tripled from 1945 to 1955 (see Tables 1.9 and 1.10).[15]

---

12 A. Surminski, *Versicherung unterm Hakenkreuz* (Berlin, 1999), p. 230.

13 G.D. Feldman et al., *Österreichische Banken und Sparkassen im Nationalsozialismus und in der Nachkriegszeit*, 2 vols (Munich, 2006).

14 H. Seidel, *Österreichs Wirtschaft und Wirtschaftspolitik nach dem Zweiten Weltkrieg* (Vienna, 2005).

15 G. Bischof and D.Stiefel, *80 Dollar. 50 Jahre ERP-Fonds und Marshall-Plan in Österreich 1948–1998* (Vienna, 1999).

Table 1.9   GNP, 1990 international Geary-Khamis dollar

	per capita	total, in millions
1945	1,736	11,803
1946	1,969	13,786
1947	2,181	15,203
1948	2,783	19,357
1949	3,315	23,016
1950	3,731	25,873
1951	3,985	27,643
1952	3,993	27,667
1953	4,164	28,871
1954	4,585	31,822
1955	5,087	35,339

Source: Maddison, *Monitoring the World Economy*, The World Economy: Historical Statistics, pp. 181, 195.

Table 1.10   Economic development in Austria, 1947–1955

	GDP	Inflation	Share of external support for the development of Austrian import
1946	16.8	—	88% (1945/6)
1947	10.3	103.2	68%
1948	27.3	52.4	57%
1949	18.9	28.1	50%
1950	12.4	13.1	43%
1951	6.8	27.8	31%
1952	0.1	17.0	16%
1953	4.4	−54	
1954	10.2	3.7	
1955	11.1	0.8	
1947–1955	11.27	26.74	

GDP: real Gross Domestic Product, annual percentage changes.

Source: Maddison, *Monitoring the World Economy*; The World Economy: Historical Statistics, p.181.

Inflation: Index of consumer prices, annual percentage changes. Foreign support.
Source: F. Butschek, *Statistische Reihen zur österreichischen Wirtschaftsgeschichte. Die Österreichische Wirtschaft seit der Industriellen Revolution* (WIFO, Vienna, 1996).

Political Conditions

In the reconstruction era, economic activity was inevitably subject to considerable political influence. A distinction should be drawn between foreign influence and that of the Austrian Republic. The Marshall Plan (1948–52) also marked the beginning of the Cold War. With the emergence of the Eastern Bloc, Austrian enterprises lost their foreign capital in these lands and economic relations regressed remarkably. Whereas exports and imports with Czechoslovakia in 1929 had made up 14 per cent and 18 per cent of Austrian foreign trade respectively, these figures decreased to 2 per cent by 1955. There was also the problem of 'German property'. The Allies laid claims to German property abroad as reparations. As a result of the ownership changes during the National Socialist period, this would have had considerable consequences for Austria. In order to prevent this transition of property to foreign countries, in 1946 Austria nationalized 71 large industrial enterprises, i.e. about 20 per cent of the national industry. In 1947 the three big banks and 85 per cent of the electricity industry were also nationalized, giving Austria the highest proportion of nationalized industry among market-economy countries. The Western occupying powers accepted this measure with some reservations, but the Soviet Union confiscated the 'German Property' in its zone of occupation and founded a corporation, USIA, which soon boasted between 30,000 and 60,000 employees and sapped the Austrian economy substantially.[16] An additional problem was Austria's coming to terms with its past. The political necessity of restoring confiscated property and of denazification were a considerable burden for the state's administration and for enterprises.[17] Such tasks were economically counterproductive, but the Allies regarded them as a *sine qua non* for the international treaty. The 1955 state Treaty had considerable economic importance, as it helped settle ownership relations with Germany.

In a systemic crisis, such as the one after 1945, the state is the only authority able to work. It had to put the currency on its feet again (introduction of the schilling in 1945 and monetary laws in 1945/48), regulate foreign trade and the circulation of foreign currencies, fix prices and wages ('Wage and Price Agreement') and make decisions on investments. The war economy was a planned economy and even the reconstruction period was characterized by planned-economy methods in order to achieve market-economy conditions again. In this time of intense cooperation between employers, employees and the state, there also emerged the 'social partnership system' (*Sozialpartnerschaft*), able to guarantee influence over economic policy for the associations representing the economic interests of employers and employees. In addition, the nationalized economy was subject to a political orientation. In order to reach a unified position before the Allied occupying powers, the governments were formed from the ranks of the People's Party (*Volkspartei*) and the Socialist Party, which together had 90 per cent of votes in parliament. The nationalized economy acted in accordance with the principles of proportional representation, and thus it

---

16 D. Stiefel, '50 Years State-owned Industries in Austria 1946–1996', in F. Amatori (ed.), *The Rise and Fall of state-Owned Enterprises in Western Countries* (London, 2000).

17 D. Stiefel, 'Has the Course of Denazification been Determined by Economic Necessities?', in S.U. Larsen (ed.), Modern Europe after Fascism 1943–1980s (New York, 1998).

either appointed members of both parties to leading positions, or assigned individual enterprises to one specific party. Although a banker of that time saw the state's influence as indispensable and its help as necessary, he could only look on with scepticism at the politicization of staff and business strategies, and at the influence of the social partnership system.

Competitive Status

Even from a banker's perspective, the situation in 1945 appeared quite confused. Part of his staff had either been murdered or had died in the war, others were still in captivity or had to be dismissed or downgraded as a result of denazification (the higher echelons of the Reich's leadership had already disappeared). The ownership status of many customers was unclear; accordingly, about 7,000 enterprises had to be put under public administration. Real-estate ownership had been severely damaged and the value of receivables against Austrian businesses had yet to be determined. Holdings and property in Eastern Europe had to be written off, and the value of receivables against the Reich and German companies was completely uncertain. Under normal circumstances, Austrian banks in 1945 would have had to declare themselves bankrupt. So the nationalization was ultimately a relief for the three remaining big banks, because the banking business was subject to strict conditions imposed by the state. As a result of the currency laws, over 60 per cent of bank accounts and cash were confiscated, the bank lending system was subject to public control and the central bank afforded banks new liquid capital.[18] As a bank owned by the state, the Creditanstalt had the advantage of having a central role in public financial transactions and was also responsible for transactions within the framework of the Marshall Plan, which was by any account a considerable business.

Nationalization in Austria did not lead to the emergence of public enterprises; rather, a form of organization based on a private-enterprise system – mainly *Aktiengesellschaften* (PLCs) – was still preserved, and the state simply became the main shareholder. Significantly, the Ministry of Finance acted as the owner in the case of banks, whereas for industry this role was assumed by a separate nationalized ministry. The Ministry of Finance had already supervised banking for a long time (with the Nationalbank); it knew this business well and left banks more margin for activity in the private sector than was the case for nationalized industries. At any rate, in this case too the principle of proportional representation was followed: the Creditanstalt was assigned to the Volkspartei and the Länderbank to the Socialist Party. With the proprietary regulation through the 1955 state Treaty (and the 1958 property agreement between Germany and Austria, also known as *Vermögensvertrag*) banks were able to draw up a proper balance sheet again. They drew up a record of the reconstruction costs of the years 1945–54, which would then become the foundation for the first balance sheet denominated in Austrian schillings. From then onwards, it is once again possible to speak of normal business activity in the line of Austria's economic tradition.

---

18 K. Bachinger et al. (eds), *Abschied vom Schilling. Eine österreichische Wirtschaftsgeschichte* (Graz, 2001), pp. 159–76.

The Period from the 1950s to the Present

Economic Conditions (see Tables 1.11 and 1.12)

Table 1.11   GDP per capita, in 1990 international dollars (Germany East and West)

	1950	1973	2001
Austria	3,706	11,235	20,225
Germany	3,881	11,966	18,677
USA	9,561	16,689	27,948

Table 1.12   GDP per capita, annual growth

	1950–1973	1973–2001
Austria	4.94	2.12
Germany	5.02	1.60
USA	2.45	1.86

Source: Maddison, *Monitoring the World Economy*, The World Economy: Historical Statistics, pp. 181, 195.

The economic development from 1950 on is a success story, even if on closer inspection it is plagued by numerous difficulties and problems. Austria's GDP increased from the 69 per cent of the OECD average in 1950 to 107 per cent in 2000 and was thus also clearly above the average of the EU 15 countries (95 per cent). This last phase is divided into two sections. The first one, from the 'Golden Twenty Years' until the mid-1970s, in which Austria's growth rate was twice as high as that of the USA. This period of the economic miracle was the expression of a catching up process triggered by the 'Second Thirty Years' War' (1914–45). Just when people had become accustomed to it, the economic miracle ended in the mid-1970s with the collapse of the petroleum price, the end of the Bretton Woods monetary system and the beginning of stagflation. Afterwards, economic growth slowed down and unemployment in particular became a chronic problem. Nevertheless, Austria's economic record (GDP growth, inflation and unemployment rates) was in most cases better than that of the other OECD countries. The driving force of economic growth was mainly exports, which until 1973 showed double-figure growth rates (annual average 11 per cent) and since then an average of 6 per cent. Austria has become a country of exportation and has integrated itself increasingly in world economy, notably through its intense economic relations with Germany. This period was concluded by the opening of the Eastern markets in 1989, which was a stroke of luck for the Austrian economy. The neighbouring countries, once characterized by planned economy, returned to a free-market economy and thus paved the way for investment and business opportunities for the first time in over fifty years. It was an historical irony that the 'Away from Vienna' movement from the year 1918 should reverse its course seventy years later, and that the successor states should leave Austria enough time to consolidate its finances and become economically efficient to play a leading role in those territories again.

Political Conditions

Austria's economic policy has been characterized by two contradictory approaches since World War II. On the one hand, energy has been vigorously invested in the promotion of liberalization and integration into the world economy. Austria joined the IMF in 1948 (the schilling became convertible in 1968), the GATT in 1950, and the EFTA in 1960; in 1972 it signed an association treaty with the EC and joined the European Union in 1995. Thus, the economic policy, albeit slowly and by degrees, developed towards a liberal market economy. On the other hand, the basis of the economic policy of the Second Republic was the social partnership system. This was a system of restricted market economy, in which market mechanisms were replaced or supplemented by negotiations. It was practically a political economic corporation in which wages, prices and partly also output were fixed. This system was further supplemented by the governmental form of the great coalition, nationalized industry and the state's influence over the banking system. That such an economic system could be successful does not appear in any theory. The success of the social partnership system was mainly due to the moderateness of the trade unions, the limited number of public conflicts and a largely protected market. The weaker growth from the mid-1970s and the increasing liberalization endangered this form of economic and social policy. The turning point was the crisis of nationalized industry in the mid-1980s. Its symptoms – worldwide crisis of the iron and steel industry etc. – had already been recognized long before, but a rehabilitation was not possible under the conditions of the social partnership system, as it would have required the forceful closure of firms and lay-offs. However, losses in 1986 were so high that even Social Democrats accepted the privatization. The privatization of nationalized industry has by now largely been completed; in nationalized banks it had already begun with the *Volksaktien* (literally, the 'people's shares') in 1957, as 40 per cent of the share capital of the Creditanstalt-Bankverein and the Österreichische Länderbank were privatized. In the foreseeable future public enterprises, such as railway and post, will also attain private-sector structures; thus, the social partnership system can be seen as an historical phenomenon, whose importance was reduced by the increasingly liberal economic conditions and the EU membership. Hence, the economic policy from the 1990s dealt with numerous reforms, in order to adapt Austria to these new conditions. With these reforms the cards are re-dealt. They also concern every Austrian personally, and are therefore, understandably, fiercely disputed.

Competitive Status

The history of Austrian banks from the nineteenth century until World War II is relatively well established. For the period after 1945, however, our historical knowledge does not fully match the considerable importance of this branch of business. The Creditanstalt closed its historical project years ago, after its investigation of the interwar years, and only recently have external influences led it to investigate the National Socialist period and its consequences. Our knowledge of the last 60 successful years is therefore rather limited, and they can only be outlined in broad terms.

According to Gunter Tichy, it is possible to divide the development of banks after World War II into various phases.[19] The first one was characterized by the overcoming of the consequences of the war. The considerable losses in income and wealth inevitably generated little savings activity. Hence, sight deposits were the first to recover, reaching a normal level as early as in 1953. As a result, the participation of banks in the balance sheet total of the lending system in 1953 was 47 per cent, thus higher than before the war. In the second phase, the savings activity recovered and savings banks and cooperative credit associations increased their market share. Both phases represent the period of the overcoming of the consequences of the war (see Tables 1.13 and 1.14).

The third phase, during the 1960s, was characterized by a differentiated growth of the groups of customers. This is the beginning of what may be called the 'democratization of the credit system' and the 'transition to a mass business'. Especially private individuals resorted to the services of a bank now. From this time, companies no longer paid wages and salaries in cash, and thus forced dependent workers to open bank accounts. Credit institutions encouraged this development by keeping salary accounts free of charge. Savings banks and cooperative credit associations were the first to profit from it, as their customers traditionally stemmed from this population group. Until the beginning of the 1970s, there was therefore almost no competition; rather, there was an expansion of the financial services offered by the bank to its already existing pool of customers (see Tables 1.15 and 1.16).

Table 1.13   Importance of the various types of deposit (% values)

Year	Sight and time deposits		Savings deposits	
	Percentage/ Deposits	GNP	Percentage/ Deposits	GNP
1937	29.9	9.8	70.1	23.2
1954	67.8	17.0	32.2	8.1
1960	40.9	13.8	59.1	19.8
1970	27.8	13.6	72.2	35.3

19 G. Tichy, 'Strukturwandel im Kreditapparat und die auf uns zukommenden Finanzierungsprobleme', in *Aktuelle Beiträge zum Geld- und Bankwesen, Österreichisches Forschungsinstitut für Sparkassenwesen*, no. 4, 1980, pp. 55–86; G. Tichy, 'Drei Phasen des Strukturwandels im österreichischen Kreditapparat', in *Bankarchiv*, no. 8, 1977, pp. 307–19; G. Tichy, 'Zu einigen wichtigen Strukturmerkmalen des österreichischen Kreditapparates', in *Bankarchiv*, no. 9, 1977, pp. 322–40.

Table 1.14   Contribution to total

	1953	1979
Banks	47	36
Savings banks	22	25
Rural credit unions	7	18
Industrial credit unions	4	6
Other	20	18

Source: Tichy, *Strukturwandel*.

Table 1.15   Total deposits market share

	1953	1970
Joint-stock banks (*Aktienbanken*)	44.2	21.2
Individual bankers	2.3	2.4
Savings banks (*Sparkassen*)	24.3	35.6
Regional mortgage banks (*Landeshypothekenanstalten*)	4.8	3.2
Credit cooperatives for agriculture (*Raiffeisenkassen*)	7.3	18.3
Credit cooperatives for trade (*Volksbanken*)	4.5	7.8
Building Societies (*Bausparkassen*)	0.3	6.3
Special credit institutions	12.3	5.2

Table 1.16   Loan market shares

	1953	1970
Joint-stock banks (*Aktienbanken*)	56.4	25.7
Individual bankers	4.2	2.2
Savings banks (*Sparkassen*)	16.9	27.0
Regional mortgage banks (*Landeshypothekenanstalten*)	6.2	9.2
Credit cooperatives for agriculture (*Raiffeisenkassen*)	9.5	16.7
Credit cooperatives for trade (*Volksbanken*)	6.5	6.6
Building Societies (*Bausparkassen*)	—	7.4
Special credit institutions	0.3	5.2

Source: Tichy, *Strukturwandel*.

From the 1970s onwards, all credit institutions endeavoured to acquire their competitors' share of customers. Banks now also dedicated themselves to mass business and savings banks and unions devoted resources to the financing of the industry. All credit institutions thus joined the trend of the universal bank, which was favoured by legislation. In the case of corporative societies, it was leading institutions in particular that developed into big banks. This development was accompanied by the strong expansion of a branch network, which increased by half its size in the 1970s (see Tables 1.17–1.19).

Table 1.17   Main institutions and branches of the banking sector

	Main Institutions	Branches	Total	Increase (%)
1960	2,169	660	2,829	
1970	2,024	1,237	3,261	15%
1980	1,595	3,376	4,971	52%
1990	1,210	4,497	5,707	15%
2003	896	4,401	5,297	(−) 7%

Source: Butschek, *StatistischeReihen*, 1996; *Finanznachrichten*, 2003.

Table 1.18   Branches per capita 1976

USA	4,674
Japan	4,135
GB	2,868
France	2,818
Spain	2,263
Austria	2,003
Sweden	1,983
Netherlands	1,876
FRG	1,420
Switzerland	1,368

Source: *Tichy*, 'Strukturmerkmalen'.

Branches functioned above all as collection points for capital. After the speculative losses of the 1920s and the loss of capital as a result of two periods of inflation, Austrian savers had become extremely risk averse. Private individuals do not invest their financial reserves for long periods or in high risk capital. The importance of bond market and share market therefore remained slight, in spite of some successes in the Austrian share market. Thus, the capital market became dependent on the money market. The capital market also became an inter-banking market: the financial sector inserted itself between supplier and customer as a mediator, and grew six times as much as the GNP from 1950 until 1980. In the 1950s and 1960s deposits and loans

Table 1.19   Deposits per branch in 1975, values in million schillings

Joint-stock banks (*Aktienbanken*)	238
Savings banks (*Sparkassen*)	178
Banks (*Banken*)	، 160
Cooperative credit associations for trade (*Gewerbliche Kreditgenossenschaften*)	76
Cooperative credit associations for agriculture (*Ländliche Kreditgenossenschaften*)	37

increased twice as quickly as the GNP. This was an immediate consequence of risk-free mass savings instead of raising capital with stocks and shares. This also had repercussions for the banks' own equity capitalization. The equity capital in 1953 was still low as a result of the war, but increased thanks to the Bank Reconstruction Law of 1955, which permitted a re-evaluation. In the 1950s and 1960s, however, when deposits and loans increased about twice as quickly as the GNP, the equity capital could not keep up with it because of the state as the principal shareholder. In 1980 it was practically at the same level as in 1953. However, the equity quota has increased since then, partly also as a reaction to Basel 2, from the end of the 1990s (see Table 1.20).

Table 1.20   Equity capital as percentage of balance sheet total

1953	2.41
1960	5.22
1970	4.70
1980	2.70
1990	4.10
1995	4.43
2003	7.30

Source: Butschek, *Monatsberichte*, WIFO 4/2004.

Whereas savings were predominantly invested for short periods, loans were mainly granted for longer periods, so that the lending system now bore the risk of the long-term commitment which savers were reluctant to take (see Table 1.21).

The state's strong influence on the financial sector also remained a distinctive feature. This concerned not only the national property in big banks and the influential position of regional corporations as customers in the capital market. This influence was also apparent in the state's promotion of savings and in the case of loans. In 1975, 14 per cent of all loans were subsidized by public institutions through interest allowances and redemption allowances. This particularly affected long-term loans for the construction of houses, and the promotion of exports and investments. In 1988 the share of subsidized loans to domestic business enterprises and private individuals must have already amounted to 41.6 per cent (see Table 1.22).

Table 1.21   Structure of savings activity

	1950–1959	1960–1969	1970–1979
Private households	25	40	70
Self-financing of companies	35	30	10
State	40	30	20

Source: W. Ehrlicher, 'Strukturwandlungen des Kapitalmarktes',
in *Aktuelle Beiträgezum Geld- und Bankenwesen,*
ÖsterreichischesForschungsinstitutfürSparkassenwesen, vol. 4, 1980, p. 77.

Table 1.22   Public subsidies for long-term loans

Regional mortgage banks (*Landeshypothekenanstalten*)	32.0%
Special credit institutions (*Sonderkreditunternehmen*)	28.5%
Savings banks (*Sparkassen*)	18.0%
Credit cooperatives for agriculture (*Raiffeisen*)	13.5%
Credit cooperatives for trade (*Volksbanken*)	9.5%
Banks (*Banken*)	8.0%

Source: Tichy, 'Strukturmerkmalen'.

From the 1980s it is possible to speak of a saturation of the Austrian financial market: asset growth as well as economic growth receded, and banks – with their costly services and numerous staff – saw their profitability seriously threatened. The principles of the social partnership system led to the attempt to solve this problem by means of agreements. At the end of the 1980s, price-fixing began in the form of 'regulatory agreements' (OPV) to make domestic business more profitable. Until then, the Austrian banking sector was an oligopolistic market, a 'protected sector', and strictly regulated by the Banking Act (KWG). Only after joining the European Union in 1995 did Austria understand at its own expense that even informal agreements could lead to a fierce reaction in Brussels.

As domestic business began to lose its impetus, the connections of Austrian banks with foreign ones increased considerably. This was not exclusively seen as positive: We borrow from the West and basically pass it over to the East, Gunter Tichy has observed. But this was probably more of a memory of the interwar years, because loan procurement did not exhaust the whole network of these foreign relations (see Tables 1.23 and 1.24).

If 1970s international relations were epitomized by the formation of consortium banks, the mid-1980s also brought about the development of representative offices and at the end of the 1980s networking via Joint Ventures had become typical. Additionally, holdings in foreign banks and banking groups increased. This development was accompanied by a shift from interbanking transactions to ultimate customer transactions and to specialized foreign units, such as subsidiary

Table 1.23   Interconnectedness with foreign countries, assets and liabilities in percentage values, all sectors

	Assets abroad	Liabilities abroad
1960	1.0	1.8
1970	7.7	7.1
1980	16.9	19.5
1990	23.0	25.5

Table 1.24   Joint-stock companies (*Aktienbanken*) and bankers

	Assets abroad	Liabilities abroad
1960	2.4	3.9
1970	20.2	19.6
1980	29.7	35.1
1990	33.7	39.5

leasing companies. The strategy followed abroad was a niche policy rather than the plan of universal banking implemented at home. Banks avoided the saturation of the domestic market and reacted to the infiltration of foreign banks into Austria. They also followed their customers, however, and their activity abroad was thus an expression of the increasing internationalization of the Austrian economy. This interconnectedness with foreign countries reached over 40 per cent in the case of the Österreichische Länderbank, Girozentrale and Creditanstalt-Bankverein in 1990. Overall, Austria thus found itself at the same level as the Netherlands, Ireland and Switzerland.[20] The activity abroad, however, was no one-way street: foreign financial institutions, too, settled in the Austrian market. In 2003, the majority shareholders of 29 banks were foreigners, foreign banks had 22 branch offices in Austria and 225 credit institutions conducted their activity on the basis of the freedom of services (mainly from the EU). In 2003, Austrian banks could boast a number of branches and representative offices abroad amounting to 27 and 44 respectively, compared to 9 and 66 in 1990.

Initially, the activity abroad was an international expansion, with branches in New York and London. From the 1990s, it became clear that Austrian banks – first and foremost because of their size – were not among the global players. As a result, there was a reorientation towards the domestic and neighbouring markets. Additionally, as a result of capital market regulation and the adoption of EC guidelines, foreign business practically became a domestic business again. This was facilitated by the communications revolution (computer), thanks to which it was no longer necessary to have direct representatives at the big financial centres. Overall, however, the

---

20 P.R. Haiss, 'Internationale Aktivitäten österreichischer Banken', in *Zeitschrift für das gesamte Kreditwesen*, Sep. 1991.

orientation of Austrian banks towards foreign markets is not as much a globalization as a regionalization. This is especially evident in the last phase of the history of Austrian banking, which is strictly tied to the opening of the Eastern markets.[21] Because of its geographical position and its tradition, Austria had, compared to other market-economy countries, very intense foreign trade relations with planned-economy states – and this foreign trade had repercussions for banking services. This was facilitated by a well-developed system of governmental guarantees and export credit insurance. Already before the opening of the Eastern markets, Austrian banks had a 15 per cent market share of Eastern Bloc financial activity. The Austrian economy could therefore react quickly to the change of system in the former Eastern Bloc countries and the early presence of banks guaranteed a business basis before most competitors, by means of branches and holdings, consultancy services and staff training. Above all in the neighbouring countries, Austrian banks are today either leaders of the market or have a top position.

From the 1990s there was also a series of bank mergers and holdings abroad. The most striking and important example is that of Bank Austria. In the early 1980s, the Österreichische Länderbank entered a crisis as a result of a whole series of irrecoverable big loans. The rehabilitation, which was carried out with the intervention of the state, led to the merger of Länderbank with Zentralsparkasse and Kommerzialbank AG in 1991 – the result of which was Bank Austria AG. At that time, the social-democratic political orientation of the Länderbank was an obstacle to its merger with the ÖVP-oriented Creditanstalt-Bankverein – although this certainly presented itself as perfectly viable in pure business terms. Therefore, it was the former municipal savings bank, the Zentralsparkasse of the City of Vienna, which was considered. With this merger, it augmented its volume, the number of its customers and its know-how considerably, becoming the largest of the Austrian banks (it would be interesting to imagine how the history of Austrian banks would have developed if the Creditanstalt had absorbed the Länderbank). In 1997 the privatization of the Creditanstalt was announced. After long negotiations, Bank Austria surprisingly made a takeover offer which was considerably higher than that of its competitors and left the government no other option than to accept it. This brilliant move had considerable consequences. First, it led to agitation among the employees of the CA, who felt their corporate culture to be very different from that of the Bank Austria. But above all, it caused the People's Party (ÖVP) to feel ambushed by its social-democratic coalition partner (SPÖ), and this is one of the reasons why, after the next elections, the ÖVP no longer associated with the SPÖ; rather, in spite of a general international opposition, it began a coalition with the Freedom Party (FPÖ). In the following years, following the trends of that time, Bank Austria-Creditanstalt (BA-CA) sought a strong parntner in order to secure its own existence in international business. Thus, by means of a share swap, it joined forces with the German bank HypoVereinsbank (HVB) in 2000. As a part of the HVB group, BA-CA answers to the Austrian market as well as Central and Eastern-European ones. In July 2003, BA-CA carried out a capital increase through an initial public offering. The bank employs the revenues from this

---

21 P.R. Haiss, 'Central European Strategies of Austrian Banks', in *Österreichisches Bankarchiv*, no. 5, 1991.

operation to finance its further expansion in Central and Eastern Europe. In the year 2005 HVB was taken over by the Italian Unicredit. BA-CA remained the centre for Central and Eastern Europe with the exception of Poland. For an historian it is too early to say anything about the results of this new development. Today the BA-CA is no Austrian bank anymore but, like the Creditanstalt until the 1930s an international bank situated in Vienna.[22]

Overall, the history of Austrian banking can be divided into three periods, namely the second halves of the nineteenth and twentieth centuries and the phase represented by the two World Wars and the interwar years. The period from 1914 to 1945 was one of the politically determined catastrophes and crises which almost reduced the Austrian banking system to insignificance. Twice, in the 1930s and in 1945, the whole sector faced a systemic crisis, from which it could only be rescued by the state's intervention. The second halves of the nineteenth and twentieth centuries, instead, saw the economic rise and internationalization, so that Austrian banks occupy a position today which they basically already held a century ago. The last 150 years were almost without exception a turbulent period, both politically and economically, but for the banker they were certainly never boring.

---

22 O. Rathkolb et al. (eds), *Bank Austria Creditanstalt. 150 Jahre österreichischer Bankgeschichteim Zentrum Europas* (Vienna, 2005).

CHAPTER 2

In the Centre of Europe:
Vienna as a Financial Hub, 1873–1913

Peter Eigner

'They served every relatively important operation in all areas: share issues, formation of syndicates, placing of loans or any larger industrial credit. Relations with international finance are concentrated in Vienna – here foreign credits were taken up and administered for the entire Empire. Viennese banks led the penetration of Eastern and Southeast Europe with Austrian capital.'[1]

This is a famous quotation from the report on the economic situation of Austria written by Charles Rist and Walter Layton directed to the League of Nations in the mid 1920s. It describes the significance of Vienna as a financial centre before World War I or better it stresses the central and dominating role of the banks in the Habsburg Monarchy's financial system. Most historians would agree. What is certainly true is that it was the Austrian banks that were heavily involved in financial transactions and operations, while the Vienna stock exchange did not mirror that significance to the same extent. Defining financial centres as 'urban locations specialising in the provision of financial services',[2] the purpose and function of financial centres is financial intermediation, and this task in the Austrian case was mainly concentrated upon the banks. The question is: Why was this so?

The time period analysed is the period from 1873 up to 1913, but considering the fact that the First World War brought no discontinuity neither in the bank-industry relationships nor in the dominance of the banks, some remarks on the further development of the financial centre of Vienna in the interwar period proved to be necessary. One should also bear in mind that the Austrian situation shares some common features with other countries, but there seem to be some Austrian peculiarities. Banking systems based on so-called universal banks spread almost

---

1   W. Layton and C. Rist, *The Economic Situation of Austria. Report presented to the Council of the League of Nations* (Geneva, 1925). Eugen Lopuszánski, high official of the Austrian Ministry of Finance, describes the strength of the Viennese banks almost analogously: 'Ohne ihre (die der Mobilbanken, P.E.) Zustimmung und Mitwirkung kann fast keine, irgendwelche größere Geld- und Kapitalsbewegung bedingende Transaktion durchgeführt werden. Sie bestimmen schon fast die Grenzen für die Tätigkeit des freien Kapitalmarktes, dessen Zentralorganisation die Wiener Börse bildet.' E. Lopuszánski, 'Einige Streiflichter auf das österreichische Bankwesen', in *Volkswirtschaftliche Wochenschrift von Alexander Dorn*, 31 Dec. 1908, no. 1305, quoted after E. März and K. Socher, 'Währung und Banken in Cisleithanien', in A. Brusatti (ed.), *Die wirtschaftliche Entwicklung der Habsburgermonarchie* (Vienna, 1973), p. 348.

2   Cp. R. Roberts, 'The Economics of Cities of Finance', in H. Diederiks and D. Reeder (eds), *Cities of Finance* (Amsterdam 1996), p. 7.

throughout Europe from the 1880s to 1914.[3] One characteristic was the banks' close relationship to industry and commerce which was especially marked in Central Europe. Nowadays a growing number of historians tend to agree that Austria-Hungary from the last quarter of the nineteenth century onwards was the country where the 'purest form' of universal banking – even compared to Germany – could be found.[4]

Starting Position: Institutional Innovations Complementing Austria's Banking System

The 1850s and 60s had seen a widening of different needs for financial services – the Austrian credit market was in no way organized to fulfil the requirements of a growing commerce – and thus new bank types had to be founded, one could add as a kind of institutional response to existing market failures.

Up to that time, the Austrian banking system had been dominated by three actors: The Austrian National Bank (the bank of issue acted as the banker of the state which had mainly because of military reasons a strong need for credit), the savings banks and the private banks.[5] The most important among the latter, for example the houses of Rothschild, Arnstein, Fries, Geymüller and Steiner, had dominated the financial life before 1848 and had been mainly concerned with government finance as well as providing credits for the estates of the high aristocracy. Since the second half of the nineteenth century due to the economic crises of 1857 and 1873 the private banks lost importance – with the exceptions of the Viennese Branch of the House of Rothschild and some others. The first banks to follow were either banks concentrating on granting short-term commercial credits, one could say commercial banks in the narrow sense, considering the discounting of bills of exchange as their main function, like the Niederösterreichische Escompte-Gesellschaft (1853) or the Banca Commerciale Triestina (1859). Later, these became universal banks, too. Or they were founded as mortgage banks with the task of granting long-term agricultural credit, among them the provincial banks (Landesbanken). A new type of these banks, Köver speaks of 'corporate "immobile" banks'[6] was the Allgemeine Österreichische Boden-Credit-Anstalt which besides the mortgage business also dealt in the issue of

---

3   Universal banks in general offered almost all possible banking transactions and services, they 'combined the short-term business of deposit banking with the long-term activity of investment banking, and in addition, they performed stock-broking functions, managed clients' portfolios, acquired shares and voting rights in joint-stock companies on their own and their clients' account'. A. Teichova, 'Banking and Industry in Central Europe, Nineteenth to Twentieth Century', in A. Teichova et al. (eds), *Banking, Trade and Industry. Europe, America and Asia from the Thirteenth to the Twentieth Century* (Cambridge, 1997), pp. 214–15.

4   Ibid., p. 216.

5   Cf. the following G. Köver, 'The Austro-Hungarian Banking System', in R. Cameron and V.I. Bovykin (eds), *International Banking 1870–1914* (New York: Oxford, 1991), pp. 322–6.

6   Ibid., p. 323.

securities and after the turn of the century turned to the industrial business and took part in current business transactions.

A real turning point and one could even say the most important institutional innovation in Austria's financial system of the nineteenth century was the creation of joint-stock (mobilier and then universal) banks following the type of the French Crédit Mobilier but adapted to Austrian needs with the function of issuing securities by absorbing short- and long-term financial credits, the first – and remaining the most important one – the k.k. priv. Österreichische Credit-Anstalt für Handel und Gewerbe founded in 1855. In 1854 the Monarchy had been forced due to financial reasons to privatize railway construction and was thus more and more confronted with the necessity to create an efficient banking system. The foundation of the Credit-Anstalt can be interpreted as the Rothschild's victory over the Pereires in the Habsburg Monarchy.[7] The start of its industrial business was not very lucky, as the severe stock exchange crash in 1857 cut the first industrial ties for decades. Some banks like the Anglo-Austrian Bank started as foreign or quasi-international banks with the purpose of meeting international capital demand but did not succeed; they either failed during the crash in 1873 or were transformed to Austrian institutions. The last foundation to be mentioned in the series of important Austrian universal banks was the Länderbank founded in 1880/81 with French capital.[8] Bohemian and Hungarian banks followed the same path.

According to Alexander Gerschenkron the universal bank could be characterized as 'an institutional substitute for the missing prerequisite of "original accumulation"'.[9] Today, researchers are more or less convinced that in the Habsburg Monarchy it was not the lack of capital or better not alone, that was responsible for this institutional innovation in the field of finance, but the lack of possibilities for more risky sorts of investment or the risk-hostile business attitude in general. Although founded with the purpose to finance industry, the business policy of the banks from the beginning followed the rules of 'profit-maximizing and risk-minimizing',[10] the banks preferred in their pioneer days the safer funding of railway construction and public borrowing to the more risky business of industrial financing.[11]

---

7   The most active supporter and main subscriber was the Viennese House of Salomon M. von Rothschild which forestalled the Pereire brothers' intention to open a branch in Vienna. Important to note is furthermore the fact that the Austrian Minister of Finance, Carl Freiherr von Bruck, strongly supported the project being aware of the urgent need to reform the finances of the state and to build a transport and banking system as well as of the lack of capital. See Teichova, 'Banking and Industry in Central Europe', p. 216.

8   The Länderbank remained international, mainly French, up to World War I: In 1913 31.4 per cent of its capital was still in foreign hands. F. Bartsch, *Statistische Daten über die Zahlungsbilanz Österreich-Ungarns vor Ausbruch des Krieges* (= Mitteilungen des k. k. Finanzministeriums, XXII) (Vienna, 1917), p. 144.

9   D. Ziegler, 'The Influence of Banking on the Rise and Expansion of Industrial Capitalism in Germany', in A. Teichova et al. (eds), *Banking, Trade and Industry. Europe, America and Asia from the Thirteenth to the Twentieth Century* (Cambridge, 1997), p. 132.

10   R. Cameron (ed.), *Banking in the Early Stages of Industrialization* (New York, 1967), p. 13.

11   See Teichova, 'Banking and Industry in Central Europe', p. 217.

A False Start: Boom, Crash and Shock Waves

In our search for the origins of the peculiarities of the Austrian capital market important traces lead us back to the so called 'Gründerzeit', a first real economic boom phase for the Monarchy dating from 1867 to May 1873 (ending with the spectacular crash of the Vienna stock exchange) and often characterized as a false start of industrialization. And one could add a false start for the stock exchange in developing more features of a functioning modern capital market. The impressive rise of the number of joint-stock companies in these years (among them many banks and building companies, their background were the extreme growth of the Viennese population, the preparations for the World Exhibition in Vienna in 1873, the regulation of the River Danube and the construction of the Ringstraße) was mainly due to speculation; Vienna developed into the biggest speculation market in Europe.

What proved even worse than the direct economic losses caused by the crash were its long-term consequences: Psychologically one could notice a spread of anti-liberal, anti-modernistic or anti-capitalistic sentiments which were connected with a heavy anti-Semitism. This conservatism and anti-liberalism found an equivalent in some legislative measures. Legal and fiscal regulations determined the specific nature of the relationship between banks and industry within Austria-Hungary, tax and company laws unfavourably affected the growth of both joint-stock enterprises and the capital market.[12] According to Alois Mosser's analysis of Austrian company balance sheets for the period 1880 to 1914, the majority of joint-stock companies obtained capital in two main ways: first, through ploughing back their own financial resources (the prime source up to 1900); and, second, by taking up frequently prolonged short-term credit from the banks, with the latter being eventually – depending on the financial success – amortized by the issue of shares.[13]

The Vienna stock exchange lost significance as direct entrance possibility to the capital market. Among the quoted types of securities investment bonds predominated. Turnover figures of the stock exchange showed a declining tendency. The functions of a capital market were largely taken over by the Vienna universal banks, though one has to underline that the banks – if they had been key actors in the speculation or not – acted very cautiously too after 1873. With regards to the turnover of securities, banks and stock exchange became competitors, banks proving to be stronger.

To summarize: The purchase of shares lost attraction, the capital market was dominated by the banks and again by state loans, and the development of joint-stock companies lagged behind in comparison with other countries. The hesitating attitude towards industrial financing had been strengthened by the crash of the Viennese stock exchange in 1873. This was true for the great commercial banks of Vienna, too,

---

12 Ibid., p. 218.

13 A. Mosser, *Die Industrieaktiengesellschaft in Österreich, 1880–1913* (Vienna, 1980), p. 105. Mosser speaks of a proportion of 2:1 between financing with own resources and credits up to 1900, then the share of own resources fell to 60 per cent, ibid. A. Mosser and A. Teichova, 'Investment Behaviour of Industrial Joint-Stock Companies and Industrial Shareholding by the Österreichische Credit-Anstalt: Inducement or Obstacle to Renewal and Change in Industry in Interwar Austria', in H. James et al. (eds), *The Role of Banks in the Interwar Economy* (Cambridge, 1991), pp. 135–6.

which until the late nineteenth century did not fulfil the expectations placed in them as promoters of industry.[14] The following data underline the fact of a widespread 'aversion to shares' ('Scheu vor der Aktie') in Austria underlining the argument of a risk-avoiding business attitude: In 1910 the percentage of railway and industrial shares was only 2.3 on all stock, compared to 29 per cent in Germany and 63 per cent in Great Britain. Eighteen per cent were bank shares, 80 per cent the share of government bonds and other public securities (see Table 2.1).[15]

Table 2.1   Number of securities quoted on the Vienna Stock Exchange, 1771–1945

	Investment Bonds/Other Loans	Mortgage/ Communal Bonds	Total of Shares Thereof	Industrial Shares
end 1771	16	–	–	
end 1820	44	–	1	
end 1848	35	1	8	n.a.
end 1854	42	1	11	n.a.
end 1867	96	9	39	39
beginning 1873	154	47	378	62
1878	251		137	49
end 1885	217	69	114	54
end 1900	253	127	200	110
July 25th 1914	361	197	262	176
Oct.1st 1922	327	187	369	281
end 1930*	266	102	284	n.a.
March 11th 1938	175	81	203	n.a.
end 1940*	131	57	193	n.a.
April 3rd 1945*	108	127	180	n.a.

Source: F. Baltzarek, *Die Geschichte der Wiener Börse* (Vienna 1073), table 3, p. 161.
* without so-called 'Exoten'
n. a. ... not available

The selection of years/dates is based on important turning points of Austria's political and economic history.

---

14 Ibid.

15 H. Matis and F. Weber, 'Kaisertum Österreich – Donaumonarchie', in H. Pohl (ed.), *Europäische Bankengeschichte* (Frankfurt, 1993), p. 327.

But the 1870s and 80s were not only a period of withdrawal from the industrial business. The banks were confronted with old and new competitors. After the Compromise in 1867 establishing the Dual Monarchy Austria-Hungary the bureaucratic limitations (prescribing humanitarian and socio-political aims) of the savings banks were largely eliminated (by new 'Musterstatuten' in 1872 stressing the banking function), and savings banks from then on did not differ much from the joint-stock banks. It seems worth mentioning that in contrast to France or England, government finance was not a priority, and their contribution to the industrial business has not been analysed in detail. Another new element in the Austro-Hungarian banking structure were the credit cooperatives with two significant types, the Schulze-Delitzsch (serving the needs of urban craftsmen) and the Raiffeisen cooperatives (turning towards rural communities and especially expanding enormously in the 1880s, a time of depression in agriculture). At least one should mention the foundation of the Österreichische Postsparkasse (Austrian Post Office Savings Bank) in 1882/83, not only important because of its wide net of branches in the form of post offices and thus its outstanding capacity to collect small savings and of its innovation of introducing cheque transactions but especially because of its later important role in state financing. And finally because of the political background of its foundation: The Postsparkasse was meant as a conservative counterpart to Rothschild, the liberal great banks in general and their dominant position in the Habsburg Monarchy's financial system. With regards to the total assets joint-stock banks lost their leading position after the crisis of 1873, the savings banks then – less retarded by speculation and crisis – played the main role in lending, which they lost only in the last decade before World War I, the so called 'Second Gründerzeit',[16] again to the joint-stock banks (see Table 2.2).

It is important to note that the great banks left an important part of the economy's financial business to other credit sectors; there was a clear division of labour between different kinds of financial institutions. The 'second credit sector', a term used by März and Socher for mortgage banks and credit cooperatives,[17] proved to be of increasing importance since the 1880s and concentrated on the financing of agriculture, home building and the local infrastructure. Another observation was that especially these credit sectors were organized mostly on a local basis (to get closer to the potential depositors the banks soon reacted with an enlargement of their branch nets) and arranged in a national framework within the multinational monarchy.[18] The existence of regional/provincial constituents, of Bohemian, Galician, Hungarian institutes, mirrored both the multinational and multilingual character of the Monarchy and the conflicts resulting from that situation. For example, the savings banks established in the Czech crownlands (=Kronländer) got two central institutions, a German speaking one and a Czech speaking one. Nonetheless, the financial system on the whole showed strong centralistic features. The result was that Viennese banks dominated the industrial business in the Czech provinces, so domestic Czech banks

---

16 März, 'Währung und Banken in Cisleithanien', p. 358.
17 Ibid., p. 349.
18 Köver, 'The Austro-Hungarian Banking System', p. 324.

Table 2.2   Total assets of financial institutions in Cisleithania, 1873–1913 (in millions of crowns)

	1873	1883	1893	1903	1913
Austro-Hungarian Bank	1,111.26*	1,186.26	1,531.04	2,523.04	3,344.59
Joint-Stock Banks	2,233.96	1,712.43	2,323.30	3,794.90	9,766.30
Savings Banks	1,030.00	1,894.90	3,242.40	4,813.30	7,092.90
Post Office Savings Bank	—	8.20	166.20	450.60	590.40
Mortgage companies	170.47	390.37	798.01	2,020.20	3,592.70
Credit cooperatives	29.74†	452.05	839.06	1,822.26	3,880.24

* Oesterreichische Nationalbank
† This estimate is according to Komlos, John, *The Habsburg Monarchy as a Customs Union*, Princeton 1983, p. 247, 'clearly wrong'.

Sources: Good, David F., 'Stagnation and Take off in Austria, 1873–1913', in: *Economic History Review*, 27 (February 1974), Appendix 1; Köver György, 'The Austro-Hungarian Banking System', in: Cameron, Rondo, Bovykin, V.I. (eds), *International Banking 1870–1914*, New York-Oxford 1991, p. 325.

and other financial institutes tried to direct more activities to the South-Slav areas of the Monarchy, an area widely neglected by the Viennese banks.

The Banks at their Zenith of Power

It took until the late 1890s – before the background of declining profits from handling government loans, the end of the railway boom and some other factors – that the Viennese banks began to turn to industrial lending. From then on they were not only heavily involved in transforming mainly profitable and longstanding client enterprises into joint-stock companies but also – still remaining cautious – in the industrial foundation business itself.[19] Sometimes their participations were due to cases of financial emergencies (e.g. the transformation of the sugar refinery in Pecek into a joint-stock company in 1888 by the Credit-Anstalt), a real missionary role of the banks in the sense of Gerschenkron was seldom found. An active industrial policy, for example, stood behind the foundation of the mineral oil refinery in Fiume by the Credit-Anstalt and the House of Rothschild. The banks' importance grew; in the period from 1907 to 1913 banks were active in more than half of the industrial foundations and they were responsible for more than two thirds of the capital

---

19 As to the various stages of the relationship banks-industry cf. R. L. Rudolph, *Banking and Industrialization in Austria-Hungary. The Role of Banks in the Industrialization of the Czech Crownlands, 1873–1914* (Cambridge, 1976).

needed.[20] It was during this period when the relationship between banks and industry could be called more and more symbiotic,[21] seemingly even more symbiotic than in Germany. Among Austrian banks a higher percentage of the own capital was bound in securities and syndicate transactions (in 1913 between 38 and 64 per cent against 20 to 29 per cent in Germany).

Fast growth characterized the development of balance sheets, debtors and creditors, of the banks' equities and so on. Their expansionist drive is also shown by the growth of bank branches; the ten largest Vienna banks had 34 branches in 1896, 92 in 1905 and 127 in 1913. Their focus lay on the domestic business and market – in contrast to the major economies of Northern and Central Europe. Only eight of these branches were outside the Habsburg Monarchy. Foreign activities of the Austrian banks on the whole were seldom found, and then primarily in the Balkans and in the Ottoman Empire and basically functioning as junior partner to mainly French financial institutes.

We have already mentioned that even among the group of countries with a similar universal bank system and with similar bank-industry relations Austria was outstanding in some respects. While the Austrian banking system performed the usual functions of accumulating and mobilizing capital like that of other developed countries it played a much greater and active role in employing resources in industry and trade, in the allocation of capital.[22] Banks not only provided advances; without any legal constraints to the ownership of shares they secured their credits by acquiring equity preferably in the largest and soundest enterprises, mainly in those they had changed into public companies and in those whose comparatively frequent share issues they organized; they strengthened or tried to strengthen their supervision of client companies through interlocking directorships, a means which at least provided important information channels but due to the accumulation of 40 and more mandates proved to be inefficient especially thinking of the bank crashes in the 1920s. Furthermore Austria-Hungary's industrial development before 1914 took place with increasing concentration in major branches of manufacturing consisting of cartelization or vertical or horizontal integration, and some of the domestic universal banks were important, often leading actors in these processes.[23] They encouraged cartelization and were initiators or mediators of mergers. In a number of industries (sugar, coal, wood, coke, petroleum) the banks even assumed marketing functions through commission sales or, in the case of the existence of a cartel, acted as cartel bureaux.

---

20 Cf. W. Reik, *Die Beziehungen der österreichischen Großbanken zur Industrie* (Vienna, 1932).

21 This phenomenon not only inspired Rudolf Hilferding in developing his theory of the finance capital. The important role of banks is also mirrored in the works of Alexander Gerschenkron, who lived in Vienna after 1918. Lastly, the role of banks and of bank credits forms an important part of the works of the Austrian economist Joseph A. Schumpeter.

22 Rudolph, *Banking and Industrialization*, p. 159. Mosser, 'Investment Behaviour', p. 135.

23 Rudolf Hilferding already stated in 1909 in his Finance Capital: 'Austria ... provides the clearest example of the direct and deliberate influence of bank capital upon cartelization.' R. Hilferding, *Finance Capital. A Study of the Latest Phase of Capitalist Development* (London, 1981), p. 213.

The sum of these activities was that on the eve of the First World War the great Viennese banks had secured strategic positions in most branches of industry and their influence reached to all the empire's territories, with a focus on Cisleithania, the Austrian half of the Dual Monarchy, and here concentrating on the more industrialized regions like Bohemia and Lower Austria.[24] By 1914 the eight great Viennese banks accounted for about two-thirds of the total capital of all the financial institutions of the Habsburg Empire. They were at their zenith of power.[25]

Relatively stable frame conditions marked by a successful currency policy had been the favourable background for the development of the financial centre of Vienna from the late 1870s onwards. Vienna was considered to be an international centre of the money market – though comparably only a secondary one.[26] It was Belgian and especially French short-term credits that played main roles in the Vienna money market.[27] The efforts of Hungarian and Bohemian banks and of the stock exchange in Budapest – all of growing importance before World War I – to get in the same position were in vain.

Trying to describe and analyse Vienna's role and function as a financial place before World War I the historian is confronted with a very specific situation showing some peculiarities:

1. On the eve of World War I Vienna could be characterized as a relatively important international financial centre and as a non negligible capital market. Vienna's significance was based on numerous financial transactions for the region of Central, Southeast and Eastern Europe.[28] Trying to include Vienna into one of the common typologies of financial centres Vienna seems to be a 'hybrid' between different categories. According to Geoffrey Jones' typology[29] based on geographical ties Vienna's position would be between a sub-regional financial centre and a regional financial centre as regional centres are understood to supply financial services to an entire region (such as Europe). The same is true for Richard Roberts' typology,[30] where Vienna could be characterized as a domestic financial centre but also shows at least some features of a regional financial centre.

---

24 Only the Hungarian General Credit Bank, a foundation of the Credit-Anstalt but emancipating from Austrian influence, seemed to have been on a par with the leading Viennese institutions. The rise of Czech banks, especially the Zivnostenská banka, had started slowly but should mainly fall in the period after 1918. Cf. Teichova, 'Banking and Industry', p. 219.

25 F. Weber, 'Universal Banking in Interwar Central Europe', in H. James et al. (eds), *The Role of Banks in the Interwar Economy* (Cambridge, 1991), p. 19.

26 Cf. Köver, 'The Austro-Hungarian Banking System', p. 326.

27 Bartsch, *Statistische Daten über die Zahlungsbilanz*, p. 45.

28 Cf. A. Teichova, 'Peripetien des Finanzzentrums Wien', in K. Bachinger and D. Stiefel (eds), *Auf Heller und Cent. Beiträge zur Finanz- und Währungsgeschichte* (Frankfurt Vienna, 2001), p. 530, and A. Teichova, 'Wiens wechselhafte Rolle als Finanzzentrum in Europa während des 20. Jahrhunderts', in *Geld und Kapital. Jahrbuch der Gesellschaft für mitteleuropäische Banken- und Sparkassengeschichte*, vol. 1997, pp. 24–5.

29 Cf. Roberts, 'The Economies of Cities of Finance', p. 9.

30 Ibid., p.11.

2. Strong banks – weak stock exchange: After 1873 the Viennese great banks had taken over the functions of a capital market from the Vienna stock exchange: The majority of capital transfers was performed by the Vienna banks; only a modest part was initiated and mediated by the stock exchange. The banks' importance and thus the importance of Vienna as a banking centre is mirrored in a ranking of banking centres in Northern and Central Europe for the year 1914.[31] Vienna reaches – in terms of the aggregate balance sheet total – fourth position after London, Paris and Berlin. Among a list of the 25 largest banks in Northern and Central Europe in 1913 ranked by balance sheet total you find three Austrian banks, the Credit-Anstalt on position 15, the Boden-Credit-Anstalt on position 21 and the Länderbank on position 23.[32]

But stressing the banks' strength and importance, their efforts to replace the stock exchange's capital market function does not mean that all banks fulfilled their role successfully. The state of the Viennese banks before World War I was worse than was believed and realized by contemporaries as well as by later historians. Already in 1913 'one could … observe signs of frozen industrial credits and an over-accumulation of the banks' share portfolios'.[33] The 'lucky chance' of the war boom stopped that development.

3. Creditor, debtor or both? The Habsburg Monarchy was among the indebted states on European capital markets, one third of its state debt accumulated by the time of the Compromise was owed to foreign creditors.[34] From the late 1870s onwards the Austrian and the Hungarian governments began to raise more and more loans. In 1912/13, 24.7 per cent of the debt of the hereditary provinces and 39 per cent of that of Hungary were in foreign hands.[35] Throughout the era 30 to 40 per cent of the budgets of both the Austrian and the Hungarian governments went to debt service.

It is important to stress that Cisleithania, the Austrian half of the Habsburg Monarchy, was a creditor with respect to the Hungarian half (Transleithania), but the monarchy as a whole was a net debtor.

The biggest foreign investor in the Habsburg Monarchy was Germany, the sum invested in 1914 coming to three billion marks.[36] German bankers did a relatively large financial business in Austria-Hungary, concentrating mainly on government and railway securities.[37] This business grew substantially from 1890 onwards. After

---

31 Cf. P.L. Cottrell, 'Aspects of Commercial Banking in Northern and Central Europe, 1880–1931', in S. Kinsey and L. Newton (eds), *International Banking in an Age of Transition. Globalisation, Automation, Banks and their Archives* (Aldershot, 1998), pp. 105–6.

32 Ibid., p. 109.

33 Weber, 'Universal Banking', p. 19.

34 After the Compromise the national debt was divided between the two halves, leading to the exclusion of Austro-Hungarian securities from the London Stock Exchange in May 1870. Köver, 'The Austro-Hungarian Banking System', p. 321.

35 Bartsch, *Statistische Daten über die Zahlungsbilanz*, p. 198.

36 According to H. Feis, *Europe, the World's Banker, 1870–1914* (London, 1930).

37 R. Tilly, 'International Aspects of the Development of German Banking', in R. Cameron and V.I. Bovykin (eds), *International Banking 1870–1914* (New York Oxford, 1991), p. 101.

1900 larger sums were invested in private industrial enterprises, especially in the manufacture of electrical equipment.

4. After 1873, intensified after 1918 one might add, Vienna had to compete with foreign financial interests. Insofar as joint business operations were concerned, the Austro-Hungarian banks were involved in most of the larger capital transfers to and foreign operations with Southeast Europe, but appeared most often as junior partners to other banks.

Köver speaks of a Central European division of labour in the lending and loan mediating activity of the banks.[38] When the Austrian state debts were unified and the common state debts were repatriated in the Monarchy, the Hungarian government bonds were repaid on the international money market. From the mid 1870s on the Vienna banks placed the Hungarian government loans increasingly in Cisleithania. In the 1890s after stabilizing the proportion of government debts being placed abroad and at home, the Vienna banks began transactions on their own, with German or French capital aid or through the mediation of Budapest to finance business in the Balkans. Capital from West Europe was directed to investment projects in the Central and Southeast European area. The role of the Monarchy's banks as mediators of international capital flows can be considered as characteristic. For all that, before World War I they lost their ability to finance the Balkan government loans.

5. Austrian banks and their role in international investments: With the exception of the period between 1903 and 1908, the Dual Monarchy generally had an export surplus of securities – i.e., it was a net importer of long-term capital.[39] In the years before World War I the Austro-Hungarian Monarchy was not merely a capital importer, but owing to the leading banking groups it could also cover the deficit partly by re-exporting foreign bonds.[40] The original sources of capital imports looking at the state loans were Amsterdam, Brussels, Frankfurt and Paris, later primarily Berlin. The percentage of Austrian securities held abroad was shrinking after 1890, mirroring the fact that after the stabilization of currency and the conversion of debts the domestic accumulation increased, with from 1903 onwards one fourth of the Austrian state securities being held abroad. Germany became the number one foreign creditor for both halves of the empire. In terms of state debts the Monarchy seems to have been a debtor towards Western and (parts of) Central Europe, while at the same time it acted as a creditor – in most cases joining German capital – towards the Balkans, here especially in Bulgaria.

While lending for the infrastructural development of economically more backward countries, the Monarchy built its own railway system with the help of foreign capital.[41] In contrast, the actual foreign investment in domestic industry was

---

38 Cf. Köver, 'The Austro-Hungarian Banking System', pp. 343–4.

39 Cf. Köver, 'The Austro-Hungarian Banking System', pp. 332–3.

40 Ibid., p. 341.

41 In spite of diverse phases of railway nationalization more than 70 per cent of the railway priority bonds of the hereditary provinces were in foreign hands at the beginning of the twentieth century, more than two thirds still at the beginning of World War I, cf. ibid., p. 334.

small, only 12 per cent of all industrial shares and bonds and only 0.5 per cent of all Austrian securities at the beginning of the century.[42]

In Hungary Austrian capital investments after 1900 were of shrinking importance and played a decisive role only in some modern branches with a high demand for capital (machinery and chemicals). The capital exports of the Monarchy to the Balkan region were not inaptly called 'reluctant imperialism' in modern literature.[43]

On the whole the share of international finance of the Austrian banks was relatively low, business was concentrated on the Habsburg Monarchy's territory. Nobody could foresee the sudden internationalization of that business, caused by the new borders and national states after the breakdown of the Monarchy.

6. The high demand for investment capital of the economically more backward crownlands explains the small radius of action of the Vienna stock exchange. This is underlined by the proportion between domestic and foreign securities at the Vienna stock exchange: In 1912 the share of foreign bonds in total registered securities – taken as a measure of the international importance of different stock markets – was 48 per cent of the London stock exchange, 37 per cent in Paris, 5.6 per cent in Berlin and in Vienna it was 0.27 per cent.[44]

7. Banking groups and state finance: The expansion of international capital movements brought about the establishment of international banking groups.[45] While the groups built as consortia of independent banks remained relatively stable, its components, the single banks, were often competing with each other. One of their main activities was the financing of the state.

A major characteristic of the Austrian financial system was the dependence of banking upon the state. The state dealt almost exclusively with Viennese banks, hardly concerning itself at all with provincial banks.[46] The government bonds market, monopolized by the Rothschild consortium until 1910, was of great importance in Viennese banking. The Austro-Hungarian development in the field of government bonds can be interpreted as an attempt to break the monopoly of the Rothschild-Credit-Anstalt consortium. The Rothschild Consortium, a kind of cartel-like collection of roughly a dozen firms, five of them German (the most important German partner was the Disconto-Gesellschaft), had been formed to handle all types of large-scale financing involving security issues by Austro-Hungarian government bodies or firms.[47] Created as an *ad hoc* arrangement to limit competition among

---

42 Rudolph, *Banking and Industrialization in Austria-Hungary*, pp. 174–5.

43 J. Lampe and M. Jackson, *Balkan Economic History, 1550–1950: From Imperial Borderlands to Developing Nations* (Bloomington 1982), p. 208.

44 F. Baltzarek, 'Finanzplatz Wien – die innerstaatliche und internationale Stellung in historischer Perspektive', *Quartalshefte der Girozentrale*, vol. 15, 1980, p. 59.

45 Cf. the following Köver, 'The Austro-Hungarian Banking System', pp. 335–6.

46 D.L. Augustine, 'The Banking Families in Berlin and Vienna around 1900', in H. Diederiks and D. Reeder (eds), *Cities of Finance* (Amsterdam, 1996), p. 230. The banks' 'inferior, dependent position' in their relationship with the state was 'the result of the hostility of society in large', ibid., p. 234.

47 Tilly, 'International Aspects', p. 100.

bankers for Austrian government loans it developed into a virtually permanent organization.

Other associations were only temporarily successful, so the group around the Wiener Bankverein formed in the 1870s (foreign partners were the Deutsche Bank and the French Banque de Paris et des Pays-Bas). With regards to the – as it seems most effective – Austro-German coalitions (between Credit-Anstalt and Disconto-Gesellschaft, between Wiener Bankverein and Deutsche Bank), Vienna had the role of the 'little brother',[48] until 1897 when the Postsparkasse participated for the first time in state loan transactions without joining the consortium. In the conversion of 1903 five Vienna banks participated under the leadership of the Wiener Bankverein and joined the Rothschild consortium. In 1910 a real 'court revolution'[49] took place when the Austrian Minister of Finance concluded a contract for the issue of certain bonds only with the Postsparkasse (establishing a group of regional German, Bohemian, and Slovenian banks). It is interesting to remember that the creation of the Postsparkasse in 1883 was an attempt of the Feudal-Conservative government of Taaffe to free itself from the hold of the Liberal Rothschilds over imperial debt management.[50] In 1911 the Rothschilds were successful in uniting the former rivals.

This shift of the role of the Rothschild-Credit-Anstalt consortium was accompanied by a change of the banks' business policy: the banks left out the loans of the dual governments after 1873 and began – as partners of international consortiums – to turn toward the Balkan states.[51] When the Balkan countries were more and more involved in the foreign policy of the great powers, Austria's banks lost significance. A kind of compensation was the increased turning to industrial business. The Viennese banks widened their nets of industrial participations, a development finally culminating in the foundation of the Österreichische Kontrollbank as a joint undertaking of ten Cisleithanian banks in 1914 meant as supervisor for syndicates and controlling institution of cartels and trusts.

The establishment of international banking groups was in many cases accompanied by the emergence of international holding companies, especially in such international branches as railways and new energy producers.

8. Vienna kept its position as *the* financial centre on the territory of the Habsburg Monarchy. Budapest and Prague expanded, but did not reach Vienna's significance.[52] The Viennese great banks were able to enlarge their central position, although the degree of concentration in an international comparison as well as from the present perspective was relatively low. While the percentage of Czech institutes rose from 7 (1881) to 23 (1912) of the total share capital of Cisleithanian financial institutes,

---

48 Köver, 'The Austro-Hungarian Banking System', p. 343.

49 Term used by B. Michel, *Banques et Banquiers en Autriche au Debut du 20e Siècle* (Paris, 1976), pp. 130–31.

50 M.J. Daunton, 'Finance and Politics: Comments', in Y. Cassis (ed.), *Finance and Financiers in European History, 1880–1960* (Cambridge, 1992), p. 287.

51 Köver, 'The Austro-Hungarian Banking System', p. 337.

52 This is also true for the position of single banks – perhaps with the exceptions of the Hungarian General Credit Bank and the Czech Zivnostenská banka.

the 12 largest Vienna banks increased their share from 57.2 per cent (1904) to 64.7 per cent (1913).[53]

According to Cottrell's estimate on the degree of banking concentration in Northern and Central Europe (by share of aggregate balance sheet total) in 1914 Austria's position among nine countries was in the middle taking either the share of the largest bank or of the three largest banks.[54]

The Power of Banks – a Myth, and Other Open Questions

It is important and perhaps astonishing to note that research on Austria(-Hungary) did not cope or coped less well with the question why the Vienna stock exchange had such a weak position and the banks such a strong one. It was the banks that attracted the main interest, especially – with regards to the close relationship between banks and industry – the question of bank power or dominance. The discussion about the power of banks is almost as old as banks themselves. The fact is that due to the accumulation of various functions performed by the banks, the relationship between Austrian universal banks and industry before 1918 was not that of equal partners. These functions were:

1. the long-run current account connected with the decision-making power of the banks in the granting of credits, often leading to the ownership of stock of non-bank corporations,
2. the participation of banks in non-banks' corporations connected with the representation on their supervisory boards (the phenomenon of interlocking directorates),[55] and finally
3. the proxy voting of shares in client companies (=Depotstimmrecht – the right to vote in stockholder meetings of non-bank corporations on behalf of those who have deposited their securities with the banks).[56]

This kind of disproportion led to the argument of an alleged bank dominance over industry. Others, more cautiously, speak in this context of far-reaching influence potential of the banks. The credit demand of an industrial enterprise and the offer of credit supply by a certain bank were the starting point for the mutual relationship. The

---

53 E. März, *Österreichische Bankpolitik in der Zeit der großen Wende 1913–1923. Am Beispiel der Creditanstalt für Handel und Gewerbe* (Vienna, 1981), p. 54.

54 Cottrell, 'Aspects of Commercial Banking', p. 115.

55 The author is still working on a revised version of his dissertation 'Die Konzentration der Entscheidungsmacht. Personelle Verflechtungen zwischen den Wiener Großbanken und Industrieaktiengesellschaften, 1895–1940', unpublished diss., 2 vols. (Vienna, 1997). For a survey cf. P. Eigner, 'Interlocking Directorships between Commercial Banks and Industry in Interwar Vienna', in A. Teichova et al. (eds), *Universal Banking in the Twentieth Century. Finance, Industry and the State in North and Central Europe* (Aldershot, 1994), pp. 260–93.

56 Cf. H. Wixforth and D. Ziegler, 'Bankenmacht: Universal Banking and German Industry in Historical Perspective', in Y. Cassis et al. (eds), *The Evolution of Financial Institutions and Markets in Twentieth-century Europe* (Aldershot, 1995), p. 250.

other 'institutional' factors mentioned above will, not necessarily but often, follow. One of these 'institutionalized bridgeheads'[57] was the phenomenon of interlocking directorates.

The close connections with industry made supervision an important prerequisite, thus banks created an institutional way of assembling and exchanging large quantities of information about the situation of 'their' enterprises and their competitors, about certain branches or the economic conditions in general.[58] Bank control was facilitated by the legal division between an executive and a supervisory board within corporate organizations. Larger credit contracts often included a seat for the bank on the supervisory board. This allowed bank representatives, and to a lesser degree also non-bank representatives, to create networks of business and of personal relationships. Systems of interlocking directorates led to a superior and intimate knowledge of many branches and companies and provided a greater input to rational decision making than that derived from a stock market where the rewards for concealment were high. The existence of such networks of interlocking directorates provided ways of reducing market uncertainty and risk, and represented a response to a high degree of competition in the financial market. The accumulation of mandates allowed the banks to engage in processes of cartelization or industrial concentration, the directors thus not only becoming 'agents for the direction of funds, but also agents of market integration and regulation'.[59]

Accumulating up to 40 positions on supervisory boards, real information traders, often called 'big linkers', came into existence.[60] What could be an advantage for coordinating businesses, transactions etc., proved to be an over-burden in most cases, especially in Austria after 1918, perhaps also due to the now international character of Austrian bank business. Such big linkers were to a large degree dependent on their staff, on the information delivered by others. Even if they visited the board meetings, what seems impossible in the case of more than 30 companies, this was not the place and the time to obtain all the information one needed. So board representation was a sign of strength (and bankers had much more mandate than industrialists), but in the interwar period proved to be an insufficient instrument for the control of and for getting insider information from client companies.

Equity ownership is another example that confronts us with two possible explanations. It could be explained as a means of bank power, but also as expression of weakness, caused by a non-functioning capital market. Not all participations were voluntary, some were due to business difficulties, to debts a company could not repay, and so on.

The establishment of a bank-oriented system in Austria compared to market-oriented banking systems leads to some questions. Have bank-oriented systems been more efficient than market-oriented ones in channelling funds to industry?[61]

57 Cf. Wixforth, 'Bankenmacht', p. 255.

58 H. James, 'Introduction', in H. James et al. (eds), *The Role of Banks in the Interwar Economy* (Cambridge, 1991), p. 10.

59 Ziegler, 'The Influence of Banking', p. 133.

60 Wixforth, 'Bankenmacht', p. 252.

61 Cf. Y. Cassis, *The Evolution of Financial Institutions and Markets*, p. 3.

Have small and medium-sized enterprises been properly served by their respective banking systems? Caroline Fohlin's research on Germany[62] focuses attention on the effectiveness of the credit banks as financial institutions (and information-improvers). Her basic finding, covering roughly the period from 1880 to 1913, is that bank influence had no persistent, significant effects on financial structure, performance and investment. There are no comparable studies on Austria based on these questions. Confronted with the task to measure efficiency of the financial sector we have to analyse the ability of the institutions and market to reduce the asymmetry of information existing between lenders and borrowers. Following Dieter Ziegler and Harald Wixforth, at a macroeconomic level the superiority of the universal banks over the market in the collection and distribution of information remains a controversial issue.[63] At a microeconomic level, however, there is mounting evidence that the alleged power of German banks over industrial companies has been greatly exaggerated.[64] The assumption of the banks' supremacy over industry was tested with regards to Wilhelmine and Weimar Germany and was found to require revision for both time periods.[65]

Austria's development seems to be an exception. According to Gerschenkron's theory the dominant position of banks disappears and their effectiveness as intermediaries deteriorated in the course of industrialization when self-financing becomes more important and non-bank enterprises can gradually emancipate themselves from the bank influence. Again, while there seems to be widespread agreement that the power of the great banks declined and while this has been investigated for Germany,[66] this work has not been done for Austria, but there are indications that the Austrian development differs from the German one. Austrian companies missed the chance to emancipate one could say after 1918 (if there was such a chance). Inflation even strengthened the ties between banks and their industrial clients and even led to a renewal of the industrial foundation business performed by the banks while in Germany during the Weimar Republic the strength of the banks was seriously shattered.[67] One of the reasons was the internationalization of capital markets in the 1920s which gave larger companies the possibility to enlarge their credit sources, to borrow from abroad.[68] In Austria there were only a very few among

---

62 C. Fohlin, 'Universal Banking in Pre-World War I Germany: Model or Myth?', in *Explorations in Economic History*, vol. 36, 1999, pp. 305–43.

63 Wixforth, 'Bankenmacht', pp. 261–4.

64 Ibid., pp. 255–61.

65 H. Wixforth, *Banken und Schwerindustrie in der Weimarer Republik* (Cologne Weimar, 1995). K.E. Born, 'Die Deutsche Bank in der Inflation nach dem Ersten Weltkrieg', *Beiträge zu Wirtschafts- und Währungsfragen und zur Bankengeschichte*, vol. 17, 1979, pp. 27–8.

66 Cf. for the Kaiserreich V. Wellhöner, *Großbanken und Großindustrie im Kaiserreich* (Göttingen, 1989); for the Weimar Republic Wixforth, *Banken und Schwerindustrie*, and T. Balderston, 'German Banking between the Wars: The Crisis of the Credit Banks', in *Business History Review*, vol. 65, 1991, pp. 588–96.

67 Wixforth, *Banken und Schwerindustrie*, and Balderston, 'German Banking between the Wars'.

68 Examples see Wixforth, 'Bankenmacht', p. 259.

the largest industrial companies (like the Alpine Montangesellschaft in mining) that were in such a privileged position.

Another question deals with the adequacy and/or efficiency of the Austrian banking system. How efficient have the Austrian banks been in channelling funds to industry and – considering Richard Tilly's judgement on the German great banks' business policy as 'development assistance for the strong'[69] – was the universal bank system also efficient and adequate for the important small- and medium-sized Austrian industry? Even if one were to assign crucial importance to the corporate sector of the economy where large-scale enterprises operated (and where the great banks definitely were disproportionately involved), this need not imply a crucial role for the great banks, for even here, self-financing predominated.

To the question of the small- and medium-sized companies and the role of the great banks in that respect, it seems that local and regional banks were important 'players' and had at least an important additive and complementary function, the problem is lack of research in Austria on this topic. But even at their summit of power, credit banks as a whole held only a minor percentage of the total assets held by all financial institutions. This fact calls for more attention to other institutions, e.g. the public savings banks or credit cooperatives. So although Austria's financial system can clearly be characterized as a bank-oriented financial system, it has become evident that such a system did not lack any division of functions. A broad analysis of Austria's banking system should thus not be narrowed to credit banks. A final judgement whether the relatively dominant position of the great banks has led to a misallocation of monetary capital is not possible. Thinking of the huge territory of the Habsburg Monarchy it also was a question of the existence or non-existence of a branch of a Viennese big bank in a certain area and whether other provincial banks were represented there. And it seems important to mention that the Habsburg Monarchy, in contrast to Germany for example, only had one financial centre – Vienna. Budapest and Prague were of growing importance from 1890 onwards but did not reach the position of Vienna.

Sequel: The Period of Illusions and of Definite Failure

Austria's financial market was still dominated by its large banks in the interwar period, they usually engaged in long-term financing of industry as well as in more conventional short-term businesses.[70] They issued shares, gave current account credits and discounted bills; they also often held large share parcels so that on occasion they appeared to be industrial holding companies rather than more conventionally understood banks. The market operated relatively independently of central banks except in times of crisis when central banks played a prominent role in discounting bills from the portfolios of commercial banks.

---

69 R. Tilly, 'German Banking. Development Assistance for the Strong', in *Journal of European Economic History*, vol. 15, 1986, pp. 113–52.

70 Cf. James, 'Introduction', p. 4. Cf. also to the following A. Teichova, 'Commercial (Universal) Banking in Central Europe – from Cisleithania to the Successor States', in M. Fase et al. (eds), *How to Write the History of A Bank* (Aldershot, Brookfield, 1995), pp. 130–32.

But what soon became apparent was that the mechanisms before 1914 did not function anymore. Shares held in the expectation of favourable future developments in the capital markets often were retained for longer than anticipated when those improvements did not arise – and in the worst cases finally had to be written off.

The outcome of the First World War radically changed the frame conditions for Austrian banks. On the other hand the war brought no discontinuity for concentration of either industrial or financial capital.[71] After the break-up of the Habsburg Monarchy the banks found themselves suddenly standing at the head of multinational diversified industrial concerns in the new successor states, thus bank-industry relations were dramatically affected by the disintegration of the Empire, even more while these new states in their first years tried to emancipate from former Austrian influence and dominance. In their efforts to uphold their former spheres of influence the Austrian banks definitely failed. Making 'business as usual' they refused to adapt their business policy to the very much changed circumstances. In addition, their function underwent a change. Although we stressed the mediating function of the banks before 1918, the leading Viennese banks after 1918 served to a much greater extent as intermediaries between West European and US-American capital groups, which had acquired substantial share packages of these banks very cheaply, especially in the inflation period between 1919 and 1923, in order to gain entrance to the new markets in South-East Europe. Foreign shareholding increased enormously, two of the Viennese universal banks, the Länderbank and the Anglo-Austrian Bank had become fully foreign-owned Paris- and London-based institutes. Foreign capital had furthermore burst directly into former industrial holdings of the Austrian banks located in Austria and other successor states of the Monarchy. The banks' position was also weakened by new competitors in the successor states. These had developed their own universal bank systems, and banks like the Czechoslovak Živnostenská banka – strengthened also by the results of the 'nostrification', a kind of nationalization process by transferring the head offices of companies from Vienna to the new states – replaced and followed the Austrian banks.[72] Not only did the banks lose most of their branches outside Austria and part of their subsidiary industrial enterprises through these measures, they also lost their former predominance in financing these companies, among them some very profitable clients, especially in Czechoslovakia.

The turmoil of post-war inflation and financial crises had even intensified the demand for capital. So the relationship between banks and industry at the beginning of the Austrian interwar period – the period culminating in hyperinflation – was strengthened. No sign of industrial emancipation was visible. But after 1918 the

---

71 Teichova, 'Banking and Industry in Central Europe', p. 218.

72 In spite of structural similarities the development of the Czechoslovak banking system differed from the other successor states. While the Czechoslovak economy and banking system remained rather independent from foreign capital influence, the share of foreign ownership of Romanian, Yugoslavian, less Polish and Bulgarian commercial banks was high. A. Teichova, *An Economic Background to Munich. International Business and Czechoslovakia 1918–1938* (Cambridge, 1974), p. 342; idem, 'East-Central and South-East Europe, 1919–1939', in P. Mathias and S. Pollard (eds), *The Cambridge Economic History of Europe* (Cambridge, 1989), p. 924.

banks were not so much promoting industrial enterprise as rescuing their own industrial subsidiary enterprises from collapse.[73] A policy of 'Veraktionierung', forcing firms to repay frozen credits by new share issues, strengthened the links between banks and industry.[74] And the banks, although willing to get rid of their over-expanded holdings, never succeeded. On the other hand, banks should have been aware earlier that their policy to keep their industrial debtors afloat, to cover industrial losses and sustain industrial dividends was more and more based on an 'illusion of prosperity'.[75] The banks should have rather invested in the necessary restructuring of Austrian industry but missed this change in their business policy. In their need for external capital help the short-term indebtedness of the Viennese banks was steadily growing.[76] The banks' credit financing relied to an ever growing extent on borrowing short-term abroad and lending funds on a long-term basis.[77]

The necessary process for banks and industry of adjusting to the new market conditions obviously failed, as Mosser states 'because of the paucity of investment' which was 'not a result of a lack of capital but due to the absence of promising opportunities for investment'.[78] The enterprises preferred internal sources of capital or – in the case of joint-stock companies – financing by issuing shares, while long-term credits played a subordinate role as before World War I. Causes for the relatively poor investment activity can be seen in the predominant forms of provision of credits and the conditions attached to them. Another reason behind the companies' preference for self-financing of investments could be found in the Austrian tax system which rendered certain forms of credits unprofitable (e.g. the issue of bonds), because interest as well as dividends emanating from them were taxed.[79] And even Austria's largest industrial companies – with a few exceptions – were not in the position to obtain long-term foreign capital. By procuring cheap Western credits especially to big industrial companies and so trying to ease the weight of interest rates, the banks created a split credit market, with small- and medium-sized firms as underdogs paying interest rates often twice as high as for dollar or sterling advances.[80]

Mosser's research shows that industrial joint-stock companies were inadequately supplied with working capital and until 1929 developed an increased demand for

---

73 H. Rosovsky, 'Alexander Gerschenkron: A Personal and Fond Recollection', in *Journal of Economic History*, vol. 39, 1970, pp. 1009–13.

74 Weber, 'Universal Banking', p. 21.

75 Teichova, 'Banking and Industry in Central Europe', p. 222.

76 H. Kernbauer and F. Weber, 'Multinational Banking in the Danube Basin', in A. Teichova et al. (eds), *Multinational Enterprise in Historical Perspective* (Cambridge, 1986), pp. 185–99.

77 P.L. Cottrell with C.J. Stone, 'Credits, and Deposits to Finance Credits', in P.L. Cottrell et al. (eds), *European Industry and Banking, 1920–1939: A Review of Bank Industry Relations* (Leicester, 1992), pp. 43–78.

78 Cf. here and in the following A. Mosser, 'Financing Industrial Companies in Interwar Austria: Working Capital and Liquidity', in A. Teichova et al. (eds), *Universal Banking in the Twentieth Century. Finance, Industry and the State in North and Central Europe* (Aldershot, 1994), p. 208. Cf. also Mosser, 'Investment Behaviour', p. 134.

79 Ibid., p. 131.

80 Weber, 'Universal Banking', p. 23.

short term bank credits.[81] One of the banks' difficulties was the fact that savings banks provided insufficient domestic resources or as Fritz Weber argues passed on funds but on conditions quite unfavourable to the banks,[82] so the Austrian financial sector's foreign debts grew, which was reflected in the banks' rising short-term indebtedness. The Viennese stock exchange remained weak except for a period of feverish activity culminating in 1923 in rocketing prices and ending abruptly in 1924 with an unsuccessful speculation in French francs.[83] The banks were forced to intervene on behalf of their industrial combines. The Austrian capital market stagnated from that moment on, and the banks were condemned to financing industry on a greater scale than ever before. The banks became more than ever industrial holding companies though it should be stressed mainly as a result of involuntary investment banking. Questionable methods of window dressing, such as paying high dividends in spite of losses, revaluing their so-called secret reserves or hiding their difficulties by presenting optimistic balance sheets, were often used to hide actual losses before the public.[84]

When prices collapsed in the wake of the excessive speculation of the mid-1920s and the world economic crisis in the 1930s the banks' illiquidity led to insolvency and mergers, the merger process starting in the mid-1920s and peaking in 1929 when the Credit-Anstalt absorbed (or rather was forced by state pressure to take over) the Boden-Credit-Anstalt. The crash of the Credit-Anstalt in 1931[85] was not only caused by management mistakes, organizational failures and by a business policy of expansionism but also due to the takeovers of quite a number of important Austrian universal banks and their industrial holdings since the 1920s. The CA-breakdown was followed by the tightest state-aided bank mergers forcing the Austrian economy, already strained by the world economic crisis, into a shrinking process and resulting more or less in a one-bank system when the process of banking concentration came to an end in 1934.[86] The debt burden of the insolvent banking system was shouldered by the government,[87] finally by the tax payers. The state was obliged to intervene: Banks were either liquidated, amalgamated or taken over fully or partially by the state, their losses socialized, their capital slimmed down.

---

81 Mosser, 'Financing Industrial Companies', pp. 211–12.

82 F. Weber, 'Central European Banking Between 1850 and 1950', in M. Fase et al. (eds), *How to Write the History of a Bank* (Aldershot Brookfield, 1995), p. 140.

83 Cf. ibid., p. 138.

84 Ibid., pp. 141–2.

85 Cf. D. Stiefel, *Finanzdiplomatie und Weltwirtschaftskrise. Die Krise der Credit-Anstalt für Handel und Gewerbe 1931* (Frankfurt, 1989).

86 Teichova, 'Banking and Industry in Central Europe', p. 223. While measured concentration among the credit banks had increased, somewhat paradoxically the increased centralization of decision-making power had gone hand in hand with a weakening of bank monitoring of its customers (the accumulation of often 40 seats on supervisory boards by bank representatives had led to a 'loss of survey').

87 Ibid.

The subsequent shrinking process in banking and industry[88] (known as 'Austrification',[89] as the banks sold almost all of their foreign holdings from 1931 on) characterized by reconstruction and rationalization measures strengthened the highly concentrated structure within banking and industry. The crisis of 1931 proved impressively that the attempts to uphold the former significance of the financial centre of Vienna after 1918 had been in vain.

The financial crash of 1931 in the context of the world economic crisis of the 1930s marked an end to the form of mixed banking that had functioned in Central Europe since the 1880s.

---

88 'The method usually chosen was the extensive writing off of advances, the cancelling of shares … and the conversion of a part of the credits into new share capital', Weber, 'Universal banking', p. 24.

89 The term was introduced by D. Stiefel, 'The Reconstruction of the Credit-Anstalt', in A. Teichova et al. (eds), *International Business & Central Europe, 1918–1939* (Leicester New York, 1983), p. 426.

CHAPTER 3

Torn between Monetary and Financial Stability: An Analysis of Selected Episodes of Austrian Central Banking History

Aurel Schubert

Introduction

To maintain monetary stability is the primary goal of most central banks. In addition, it is in the interest of central banks that financial stability be secured.[1] The two are closely interlinked. Most of the time, the pursuit of these two goals is complementary. However, in times of crisis the pursuit of these two goals may require different actions; they may become conflicting goals. In these cases, hard choices have to be made by the central bank.

This chapter reviews three episodes of Austrian central banking history. These were three episodes of crisis management by the Oesterreichische Nationalbank in times when financial stability was endangered and the Bank was called to contribute to the resolution of the crises. However, attempting to ensure financial stability had repercussions on the pursuit of monetary stability and at times the Bank's management was torn between giving priority to one or the other goal. Emergency liquidity assistance given by the lender of last resort potentially interfered with the monetary policy mandated by the respective statutes and pursued by the Bank.

In the next section we briefly review the concepts of monetary and financial stability and the possible interrelation between them. We then focus on the charters of the Oesterreichische Nationalbank before the crisis of 1873, before we deal with this first episode, the stock-market crisis. Only six years following its reestablishment after the break-up of the Austro-Hungarian Monarchy, the Oesterreichische Nationalbank had to deal with the next crisis, the illiquidity of the Boden-Credit-Anstalt in 1929, the second episode reviewed here. Next we analyse the largest financial crisis in Austrian history, the collapse of the Credit-Anstalt in 1931 and its consequences for financial stability, monetary stability and central banking. Tentative conclusions form the end of the study.

---

1   The Statutes of the European System of Central Banks and of the European Central Bank, for instance, define as the primary objective of the ESCB 'to maintain price stability' (Article 2). As far as financial stability is concerned, the ESCB shall (only) 'contribute to the smooth conduct of policies pursued by the competent authorities relating to the prudential supervision of credit institutions and the stability of the financial system' (Article 4).

Monetary Stability vs. Financial Stability

In central banking we can usually distinguish between the internal and the external stability of the currency; internal and external monetary stability. Internal stability means that the value of the currency in terms of its purchasing power is maintained over time. External stability refers to the maintenance of a stable exchange value of the domestic money relative to some foreign currency or other external anchor.

If the goal is the maintenance of the domestic purchasing power of the currency, the rate of inflation – in whichever way it is actually measured – must be kept low (e.g. below a certain threshold). Inflation usually refers to consumer prices but can also refer to asset prices, like real estate or stocks.[2]

Maintaining the external value might be achieved by successfully pegging – either announced or unannounced – to another currency or to a currency basket, or by maintaining the exchange value relative to a commodity, like gold or silver. It can also be defined as the commitment to exchange paper currency into specie at the fixed rate.

Defining what financial stability means is much more difficult than for monetary stability. There is no single agreed definition of financial stability, except that it is equal to the non-existence of a financial crisis.[3] Actually, there is a myriad of definitions.

There is neither a consensus on how to define the concept of financial stability, nor on how to assess developments under this objective, nor on what role public policy should play.[4]

In a modern economy, finance and the financial sector play a crucial role. However, there are potential benefits but also risks associated with finance. Finance enhances the private and social benefits of fiat money, in part by enlarging the pool of pure liquidity available for production and consumption and exchange. On the other hand, finance inherently embodies uncertainties and therefore risks. Repayment of deposits to the saver depends on the continued existence of the financial institution and on its liquidity and solvency. This uncertainty represents a potential instability in the financial markets.[5]

The analysis of financial stability therefore involves a continuous examination of potential risks and vulnerabilities that may threaten the health of the financial system. The sources of risks to financial stability are manifold. They may be endogenous or exogenous.

A single target variable cannot be found for defining and achieving financial stability as developments in financial stability cannot be summarized in a single

---

2   Other price indices, like producer prices or wholesale prices, can also serve as inflation indicators.

3   Even the definition of a financial crisis is not universal. The term is used in the literature to describe very diverse facts; see A. Schubert, *The Credit-Anstalt Crisis of 1931* (New York, 1991), p. 19.

4   A. Houben, J. Kakes and G. Schinasi, *Towards a framework for financial stability*, De Nederlandsche Bank, Occasional Studies, vol. 2, 1, 2004, p. 8.

5   Houben, *Towards a framework*, p. 9.

quantitative indicator, as it is usually considered to be the case for monetary stability.[6] In addition, analysis of financial stability is still in an infant stage of development.

Financial stability is occurring along a continuum rather than as a static condition or situation. It is a very broad concept that includes different aspects of finance or the financial system: institutions, markets as well as infrastructure.[7] As these are interlinked, disturbances in one of them can easily lead to disturbances in others or in the overall financial system. Ensuring financial stability therefore includes both preventive and remedial dimensions.

There is an additional aspect to financial stability. Policy requirements for financial stability may be time-inconsistent. As some of the policy initiatives to maintain or rescue financial stability might be against market forces, the short-term stability gain might be at the cost of a longer-term stability loss, as they might undermine market discipline and lead to moral-hazard effects.[8]

Developments in financial stability are inherently difficult to forecast. In addition, they are only partly controllable, as the policy instruments available may have other original purposes and other consequences, too. Financial stability is also very directly susceptible to exogenous shocks. This makes it even harder to control.

Why should a central bank bother about financial stability? '… central bank concerns with financial stability are as old as central banks themselves, given their ultimate responsibility for the confidence in the national currency'.[9] There might be a scramble for high-powered money, resulting in a squeeze on the reserves of the banks.

In addition, disturbances at individual institutions or in individual markets can damage overall economic activity, i.e. have negative repercussions on macroeconomic developments. If that danger does not exist then central banks do not need to get involved. Poorly-managed individual institutions should not be rescued. It is only the stability of the overall system that needs to be maintained in order to avoid any contagion of the macro economy. But it is the potential for damage rather than the actual damage which matters.[10] Therefore, just to be on the safe side, there will be an inherent bias towards too much involvement.

How are the two goals related? Are they really conflicting goals, as is often claimed, or are they actually complementary?

The lender-of-last-resort function is often portrayed as being in conflict with maintaining monetary stability, as the central bank has to open the 'money tap' by lending large amounts to the market or to individual institutions, thereby creating (excessive) liquidity. This liquidity might endanger the internal and/or the external stability of the currency. 'The pursuit of financial stability by direct intervention may

---

6   However, there is increasing discussion whether monetary stability is really adequately reflected by the development of consumer price inflation, as asset price inflation might occur even with a stable level of consumer prices. With rising asset prices the value of money declines.

7   G. Schinasi, *Defining Financial Stability*, International Monetary Fund, Working paper WP/04/187, 2004, p. 6.

8   Schinasi, *Defining Financial Stability*, p. 12.

9   Houben, *Towards a framework*, p. 7.

10   A. Crockett, *The Theory and Practice of Financial Stability*, GEI Newsletter Issue No. 6, U.K., 1997.

divert the central bank from achieving its primary goal of controlling the monetary aggregates so as to achieve price stability.'[11]

However, one can also argue that, at least in the longer run the two goals are actually complementary. They both serve the same rationale, namely to maintain the confidence of the general public in the functioning of the monetary system. This monetary system is composed of both financial institutions and money itself. Therefore, both are necessary for securing and maintaining confidence in the system. One has to trust both, the medium of exchange and store of value, namely money, as well as the financial intermediaries and markets where money is created, transferred or stored. A monetary policy that maintains price stability would thus also promote financial stability.[12] Or as other analysts conclude: '… financial stability and monetary stability overlap to a large extent'.[13] In addition, 'price-level instability … can exacerbate financial instability by increasing the uncertainty both borrowers and lenders face about potential real returns to a project'.[14]

However, there might be differences in the time horizon between measures to support financial stability and monetary stability. Supporting financial stability usually requires urgent action. Maintaining external monetary stability in times of crisis might also require fast action. The transmission mechanism for internal monetary stability, i.e. price stability, has much longer lead times ('long and variable lags', as Milton Friedman once concluded). Therefore, eventual negative consequences for internal stability can often be offset once financial or exchange-rate stability has been restored.

The *privilegirte oesterreichische Nationalbank*

The *privilegirte oesterreichische Nationalbank* (OeNB) was established in 1816, after the Napoleonic wars. These wars and their financing by different forms of paper money had completely destroyed the Austrian monetary system. During those wars the Austrian government had borrowed heavily by issuing paper notes, which could be used for payment of taxes and circulated as media of exchange.[15] This overissue led to large depreciations in the value of the notes and repeatedly caused large monetary disruptions. A bank of issue, independent of the government and the state, was to restore monetary order. This was the 'privilegirte oesterreichische Nationalbank'.

The OeNB was created as a private joint-stock bank independent of the state and charged with the task of re-establishing a solid money supply and a reliable supply of credit for the economy throughout the monarchy. As its first task it had to reduce the

---

11 C. Goodhart and H. Huang, 'The lender of last resort', in *Journal of Banking and Finance*, vol. 29, 2005, p. 1060.

12 M.D. Bordo and D. Wheelock, 'Price Stability and Financial Stability: The Historical Record', *Review, Federal Reserve Bank of St. Louis*, September/October, 1998, p. 41.

13 Houben, *Towards a framework*, p.15, and Schinasi, *Defining Financial Stability*, p. 6.

14 Bordo, 'Price Stability', p. 42.

15 F. Capie, C. Goodhart and N. Schnadt, *The Development of Central Banking. Monograph prepared for the Tercentenary of the Bank of England* (London, 1994), p. 161.

amount of paper money in circulation, and especially to gradually replace the notes issued by the government with its own notes. Its notes were covered by its metallic assets as well as by a special mortgage on all mines of the state. It was given the exclusive right to issue notes convertible into silver. It was not, however, obliged to maintain a specific ratio of specie to the notes issued. The Bank was authorized to discount bills and to accept deposits. The management of the Bank was in the hands of the governor and the directors, representatives of the shareholders. The state Commissioner as the representative of the state only had one power, to watch over the Bank's respect for its statutes. The government was explicitly limited in its ability to borrow from the Bank.

Its charter was granted for a period of 25 years and was then renewed for the first time in 1841. On the occasion of the renewal of the Bank's privilege the state increased its influence over the Bank by appointing a second state Commissioner with the task of overseeing the discount and loan business of the Bank. The accounts of the Bank and their developments were kept secret, with only a very small group of high officials having access to this information. A balance sheet of the Bank was published for the first time only in 1848.

In the aftermath of the political crisis of 1848 the convertibility of the notes into silver was suspended. The state had borrowed heavily from the Bank and resumed issuing its own unbacked notes, some of which were declared to be legal tender. In 1857, the *Österreichische Währung* was introduced as the only legal tender. On 30 August 1858 the government issued a decree obliging the Bank to introduce specie payment and a metal cover of one third.

This was an important step towards a credible commitment to monetary stability. However, it also showed the limits of the Bank's political power, as it had not been consulted by the government before the issuing of this decree. In the event, this strong political commitment to monetary stability did not last more than half a year. Another war and its financial needs led to the 'temporary suspension' of the obligation to redeem notes with metal. The Bank – despite its heavy opposition – had to advance a loan to the government, make an advance payment for a planned issue of government bonds, issue new notes in a denomination of five florins and advance silver to the government. The financial strains of war led to the 'death' of central-bank independence and of specie payment. The commitment to monetary stability was the first victim of the war.

The silver agio, the difference in price between a silver coin and a bank note (or the discount of a paper currency against specie), was the market signal with respect to the perceived stability of the currency. During 1859 it jumped from (almost) par to its all-time high of about 153 (see Table 3.1) as people started to hoard silver coins as a hedge. The confidence that had been slowly acquired during the previous years was (suddenly) lost. By that time, the *Österreichische Credit-Anstalt für Handel und Gewerbe* had already been established (in late 1855).

The second privilege was intended to run through 1866. However, in 1861, a new initiative was started by the Emperor to reform the privilege of the Bank. For the first time, it was not simply declared by the monarch but was negotiated in parliament. The government announced its intention to settle the question of the government's debt to the Bank, together with a reformulation of the Bank's independence and the

Table 3.1   Silver agio, 1848–1863

Year	lowest rate	highest rate	average rate	Year	lowest rate	highest rate	average rate
1848	101	117	109,36	1864	113,39	119,82	115,72
1849	105	127	113,85	1865	105,39	114,28	108,32
1850	111	150	119,82	1866	101,75	129,75	119,76
1851	116,75	134	126,05	1867	118,75	130,00	123,95
1852	110	125	119,45	1868	111,75	118,75	114,43
1853	107,75	116,75	110,57	1869	118,06	122,38	121,02
1854	114,75	146,60	127,85	1870	118,48	125,40	121,89
1855	109,12	129,25	120,9	1871	116,57	122,55	120,38
1856	101,25	113,5	104,64	1872	107,09	113,75	109,27
1857	103,87	109,37	105,5	1873	106,24	110,81	108,14
1858	100,25	106,75	104,11	1874	103,56	107,04	105,25
1859	100,25	153,2	122,16	1875	100,94	105,64	103,4
1860	124,65	144,3	132,32	1876	100,9	108,25	104,6
1861	135,62	150,03	141,25	1877	103,95	107,70	106,36
1862	117,19	138,67	128,07	1878	99,85	112,50	103,15
1863	110,16	118,84	113,79				

Source: E. März and K. Socher, 'Währung und Banken in Cisleithanien', in: A. Brusatti (ed.), *Die Habsburgermonarchie 1848–1918* ,vol.1, *Diewirtschaftliche Entwicklung* (Vienna, 1973).

issuing of a new privilege. These three issues would be closely linked. A central point in the discussions was the question of sequencing: should the government finances or the currency be reformed first?

These negotiations led to the Bank Act of late 1862, including a new privilege of the Bank, new statutes of the Bank and a settlement of the government's debt with the Bank. The negotiations were rather controversial, especially the question of the interest on the Bank's permanent loan to the government. The representatives of the Bank were fighting up to the last moment to secure a fixed interest payment and not just a conditional one. But the government prevailed. This third privilege lasted for 16 years, from 1863 to 1878.

The new agreements with the Bank contained a few elements with great importance for our focus of attention, the question of monetary stability vs. financial stability. Relevant in this respect were especially the issues of the monopoly of issue, specie payment, metal cover and the level of independence of the Bank.

The Bank received the exclusive right to issue banknotes but they were not allowed to be in smaller denominations than ten florins. Bank notes had to be redeemed for silver on presentation. Should the Bank be unable to honour this obligation it would lose its privilege. However, there was an escape clause. The Bank was not obliged to redeem paper notes into silver in case of a temporary suspension by law. In order to be able to fully honour its obligation the Bank had to hold an adequate ratio of silver to paper notes. Any notes issued in excess of 200m florins had to be fully covered by silver reserves. Up to one fourth of the metal cover could be in gold instead of silver. Notes not covered by metal had to be covered by discounted paper or mortgage paper.

The privilege gave the Bank a large degree of independence from the government and from fiscal policy. The Bank was not allowed to give loans to the government and the government was not allowed to influence the Bank. The existing government debt to the Bank was to be settled. Eighty million florins of the government's outstanding debt were turned into a permanent loan in exchange for granting the privilege of issue. This loan was interest-free unless the Bank's profits fell short of paying for a 7 per cent dividend to shareholders. In that case the government would pay a fixed amount of 1m florins in interest on this 80m loan.

The question of the interest on this permanent loan proved to be the most contentious part of the negotiations of the new privilege between the government and the Bank. It showed also where the priorities of the Bank's management were as it tried repeatedly to convince the government to pay a fixed rate of interest. The commercial interest – dividends to shareholders – received more attention than those aspects of the privilege relevant for monetary policy and stability.

The Bank was a publicly traded joint-stock company with 150,000 shares outstanding, held by private investors. These shareholders had an interest in receiving dividends, and the Bank's management was under considerable pressure to generate them. Therefore, the development of profits always received special considerations in the thinking and the actions of the Bank's management (see above). One could argue that the central-banking policy of the Bank was torn between *three* stability goals, monetary stability, financial stability and dividend stability; between public policy and private profits.[16]

In the view of many analysts[17] the Bank's management considered profits more important than its role in the economy. In 1867 and 1868, for instance, the management neglected the rapidly changing political environment in Hungary following the Ausgleich. Instead of dealing with the potential threat of losing its business in Hungary – to a Hungarian note-issuing bank – it was busy demanding financial compensation for the violation of its charter during the war with Prussia in 1866.[18]

The Bank always played an important and active role in the development of the financial sector in Austria. It lent its active support in many ways. It served as an 'incubator' for new commercial banks, as in the case of the establishment of the Niederösterreichische Escompte-Gesellschaft (NOEG), the first private Austrian joint-stock commercial bank in 1853. As the Bank had been very restrictive in accepting and discounting bills of exchange only a few and large enterprises could have their bills discounted at the Bank. All the others had to find commercial banks. This was one of the aspects for the establishment of the NOEG and the Bank

---

16 The profit distribution was in the following way: an amount equal to 5 per cent of the bank's capital would go to the shareholders. The reserve fund would receive a quarter of the profits if its volume was smaller than 20 per cent of the Bank's capital. The rest of the profits would go as a superdividend to the shareholders. If, however, there was not enough profit for the 5 per cent dividend the money had to be taken from the reserves (as long as they did not amount to less than 10 per cent of the Bank's capital).

17 E.g. C. Jobst, *How to Join the Gold Club: The Credibility of Austria-Hungary's Commitment to the Gold Standard 1892–1913* (thesis, University of Vienna, 2001).

18 Jobst, *How to join*, p. 43.

supported its establishment by active involvement in the subscription process of the shares of the new bank. Two years later – in 1855 – the Bank did the same in the case of the establishment of the Credit-Anstalt für Gewerbe und Industrie (CA).

These first joint-stock banks did not – initially – have the broad scope which was to typify them in the course of later developments. Their primary function was to act as intermediaries between demand and supply of credit, and trade in securities.[19]

Soon the Bank had to get involved again, not to support new financial developments but to secure financial stability. Both newly-established commercial banks, the NOEG and the CA, needed support. The CA lost money on the stock exchange and the Bank advanced a special loan amounting to 5m florins in 1857. The NOEG asked for a lowering of the interest rate on part of its discount portfolio and the Bank accepted that too. In the same year, the Bank also tried to support the failing private bank, Arnstein & Eskeles, by providing emergency loans without adequate security, loans that had to be written off after the collapse of this bank.

All these episodes already show that from the very beginning of commercial banking in Austria the Bank accepted an active role in maintaining financial stability – even on a micro, i.e. company level. It is therefore not surprising that it was asked and expected to get involved whenever financial problems arose during the next decades.

The Bank received the exclusive privilege to issue bank notes (Article 12). It was agreed between the government and the Bank that specie payment should resume by 1867. The necessary details should be decided by the Reichsrat by 1866. If, however, the Bank did not fulfil its obligations with respect to specie payment it would lose its privilege, except for the cases of temporary suspension prescribed by law.

As far as the metallic cover for the bank notes issued was concerned, after long negotiations in parliament agreement was reached on the following rule, modelled after Peel's Act in Britain (Article 14 of the Bank Act). The Bank was required to ensure that the ratio between the notes issued and the metal cover was such as at all times to meet the requirement of specie payment. This ratio was not, however, numerically fixed. It was only stated that any amount of bank notes in excess of 200m florins had to be fully covered by silver or – at most one quarter – by gold. Notes not covered by specie had to be covered by discounted securities.[20]

Transparency was increased with the introduction of the requirement to publish a weekly statement of the amount of notes in circulation and their cover. In addition, the Bank had to publish monthly its assets and liabilities and biannually its profit-and-loss account.

Nominal independence of the Bank was restored and the role and power of the state Commissioner in the Bank reduced. While the governor was still to be appointed by the Emperor, the vice-governors were elected by the directors, the representatives of the shareholders.

The silver agio – the external gauge of the credibility of the currency – reacted positively to the new developments. It fell to about 110 by 1863 (see Table 3.1).

---

19 M. Sokal and O. Rosenberg, 'The Banking System of Austria', in H.P. Willis and B.H. Beckhart (eds), *Foreign Banking Systems* (New York, 1929), p. 107.

20 The underlying principle of this rule was that all notes issued above a certain minimum required by the economy needed to be covered by metal.

Before that, the government debt with the Bank, amounting to about 220m florins had to be settled. There was a mixture of repayments, transfers of government assets to the Bank for sale and reduction of note circulation. The government received a permanent loan of 80m florins in exchange for the privilege.

But again monetary reconstruction was stopped by war, this time in 1866 and against Prussia. All institutional safeguards 'came to nothing'.[21] The Bank was forced by law to finance the war effort – despite the Bank Act. The minister of finance received an advance amounting to up to 200m florins. This money should have been repaid via a bond issue or via the issuing of state notes. In July 1866 – after the defeat at Königsgrätz – the Bank Act was formally suspended, including the obligation to ensure specie payment by 1867.

In order to finance war reparations to Prussia in silver, the Bank had to discount bills of exchange written by a banking consortium under the leadership of the Credit-Anstalt. In this way, the government avoided violating the Bank Act again, but it was an expensive deal for the government and a good one for the banks.

In August 1866, the Bank again had to advance money to the government, this time by issuing new banknotes. The protests of the Bank's management were again in vain.

The year 1866 turned out to be an 'annus horribilis' for the Bank, for its independence and for monetary stability in Austria. (But the shareholders received a sizeable dividend!) The Bank lost control over the money supply as state notes dominated over the bank's notes. As a consequence, the Bank missed out on the discussions with Hungary about the creation of the dual monarchy, as its main focus was on getting compensation for the violation of its privilege.

The 1867 Ausgleich (compromise) between Austria and Hungary declared money a dualistic matter. However, what to do with the OeNB and its privilege was not part of the treaty. That matter was left for later negotiations. It was not until 1878 that the common central bank, the Oesterreichisch-ungarische Bank, was established. In the meantime, the Hungarian minister of finance agreed not to establish a separate note-issuing bank in Hungary. Accordingly, even the new privilege of 1868 did not include any big changes from the previous one. It was the legal base for the central bank when the crisis hit in 1873.

Episode One: The Challenges of 1873

One cannot understand the events of 1873 without remembering that the years between 1867 and 1873 were the so called 'Gründerzeit', a period of great economic boom, of the establishment of many new businesses, of a construction boom, and of a stock-market craze (see Table 3.2). There was an

> enormous extension of stock-exchange speculation consequent upon the large number of company promotions which set in soon after the war of 1866. This was a time of unrestrained gambling in many countries, which led in Austria to the precipitate foundation of enterprises, some on a fraudulent basis, aiming in many cases only at the

---

21 Jobst, *How to join*, p. 45.

profit obtainable through the issue of shares. The hypertrophic growth of stock-exchange transactions relegated to the background the regular banking business.[22]

Table 3.2   Number of stocks at the Vienna Stock Exchange, 1869–1878

Year	Banks	Transportation	Industry
1869	42	43	38
1870	45	54	45
1871	55	69	53
1872	98	140	61
1873	117	199	62
1874	101	182	61
1875	90	167	59
1876	47	75	50
1877	35	63	50
1878	33	55	49

Source: F. Butschek, *Statistische Reihen zur österreichischen Wirtschaftsgeschichte* (Vienna, 1997).

On 9 May 1873 this boom came to an abrupt end: 'Black Friday' – the day the bubble burst. Stockbrokers went bankrupt, margin requirements were not paid, the stock exchange was paralysed. An important element of the Austrian financial system could no longer perform its functions. Bank representatives, brokers, and clients were in panic. A Viennese Support Committee and an Emergency Fund were set up with the aim of lending against collateral, especially by discounting bills of exchange, by extending extraordinary loans. The OeNB was invited to participate in the Fund with 5m florins, the Ministry of Finance with 3m. The Credit-Anstalt also participated. This participation by the OeNB, and its financial volume, led to heated discussions among the Bank's leading managers.[23] Some wanted a limited contribution of 3m florins at most, others wanted more. At the end, a 5m florin contribution was agreed, but at a higher interest rate, and the Bank would restrict its acceptance to those securities that were allowed by its statutes. This was a compromise between support for financial stability (a larger contribution) and securing monetary stability (a higher interest rate and a limited set of securities).

But the Emergency Fund was not able to reverse the downward spiral at the Viennese stock exchange. Share prices were tumbling and there was the repeated call for the Bank Act with its limits on the circulation of bank notes (Article 14 of the Statutes of the Bank) to be suspended. The OeNB should be allowed to lend freely without the limitations of the coverage rules in the Bank Act. But the Bank's management was very much against this suspension of Article 14 of the

---

22 Sokal, 'The Banking System', p. 108.

23 See W. Antonowicz and B. Mussak, 'Torn between monetary and financial stability – What do the archives of the Oesterreichische Nationalbank reveal?', Paper presented at the EABH Conference 'Finance and Modernization' (Vienna, 2005).

Statutes. The basis for this push to suspend the coverage rules was the (mistaken) assumption that there was a shortage of liquidity in the market. But liquidity was not the problem, and therefore lending freely was not the required solution either. (By the way, the Credit-Anstalt's management had not supported a motion to call for suspension of the coverage rules of the Bank Act.) Accordingly, publication of the imperial decree suspending Article 14 of the Statutes in mid-May did not manage to calm the markets.

Torn between supporting financial stability by providing additional funds to the market and protecting monetary stability by avoiding an overissue of bank notes, the Bank clearly had to side with those trying to keep the Vienna Stock Exchange afloat. The Stock Exchange was considered to be a crucial part of the infrastructure of the financial market. The Bank pursued a liberal lending policy – especially in Hungary – but at the same time tried, as far as possible, to keep monetary conditions stable. It charged a higher interest rate for its loans: in this way, it tried to bridge the gap between maintenance of monetary stability and financial stability. The rationale for helping those who had participated in or even enabled the speculative frenzy was to avoid negative repercussions on solid, healthy companies, on trade and investment, on the real economy in general. Contagion to the real economy should be avoided.

However, the suspension of Article 14 of the Bank's Statutes did not result in a large overissue of money. On 21 May 1873, the Bank reported its weekly statement showing that there was a (first) small reduction in silver cover below the statutory limits (or an overissue of notes). During the 7½ months' period from 14 May 1873 until the end of the year, the right to issue beyond the metal cover was only used on 93 working days.[24] Accordingly, no significant direct effects arose for either internal or external monetary stability. The monetary flood gates were not opened – and did not have to be – as there was no special demand for additional liquidity. Bank notes in circulation fluctuated between a low of 299m florins at the end of March and a high of 367m florins at the end of November. By December 1873 they were only about 12 per cent above the level of 1872 (see Table 3.3). The silver agio (the premium on silver relative to paper) – the indicator for the confidence in the currency and in monetary stability – stayed very stable throughout the year, with a high of 110 in May and a low of 106 in August[25] (see Table 3.1).

However, there was a general loss of confidence. This lack of confidence in stocks in general and in the Viennese stock exchange in particular was the real problem and not a lack of liquidity. The Bank shouldered its responsibility for the maintenance of the stock market as an important part of the financial infrastructure of an economy. However, it did not want to give speculators an easy way out without losses. A cleaning-up process was necessary and did actually occur.

---

24 The weekly statement of 20 January 1874 was the last one showing notes in circulation in excess of the statutory limits. The formal end of the temporary suspension of Article 14 was with an Imperial decree of 11 October 1874, see S. Pressburger, *Das österreichische Noteninstitut 1816–1916* (Vienna, 1962), 1st Part, 3rd Volume.

25 Pressburger, *Das österreichische Noteninstitut*, p. 1183.

Table 3.3   Banknote circulation and cover, 1859–1877

End of the year	Banknotes (1)	Cover (2)	Index for (1)	Index for (2)	Cover ratio in %
	Florins bn		(1859 = 100)		
1859	466,8	80,1	100	100	17,2
1860	474,8	89,1	102	111	18,8
1861	468,8	100,4	100	125	21,4
1862	426,8	105,1	91	131	24,6
1863	396,6	110,7	85	138	27,9
1864	375,8	112,2	81	140	30,0
1865	351,1	121,5	75	152	34,6
1866	283,9	104,0	61	130	36,6
1867	247,0	108,3	53	135	43,9
1868	276,1	108,6	59	135	39,3
1869	283,7	116,8	61	146	41,2
1870	296,9	147,3	64	184	49,6
1871	317,3	147,4	68	184	46,4
1872	318,3	147,4	68	184	46,3
1873	358,9	147,5	77	184	41,1
1874	293,7	143,8	63	179	49,0
1875	286,2	145,7	61	182	50,9
1876	295,9	147,7	63	184	49,9
1877	282,3	148,7	60	186	52,7

During 1873 alone, approximately 40 banks entered into liquidation (see Table 3.4). Most of them had been established only a few years earlier, during the boom years. Many had been very heavily involved in the speculative frenzy, earning a lot of money by bringing new public offerings to the market. Cleansing the market of speculative objects was a healthy process; however, contagion effects and a systemic crisis needed to be avoided. By 1879, the number of banks and banking firms in Austria dropped from 141 in 1873 to only 45.[26] It was for this latter reason that the OeNB participated in the rescue of the Boden-Credit Anstalt and the Wiener Bankverein in autumn 1873 by rediscounting bills of those banks that had been accepted by a rescue group including the Credit-Anstalt.

From a commercial point of view, however, 1873 turned out to be a successful year for the OeNB and its shareholders. It had survived this difficult year with an increased profit. The dividend amounted to 11.16 per cent, more than in 1872. The suspension of Article 14 of the Statutes had yielded an extra return of 123,000 florins.[27]

In summary, 1873 had witnessed the OeNB fighting at the frontline for maintaining financial stability, having to give in on the issue of monetary stability – however, without any major consequences – and having succeeded in maintaining dividend stability.

The crisis of 1873, however, had serious and lasting consequences on the real economy throughout the Monarchy. It resulted in a deep and prolonged economic stagnation and deflation (see Table 3.5). 'Seen from a distance…[it] was a blessing in disguise, in so far as it did away completely with the rank growth of unsound

26 Sokal, 'The Banking System', p. 108.
27 Pressburger, Das österreichische Noteninstitut, p. 1176.

Table 3.4   Liquidation of banks in 1873

BANKS	CAPITAL
	in 1000 florins
Allgemeine Escompte-Anstalt	6.000
Allgemeine Vorschussbank	6.000
Bank für den Wiener Börsen-Verkehr	8.000
Börsen- und Arbitrage Maklerbank	5.000
Börsen- und Credit-Bank	4.000
Italisch-Oesterreichische Bank	4.400
Oesterreichische Börsen- und Wechsler-Bank	5.000
Oesterreichische Industrial-Bank	2.500
Oesterreichischer Spar-Verein	2.000
Oesterreichische-ungrische Escompte- und Creditbank	5.490
Oesterreichischer Vorschuss-Cassen-Verein	6.000
Provinzialbank in Wien	2.000
Raten- und Renten-Bank	3.000
Spar- und Lombard-Verein	845
Universal-Bank	5.000
Wiener Agentur- und Credit-Bank	10.000
Wiener Boden-Credit-Gesellschaft	2.400
Wiener Börsen-Bank	2.000
Wiener Capitalisten-Vereins-Bank	10.000
Wiener Cassen-Verein	2.000
Wiener Commercial-Bank	2.400
Wiener Effectenbank	5.000
Wiener Maklerbank	4.000
Wiener Spar- und Credit-Bank	3.000
Credit-Bank in St.Pölten	500
Nieder-Oesterreichische Bank	500
Bank in Stadt Steier	500
Allgemeine Triesterbank	3.000
Triester Bodencredit- und Sparverein	2.000
Allgemeine Credit- und Handelsbank in Pilsen	800
Böhmische Hypothekar-Renten-Bank	3.200
Crédit foncier für das Königreich Böhmen	4.000
Erste Ratenbank in Prag	1.000
Prager Wechslerbank	3.000
Bank für Handel und Gewerbe des Riesengebirges in Trautenau	500
Depositen- und Wechsler-Bank	4.000
Zwittauer Commerzialbank	100
Schlesischer Bankverein	1.000
Galizische Landes-Bank	1.500
Lemberger Bank	1.200
SUM 40	132.835

Source: K.K. Statistische Central-Commission (1876).

Table 3.5   Consumer price index, 1870–1880

Year	Index
1870	87,0
1871	89,7
1872	96,2
1873	98,3
1874	97,1
1875	94,1
1876	92,7
1877	93,0
1878	89,4
1879	89,3
1880	89,8

Source: Butschek, *Statistische Reihen.*

foundations, thereby clearing the ground for a healthy development of the remaining solid enterprises along lines of commercial respectability.'[28] However, the banks were obliged to support the market by buying the shares of the sounder undertakings, leading to the 'peculiarly close connection which exists in Austria between the financial institutions and the other branches of economic life'.[29] This was then one of the main factors that led – some 50 years later – to new challenges for the OeNB, to new conflicts between maintaining financial stability and monetary stability.

The crisis left its mark on the Austrian population, too. There was a strong increase in the number of deaths, by more than 12,000 – a temporary rise of more than 8 per cent – compared to the year before and the year after (see Table 3.6).

Table 3.6   Changes in population, 1871–1876

Year	Births	Deaths	Net changes
1871	153.500	135.800	17.700
1872	158.400	144.600	13.800
1873	162.600	156.500	6.100
1874	162.900	143.700	19.200
1875	164.900	140.500	24.400
1876	169.900	136.600	33.300

Source: Butschek, *Statistische Reihen.*

---

28 Sokal, 'The Banking System', p. 108.
29 Sokal, 'The Banking System', p. 109.

The (Re)establishment of the Oesterreichische Nationalbank in 1923

After World War I and the dissolution of the Austro-Hungarian Monarchy the Oesterreichisch-ungarische Bank was liquidated. Following the end of the hyperinflation of 1921–2 and the signing of a loan agreement with the League of Nations, on 1 June 1923 the Oesterreichische Nationalbank (OeNB) started to operate as the central bank of the small, remaining Austria, with new statutes. One of the first tasks – after restoring monetary stability – was to replace the defunct crown with a new and reliable currency, the schilling. It was intended to be the symbol of the regained monetary stability.

The new statutes of the OeNB contained, as the main function of the Bank, 'to prepare the introduction of cash payments (redemption of bank notes in specie) by forming a reserve of precious metal and of deposits payable in stable currencies …'. In addition, there was the obligation of the Bank 'to use all the means at its disposal to ensure that until the redemption of paper money (bank notes) in specie has been regulated by law, the value of its notes, when expressed in the currency of a country having a gold standard or a stable currency, shall at least not depreciate'. In case of breaching this obligation, it would lose its privilege (unless it was prevented from doing so by some forces beyond its control and accepted as such by government). Monetary stability was thus the mandate of the Bank.

As far as the prohibition of financing of the state is concerned, the statutes of the OeNB were very modern: the state was only allowed to borrow from the Bank against an equal deposit of gold or foreign exchange, as 'neither the federation nor the provinces nor the municipalities shall in any way, either directly or indirectly, have recourse for their own purposes to the resources of the bank unless they shall have paid in the equivalent of the notes received in gold or in foreign credits'.

With respect to coverage of the Austrian schilling, the statutes obliged the Bank to hold an increasing amount of appropriate cash reserves (foreign currency and foreign credits), i.e. during the first five years at least 20 per cent of the notes and deposits at the Bank, then for five years 24 per cent, then 28 per cent and finally and permanently at least 33.3 per cent. If the cover was inadequate a penalty (banknote) tax would be due.

In addition, the statutes contained rules concerning the composition of the decision-making bodies of the Bank which might have had repercussions on the policy preferences between financial and monetary stability. The General Council, the highest decision-making body, had to include representatives of institutions engaged in the banking business, of savings banks, of industry, of commerce and trade, of agriculture and of labour. Up to but not more than four of the 14 members of the General Council were allowed to have a seat on the board of an institution engaged in regular banking business.

The 1920s had also been challenging years from the financial stability perspective, with a stock-market crash in 1924 and many banks in trouble, being either closed or merged. But 1929 was again a very special year for the Austrian financial sector and for the OeNB.

Episode Two: The Challenges of 1929

The Allgemeine österreichische Boden-Credit-Anstalt (BCA), the second largest Bank in Austria, which was founded in 1863 and had followed a very ambitious lending policy, got into trouble. It had – like other banks in Austria too – not adjusted to the reduced business opportunities after the end of the Monarchy. In addition, it owned a very large industrial portfolio which immobilized the bank.[30] For years – as it turned out later – it had paid its dividends from its capital as there were no (or not enough) profits.

Now, in the autumn of 1929 political unrest in Austria resulted in massive withdrawals of deposits and the recalling of loans. The volume of refinancing of the BCA had been rising rapidly since April 1928. By October 1928 the volume had surpassed the rediscounting limit of 60m schillings. The OeNB had tried repeatedly to get the BCA to reduce its rediscount loans but without success. This led the OeNB to stop providing discount loans to the BCA. The Bank urged the BCA to find other banking partners. As a large foreign loan of the BCA was also called at the same time, the bank became illiquid and turned to the government for help.

On 30 September 1929 there were long negotiations between the BCA and the OeNB about an additional loan of the Bank for the BCA amounting to 12m schillings, on top of the 121m schillings of already existing loans. The normal ceiling for refinancing for the BCA at the OeNB had been 60m schillings only. This additional loan was finally granted by the Bank as a 'last loan' in order to buy time for the BCA for negotiations concerning a merger. The OeNB accepted a limited lender-of-last-resort function in order to defend financial stability.

A fast merger with the Credit-Anstalt (CA) – the largest bank in Austria – was seen as the only way to proceed. The CA was considered to be the only Austrian bank large enough to be able to 'digest' a merger with the BCA. With the strong involvement of the OeNB (and the government) the Credit-Anstalt's management was convinced ('with a pistol to its chest') to take over the BCA. In exchange, the OeNB granted the CA the right to repay the debt of the BCA to the OeNB over a period of up to three years.

The fast and determined actions, especially by the OeNB, were driven by the overriding goal of maintaining financial stability in Austria. At the same time, the limits on the rediscounting of the BCA were due to concern for the stability of the Austrian currency as well as for the value of the Bank's rediscounting portfolio.

In this episode, however, there was no apparent conflict to be managed by the Bank. Both stability considerations, monetary as well as financial stability, led to the same conclusions and actions, namely closing the discount window and organizing a merger with the largest bank. The OeNB acted as a crisis manager more than a crisis lender. It saw its role in helping to overcome the coordination problem. Its instrument was moral suasion rather than money.

However, as it turned out years later, there was disagreement within the Bank's management about the issue of closing the discount window for the BCA and forcing it to merge with the CA. To use categories of present-day monetary analysts, the

---

30 S. Pressburger, *Oesterreichische Nationalbank 1816–1966* (Vienna, 1966), p. 421.

president was a monetary dove and the director general a monetary hawk. According to the then President of the OeNB, Reisch, the director-general Brauneis's insistence on the credit stop for the BCA resulted in a first wave of distrust in banks in general and so laid the basis for the crisis to come in 1931.[31]

The (temporary) resolution of this crisis was – again – a joint action of the OeNB and the Credit-Anstalt. It was 1½ years later that the (inherent) risks of this action became apparent, when the Credit-Anstalt's own problems emerged. The OeNB had expected that the merger would generate synergies, especially in the area of the industrial conglomerates, and would be commercially viable.[32] However, this merger was to become the reason for a considerable part of the CA's financial problems in 1931.

Episode Three: The Challenges of 1931

On 8 May 1931 the Credit-Anstalt informed the OeNB – as well as the government – that in 1930 it had incurred losses of 140m schillings. With these it had lost its equity of 120m schillings as well as a considerable part of its reserves amounting to another 40m schillings. This fact was to be kept secret until a decision on a rescue package had been taken.

The Credit-Anstalt was not a 'normal bank' for Austria. It was by far the largest bank in Austria, the largest in Central Europe, the largest Austrian debtor abroad, and large parts of Austrian industry were dependent on it. Its collapse would have had unpredictable consequences for the Austrian economy and the country as a whole and therefore had to be avoided, at whatever cost.

On 11 May a government communiqué presenting the rescue plan – crafted with the active participation of the OeNB – to the public was issued. The share capital of the CA was to be reduced by (only) 25 per cent and new capital was to be injected by the OeNB and the government as well as the Rothschild family, who owned considerable parts of the Credit-Anstalt. The OeNB committed to contribute 30m schillings to recapitalizing the CA and covering the losses. The Bank opted for contributing to the maintenance of financial stability in Austria – even with its own money – because it feared systemic financial consequences as well as very negative repercussions of a failure of this bank on the Austrian economy in general. There was no apparent conflict with monetary stability yet.[33] However, both the Bank and the government were immediately aware of potentially negative consequences on the currency. Therefore, they tried – even before the public announcement of the CA problems together with the rescue package – to get a commitment from the Bank of England to support the currency if need be. The Bank of England declined and referred the OeNB to the Bank for International Settlements.

---

31 H. Kernbauer, *Währungspolitik in der Zwischenkriegszeit* (Vienna, 1991), p. 282.

32 The Wiener Börsen-Kurier (14 October 1929, p. 3), for instance, reported that it was quite sure that the CA would not lose and not even risk anything since the 'BCA was and is solvent'.

33 The international reactions to the rescue initiative were actually rather enthusiastic. The Banker, for instance, wrote: 'financial opinion is mainly disposed to congratulate all concerned for the masterly way in which they have handled a very delicate situation' (*The Banker*, June 1931, p. 213).

A few days later, a law was passed in the Austrian parliament – the first of eventually nine Credit-Anstalt laws – changing certain provisions of the Bank's statutes. In particular, the requirement to accumulate enough reserves in metal in order to be able to resume specie payment was suspended. This was mainly done to allow the OeNB to advance the government's financial contribution to the rescue package, as the government did not have the funds needed. Maintaining financial stability by rescuing the largest bank was more important than preserving internal as well as external monetary stability.

However, as the rescue package could not convince the public and the markets about the re-established health of the CA, large-scale deposit withdrawals occurred, not only at the CA but also at other commercial banks in Austria. At the explicit request of the Bank, the CA honoured all demands for withdrawals. At the same time, several foreign loans were recalled. The situation was worse than initially expected. The central bank injected emergency liquidity by rediscounting financial bills i.e. promissory notes, from the Credit-Anstalt. The Bank honoured all requests for discount loans and the volume of discounts rose very quickly. Within one week the volume of discounted bills of exchange more than quadrupled to almost 300m schillings, and it rose by another 50 per cent during the following two weeks. Soon the amounts became so large that implicit rediscounting limits of the OeNB were reached. The amount of high-powered money increased very strongly while the money multiplier declined (due to declines in the deposit/currency ratio and the deposit/reserve ratio).

At the same time, the Bank's foreign-exchange reserves increasingly melted away and the cover ratio declined rapidly. The Bank was lending freely, and the money left Austria and the schilling (see Table 3.7). The banking crisis turned into a currency crisis; financial instability led to monetary instability. 'Since inflation is usually combined with an increase in note circulation', as the Wiener Börsen-Kurier remarked, 'inflationary fears have been created in the public by the rise in currency'.[34]

These were signals for the Bank's management to ask the government to announce a general moratorium. This was thought to protect the banks from a rush by depositors (i.e. contribute to financial stability) and protect the OeNB from the demands for discount window lending and for foreign exchange (i.e. contribute to monetary stability).[35] But neither the government, the Bank of England nor the BIS were in favour of such a moratorium. Actually, they were very much against it. The BIS insisted on a governmental guarantee for the Credit-Anstalt's liabilities instead. Only in this case would international help be granted. Therefore, at the end of May, the government saw itself obliged to announce a blanket guarantee for all the loans extended to the CA for its reconstruction. This allowed the OeNB to advance further loans to the Credit-Anstalt. The Bank acted as a lender of last resort, accepting bills of exchange – even purely financial bills – going far beyond its statutory limits. But the Bank pointed out that the bills of exchange presented by the CA could not be counted towards the Bank's note cover.

---

34 Schubert, *The Credit-Anstalt*, p. 54.
35 Kernbauer, *Währungspolitik*, p. 306.

Table 3.7   Notes and deposits, foreign reserves and bills discounted at the outbreak of the crisis, weekly (in million schillings)

Day	Notes and deposits at OeNB	Foreign reserves	Bills discounted
April 30	1,048.5	860.0	89.2
May 7	1,024.6	855.5	69.5
May 15	1,223.8	826.4	297.6
May 23	1,230.4	780.5	350.0
May 31	1,282.9	732.2	451.3 **a**
June 7	1,251.9	677.1	475.4
June 15	1,286.4	698.7 **b**	488.2
June 23	1,255.4	661.0	490.2
June 30	1,290.9	658.6	528.7
July 7	1,252.6	639.0	511.3
July 15	1,259.7	622.4	533.9
July 23	1,285.2	592.6	588.4
July 31	1,299.7	566.7	632.1

a Bills discounted do not include the 100m schillings worth of discounts rediscounted by the OeNB at the BIS and the other Central Banks participating in the BIS credit.
b Includes about half the Bank of England loan of 150m schillings.

Source: Mitteilungen des Direktoriums der Oesterreichischen Nationalbank, various issues.

The goal of maintaining the functionality of the Austrian financial system became the overriding one. The key concern was to avoid contagion from the collapse of the largest bank in Austria on Austrian industry and its economy in general and on the rest of the financial system in particular.[36] However, the Bank raised the discount rate, first on 8 June – one month after the outbreak of the crisis – by one percentage point to 6 per cent and then again one week later, this time to 7½ per cent. (This was meant to be a penalty rate in Bagehot's sense.[37]) At the same time it was decided to increase the volume of discount loans to the CA only 'if it was economically unavoidable'.

However, disagreement developed within the Bank about the priorities in the fight against this financial crisis. While the vice-president (as well as the general manager) was in favour of defending the currency (monetary stability) with a restrictive discounting policy, the President preferred a more liberal lending policy in order to support the needs of the Austrian economy (financial stability). The Bank was torn between these two approaches, with the president as the monetary dove and

36   This was consistent with the conclusions in Goodhart, 'The lender of last resort', p. 1079, that 'the likelihood of contagion is the key factor affecting CB's incentive in providing lending of last resort'.

37   W. Bagehot, *Lombard Street* (1873; reprinted Homewood, Ill., 1962), stated that 'in a crisis, the lender of last resort should lend freely, at a penalty rate, on good collateral'.

vice-president and director-general as the monetary hawks. The conflict escalated, even leading to the (temporary) resignation of the vice-president. He pointed out that even a foreign loan to the Bank would not be more than window dressing as no capital inflows could be expected before these loans would be due. Therefore, the Bank would not be able to ensure monetary stability, as its statutes required it to do. This prompted the General Council of the Bank – contrary to its earlier decision – to restrict the volume of additional loans to the CA to 30m schillings. But also within the General Council the positions were very diverse. In mid-June some members of the Council even requested the liquidation of the CA. (As mentioned above, several members of the Council were on the boards of competing financial institutions.) However, this was rejected by the director-general.[38] The Council sent a letter to the Minister of Finance requesting restrictions on withdrawals from banks and savings banks as they saw the danger that the Bank's liberal lending policy might 'become inflationary':[39] However, no restrictions were imposed.

Parallel to that, the Bank of England as well as the Bank for International Settlements acted as international lenders of last resort and extended foreign currency loans to the OeNB; however, too late and in too small amounts.[40] In addition, the foreign creditors as well as the foreign advisor attempted to put pressure on the Bank's management. The disagreements were so deep that the director-general decided to go on holiday for a period of more than three months. In this way he hoped to avoid the negative public reaction to a resignation.

In July 1931 the situation became even more difficult and dramatic with the crisis in Germany. As one reaction to the re-emerging capital flight the OeNB – at the request of its foreign advisor and foreign creditors – raised the discount rate to 10 per cent, a rate that – according to Kindleberger – was high enough to 'draw gold from the moon'. However, this drastic move was very controversial. Many members of the General Council but also the Minister of Finance and the Chamber of Labour disagreed with this raise and demanded a lowering of the rate. Yet the president insisted on the independence of the Bank and did not give in.

On 9 October 1931 strict foreign-exchange controls were finally introduced in Austria, two weeks after Britain had left the Gold Standard. But the Bank did not change the parity of the schilling until early 1932. The inconvertibility of the schilling managed to stop the depletion of the foreign-exchange reserves, but did not stop the depreciation of the schilling; it did not restore external monetary stability. The gold agio of the schilling rose to 144 in November 1931 (see Table 3.8).

This episode shows how banking problems can immediately lead to monetary problems as well. In comparison to the other Austrian banks, the CA was very large and help for it needed to be large as well. The liberal rediscounting created monetary instability and resulted in a flight from the Austrian schilling into foreign currencies.

---

38 Kernbauer, *Währungspolitik*, p. 314.

39 Kernbauer, *Währungspolitik*, p. 318.

40 The OeNB and the Austrian government had – for some time – expected to receive help from France. This help did not materialize, as France set unacceptable political preconditions for any form of support. It was only then – in mid-June 1931 – that the Bank of England extended a short-term loan amounting to 150m schillings.

Table 3.8   Agio on the schilling price of gold in 1931–1932 (in percentages)

1931		1931		1932		1932	
September		**November**		**January**		**February**	
Day	percent	Day	percent	Day	percent	Day	percent
23	2	2	28	6	30	2	42
24	3	3	24	27	32	11	36
25	8	7	20	30	35	17	34
28	2.5	9	28				
29	5	16	24				
		20	32				
October		23	36				
1	8	24	44				
2	13						
6	20	**December**					
21	30	16	41				
27	32	17	39				
		22	36				
		24	32				

The monetary problems resulted in strains on the Bank's foreign-exchange reserves and a full-blown currency crisis: 'The cost of salvaging the Credit-Anstalt was the gold schilling.'[41] The attempt of the authorities to resist a rational evaluation of the value of the schilling without changing the underlying policies resulted in the currency crisis.[42]

This was a rational response by the market and the public as they immediately recognized the danger for monetary stability. The weekly statements of the central bank and especially the behaviour of the note cover (see Table 3.9) became the centre of attention,[43] as people saw the volume of discount loans mounting and the volume of foreign-exchange reserves dwindling (see Table 3.7; although these statements did not show the whole truth). This flight from the currency got another push when the government accepted a blanket guarantee for the liabilities of the CA. It was clear that this guarantee overstrained the government's finances, and memories of the hyperinflationary periods re-emerged.[44]

Torn between defending monetary or financial stability neither one of the goals could be achieved. Internal monetary stability in the sense of a low inflation rate was, however, maintained. Actually, deflationary tendencies occurred in 1931 (see Table 3.10).[45] The fundamental problems triggering the crisis/crises were too large and the initial reactions by both the domestic and foreign authorities too hesitant to stop the flow of events once the avalanche had been set in motion.

---

41 H.S. Ellis, *Exchange Control in Central Europe* (Cambridge, Mass., 1941), p. 35.

42 A. Schubert, 'The Causes of the Austrian Currency Crisis of 1931', in J. Komlos (ed.), *Economic Development in the Habsburg Monarchy and in the Successor States* (New York, 1990), p. 90.

43 Schubert, *The Credit-Anstalt*, p. 56.

44 Schubert, *The Credit-Anstalt*.

45 The money supply declined sharply as the large increase in high-powered money was offset by a strong reduction in the money multiplier due to an increase in the currency-deposit ratio (see Schubert, *The Credit-Anstalt*).

Table 3.9   Note cover in Austria, May–October 1931 (in percentages)

		Days		
Month	7	15	23	Last Day
May	83.5	67.5	63.8	57.1
June	54.1	54.3	52.7	51.0
July	51.0	49.4	46.1	43.6
Aug.	48.7	43.1	42.3	40.3
Sept.	39.6	39.3	35.6	33.0
Oct.	29.9	29.1	28.7	28.1

Table 3.10   Consumer price index, 1925–1937

Year	Index
1925	100.0
1926	99.0
1927	102.0
1928	104.0
1929	107.0
1930	108.0
1931	103.0
1932	104.0
1933	102.0
1934	101.0
1935	101.0
1936	101.0
1937	101.0

Conclusions

In this chapter we have revisited three episodes of Austria's central-banking history when the central bank had to decide between contributing to the maintenance of financial stability and securing internal or external monetary stability. In all three episodes, a financial crisis –in the form of the collapse of either a large bank or the stock market – was the trigger and the Bank was drawn into the rescue initiatives. However, the three episodes evolved in very different ways. The Bank's role and involvement fluctuated between being mainly a crisis manager (in 1929) to being a crisis lender (1873 and 1931). However, this lending role was more symbolic in 1873 and very real in 1931. In the latter episode, the Bank had to act as a real lender of last resort, opening the monetary floodgates. With the flood the stability of the currency and the monetary system in general was swept away. The attempt to secure financial stability had destroyed monetary stability.

Although the Bank was nominally independent, its roles and actions in these three episodes were very much driven by political decisions of the government. The actual degree of independence of the Oesterreichische Nationalbank was not based on an explicit rule but was rather the result of an endogenous process. As Jobst[46] concludes, ever since the establishment of the Bank in 1816 to calm the monetary

---

46 Jobst, *How to join.*

chaos around the 1811 state bankruptcy, the government had switched between the granting of large autonomy to increase trust in the currency in times of peace and heavy interference and monetizing of debt in times of crisis. The charters did not matter once large demands on public expenditures arose, as in times of military conflict or of financial crisis. At times, there was a large gap between nominal independence and factual weakness *vis-à-vis* the government, or, as Flandreau put it, there were 'leads and lags between printed norms and actual behaviour'.[47]

This discrepancy was very apparent in the three episodes. In such times of crisis the Bank was not free to choose between monetary stability, as its charter dictated, and contributing towards efforts to maintain financial stability. The Bank had to bow to external influences, mainly the Austrian government but also foreign central banks or foreign creditors.

Comparing the three episodes, in 1873 the conflict was more theoretical than actual, as no major monetary consequences occurred. In 1929, again, no major conflict arose, as the problems of one large bank were resolved without large monetary consequences. On the contrary, solving the bank's problems avoided the danger of a continued extension of discount loans. In 1931, however, a full-blown financial crisis almost immediately led to a currency and monetary crisis. The problems were just too big to be resolved by the Austrian authorities and especially by the central bank alone. The management of the OeNB was torn between its duty to preserve the value of the currency and its *de facto* responsibility to aid the ailing banking system. The banking problems were so big and systemic that the people lost confidence in the currency too.

In all three episodes, but especially in 1931, the Bank had to act under uncertainty. It was called to act on the basis of very incomplete information. And there was also an asymmetry of information between the Bank and some other parties involved. According to Goodfriend and Lacker[48] the OeNB did what central banks in such situations tend to do: '… central banks responsible for the stability of the entire financial system are inclined to lend whenever not lending could plausibly trigger a systemic crisis'.

---

47 See M. Flandreau, *The Bank, The States, and the Market: An Austro-Hungarian Tale for Euroland, 1867–1914*, Working Paper 43, Oesterreichische Nationalbank (Vienna, 2001).

48 M. Goodfriend and J.M. Lacker, *Limited Commitment and Central Bank Lending*, Federal Reserve Bank of Richmond Working Paper 99-2, p. 3.

CHAPTER 4

Austrian Banking Between Two Great Depressions: The Creditanstalt from the 1870s to the 1930s

Fritz Weber

Banking as Part of Economic Development

The history of the Creditanstalt (CA) during the eight decades between 1855 (when the bank was founded as the k.k. privilegierte Österreichische Credit-Anstalt für Handel und Gewerbe) and the 1930s (when it failed and had to be reorganized) can clearly be divided into two great periods: The first (and successful) one extends until World War I, thus covering the last part of the 'long' nineteenth century. The second one spans the relatively short phase from the break up of the Habsburg Monarchy until the dramatic events, which started with the collapse of the Boden-Credit-Anstalt (BCA) in 1929 and reached their height with the crisis of 1931 and the big bank fusion of 1934.

The crisis of 1931 was not the first and only one in the history of the modern Austrian banking system. The first dangerous situation arose in 1857, only two years after the Creditanstalt had opened. The next crisis occurred in 1873, after the burst of a speculative bubble at the Vienna stock exchange, which marked the end of the so-called *Gründerzeit*, a phase of rapid economic and financial expansion, which started in 1867 accompanied by the fast spreading and adoption of the joint stock company in the Austrian (Cisleithanian) part of the Monarchy. The Creditanstalt itself was not exposed to substantial danger.

The stock exchange crash of 1924, too, seemed at first sight not to affect the Creditanstalt and the other Viennese big banks. However, as it turned out in the subsequent years, 1924 marked the start of a creeping crisis of the Austrian banking sector, which anteceded the open calamities of the 1930s.

When the Creditanstalt was founded as a Crédit mobilier bank in 1855, it held a monopolistic position in the field of commercial banking in Austria. The same could be said about the late 1930s, when the bank – after the amalgamation with the *Wiener Bankverein* – combined two thirds of the accounts receivable of all Austrian banks. Was it just a return of the old structure at a higher level? The contrary was the case: The 1850s mark the inception of a long period of economic growth, which ended in the First World War. In Central Europe the 1930s were the sad aftermath of heavy turbulences, which in the final analysis had been set into motion by the breakdown of the Austro-Hungarian Empire.

On the eve of World War I, the ten biggest Viennese banks combined two thirds of the share capital of all the banks of Cisleithania. They dominated – despite the challenge by the emergent 'national' (= Czech banks like the *Živnostenska banká*) – the financial market of Prague, and cooperated closely with the Budapest banks. In short, they controlled the financial system of the Monarchy. They disposed of a widely ramified network of branches all over the Western part of the Empire, and sustained intimate relations to the most important industrial firms all over Austria-Hungary.

In the end of 1934, only three big commercial banks had remained in Vienna. Two of them – the *Länderbank* and the *Mercurbank*, were hardly more than branches of the foreign banks. The third one, the Österreichische Creditanstalt – Wiener Bankverein-(CA-BV), was – as well as the Österreichische Industriekredit AG, a holding company, which ran the remainder of the industrial empire of another big bank, the Niederösterreichische Escompte-Gesellschaft in public hands (= State and Nationalbank). In the domestic credit market the CA-BV disposed of 57 per cent of the all liabilities of the Austrian banks; abroad, however, – i.e. in the successor states of the Monarchy – it had ceased to play any decisive role after the banking crisis of 1931.

But where had the rest of the ten big banks of 1913 gone? One, the Depositenbank, had been closed in 1924 after the disastrous stock exchange crash in Vienna. The other six had, directly or indirectly, ended up in the arms of the Creditanstalt. Crude figures like these tell perhaps more about the fate of the Viennese banks in the interwar years than any lengthy analysis. The crisis of 1931, the history of which can be only touched upon here,[1] was just the dramatic climax of a development, which started in 1918, and which can be described as a process of *contraction* rather than of *concentration*. This story cannot be separated from the break-up of the Danubian Monarchy in autumn 1918.

The Creditanstalt had been founded by the Austrian branch of the Rothschild family, and it remained a 'Rothschild bank' until the early 1930s, when it had to be reconstructed by the Austrian State. In the late 1930s the Creditanstalt was a quasi nationalized bank. The majority of shares were in the hands of the Austrian State and the National Bank, although they did not interfere in the daily business transactions of the bank. The bank was conducted along a strictly private route by a foreign General Manager, Adrianus van Hengel, a confidant of the foreign creditors of the bank.

It is evident, that the history of a big bank like the Creditanstalt can neither be separated from nor understood without taking into account the general economic development of the country, particularly the region, in which banking takes place. The foundation and the rise of the Austrian big banks were interconnected with the economic rise of the Monarchy, in particular of *Cisleithania*, a moderately underdeveloped region in the sense of Alexander Gerschenkron.[2] Of this first and 'glorious' period we shall focus in this chapter mainly on the years from the *Gründerzeit* (1867–73) until 1914, the time when the Monarchy experienced the

---

1   See F. Weber, *Vor dem großen Krach. Die Krise des österreichischen Bankwesens in den zwanziger Jahren,* unpubl. habilitation, University of Salzburg, 1991; D. Stiefel, *Finanzdiplomatie und Weltwirtschaftskrise. Die Krise der Credit-Anstalt für Handel und Gewerbe 1931* (Frankfurt, 1989).

2   See E. März, *Österreichische Industrie- und Bankpolitik in der Zeit Franz Josephs I* (Vienna Frankfurt Zurich, 1968); idem, 'Besonderheiten in der Entwicklung des österreichischen Bankwesens', in *Schmollers Jahrbuch*, vol. 77, 2, pp. 61–71.

decisive phase of industrialization, even though a marked 'take-off' or 'great spurt' in the sense of W.W. Rostow and A. Gerschenkron cannot be identified.

The *Gründerzeit* ended with the great stock exchange crash of 1873, which in the eyes of elder generations of historians called forth the so-called 'Great Depression'. In reality, the crisis of 1873 in Central Europe just cleared the air from speculative overdoing in certain sectors of the economy.[3] It was a rather short rest within the great transformation from an agrarian to an industrial society, comparable to the *Asian crisis* of 1997 in South East and Eastern Asia. The research of historians interested in quantitative analysis[4] has enduringly changed the view of the 'Great Depression' of the 1870s to 1890s: overall growth declined, but remained positive, except during the first years following 1873, when the economy was shaken by the immediate repercussions of the stock exchange crash. The rate of unemployment, too, was much lower than in the years after 1929.[5]

Hit by the crisis were mainly industries interconnected with railway construction and above all, building enterprises profiting from the speculative building construction boom, which accompanied the years prior to 1873, when a world exhibition was to take place in Vienna.[6] The quotations of these shares were as heavily hit by the crash as those of the banking sector (see Table 4.1). Many of the new banks established between 1867 and 1873 (see Table 4.2) suffered heavy losses and had to be closed during the aftermath of the crisis (see Table 4.3).

Agriculture and heavy industry were afflicted by a persistent price depression after 1873. At the same time, between 1875 and 1890 the fundamentals for the long-term upswing were laid, which seized the Monarchy between 1895 and 1914 and has with good reasons been called a 'second *Gründerzeit* in the history of Austria' by Eduard März.[7] In a long-term perspective the 'Great Depression' was a time of

---

3   See J. Neuwirth, *Die Spekulationskrisis von 1873* (Leipzig, 1874); A. Schäffle, 'Der "große Börsenkrach" des Jahres 1873', in *Gesammelte Aufsätze* (Tübingen, 1885), pp. 67ff.; M. Wirth, *Geschichte der Handelskrisen* (Frankfurt, 1883), pp. 450–614.

4   R. Rudolph, 'The Pattern of Austrian Industrial Growth from the Eighteenth to the Early Twentieth Century', in H. Matis (ed.), *The Economic Development of Austria since 1870. An Elgar Reference Collection* (Aldershot, 1994), pp. 87–117; D.F. Good, 'Modern Growth in the Habsburg Monarchy', in H. Matis (ed.), *The Economic Development of Austria since 1870. An Elgar Reference Collection* (Aldershot, 1994), pp. 66–86; J. Komlos, *The Habsburg Monarchy as Customs Union. Economic Development in Austria-Hungary in the Nineteenth Century* (Princeton, 1983); A. Kausel, 'Österreichs Volkseinkommen 1830 bis 1913', in *Geschichte und Ergebnisse der amtlichen Statistik in Österreich 1829 bis 1979* (Vienna, 1979), pp. 699–710; H. Kernbauer and E. März, 'Das Wirtschaftswachstum in Deutschland und Österreich von der Mitte des 19. Jahrhunderts bis zum Ersten Weltkrieg – eine vergleichende Darstellung', in W.H. Schröder and R. Spree (eds), *Historische Konjunkturforschung* (Stuttgart, 1980), pp. 47–59.

5   See G. Chaloupek, 'Industriestadt Wien', in G. Chaloupek et. al, *Wien. Wirtschaftsgeschichte 1740–1938, Teil 1: Industrie* (=Geschichte der Stadt Wien, vol. 4) (Vienna, 1991), pp. 364–7.

6   März, *Österreichische Industrie- und Bankpolitik*, pp. 185–8.

7   März, 'Besonderheiten', p. 69; see also idem, *Österreichische Bankpolitik in der Zeit der großen Wende 1913–1923. Am Beispiel der Creditanstalt für Handel und Gewerbe* (Vienna, 1981), pp. 21–32.

retarded growth rather than a 'crisis' in the emphatic sense of the word, so-to-speak: a breath-taking before the next long economic spurt.

Table 4.1   Market value of different categories of securities quoted at the Vienna Stock Exchange between March and October 1873

Category	Value 31 March (in m Fl)	Value 28 October (in m Fl)	Loss (in %)
Banks	1.002,0	417,0	58,4
Transportation (railways)	1.105,0	884,0	20,0
Building	258,0	67,0	74,0
Industry	349,0	178,0	49,0

Source: Neuwirth, Spekulationskrisis, p. 203.

Table 4.2   Number of newly founded banks in Cisleithania, 1867–1873

Year	Vienna	Provinces	Total
1867	—	3	3
1868	4	4	8
1869	13	12	25
1870	2	5	7
1871	12	7	19
1872	29	31	60
1873	10	6	16
1867–1873	70	68	138

Source: März, Österreichische Industrie- und Bankpolitik, pp. 146–7.

Table 4.3   Number of Austrian (= Cisleithanian) joint-stock banks, 1866–1885

Year	Number
1866	10
May 1873	141
End of 1873	102
1879	53
1885	42

Source: März, Österreichische Industrie- und Bankpolitik, pp. 146, 188–9; Steiner, Entwicklung, pp. 259–60.

The Creditanstalt in the Speculation Crisis of 1873

For the k.k. privilegierte Österreichische Credit-Anstalt für Handel und Gewerbe the years of depression had no serious consequences. This was due mainly to the very circumspect and cautious way of acting of the management, which had learnt the lessions of the first severe and threatening crisis of 1857, which afflicted the bank already two years after its foundation. During the first year of existence the Creditanstalt had – in accordance with the missionionary aims laid down in the statutes of foundation – acted as a *macroeconomic* institution and had invested a great part of the capital in the realm of company promotion business (*Gründungsgeschäft*).[8] The immobilization of capital and the great losses, which resulted from great commitments at the Viennese stock exchange, initiated a revision of the banking policy, above all a change to a more conservative investment policy,[9] which protected the bank from the mistakes done by other, 'younger' banks in the years preceding the crash of 1873. To quote the company report of the bank for 1872:

> Unschwer wäre es uns gewesen, die Erträgnisse durch ausnahmsweise Gewinne zu steigern, wären wir bei der uns so häufig gebotenen Gelegenheit zur Gründung neuer kommerzieller oder industrieller Unternehmungen mit minder strenger Auswahl vorgegangen und hätten wir, nur auf den momentanen Vorteil ... bedacht, der allgemeinen Stimmung folgend, unsere Tätigkeit der Schaffung von Werten zugewendet, die mehr nur Material für die Tagesspekulation bieten, als Mittel sind, dem kapitalbesitzenden Publikum die Teilnahme an solide begründeten Unternehmungen zu ermöglichen.[10]

The cautious policy of the Creditanstalt is obvious, too, when one compares the behaviour of the bank during the 'Gründerzeit' with the business strategy of other Austrian joint stock banks. Whereas the newly founded institutes and some banks – created by other big banks with the explicit concern to intervene heavily and aggressively in the company promotion business – suffered heavy losses in 1873, the Creditanstalt got over the stock exchange crisis on the whole in good condition. During the first half of the 1860s the equity portfolio had amounted to more than two thirds of its share capital; during the years 1874 to 1877 it never surpassed 45 per cent. Of course, after the stock exchange crash, dividends remained small compared with 1872, when the bank had distributed a dividend of 18.75 per cent; in 1873–76 it amounted to 1.25–6.875 per cent. In 1876, the worst year after the crisis, only nine out of 18 banks still in existence were able to honour the dividend coupons. The Creditanstalt never had to stop dividend payments.[11]

The bank was even able to play a leading role in rescue operations for other banks in 1873, which had been severely hit by the crisis. In May, it participated with an amount of 2m fl in a rescue fund (*Aushilfefonds*), to which the State and the Nationalbank contributed respectively 3 and 5m fl. One month later it took part in

---

8   März, *Österreichische Industrie- und Bankpolitik*, pp. 65–70.
9   Ibid., pp. 64–5, 166–7.
10 Cited in ibid., p. 151.
11 Ibid., pp. 191–201.

the foundation of an *Aushilfs-Comité*. Moreover, the bank did a good job in various smaller rescue operations for individual banks.[12]

How did the two other big banks of the time perform during the 'Gründerzeit'? The Niederösterreichische Escompte-Gesellschaft (NEG) – which had been founded in 1853 as a bank which should only deal with short term business transactions, mainly with discounting bills – invested just a moderate portion of its working capital in speculative transactions, and therefore was not affected by the crisis. The Anglo-Oesterreichische Bank (founded in 1865) invested heavily in risky railway, construction and bank promoting transactions.[13] 'For the seven fat years, which it was allotted', is the comment of a historian, 'it later had to pay with a long period of sterility.'[14] Indeed, the balance sheet total of 1868 (90m fl), could not be regained for many years: by 1890 it had not surpassed two thirds of the level of 1868 (60m).[15]

Even worse was the fate of the Boden-Credit-Anstalt (BCA), the biggest Austrian mortgage bank. Since the bank was not allowed to pursue promoting transactions, it founded an affiliate, the Wiener Bankverein (WBV), in 1869, which soon was heavily engaged in the stock exchange and promoting business. During the first years, the institute was able to pay incredible dividends. In 1873, however, the quotation of the Bankverein share fell to a level lower than the dividend of 1872.

The two banks survived the years of crisis following the stock exchange crash. However, they had to separate from one another, and were – similarly to the *Anglobank* – unable to play an active role for a long period. In November 1873, they had even to be rescued by a syndicate, in which the Creditanstalt and the NEG and some private banks took part.[16]

The Rise of the Austrian Universal Banks after 1890

The crisis of the over-extended banking sector, which succeeded the stock exchange crash of 1873, was – similarly to what can be stated for the economy as a whole – a purifying experience. Those banks, which had 'sinned' most during the speculative boom, disappeared from the scene rapidly. The other ones (among them the Bankverein, the Anglo-Oesterreichische Bank, the Escompte-Gesellschaft, the Unionbank and the Verkehrsbank, which both were to move up to reputable Viennese middle-sized banks until 1914, but also some Czech institutes as the Živnostenska banká) played an important role in the Cisleithanian economy of the *fin de siècle* and became *universal banks*, i.e. competitors and rivals of the Creditanstalt, although none of them was able to really challenge the 'Rothschild bank'.[17]

---

12   Ibid., pp. 178–80.

13   C. Natmeßnig, *Britische Finanzinteressen in Österreich. Die Anglo-Oesterreichische Bank* (Vienna Cologne Weimar, 1998), pp. 127–9.

14   März, *Österreichische Industrie- und Bankpolitik*, p. 149.

15   Natmeßnig, *Britische Finanzinteressen,* pp. 122–3.

16   März, *Österreichische Industrie- und Bankpolitik*, pp. 149–50, 180–81.

17   Ibid., pp. 289–357; See also: H. Matis and F. Weber, 'Kaisertum Österreich – Donaumonarchie', in H. Pohl (ed.), *Europäische Bankengeschichte* (Frankfurt, 1993); F.G. Steiner, *Die Entwicklung des Mobil-Bankwesens in Österreich* (Vienna, 1913).

After 1873, there was a long period of about twenty years, during which the banks kept clear of the stock exchange and the promoting business in general, and concentrated their efforts in transactions with the state. In the long run, however, they played a decisive role within a system, which has been characterized as *Finanzkapital* by Rudolf Hilferding. They became partners or, as many tended to say, 'masters' of the industry, and financed and accompanied the rapid rise of a whole phalange of industrial firms. The financing – or in many cases financing in anticipation – of the expansion of companies like the Skoda and the Steyr works, and their transformation into joint-stock companies would have been impossible without the active financial support of the banks.[18] Self financing of investments, which had emerged in the years following 1873 as a consequence of the retreat of the banks from the promotion business,[19] came up against difficulties and limits, when the economic upswing started to turn into an impetuous boom, which assumed a permanent character and was only interrupted by short recessions until 1914. The steady process of approach and amalgamation between industrial and banking capital can easily be read by the continuous increase of the number of participations of the banks in industrial joint-stock companies since the middle of the 1890s, demonstrated by Eduard März for the Creditanstalt.[20]

On the eve of World War I the Viennese commercial banks were, as Dieter Stiefel has put it, 'at the zenith of power and influence'.[21] Among the largest European commercial banks the Creditanstalt ranked no. 15 in 1913.[22] A process of emancipation of industry from the banks, similar to the development in Germany prior to 1914 (and continuing during the inflation years after the War), did not take place in Austria-Hungary. Even in the more developed Cisleithanian part no industrial enterprise would have been in the position to exercise a decisive or commanding influence on a bank. The only innovation in the relation between banks and industry was that during the last years preceding 1914 in some cases not one single, but several banks participated in promoting and – later on – in financing newly founded industrial firms.[23]

The long boom period after 1895 was interrupted by the outbreak of the First World War. And although this boom had an armament-driven list, the war completely changed the environment for the industry. Profiting from the war boom were only arms-related industries; the consumer goods industry stumbled into crisis. Soon

18 März, *Österreichische Industrie- und Bankpolitik*, pp. 302–4, 333–52; idem, *Österreichische Bankpolitik*, pp. 73–98, shows the industrial *Konzern* of the Creditanstalt in 1913.

19 See A. Mosser, *Die Industrieaktiengesellschaft in Österreich 1880–1913* (Vienna, 1980), pp. 131–53.

20 März, *Österreichische Industrie- und Bankpolitik*, pp. 305–10; idem, *Österreichische Bankpolitik*, pp. 52–64.

21 D. Stiefel, 'Austrian Banks at the Zenith of Power and Influence', in H. Matis (ed.), *The Economic Development of Austria since 1870. An Elgar Reference Collection* (Aldershot, 1994), pp. 358–74.

22 Y. Cassis, *Capitals of Capital. A History of International Financial Centres, 1780–2005* (Cambridge, 2006), p. 92, Table 3.3.

23 März, *Österreichische Bankpolitik*, pp. 73–95; see also: W. Reik, *Die Beziehungen der österreichischen Großbanken zur Industrie* (Vienna, 1932).

scarcity of resources, 'planned' interventions and the requirements of war financing determined the economic scenario and thus also the compass for the banking policy.

For the banks the war meant a new period of concentration on transactions with the state (the allocation of short-term credits, the subscription and intermediation of war loans), whereas the relations with industry loosened, because the firms – as far as they profited from the armament boom – were in the position to pay back advances and to finance investments out of the cash flow. Only the approaching collapse of the Austrian war economy brought banks and industry near to one another again.[24]

Just like the history of the economy of the new small state, the development of the Austrian banking sector after 1918 cannot be understood without taking into account the economic consequences of the dissociation of the Habsburg Monarchy and of the lost war on the Austrian economy, currency, value of money, state finance, and the various micro-economic problems caused by the macro-economic crisis. It is, however, important to state that the Viennese big banks did *not* directly suffer dramatic losses from lending to the Austrian-Hungarian state.[25]

What did the decay of the Monarchy mean to the banks? The Viennese banks had, from their very inceptions in the second half of the nineteenth century, been 'multinational' institutions, as their radius of action always had tended to cover the whole scope of a multinational empire. The territory of the later Republic of Austria had played a secondary role. The most important branches and affiliates (and the focus of the banking business) lay in Budapest, Upper Italy (Trieste) and above all in Bohemia, in other words in those regions where the industrial centres of the Monarchy were to be found.

On the eve of World War I the ten biggest Viennese banks disposed of 149 branches outside the capital; 115 of them were situated in the territory of the later successor states. Among the industrial affiliates of the banks were the Skoda works and other important companies of the mechanical engineering sector, metallurgical and heavy industry firms in Bohemia such as the Berg- und Hüttenwerke, the leading Hungarian mining companies and the Rimamurány iron works, the coal mining company of Trifail in Slovenia, the big oil companies of Galizia, and the Stabilimento Tecnico Triestino, the Monarchy's biggest shipbuilding yard. The factories of big textile companies like the Mautner works or the Fezfabriken conglomerate were dispersed all over the territory of the Monarchy. To cite the example of the Creditanstalt: in 1913, 57 of the 85 industrial companies belonging to the *Konzern* of the bank had their main manufacturing centres outside the borders of the later Austrian Republic.[26]

After the War: New Challenges

After the end of the Monarchy the new successor states were seized by a wave of economic nationalism, which was levelled against the influence of the Viennese

24 H. Kernbauer and F. Weber, 'Die Wiener Großbanken in der Zeit der Kriegs- und Nachkriegsinflation 1914–1922', in G.D. Feldman et al. (eds), *Die Erfahrung der Inflation im internationalen Zusammenhang und Vergleich* (Berlin New York, 1984), pp. 146–7.

25 Ibid., pp. 148–50.

26 See: März, *Österreichische Bankpolitik*, pp. 73–98 and pp. 535–40.

banks as shareholders and creditors of the 'national' industry. What was called *nationalization* in the diction of the time, aimed at the takeover of the banking branches and the industrial affiliates of the Viennese banks by 'national' capital groups, which acted, in many cases, in close cooperation with Western (i.e. French or British) business partners.[27]

Two answers to that challenge could be given by the Viennese banks:

1. *Austrification*, i.e. the general retreat from the Danubian area, the selling of the so-called 'new foreign' (*'neuausländischen'*) holdings, and the concentration on the small Austrian economy. This strategy was favoured by a small group of Austrian economic experts; it would have implicated a fast, conscious and 'planned' shrinking of the Austrian banking apparatus.[28]
2. *Multinationalization*, i.e. the attempt to stand up for the traditional spheres of influence in the Danube area, and ultimately even to strengthen it against national and Western rivals. This strategy of pursuing *business as usual* meant more than the words *prima vista* suggest: namely continuing the old policy by *new* means. Because it was clear that the financial resources to maintain the existing connections with the *new foreign states* (*Neuausland*) could not be provided by Austrian capital.

The Viennese banks soon decided in favour of the second alternative. They were supported by a long list of renowned economic brains in Austria as well as in the West. Among them were Joseph Alois Schumpeter (in 1919 the Austrian Minister of Finance) and the Governor of the Bank of England, Montague Norman.[29] Only *ex posteriori* – after the failure of the strategy – a critical attitude *against* the strategy of transnationalization gained acceptance.[30] Most of the historians employed the benefit of hindsight and joined the critical forces.[31]

---

27 See A. Teichova, *An Economic Background to Munich. International Business and Czechoslovakia 1918–38* (Cambridge, 1974).

28 See A. Spitzmüller, *'... und hat auch Ursach' es zu lieben* (Vienna, 1955), p. 332. It is, however, not easy to decide, what the author did or would have done in the concrete historical situation and what is his reflection about the outcome of other persons' decisions in the past.

29 März, *Österreichische Bankpolitik*, pp. 459–60; P.L. Cottrell, 'Aspects of Western Equity Investment in the Banking Systems of East Central Europe', in A. Teichova and P.L. Cottrell (eds), *International Business in Central Europe, 1918–1939* (Leicester, 1983), pp. 330–51; A. Teichova, 'Versailles and the Expansion of the Bank of England into Central Europe', in N. Horn and J. Kocka (eds), *Recht und Entwicklung der Großunternehmen im 19. und 20. Jahrhundert* (Göttingen, 1979), pp. 366–87.

30 Cf. W. Federn, 'Der Zusammenbruch der Österreichischen Kreditanstalt', in *Archiv für Sozialwissenschaft und Sozialpolitik*, vol. 29, 1932, pp. 403–35; G. Wärmer, *Das österreichische Kreditwesen* (Vienna, 1936), pp. 37–8; J. Joham, 'Geld- und Kreditwesen in Österreich', in *Österreichische Zeitschrift für Bankwesen*, vol. 2, 3, 1937, p. 51. (Joham was confronted with the consequences of the wrong decisions of the 1920s then as the new general manager of the CA-BV.)

31 Cf. K. Ausch, *Als die Banken fielen. Zur Soziologie der politischen Korruption* (Vienna Frankfurt Zurich, 1968), pp. 312–13 and pp. 344–6; K. Bachinger, *Umbruch und Desintegration*

To state the salient facts of change briefly: Compared to the time prior to 1914 the prominence of the Viennese big banks, measured in terms of capital resources and balance sheet total, declined considerably in the early 1920s (see Table 4.4). This was the consequence of inflation and of the loss of assets in the successor states, which the banks had to face immediately after World War I.[32]

Table 4.4   Share capital and balance sheet total of the biggest Viennese joint-stock banks, 1913–1932 (in m schilling)

Year	Number of banks	Share capital	Balance sheet total
1913	8*	1.369,0	6.640,1
1925 (Gold balance sheets)	7	306,0	1.875,4
1927	5	364,9	2.926,7
1929	4	336,0	2.589,3†
1932	4	221,1	1.647,8

* Without *Länderbank* and *Anglobank*, which had become foreign in 1921.
† The dates of the *Boden-Credit-Anstalt* were shown only as a small all-inclusive sum in the balance sheet of the CA.

That the transnational strategy failed, can be presupposed as well-known. However, in this chapter it may be useful to reconsider some of the fatal consequences for the banks:

- The banks tended to 'hoard' employees, hoping that there would be future use for highly qualified staff in the realm of international business transactions.[33]
- The banks tried to defend – in a tough defensive struggle – their ancestral sphere of influence in the successor states by bringing in their branches in existing 'national' banking institutions, especially by transforming them in newly founded banks. But in most cases they proved to be unable to control the business strategy of these banks. As a consequence, the number of foreign branches of the Viennese banks declined from 143 (in 1918) to nine (in 1923).
- Until 1918 the Viennese banks disposed of the deposits of their branches all over the Cisleithanian regions of the Monarchy, which could be channeled wherever they were needed to finance investments. After the loss of the 'new

---

nach dem 1. Weltkrieg. Österreichs wirtschaftliche und soziale Ausgangssituation in ihren Folgewirkungen auf die Erste Republik, unpubl. habilitation, Wirtschaftsuniversität Vienna, 1981, pp. 958–65; Stiefel, *Finanzdiplomatie*, pp. 97–9.

32 See H. Kernbauer and F. Weber, 'Multinational Banking im Donauraum? Die Geschäftspolitik der Wiener Großbanken 1918–1929', in *Österreichische Zeitschrift für Geschichtswissenschaften*, vol. 4, 1994, pp. 585–616.

33 Kernbauer, 'Die Wiener Großbanken', pp. 155–6.

foreign' branches they were forced to search for substitutes for these deposits in the form of credits put at their disposal by Western financial institutions, but mainly as short-term deposits.

• The necessity to attract foreign money brought about a fundamental change in the property structure of the Viennese banks. In the case of the Creditanstalt the foreign part in the share capital rose from 4 per cent (1913) to 20 per cent in 1923. It was further increased by the merger with the Anglobank, decreased somewhat after the fusion with the BCA, and amounted to one third in May 1931.[34]

• In order to support their Austrian as well as their new foreign affiliates with cheap Western credits, some of the banks participated in financial institutions in Western Europe. Probably the most famous outpost of that kind was the Amstelbank in the Netherlands, which was founded by the Creditanstalt, together with Dutch banks and the Viennese private bank S.M. v. Rothschild (which was one of the main shareholders of the CA) in the 1920s.[35]

Other Viennese banks, like the NEG or the Wiener Bankverein, settled the acquisition and distribution of the Western credits via those Western banking partners, which were linked to them by capital participation with the Viennese headquarters as well as with their bank affiliates in the Danube area.[36]

Another alternative to maintain the industrial conglomerates, which often were distributed over several states, and to procure credits for them, was the foundation of *holding companies* in countries like Switzerland and the Netherlands, which – as far as doing business in the successor states was concerned – were 'neutral' ground.[37]

In 1918, the Viennese banks disposed, as did Austrian industrial companies, industrialists and private investors, of parts of firms in the successor states, about the value of which nothing certain is known. One can guess, however, that the value was quite considerable.[38] The possession of shares, however, was by no means identical with 'control' over an enterprise. Immediately after the collapse of the Monarchy, and during the years of hyperinflation, the Viennese banks were certainly able to 'hoard' shares of foreign firms like other 'real values' (*Sachwerte*); however, they were not in the position to provide substantial advances to these companies, either to ensure the maintenance of the daily business or to guarantee the financing of investments. 'Wohl waren und blieben sie', as Walther Federn, one of the most prominent economic experts of the time, wrote, 'noch Großaktionäre von Banken und Industrieunternehmungen in den Nachfolgestaaten und sie behielten auch Einfluß auf diese, aber dieser war überwiegend ein persönlicher der Wiener

---

34 Kernbauer, 'Die Wiener Großbanken', p. 166; Weber, Vor dem großen Krach, pp. 388 and 570.

35 Ibid., pp. 330–33.

36 Ibid., pp. 334–5, 354–60.

37 Kernbauer, 'Die Wiener Großbanken', pp. 156–7. See also Kernbauer, 'Multinational banking', pp. 585–7.

38 See the different estimates referred to in Kernbauer, 'Die Wiener Großbanken', pp. 161–2.

Bankleiter (...) Erst nach der Stabilisierung der österreichischen Währung wurden die Kreditbeziehungen in größerem Umfang wieder aufgenommen.'[39]

In other words the degree to which the banks were able to maintain their now foreign empires after 1918, has been considerably overestimated by most of their contemporaries. In fact, the new foreign credit business shrunk to a fraction of its 1913 value. The post-war figures may have reached, when the transnational activities of the banks were at their interwar zenith in 1928–29, barely more then two-fifths of the pre-war level.[40]

The share of the foreign business in the losses of the banks seems to have corresponded – at least in the case of the Creditanstalt in 1931 – with the quota in the overall business.[41] We shall not discuss this 'foreign' aspect of the Austrian banking crisis further.[42] It seems much more important to identify the *deeper* origins of the banking miseries. They are to be found in the years of inflation during and after the War, in the stock exchange crash of 1924, and in the mode by which the banks tried to resolve the problem of the revaluation of their assets in the Gold balance sheets of 1925.

Even though the inflation years were a time of *negative* interest rates also for the banks, the losses emanating from this seem to have remained within narrow limits, since the fall in real value of the advances was equaled by that of the deposits. Distressing losses occured only if deposits in foreign hard currency faced advances in Austrian Crowns. This, incidentally, was the main cause for the transition of Anglobank and Länderbank in British and French hands respectively.[43]

But there is a close and inner relationship between the effects of inflation on the bank balance sheets and the later problems. During the phase of inflation after World War I the banks accumulated great quantities of shares of industrial companies, attempting to escape the inflationary devaluation of assets. Moreover, they encouraged many of their clients to *Veraktionierungen*, i.e. to transform their enterprises into joint stock companies. Usually in the run of such transactions the former advances of the banks were transformed into a participation in the share capital of the industrial company. In other words, the banks 'hoarded' equities (= *Sachwerte*), hoping to be able to resell them later after the stabilization of the currency, with considerable benefit.

They succeeded in doing so, indeed, during the short period of the stock exchange boom in Vienna in 1923; however, after the crash of spring 1924 they were forced to buy back the shares of both old and new industrial affiliates. And since the Viennese stock exchange never recovered from that shock, the banks could never again get rid of their huge equity portfolios until the outbreak of the Great Depression in 1929, when the price of the shares started to decrease further, even though the quotation of

---

39 Federn, 'Der Zusammenbruch', pp. 411–12.

40 Weber, Vor dem großen Krach, pp. 347–8.

41 See also Ausch, *Als die Banken fielen*, pp. 422–3.

42 See 'Die Wiener Banken und der Donauraum – das Scheitern einer Strategie', in: J. Günther and D. Jajesniak-Quast (eds), *Willkommene oder nationaler Ausverkauf? Ausländische Direktinvestitionen in Ostmitteleuropa im 20. Jahrhundert* (Berlin, 2006), pp. 49–70.

43 See Natmeßnig, *Britische Finanzinteressen,* pp. 172–204.

most of them was as low as to leave no big margin for further devaluation. The big 'bang' for losses at the stock exchange in Vienna therefore did not take place, as one would believe, after 1929, but in 1924.[44]

During the inflation period the industrial firms suffered from a dramatic loss of operating assets, often caused by miscalculation, which further increased the demand for bank credit even after the end of inflation. And since the Viennese stock exchange remained in agony after 1924, the companies were forced to take recourse to the expensive advances of the banks, a fact which obviously lessened the profitability of industrial production, and finally brought forward conditions under which the banks had to grant ever increasing loans to their industrial clients. Those loans, however, were also partially used to pay dividends. The hope bound to those unorthodox methods was, to bridge over difficulties until economic prosperity would return, enabling the firms to pay back advances, and allowing the sale of the industrial shares by the banks.

By this strategy, however, very often nothing else was set in motion than a vicious circle, which constrained the banks to throw good money after bad. Examples are the Berndorfer Metallwerke A. Krupp, which had been reorganized several times by the Creditanstalt already in the 1920s, when the bank had to write off loans and inject fresh capital, the Steyr works, an automobile firm linked to the BCA and heavily indebted when the CA took over the bank, and some companies in the textile and oil sector, closely associated with the CA and the BCA.[45]

Those banks suffered most of the malice of these economic circumstances, which either had decided in favour of an expansionary policy of acquisition of affiliates or – as was the case with Creditanstalt and Boden-Credit-Anstalt – had over-expanded their industrial combine by the merger with other banking institutions. Since practically every bank had been affected by the virus of creeping illiquidity, each merger meant nothing less than the takeover of one ill institute by another already weakened one.[46] Moreover, the organizational apparatus of the bank taking over another one usually und regularly was over-stressed by the rapid and knee-jerk reactions of industrial affiliates.

Inflation, the depreciation of the Austrian Crown and the aspiration of the Viennese banking managers to attract foreign capital from the West led to a complete change of the ownership structure of the banks: prior to World War I their shareholders were mainly Austrian private bankers, industrialists and members of the wealthy upper classes. The foreign part in the share capital of the ten biggest Viennese banks amounted to approximately 10 per cent in 1913. After the War this share rose, as already mentioned to ca. 30 per cent in 1923. On account of the depreciation of the

44 See also Baltzarek, 'Finanzplatz', pp. 124–9.

45 Weber, Vor dem großen Krach, pp. 499–508, 532–3, 668–70; idem, 'Die österreichische Bankenkrise und ihre Auswirkungen auf die niederösterreichische Industrie', in A. Kusternig (ed.), Beiträge über die Krise der Industrie Niederösterreichs zwischen den beiden Weltkriegen (Vienna, 1985), pp. 125–41; idem, 'Die österreichischen Großbanken in der Zwischenkriegszeit', in Christliche Demokratie, vol. 4, 1985, pp. 346–7.

46 This was also discussed by the bank managers themselves in some cases, e.g. when the BCA decided to take over the Verkehrsbank and the Unionbank in 1925. Archives of BA-CA: VSP-BCA 9.7.1925.

Crown until 1922, direct investments in Austrian became even more attractive for foreigners.[47]

The Gold Balance Sheets of 1925 as a Strategic Turn of Far-reaching Consequences

The banking policy of the 1920s was influenced to an extent not to be under-estimated, by the manner by which the Viennese banks drew up the Gold balance sheets of 1 January 1925. After ten years of inflation, and after the stabilization of currency and prices, it had become necessary to vigorously revalue the assets and liabilities of the Austrian enterprises. Yet in 1924, in the books of firms Gold Crowns of 1914 and inflated Crowns of 1922 were placed side by side.

Even though the banks considerably revalued different items against the balance sheets for 1924 (dated 31 December 1924), the extent of revaluation varied from 21 per cent (Escompte-Gesellschaft) to 111 per cent (BCA); the Creditanstalt was in mid-table with 60 per cent. The Gold balance sheets indicate clearly the extent of capital losses (see Table 4.5). Years later it became evident, that the banks – in order to hide the real losses of the inflation period – had unwarrantedly revalued assets.[48] If one adds the gold value of the new capital paid in by capital increases after 1913, the losses were even higher. However, even in their distorted shape the Gold balance sheets clearly showed the imminent danger of immobilization: after the war a much bigger part of the capital resources of the banks were fastened up in the equity and syndicate portfolios than in 1913[49] (see Table 4.6).

Table 4.5   Share capital and published reserve funds of the Viennese big banks 1913 and 1925 (Gold balance sheets) (in m schilling)

Bank	1913	1925	1925 as % of 1913
Credit-Anstalt	452,5	70,0	15,7
Boden-Credit-Anstalt	308,4	50,0	16,2
Wiener Bank-Verein	389,0	60,0	15,4
Nö. Escompte-Gesell.	222,0	50,0	22,5
7 biggest banks	1.860,0	296,0	15,9

Source: Wirtschaftsstatistisches Jahrbuch der Arbeiterkammer 1926, pp. 359–70.

In the eyes of the bank managers – but also of many contemporary experts, who tended to believe that the banks tried to conceal wealth, assets and profits from the public – there still remained a good deal of undisclosed reserves (i.e. mainly the difference between book value and market value of equities) left to cover eventual

---

47   Kernbauer, 'Die Wiener Großbanken', p. 166.

48   See: Ausch, *Als die Banken fielen*, pp. 421–2.

49   Already in 1914 the ratio was higher with Austrian than with German banks See Kernbauer, 'Die Wiener Großbanken', pp. 144–5.

Table 4.6   Assessment of the capital resources of the Viennese big banks in 1913
                 and 1925 (equity and syndicate portfolios as percentage of capital
                 resources, i.e. share capital plus published reserve funds)

Bank	1913	Gold balance sheets (1 January 1925
Creditanstalt	54	89
Boden-Credit-Anstalt	20*	117
Wiener Bankverein	49	49
Nö. Escompte-Gesellschaft	57	71

* Syndicate portfolio booked amongst liabilities.

Sources: *Compass* 1915, vol. 1; Mitteilungen des Direktoriums der Oesterreichischen
Nationalbank 7/1926.

losses in the future. Only the Steyrian Christian Socialists (*Christlichsoziale*), well
known for their critical ideas on big banks, were aware of and disclosed the dilemma
of the banks.

'Aus Sorge um die Kreditfähigkeit im Auslande', the economic programme
(*Wirtschaftsprogramm*) of 1925 stated, '(sehen sich) die Banken gezwungen ..., möglichst
hohe Eigenkapitalien ... aufzuzeigen ... Die Banken stehen vor dem Dilemma, entweder
bei der Erstellung der Goldbilanzen ein hohes Eigenkapital aufzuweisen und die
laufende Betriebsrechnung mit Verlust schließen zu lassen, oder aber ... ihr Eigenkapital
entsprechend gekürzt auszuweisen und latente Reserven beizubehalten ...'[50]

A further consequence of the Gold balance sheets (window dressed to impress
or at least not to irritate the foreign investors) was, that starting with 1925, the
banks as well as their industrial affiliates, which followed suit in constructing bright
prospects for the future, had to pay high dividends in order to make believe wealth
and prosperity. They therefore continued to compensate losses of current business
transactions by secretly revaluing what they believed to be undisclosed reserves, in
order to keep up the appearance of surpluses. This dangerous policy seems to have
been very common in the Viennese banking community. Only in the very detailed
minutes of the management board of the Wiener Bankverein can one not find any
hint for permanent *window dressing*.[51] In general, it is not easy to know the ins and
outs of Viennese banking: the records of the WBV (kept in the archives of the CA)
allow at best conclusions over the real state of the bank. The minutes of the BCA
are less revealing. Those of the CA herself are the most sterile ones; however, a lot
of information about the development of the bank during the 1920s can be found

50 Österr. Staatsarchiv (ÖSTA), Archiv der Republik (AdR), HHStA, Schüller-Faszikel:
Vorschläge zur Schaffung einer österreichischen Nationalwirtschaft zwecks dauernder
Stabilisierung der Währung, pp. 17–18.

51 The records have been kept in the archives of the Creditanstalt.

in the records of the so-called *Ehrenfest-Prozeß*,[52] a trial held to shed light on the 'subjective' causes of the banking crisis of 1931.

The profit and loss account of the Creditanstalt showed for 1924,the year of the stock exchange crisis, a loss of 5.2m schilling, which was 'settled' by the construction of the optimistic Gold balance sheet. For 1926 a positive result could only be obtained by revaluing shares of the Amstelbank and by dissolving reserves of 6m. AS kept non-performing loans, which had been built on the occasion of the merger with the Anglobank. A similar strategy seems to have been chosen by the Boden-Credit-Anstalt in 1927, when, in order to show a profit and to be able to pay higher dividends – the reserves which had been built when the merger with the Unionbank and the Verkehrsbank took place, were 'consumed'.[53] In general, it seems that there was *not one* year between 1924 and 1930, for which the Creditanstalt could draw the balance sheet without taking recourse to the method of heavy window dressing (see Table 4.7).

Table 4.7   Intern revaluation of the equity portfolio (= dissolution of unpublished reserves) of the Creditanstalt, 1926–1929

	1926	1927	1928	1929
Amount of re-valuation (in m AS)	4.2	12.5	10.1	16.5
As % of the profit shown	53.3*	120.0	96.0	180.0

* If one adds the dissolution of reserves built for non-performing loans on the occasion of the merger with the *Anglobank*, the ratio is 130%.

Sources: Archives of the BA-CA: Nachlaß Georg Stern, Gutachten zur Creditanstalt.

In other words, even in the over-optimistic view of the bank managers, there remained only comparatively narrow room for manoeuvre for covering unexpected losses (see Table 4.8).

With hindsight, those unpublished reserves were – if ever existent – much too small to cover the huge amount of non-performing loans. Because in reality those bad loans were much higher than shown in the books of the CA, and the losses imminent from frozen engagements were assessed as much too small. (This follows also by a comparison with the 140m AS losses declared in May 1931.) Today we know that even these 140 millions were just a fraction of the real overall losses, which amounted to more than a billion AS, and obviously cannot have been accumulated in only one year (1930).[54]

Since 1924–25 the banks were confronted with an ever growing immobilization of their capital, and with losses emanating from credit transactions which rapidly

---

52   Kept in the Archives of the *Landesgericht Wien* (LGW).
53   LGW, Ehrenfest-Prozeß, OZ 414, Gutachten Sedlak-Neumann.
54   Weber, Vor dem großen Krach, pp. 553–62.

Table 4.8   Ratio of non-performing loans and other dubious items determined by the management of the Creditanstalt to unpublished reserves, 1925–1929 (in m AS)

Year	Non-performing loans	Unpublished reserves	Ratio of covering (un-published reserves as % of non perf. loans
Gold balance sheet (1 January 1925)	14.6	19.6	134
1925	14.6	22.8	156
1926	14.3	32.0	224
1927	42.6	46.9	110
1928	38.4	49.5	129
1929	46.8	24.7	53 (110)*

* 26,8m AS covered by the surplus of merger with BCA.

Source: LGW, Ehrenfest-Prozeß, OZ 414 and 1771.

gobbled up the small unpublished reserves. The *system of fictions*, which had been erected with the Gold balance sheets, proved to be very weak – even too friable as to be saved by the economic upswing commencing in 1927. It was during the *good* year of 1928, that the Creditanstalt started to introduce '*Besserungsscheine*' and '*bedingte Nachlässe*', new means of even more adventurous window dressing than before.[55]

By the tricky policy of high dividends paid out of the substance (of the banks as well as of industrial firms) the institutes tried – as has been already mentioned – to keep their foreign shareholders in a good mood, *and* to maintain the option to sell the huge amounts of industrial equities parked in their portfolios later. This was the *ultimate* reason to continue a credit policy, which compelled the banks ever and ever more to act offensively and riskily, and to increase credit risks with the argument that one should 'not jeopardize the international reputation' of the firms,[56] although the managers were aware of the fact, that in some cases, firms had already been paying dividends 'out of the substance' for many years.[57]

---

55 LGW, Ehrenfest-Prozeß, OZ 566: Bilanzfragen 1928.
56 Archives of the BA-CA, Verwaltungsratsprotokoll (VWP) BCA 24.1.1924.
57 Archives of BA-CA, VWP-BCA 4.1.1929 (Steyr works).

Outlook: The Financial Crisis of 1931, the General Reconstruction of the Austrian Banking Sector in the 1930s, and the Consequences of the Banking Crisis for the Economy as a Whole

The stock exchange crash of 1924 had much more aggravating consequences for the Creditanstalt and other big Austrian banks than the crash of 1873. In 1873, the CA had pursued a conservative strategy and kept away from the speculative excesses at the Viennese stock exchange. The crisis occurred – in a long-term perspective – during an epoch of transformation of Cisleithania to an industrial state. This development was slowed down by the crisis, but not decisively held up.

In contrast to 1873, the stock exchange crash of 1924 was the last act of a period of speculation and economic turbulence, which had had its inceptions during the years of war- and post-war inflation, and had been further augmented by the devaluation of the Austrian currency.[58] Thus, speculation was not the symptom of an exuberant boom (as it had been in 1873), but took place against the background of a severe social and economic crisis, called forth by the lost war and the collapse of the Danube Monarchy. In other words, the crisis was not induced by over-optimistic anticipation, but by desperation. It was further furnished – because of the depreciation of the Austrian Crown – by foreign speculators. Sustained was the speculation by the assumption that the real value (*'Substanzwert'*) of Austrian equities were much higher than the actual value based on the net income obtainable (*'Ertragswert'*). Nourished were speculations of that kind by the fact, that during the years of inflation the quoted value of the shares had not kept pace with both inflation and depreciation of the Crown, and many expected a considerable revaluation of the quotations.

Although there are no direct hints indicating that the big banks stoked up and encouraged speculation, it is evident that they must have had an eminent interest in a rise of the quotations, which could render it possible to ease the burden of their swollen equity portfolios and to obtain capital for 'normal' transactions.

The speculation in Austrian shares reached its very height after the end of hyper-inflation (in autumn 1922) in an environment of optimism set free by the Geneva reform project (*'Genfer Sanierung'*). It ended in a disaster when it had passed its peak and the speculators had discovered a new worthwhile aim: the speculation on a fall of the France franc in spring 1924. Only when this speculation, too, had failed, the equity *hausse* finally failed.

The Viennese stock exchange could never recover from that crash in the interwar period. Even in the late 1920s the quotations reached nothing like the level of 1923. The banks were left with a mountain of shares, in fact with a white elephant, which became ever more unsaleable, although equipped with a propensity to be ever cheaper. On the other hand, the banks were compelled to grant long term loans (desperately needed for modernization investments by industrial firms) to an ever growing dangerous extent for their affiliates and clients. That a considerable part of the loans – to Austrian as well as new foreign firms – were granted on the basis of short term credits, which the banks had raised in the West, only made conditions worse.

---

58 See Baltzarek, 'Finanzplatz', pp. 118–21.

Since the Austrian economy laboured under a chronic and obstinate crisis – even in 1929 industrial production as well as exports lay below the 1913 levels – advances to Austrian industrial clients started to freeze already in the second half of the 1920s. When the *Great Depression* set in, the situation became untenable, and the losses so carefully hidden beyond the polished surface of refined bank balance sheets came to light. It is clear that these 'objective' propensities of crisis were augmented and carried out to last maturity by imprudence, negligence and grave false estimations. This, however, is quite another story and must remain unwritten in this chapter.[59]

Another aspect of the stock-exchange crisis can only be touched on here: the dramatic die-off of smaller joint-stock banks founded after the war. Many of them had been founded in the Austrian Provinces with political backing by the Christian Socialists or the *Großdeutsche Partei*.[60] Many small private banks had had to shut their doors in the aftermath of the stock-exchange crash of 1924 too. The only bigger bank of note immediately hit by the crisis was the Allgemeine Depositenbank. Founded in 1871, it had been managed conservatively until 1918. After the war it was taken over by one of the big speculators of the time, Camillo Castiglioni, who used the Depositenbank to finance his private empire. The bank had to close its doors in 1924.[61]

Another reputable bank, the Biedermannbank, had to be closed in 1927. The institute emerged from the private bank Biedermann & Co, and was transformed into a joint-stock company in 1921. The President of the supervisory board of the Biedermannbank was the well-known economist and Austrian Minister of Finance in 1919, Joseph Alois Schumpeter. The collapse of the bank did not, however, result from over-speculation, but has to be attributed to the industrial crisis in Austria following the stabilization of the Crown, and to the economic consequences of the break-up of the Habsburg Monarchy. After the Gold Balance Sheet had stated a loss of 30 billion Crowns, the company meeting held in the end of 1926 determined on the liquidation of the bank.[62] The overall consequences of the 1924 crisis for the Austrian banking system can be seen in Table 4.9.

The first consequence of the creeping crisis of the Austrian banking system in the second half of the 1920s were mergers, starting with the acquisition of the Austrian network of branches of the Anglobank by the Creditanstalt in 1926.[63] In autumn 1929, the Boden-Credit-Anstalt, which had in the years before taken over the Unionbank and the Verkehrsbank, failed – independently from the crisis in America. The bank

---

59 See Ausch, *Als die Banken fielen*, pp. 343–68; Weber, Vor dem großen Krach, pp. 672–82.

60 See C. Natmeßnig and F. Weber, 'Die österreichischen Provinzbanken in den 1920er-Jahren. Zwischen politischer Instrumentierung und öffentlicher Konkursversicherung', in *Geld und Kapital*, no. 199, Jahrbuch der Gesellschaft für mitteleuropäische Banken- und Sparkassengeschichte (Bankenkrisen in Mitteleuropa im 19. und 20. Jahrhundert), pp. 101–42; Ausch, *Als die Banken fielen*, pp. 155–298; Weber, Vor dem großen Krach, pp. 264–88.

61 Ausch, *Als die Banken fielen*, pp. 155–68.

62 See Ausch, *Als die Banken fielen*, pp. 192–7; E. März, *Joseph Alois Schumpeter. Forscher, Lehrer und Politiker* (Munich 1983), *Preface*, pp. 11–12.

63 Natmeßnig, *Britische Finanzinteressen*, pp. 260–64; Weber, Vor dem großen Krach, pp. 385–92.

Table 4.9   Number of banks in Austria, 1913–1935

Year	1913*	1919	1923	1925	1927	1935
Joint stock banks	27	34	76	51	40	19
Private banks	150	146	282	230	152	131

* Territory of the later Republic of Austria.

Source: W. Federn, 'Die österreichischen Banken', in special issue *Der österreichische Volkswirt (10 Jahre Nachfolgestaaten)*, 1928, p. 56; *Compass*, vol. 1936.

had to be taken over lock, stock, and barrel by the Creditanstalt, which thus became by far the biggest bank in Austria.[64] The Creditanstalt itself, however, was – as we know from hindsight – in a weak position then, and proved to be unable to publish a positive balance sheet for 1930.[65]

The crucial year for the Creditanstalt was 1932, when the bank was anything other than a living financial body: it had lost the greatest part of its deposits, had completely ceased lending, and reduced its activities to the rigorous collecting of outstanding loans. Only after an agreement with the Austrian Government, by which the State took over the debt of the bank *vis-à-vis* the Nationalbank, was the Creditanstalt put back into a position where it could fulfil 'normal' banking functions. With regard to activities abroad, however, the Creditanstalt had already suspended them in 1931 and had started selling off parts of its conglomerate – equities as well as whole packages of assets including outstanding loans – to national groups in the successor states. Immediately after the amalgamation of 1934, came the next step: the bank divested itself of the Czechoslovakian banking assets it had inherited from the Bankverein, and retained only the Budapest branch and the banking affiliates of the WBV in Yugoslavia and Poland.[66] And although some of the connections with industrial firms (particularly in Hungary) were kept alive, the CA-BV had ceased to be a transnational player.

In 1934 a grand new grand design of Austrian banking became reality. The Creditanstalt took over the Bankverein and the regular banking business of the *Niederösterr, Escompte-Gesellschaft*. The long-term engagements of the NEG and its equity portfolio was put in a new holding company, the Industriekredit AG, which was controlled by the Austrian National Bank.[67]

The Österreichische Creditanstalt-Wiener Bankverein (CA-BV) held, as indicated earlier in this chapter, a quasi monopolistic position in the Austrian banking sector. Finally, the banks had to acquiesce in the *austrification* of their business activities by the force of a severe crisis and after having suffered heavy losses. The multinational

---

64 Ausch, *Als die Banken fielen*, pp. 307–34; Weber, Vor dem großen Krach, pp. 464–517.
65 Ibid., pp. 543–52.
66 Ibid., pp. 608–15.
67 See Stiefel, *Finanzdiplomatie*, pp. 214–25; Ausch, *Als die Banken fielen*, pp. 421–3.

dreams of 1919 had to be buried. And until 1938, the year which opened a new chapter in Austrian history in general, neither the banks nor the whole economy of Austria regained economic prosperity.[68] The price which had to be paid for the errors and the rashness of the banking policy of the 1920s, was a high one: the overall losses of the Creditanstalt amounted, following the calculations of Dieter Stiefel, to 1.068m; the overall amount invested by the Austrian state and the National Bank in rescuing actions in banks between 1925 and 1936, was even higher and came to 1.137m schilling.[69]

But the consequences of the banking crisis of 1931 did not end at the Austrian border: the crisis of the Creditanstalt was the outset of an international financial crisis which shook the banking system of, and had repercussions for, the entire world. As a consequence of the incidents in Vienna, banks in other successor states of the Danube Monarchy were affected by the turmoil.[70] In summer 1931 the crisis spread to Germany; in September the pound sterling had to be depreciated, and the whole gold exchange standard system, erected with so many difficulties in the 1920s, broke down. In short: 'the rolling deflation (of the 1930s, F.W.) started', as Kindleberger put it, with the crisis of the Creditanstalt.[71]

The consequences for the Austrian economy itself proved to be disastrous: The Creditanstalt was compelled to declare credit restrictions in 1932, the currency crisis, which followed suit to the banking crisis, ended in the devaluation of the Austrian schilling, unemployment rose to about 25 per cent (and probably more) in 1932–33, and the overall economic crisis could never be overcome until 1938. Even in the last year prior to the 'Anschluß' the unemployment rate still amounted to more than 20 per cent.[72]

In contrast to the years following 1873, the consequences and the aftermath of the banking crisis of 1931 (which has, as shown above, to be connected with the breakdown of the Habsburg Empire in 1918 and the crash of the Viennese stock exchange in 1924) proved to be detrimental, in Austria as well as in the whole of Europe and in a global perspective. True, the crisis of 1873 also had international dimensions.[73] But the big difference to 1873 was that the crisis of 1931 affected not only the economy of one or two countries, and it ignored and surpassed the limits between the financial and the 'real' economy. Already in 1933, one of the great Austrian economists of the interwar period, Karl Polányi, pointed to the new quality of the crisis of 1931:

> Das bedeutsamste Kennzeichen der Weltwirtschaftskrise im Unterschied zu früheren ist, daß sie in den ... Gang der Erzeugung viel unmittelbarer eingreift. Frühere Krisen waren mehr auf die Wert- und Kreditsphäre beschränkt ... Zum erstenmal ist in der

---

68 See Stiefel, *Krise*; K.W. Rothschild, 'Wurzeln und Triebkräfte der Entwicklung der österreichischen Wirtschaftsstuktur', in W. Weber (ed.), *Österreichs Wirtschaftsstruktur gestern-heute-morgen*, vol. 1 (West Berlin, 1961), pp. 79–90.

69 Stiefel, *Finanzdiplomatie*, pp. 230–31.

70 See: Weber, Vor dem großen Krach, pp. 571–7.

71 Kindleberger, *Manias*, p. 151.

72 See H. Kernbauer, *Währungspolitik in der Zwischenkriegszeit. Geschichte der Oesterreichischen Nationalbank von 1923 bis 1938* (Vienna, 1991) pp. 305–94.

73 Ibid., pp. 145–6. Kindleberger cites Carl Meyer von Rothschild, who in the aftermath of the crisis asserted: '(T)he whole world has become a city' (p. 146).

Weltwirtschaftskrise der Erzeugungs- und Austauschprozeß selbst optisch zum Hauptschauplatz der Krise geworden, das erstemal wurde im Weltmaßstab der naturale Prozeß der Wirtschaft auf die Dauer von Jahren zurück geschraubt. Im Vergleich mit dem Tiefgang der heutigen Krise haben vergangene Krisen sozusagen bloß die Oberfläche der Wirtschaft gekräuselt.[74]

---

74 K. Polányi, 'Das Ausmaß der Wirtschaftskrise', in *Der österreichische Volkswirt*, 20 May 1933, p. 801.

PART II
Stock Markets, Railroad Finance, and Information Networks

CHAPTER 5

Efficiency of Early German Stock Markets, 1836–1848

Hartmut Kiehling[1]

Abstract

Since more than three decades, it is generally accepted that financial markets need to have certain efficiency to fulfil market functions.[2] Until now it was granted that early German stock markets were not efficient enough to do so.[3] In recent times, some research did find that stock exchanges in German imperial times (1871–1914) were not ineffective,[4] but still no investigation has covered the times before. Further research is possible on a more reliable basis, since the Frankfurt Centre for Financial Studies published monthly data of German stocks and bonds traded at all important German stock exchanges and calculated representative indices for 1876–1914. The data are available in dBase format. This will hopefully be the basis of more detailed and representative research in this field. The present study deals with the first modern stock return cycle in the German Confederation (Deutscher Bund) 1835–48. The study uses measures from the mathematics of nonlinear dynamics, as the data in hand lack information to use common measures of market efficiency such as excess volatility. In a second step, coincidence of the mathematical findings with historical findings and economic plausibility are discussed.

There are only a few estimates of early German stock market figures, but they point to an extraordinary importance of stock financing during the country's first phase of industrialization. Hoffmann guesses that German capital stock (outside Austria) summed up to original costs of 32.08 B Mk in 1850 (1856 38.34). 6.56 B Mk of it fell to business (incl. railways, 1856 8.15).[5] According to Bösselmann the par

---

1 Prof. Dr. Hartmut Kiehling is teaching Finance at the German University in Cairo. Many thanks to the physicist Prof. Dr. Thomas Holzhüter, University of Applied Sciences Hamburg, for various calculations and discussions, which made this paper possible.

2 E.F. Fama, 'Efficient Capital Markets: A Review of Theory and Empirical Work', in *Journal of Finance*, vol. 25, 1970.

3 R.H. Tilly, 'The Berlin Securities Exchange in National Context: Actors, Rules, and Reforms to 1914', 1955 *ASSA Abstracts, Newsletter of The Cliometric Society* 9, 1995.

4 J.B. De Long and M. Becht, '"Excess Volatility" and the German Stock Market, 1876–1990', EUI Working Paper ECO 92, 1982; C. Wetzel, *Die Auswirkungen des Reichsbörsengesetzes von 1896 auf die Effektenbörsen im Deutschen Reich, insbesondere auf die Berliner Fondsbörse* (Münster, 1996); S. Eube, *Der Aktienmarkt in Deutschland vor dem Ersten Weltkrieg: Eine Indexanalyse* (Frankfurt, 1998); J. Müller, *Der deutsche Rentenmarkt vor dem Ersten Weltkrieg: eine Indexanalyse* (Frankfurt, 1992).

5 W.G. Hoffmann, *Das Wachstum der deutschen Wirtschaft seit der Mitte des 19. Jahrhunderts* (Berlin, 1965).

value of stocks issued in Prussia until the same year amounted to 506.3 M Mk. 46 per cent of it was subscribed between 1841 and 1845.[6] In 1856 nominal paid-in stock funds in Germany (excluding Austria) summed up to 2.601 B Mk.[7] German traded stocks from stock market reports of 'Allgemeine Zeitung' amounted to a nominal capital of 493.4 M Mk at 1848 year's end. The latter gives a hint that stock exchanges could have played an especially important role in financing early German industrialization.

Source and Characteristics of Data

The underlying data come from (Augsburger) 'Allgemeine Zeitung', one of the most important newspapers during the time, and the oldest one still existing. From all stock market prices mentioned, eleven time series of daily stock returns have been selected by the criteria of longitude and absence of substantial gaps (see Table 5.1). All time series cover between 45 and 128 months and have a length of 1000 to 3572 trading days. Except for Hypo-Bank, OeNB, and Taunusbahn (since September 1838) with a unit quotation, stocks included in this study had a per cent quotation. Prices were demand prices at closing time. They were only adjusted for clearly false figures, but not for dividends or capital changes. Such adjustments cause additional noise when using nonlinearity measures. ('Noise is any unwanted input, either because it is irrelevant or because it distorts the presentation of values and/or their interpretation.' Noise is assumed to be randomly distributed. Chaos researchers often distinguish between dynamic and observation noise. The former 'disturbs the information obtained on the states of the system'. The latter 'makes the measurement less accurate than is desirable'.[8]) They should make no big difference since dividends usually were paid out twice a year, and they were guaranteed and included into stock prices to a large extent, leaving only a small extra dividend subject to ex-dividend quotation. In this study only Augsburg-Münchener Eisenbahn, Taunusbahn, Hypo-Bank 1844–48 and Ludwigskanal (1845–48) bear dividends neither fixed nor guaranteed. Even in these cases the author refrains from adjusting, since in many cases we do not know frequently changing distribution conditions. In the case of purchases of stocks not bearing fixed dividends, accrued interest ('Börsenzins') was subtracted from listed prices. Accrued interest rates differed from place to place and from stock to stock, but they were often 4 per cent calculated at the beginning of each year or semester.

---

6   K. Bösselmann, *Die Entwicklung der deutschen Aktiengesellschaft im 19. Jahrhundert* (Berlin, 1939).

7   E. Laspeyres, 'Die Rentabilität der industriellen Unternehmungen, namentlich der Actien-Gesellschaften', *Neue Freie Presse* (Vienna), 27 Nov. 1873.

8   D.N. Chorafas, *Chaos Theory in the Financial Markets* (Chicago, 1994).

Table 5.1   Time series included in the study

Series	Company	Domestic Stock Exchange
1	Bayerische Hypotheken- und Wechsel-Bank	Augsburg
2	Ludwigskanal	Augsburg
3	Augsburg-Münchener Eisenbahn	Augsburg
4	Österreichische Nationalbank	Vienna
5	Nordbahn/ Bochnia-Bahn	Vienna
6	Mailänder Bahn	Vienna
7	Pesther Eisenbahn	Vienna
8	Raaber/ Gloggnitzer Eisenbahn	Vienna
9	Rheinschanze/ Ludwigshafen Berberau	Frankfurt
10	Friedrich-Wilhelm-Nordbahn	Frankfurt
11	Taunusbahn	Frankfurt

Representativeness of Data

The applied stock market prices come from three places situated in the German Confederation (Vienna, Frankfurt and Augsburg). Vienna stocks include Italian, Hungarian and Czech stocks, of which the main trading place was the Austrian capital. This doesn't seem like very many compared to 20 contemporary trading places in Germany and Austria, but only eight of them had constant trading (Berlin, Vienna, Frankfurt, Leipzig, Hamburg, Augsburg, Breslau and Cologne).[9] Augsburg probably had the lowest trading; Vienna and especially Berlin seem to have had the highest turnovers.

For a long time it was generally considered that the Frankfurt stock trading section had been number one in Germany until 1870, but this was a misinterpretation of Wormser, whose argument was based on the overall turnover of securities.[10] Wormser's argument in turn was based on Schick's statement which was made almost immediately after the revolution of 1848, when stock market turnover had collapsed and bond market turnover was of outstanding importance.[11] Gömmel therefore thinks that the Berlin stock market turnover from 1840 to 1848 was the highest.[12] Figure 5.5 shows that Vienna stock market turnovers might also have had exceeded the ones in Frankfurt.

Unfortunately only weekly data are recorded of Berlin, Leipzig, Hamburg, Breslau and Cologne stock market prices. Augsburg and Frankfurt exchanges were

---

9 R. Gömmel, 'Entstehung und Entwicklung der Effektenbörsen im 19. Jahrhundert bis 1914', in H. Pohl (ed.), *Deutsche Börsengeschichte* (Frankfurt, 1992).

10 O. Wormser, *Die Frankfurter Börse* (Tübingen, 1919).

11 E. Schick, *Handbuch des deutschen Staatspapier- und Actienhandels* (Leipzig, 1849).

12 Gömmel, 'Effektenbörsen im 19. Jahrhundert'.

dominated by market segments others than stocks: Augsburg's markets for bills of exchange and foreign notes and coins, and Frankfurt's bond market had international importance.[13] Vienna was both an important stock and bond market. It did not list foreign securities, which Augsburg and Frankfurt did. Vienna left the other stock exchanges of the monarchy (Budapest, Milan, Venice and Trieste) far behind in importance. Regulatory and *de facto* state interventions were very common in Vienna, while both Augsburg and Frankfurt were dominated by banks. In a nutshell Vienna, Frankfurt and Augsburg represent different types of stock exchanges that could be found in the 1830s and 1840s in Germany.

The number of stocks included into this study reached 2 to 10 at a time, i.e. more than 50 per cent of actually traded German stocks between 1837 and 1842 according to 'Allgemeine Zeitung's' stock market reports. When the number of stocks at the Berlin stock market exploded after 1842, this percentage fell to about 20 per cent. Therefore the number of stocks included into this study can be characterized as representative (see Figure 5.1).

The industry structure of stocks included at least in the year 1846 was clearly representative compared to stocks traded, with a slight overweighting of banks, but it was surely not representative to stocks issued. This was due to the fact that since the 1820s, dozens of stock companies were founded in Germany, including insurances, country roads, theatres, mills etc., whose stocks were held as long-term investments (see Table 5.2 and Figure 5.2).

Supposing 'Allgemeine Zeitung' mentioned all stocks regularly traded in the German Confederation, market capitalization of traded German stocks grew from 93 to 359m marks in the years 1835–47 (yearly averages). With the following crash, it went down to 253m marks in 1848. This means that the stake of stocks included

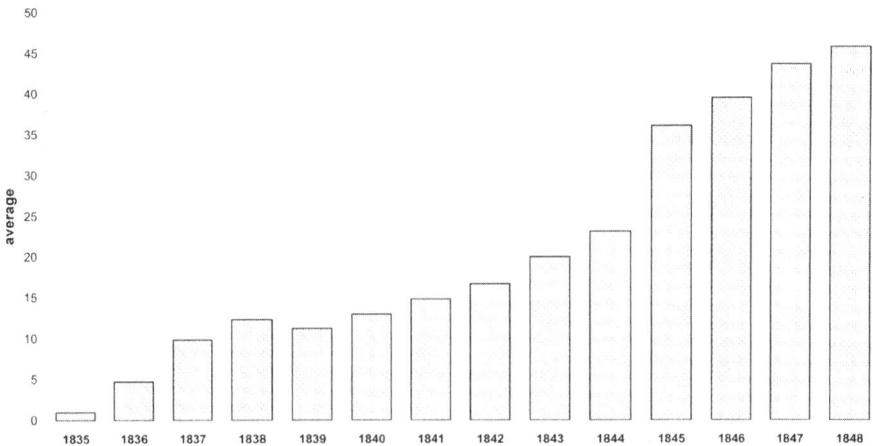

Figure 5.1   Number of stocks mentioned in the market reports of 'Allgemeine Zeitung'

---

13 O. Schwarzer et al., 'Das System des internationalen Zahlungsverkehrs', in J. Schneider, O. Schwarzer and F. Zellfelder (eds), *Währungen der Welt*, vol. I,1 (Stuttgart, 1991).

Table 5.2   Industry structure of stocks included in the study, traded and issued

Industry in %	Stocks included into the Study	Traded Stocks (1)	Stocks Issued (2)
Banks	18.2	7.1	5.5
Insurance			14.7
Railways	72.7	85.7	46.6
Steamboat		2.4	12.9
Services	9.1	4.8	10.4
Mines			
Industries			9.8
No. of Stocks	11	42	163

1) Reported in "Allgemeine Zeitung"
2) Discussed in Feller: Die Staatspapier- und Actien-Bőrse, Leipzig 1846

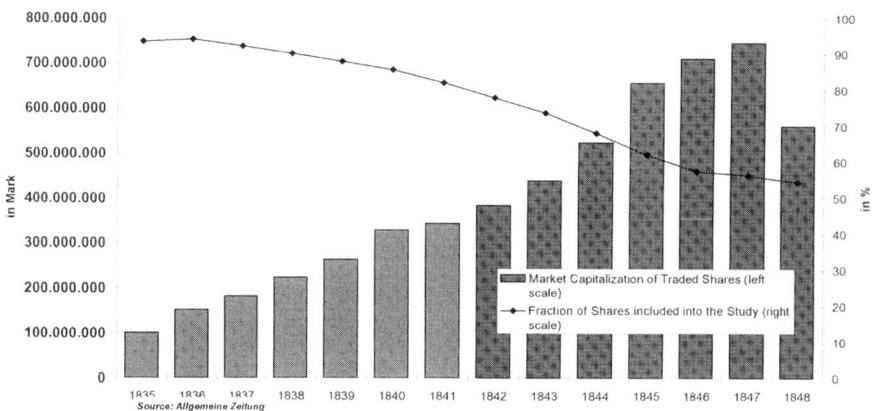

Figure 5.2   Market capitalization and representativeness of the study

in this study went down from 94 per cent in 1836 to 54 per cent eight years later. The decline is due to the growing importance of the Berlin stock market which is not included.

As a result, and besides general stochastic problems due to its smallness, the sample of stocks is sufficiently representative to all important extents.

Randomness of Data

There are only very few methods to measure market efficiency of any degree. With regards to stock markets, excess volatility was used in most cases to measure medium and strong market efficiency. It compares stock market prices before and after dividend announcements and decides if price reactions exceed certain efficiency levels. In the case of daily prices, it would be necessary to have the exact dates of the announcements as well as details of calculation like accrued interest. These data were handed down only sporadically during the time in question. Data Envelopment Analysis (DEA), mainly used to measure efficiency of sectoral factor allocation, is a theoretical alternative.[14] As it needs the effect of certain input on certain output, the same problem appears as with excess volatility.

To measure medium and strong market efficiency, it would not be necessary to assume causalities. Ideal efficient capital markets are supposed to behave like random walks, and in order to measure their efficiency it should be enough to distinguish if their price changes develop randomly or not. The Hurst exponent is a measure to do so without the need to imply causalities is. It distinguishes random behaviour from different degrees of deterministic behaviour of a time series: Let the range R of a spot's motion in an otherwise quiet system during a period m be rescaled by its standard deviation S, the process can be described by the equation of the Rescaled Range or R/S analysis:

$$(1) \qquad \frac{R_m}{S_m} = c \times m^H$$

For c = constant the Hurst exponent H can be calculated as

$$(2) \qquad H = \frac{\log\left(\frac{R_m}{S_m}\right) - \log(c)}{\log(m)}$$

H takes values between 0 and 1 with 0.5 as pure random. A significant difference from 0.5 points to a clearly deterministic data structure, with $H \gg 0.5$ indicating persistency and $H \ll 0.5$ indicating anti-persistency (i.e. persistent or trend-reinforcing series).[15] In order to calculate Hurst with sufficient accuracy, 2000–3000 data points are needed, but 500 observations might be enough for first results.

For this study, H was calculated via linear regression for sub-series, each between 20 and 200 data points. It was not calculated using the raw data, but out of day-to-day changes

$$(3) \qquad y_n = \log\frac{x_n}{x_{n-1}}$$

---

14 T. Coelli, *An introduction to efficiency and productivity analysis* (Dordrecht, 1998).
15 E.E. Peters, *Chaos and Order in the Capital Markets* (New York, 1991).

The applied algorithm follows Peters.[16]

As a first result, it turned out that behaviour of time series changed at the beginning of the year 1848. The calculation of H ceased in 1847 at year's end for the long time series 1, 2, 5, 6, 7, 9 and 11. Standard deviation S typically reaches zero in the case of short series because of the infrequency of price change. In such cases R/S values are not defined and the calculation of H is not possible.

To show results more obviously, each time series H was embedded into a confidence funnel around the H of a pure random walk. All calculations for H clearly stay within this confidence range with the only exception of series 2 (Ludwigskanal) (see Figure 5.3). Its market might have been the only one being clearly inefficient. On the whole, all other Hs cluster around one another. This is especially true for Vienna railway stocks, being the closest to a random walk, with Frankfurt Taunusbahn and Vienna OeNB staying slightly aside and Augsburg Hypo-Bank being the most distant (see Table 5.3).

Table 5.3   Hurst exponent

Series	Company	Hurst exponent
6	Mailänder Bahn	0.53150
8	Raaber/ Gloggnitzer Bahn	0.54178
5	Nordbahn/ Bochnia-Bahn	0.55094
11	Taunusbahn	0.57155
4	OeNB	0.57315
1	Hypo-Bank	0.62265
2	Ludwigskanal	NaN

Normal Distribution of Changes

Since Hurst results are often biased,[17] they need to be confirmed by other instruments. BDS statistics, a test developed by Brock, Dechert and Scheinkman, distinguishes linear from nonlinear behaviour and thus shows if time series are identical and independently distributed (IID). In other words BDS proves if their changes form a normal distribution or not. In this way, BDS statistics also should distinguish between random and deterministic behaviour of certain degrees. The measure starts from the correlation integral

$$(4) \qquad C(\varepsilon) = \lim_{n \to \infty} \frac{1}{n^2} \sum_{\substack{i,j=1 \\ i \neq j}}^{n} \Theta\left(\varepsilon - \left\| x_i - x_j \right\| \right).$$

16 Peters, 'Chaos and Order'.

17 B.W. Ambrose et al., 'Fractal Structure in the Capital Markets Revisited', in *Financial Analysts' Journal*, vol. 3, 1993.

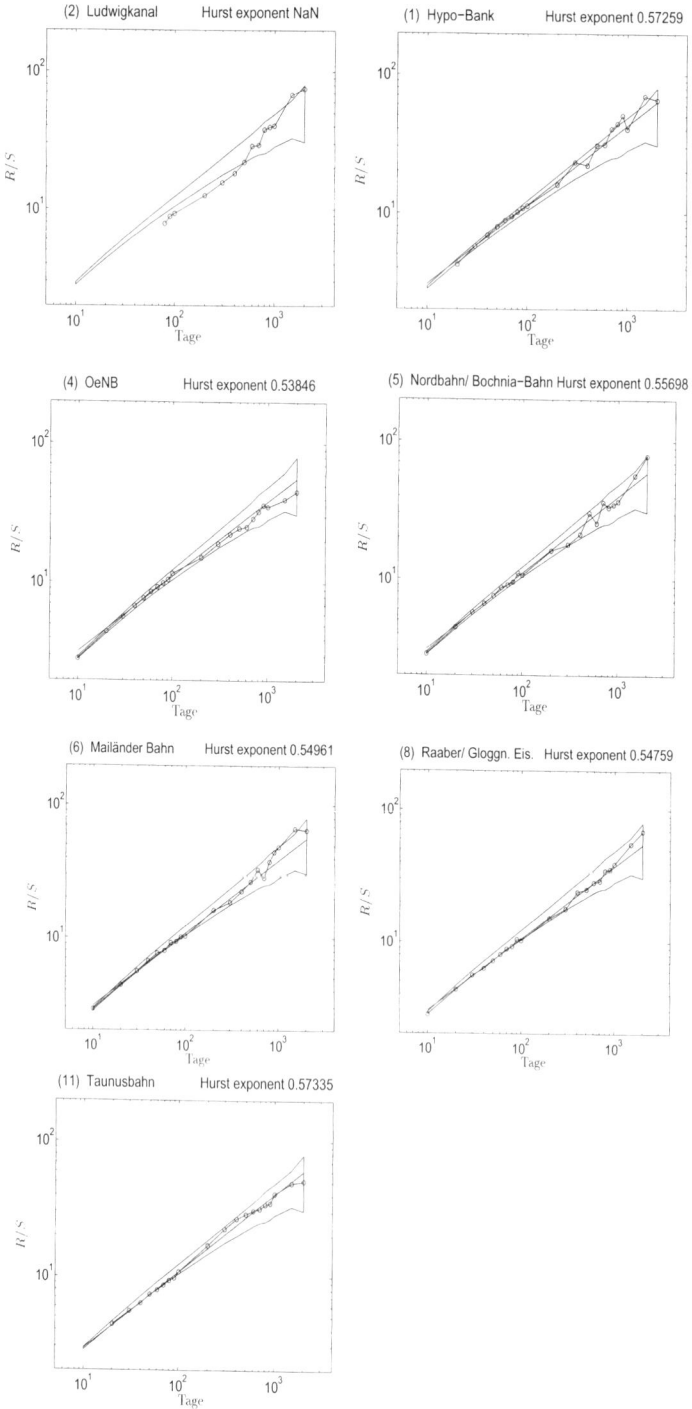

Figure 5.3   Hurst exponent

The correlation integral counts the number of values x_j, of which the difference $\left\| x_i - x_j \right\|$ to a value x_i is smaller than $\varepsilon > \left\| x_i - x_j \right\|$ and puts it into a proportion to the whole number of values. This correlation integral makes it possible to separate all unimportant values and to simplify the calculation. If one calls a sequence of IID observations $\left\{ x_t : t = 1, \dots, T \right\}$, that forms N-dimensional vectors $x_t^N = \left(x_{t+1}, \dots, x_{t+N-1} \right)$ ('N-histories'), the correlation integral can be written as

$$(5) \qquad C_n(\varepsilon) = \frac{2}{T_n(T_n - 1)} \sum_{1 \le i < j \le T_n} \prod_{k=0}^{m-1} \Theta\left(\varepsilon - \left\| x_{i+k} - x_{j+k} \right\| \right).$$

Assuming an asymptotic standard normal deviation BDS statistics show the form

$$(6) \qquad bds = w_n(\varepsilon) = \frac{\sqrt{T} \times \left[C_n(\varepsilon) - C_1(\varepsilon)^n \right]}{\sigma_n(\varepsilon)}$$

The applied algorithm followed LeBaron's original C-procedures.[18]

All calculated BDS values in this study are large enough to reject the null hypothesis of IID for all reasonable embedding dimensions $m = 2$ until $m = 10$ (see Figure 5.4 and Table 5.4). (An embedding dimension reflects, roughly spoken, a system's complexity.) This points to certain determinism within all series, but there are also differences between time series. Extremes for all embedding dimensions were Augsburg-based Hypo-Bank and Ludwigskanal at the low end, and Frankfurt-based Taunusbahn at the high end of figures, leaving again Ludwigskanal and Hypo-Bank in the order of inefficiency or near-inefficiency.

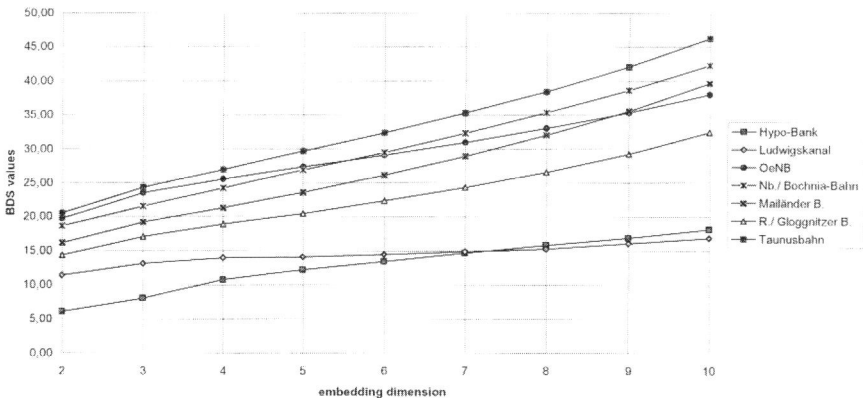

Figure 5.4   BDS statistics

---

18 B. LeBaron, 'A Fast Algorithm for the BDS Statistic', in *Studies in Nonlinear Dynamics and Econometrics*, vol. 2, 1997.

Table 5.4   BDS statistics

Series	Company	m=2	m=3	m=4	m=5	m=6	m=7	m=8	m=9	m=10
2	Ludwigsk.	11.47	13.17	14.03	14.15	14.47	14.92	15.31	16.09	16.85
1	Hypo-Bank	6.13	8.05	10.80	12.27	13.45	14.70	15.83	16.90	18.16
8	Gloggnitzer	14.41	17.08	18.96	20.49	22.34	24.33	26.58	29.27	32.46
4	OeNB	19.75	23.53	25.55	27.37	29.08	30.98	33.04	35.37	37.99
6	Mailänder	16.19	19.21	21.34	23.59	26.14	28.93	32.04	35.58	39.66
5	N./Bochnia	18.64	21.54	24.23	26.92	29.49	32.33	35.35	38.61	42.29
11	Taunusbahn	20.59	24.30	26.96	29.67	32.38	35.31	38.43	42.09	46.26

A few words should be said about consistency of efficiency and determinism. In capital market theory ideal markets follow a pure random walk without any determinism. This is only true under the assumption of relevant information occurring randomly over time (see below). Because incoming information clusters in reality, there must be at least some determinism in otherwise sufficiently efficient financial markets.

Determinism in the Data

If Hurst and/or BDS Statistics point to certain deterministic structure in the data, it is reasonable to apply further measures to find out more about the nature of the process. If a time series does not follow a pure random walk, the distribution of its changes is heteroskedastic to a normal one. One possibility is a distribution which is skewed. The measure of skewness shows both the direction and extension of a distribution's deviation from its mean. Standard normal deviations have $g_3 = 0$. $g_3 < 0$ shows that data are skewed right, $g_3 > 0$ shows that they are skewed left. If a distribution is skew, the underlying process follows a trend. Formula of skewness is:

$$(7) \qquad g_3 = \frac{1}{n}\sum_{i=1}^{n} z_i^3 .$$

z makes a z-transformation $\dfrac{x_n - \mu}{s}$ with μ = mean and ∂ = standard deviation of the time series to make results comparable.

Results show that all eleven time series are skew, but to a different degree (Table 5.5). 1848 figures once more show a dramatic increase in determinism, especially in smaller stock market places like Augsburg and Frankfurt, whereas at other times Frankfurt shows by far the lowest determinism.

Table 5.5   Skewness

Series	Company	incl. 1848	excl. 1848
1	Hypo-Bank	−26.84	−0.72
2	Ludwigskanal	−20.44	−1.21
3	Augsburg-Münchener Eisenb.	−1.41	−1.41
4	OeNB	−4.00	−0.89
5	Nordbahn/ Bochnia-Bahn	−1.47	−0.61
6	Mailänder Bahn	−1.81	−1.02
7	Pesther Eisenbahn	−0.75	−1.03
8	Raaber/ Gloggnitzer Bahn	−0.75	−0.52
9	Rheinschanze/ Ludwigsh. Berb.	−18.89	−0.28
10	Friedrich-Wilhelm-Nordbahn	−2.49	−0.27
11	Taunusbahn	−6.02	0.03

Another kind of determinism is measured by kurtosis. It compares a distribution with Gauss in view of peakedness. A value of zero points again to a standard normal deviation, negative K shows a broader peak around the mean, positive K steeper ones. The first one is called excess kurtotic or platykurtotic, the latter one is called leptokurtotic. Kurtosis follows the formula:

(8) $K = \dfrac{1}{n}\sum_{i=1}^{n} z_i^4 - 3 .$

The calculation shows all time series as being leptokurtotic but to different degrees (see Table 5.6). Again 1848 caused excess values reflecting paralysis after the crash. Again Vienna was less affected by 1848 turbulences and including that year's values brings Augsburg and Frankfurt time series to remarkably high values. Much lower differences between market places can be found when excluding the year of revolution. Nevertheless Frankfurt had substantially lower figures than Augsburg and Vienna, bringing Frankfurt's price changes nearer to Gauss in normal times.

Table 5.6   Kurtosis

Series	Company	incl. 1848	excl. 1848
1	Hypo-Bank	1059.76	28.89
2	Ludwigskanal	668.27	27.46
3	Augsburg-Münchn. Eis.	—	12.49
4	OeNB	99.75	26.56
5	Nordbahn/ Bochnia-Bahn	36.05	28.33
6	Mailänder Bahn	42.15	24.44
7	Pesther Eisenbahn	56.19	24.05
8	Raaber/ Gloggnitzer Bahn	24.62	17.80
9	Rheinsch./ Ldwh. Berb.	548.08	8.20
10	Friedr.-Wilh. Nordbahn	27.82	19.52
11	Taunusbahn	159.45	21.30

Chaos in the Data

Because it is difficult to distinguish between random and high-dimensional chaotic processes, time series should be tested additionally for chaotic behaviour. This can be done by the Lyapunov exponent L. It measures the actual chaotic behaviour of a system in the sense of sensitive dependence from initial conditions (or outside disturbance in the case of a running system). If the underlying equation is known, L shows the rate of removal between two neighbouring spots depending on these initial conditions. The system is chaotic if these spots disperse and $L > 0$, while it shows periodic behaviour if they narrow and $L < 0$. In other words: L measures how predictable a system actually is. L might change over time and with each dimension, so it has to be calculated for every time $t \leq T$ and every dimension D (for the calculation of D see below). L = max determines the system's behaviour. m-dimensional phase spaces z can be formed from an empirical time series $X = (x_0, x_1, x_2, ..., x_T)$:

(9) $z_t = \left(x_t, x_{t+1}, x_{t+2}, ..., x_{t+m+1}\right)$ with $t = 1, 2, ..., T - m + 1$.

In a m-dimensional phase space $T - m + 1$ plots can be found for all neighbouring spots (a_j, a_k), for which is true $|a_j - a_k| < \varepsilon$ with $a_j \neq a_k$. In a next step the distance δ after p periods can be calculated for these N pairs of neighbouring spots as

(10) $\delta_p^{(j,k)} = \dfrac{\left|a_{j+p} - a_{k+p}\right|}{\left|a_j - a_k\right|}$.

This lets L follow the equation

(11) $L = \dfrac{1}{p \times n} \times \sum_{j,k} \left(\ln \delta_p^{(j,k)}\right)$.

If a system with an actually negative L is disturbed, it will return to a stable attractor. Actual sensitivity of the system to changes of its starting conditions (or outside disturbance) grows with L. The larger L grows, the bigger is the system's sensitivity to changes of its starting conditions. The bigger L becomes, the more unpredictable the system becomes. The Lyapunov exponent needs even more data points than the fractal dimension D, but there are several algorithms to help this point. Our estimation of the linearized flow map follows QR decomposition according to the procedure of Parlitz.[19]

The result of Lyapunov analysis is not quite clear in this case. The Lyapunov's highest exponents exceed zero in each case giving a hint towards the existence of chaos, on one hand. On the other hand results point to very high dimensionality, which also could result from high-dimensional stochastic processes. To add on to this problem, all exponents are parasitic leaving the assumption that there are no true Lyapunov exponents at all. The calculated exponents are probably spurious because the embedded dimensions are much too low compared to the real fractal dimension of the processes (see below). Results do not contradict random behaviour despite this vagueness, as they are not exact enough to distinguish between random and high-dimensional chaos.

---

19 U. Parlitz, 'Identification of True and Spurious Lyapunov Exponents from Time Series', in *International Journal of Bifurcation and Chaos*, vol. 2, 1992.

Number of the System's Determinants

The maximum number of determinants of a system can be determined by a version of fractal dimension D. These determinants spread out an ideal phase space. D shows how much of this phase space is filled up by its attractor. An attractor maps where the degrees of freedom of a deterministic system approach after it has been disturbed ('limit cycle'). A fractal dimension shows a system's maximum number of degrees of freedom or of determinants.[20] Pure random time series have $D = 2$ in a phase space, reconstructed by the map $x_t \rightarrow x_{t+1}$. In order to calculate D the phase space of the underlying system has to be determined first with an embedding dimensional $\dim_E$, and this phase space must be divided up into cells V_i, each with an edge length of ε and a volume of $R^{\dim_E}$. By doing so, $N(\varepsilon)$ shows the minimum number of cells needed to cover the attractor and V_i runs from $i = 1$ until $N(\varepsilon)$. p_i is the probability to find a point of an attractor in cell V_i. With these definitions the fractal dimension follows the equation:

$$(12) \qquad D_q = \lim_{\varepsilon \to 0} \frac{1}{q-1} \times \frac{\log \left(\sum_{i=1}^{N(\varepsilon)} p_i^q \right)}{\log(\varepsilon)} \quad \text{for } D_q \geq D_p \text{ for } q \leq p.$$

To quantify different characteristics of attractors, physicists have developed a whole family of fractal dimensions. We have used the correlation dimension with $q = 2$.[21] D_C grows with the complexity of underlying dynamics. All fractal dimension measures ask for an excessive amount of data, growing with the number of dimensions reached.[22] In a real economic world, this means that only low-dimensional processes can be distinguished from high-dimensional ones, and it is difficult to distinguish between random and high-dimensional chaotic processes.

Again we had to deal with insufficient data: There are important quantification effects resulting from price listing mainly in 1/8. In ten out of eleven cases, time series are too short for D to tend to a saturation level. Only Ludwigskanal's D tends to this level at pretty low dimensionality, and in the case of Hypo-Bank, there is a slight possibility for that. In all other cases low-dimensional chaos can be denied. Time series 1 (Hypo-Bank), 11 (Taunusbahn) and 7 (Mailänder Bahn) probably have correlation dimensions of at least 4.5, 6 and 7.5, the other time series show even higher dimensional behaviour. In most cases there should even be very high dimensions, although time series are not really long enough to prove. The result fits into the above picture, findings being compatible with random behaviour with the exception of Ludwigskanal.

---

20 O. Loistl and I. Betz, *Chaostheorie: Zur Theorie nichtlinearer dynamischer Systeme* (1993, reprinted Munich and Vienna, 1996); Th. Buzug, *Analyse chaotischer Systeme* (Mannheim, 1994), thereafter Buzug, 'Analyse chaotischer Systeme'.

21 W.-H. Steeb, *A Handbook of Terms Used in Chaos and Quantum Chaos* (Mannheim, 1991).

22 Buzug, 'Analyse chaotischer Systeme'.

To sum up mathematical findings are relatively clear: Both Ludwigskanal and (to a lower extent) Hypo-Bank lack market efficiency, whereas railway stocks and (to a limited degree) OeNB stocks were pretty efficient. All these stocks followed more or less certain determinism, but we wouldn't have expected pure random walk in a real financial world. Vienna and Frankfurt stock exchanges seem to have been more efficient than the small Augsburg stock exchange. The whole year of 1848 was clearly inefficient, although the broad Vienna market seems to have been affected the least.

Market Information

According to Eugene F. Fama efficient capital markets have several premises. He defines efficiency as information efficiency, meaning the less information is privileged, the more markets are efficient.[23] This implies:

- In an ideal world listed companies have to publish all information that could be relevant for their stock prices, leaving no place for insider trading. Velocity of information transmission has to be fast enough to enable arbitrage.
- Markets need certain broadness to be efficient: There has to be certain market turnover and each market side as well as companies and stockholders need to be of certain variety.
- Market entry has to be free. Market efficiency can be disturbed by legal, statutory or organizational restrictions as well as by high transaction cost, lack of transferability and other economic hindrance.
- Also market interference, like backing actions and other manipulations, destroys efficiency.

The second part of this chapter deals with these premises. To have a look at the first one: Information about current market situation was very poor compared to modern standards. Professional market participants and banks subscribed daily price lists published officially by every German stock exchange. The public had to wait for printed market reports of some newspapers, published daily or even weekly. Their reports were short, but they had sufficient quality showing important information, tendency and undertone. Stock market gazettes existed only locally. We only know of 'Leipziger Actien-Zeitung'.[24] 'Der Aktionär' was founded as the first nationwide stock market gazette in 1854.

Compared to today's international standards information given by listed companies was poor. Railway and canal companies published their figures of transported persons and freight quarterly, if not monthly, and (almost) every company prepared its annual financial statement and published it during its general meeting of shareholders. These statements were only gross statements and no value adjustments, depreciation or attention obligation were deducted. This practice gave

---

23 H.V. Roberts, 'Statistical versus Clinical Prediction on the Stock Market', unpublished paper (University of Chicago, 1967).

24 *Allgemeine Zeitung*, 27 Aug. 1837.

way to all kinds of internal knowledge and speculation, suggesting a high probability that insider trading was a frequent phenomenon. We do not know much about privileged access to information at early German stock markets. Several continuous news connections existed established by Rothschild, and it is obvious that other professional market participants also built up private accelerated news transmission. Rothschild's network included Frankfurt and Vienna, but not Augsburg. Market comments paid considerable attention to all rumours and actions concerning this banking house.

The time covered by this study was a time of an upheaval of information. Velocity of information transmission grew for several reasons. Due to punctual acceleration of traffic by fast roads and stagecoaches, steamboats and railway lines, transaction times from Paris, Amsterdam and London shrank from 4, 5 and 6 days to 3, 3 and 4 days between 1839 and 1848 according to stock market reports in 'Allgemeine Zeitung'. Nationwide acceleration was even faster in some cases: Transaction times from Frankfurt and Vienna to Augsburg shrank from 3 to 1 and from 3 or 4 to 2 days, while news from Leipzig, Berlin or Hamburg still needed the same time. There are also some examples of establishing special couriers. Berlin stock exchange established one at Christmas 1846 from Hamburg to Berlin, but not in the opposite direction. In the mid 1840s a pigeon course was established between Paris and Frankfurt stock exchanges like the famous one between London and Amsterdam existing already long before. New kinds of telegraphs were invented and established in the meanwhile and they influenced stock markets' desires, although they could not yet be used for private purposes. This was both true for the optical telegraph from Berlin over Cologne to Koblenz (est. 1833) and for the first German electric telegraph from Wiesbaden to Frankfurt (est. 1846).[25]

Market Broadness

Efficient stock markets have to have a certain variety of stockholders resulting in certain free float. We know that stock subscription often found broad interest, although there were usually also major shareholders. In the case of Hypo-Bank: Augsburg banker Eichthal 29.21 per cent, Rothschild Frankfurt 15.44 per cent, in the case of Ludwigskanal Bavarian government 25 per cent, in the case of Augsburg-Münchner Eisenbahn Eichthal and some of his friends 25 per cent, five other Augsburg bankers each 4.8 per cent. In most cases a broad range of private subscribers can be found besides these 'founders': Augsburg-Münchener Eisenbahn had 64 and Hypo-Bank had 75 subscribers. A usual stock offering was publicly done in diverse cities, in some case even abroad (see Table 5.7). Rothschild placed 75 per cent of Ludwigskanal's stocks internationally while Rheinschanze/Ludwigshafen-Berberau was placed in Milan as a first step.

Companies authorized banks in other towns as paying agencies. This points to certain broadness of stock holdings (see Table 5.8). The same is true for listings

---

25 J. Steen, *Die zweite industrielle Revolution. Frankfurt und die Elektrizität 1800–1914* (Frankfurt, 1981); O. Blumtritt, *Nachrichtentechnik* (Munich, 1988).

Table 5.7   Public offering

Series	Company	Public offerings in
1	Hypo-Bank	Several towns in Bavaria
2	Ludwigskanal	Austria, Belgium, England, France, Germany, Italy, the Netherlands and Switzerland
3	Abg.-Mchn. Eis.	Augsburg and Munich
4	OeNB	Vienna
5	N./Bochnia B.	Vienna
6	Mailänder B.	Milan and Vienna
7	Pesther Eis.	Budapest and Vienna
8	R./Gloggn.Eis.	Vienna
9	Rhs./Lwh.Berb.	First in Milan, later on in Frankfurt, Mannheim and in the Palatinate
10	Fr.-Wilh.Nordb.	Frankfurt
11	Taunusbahn	Frankfurt, Mainz and Wiesbaden

Table 5.8   Paying agencies

Series	Company	Paying agencies in
5	N./Bochnia B.	Frankfurt and Vienna
6	Mailänder B.	Milan and Vienna
7	Pesther Eis.	Berlin, Leipzig, Budapest and Vienna

at several places including foreign ones (see Table 5.9). Although data material is not ideal, it is obvious that stockholders' distribution was broad enough for stock markets not to hinder certain efficiency.

Sufficient market turnover is constitutional for market efficiency. Again exact figures are not known, but there are proxies like percentage of unchanged (offer or demand) prices growing inversely proportional to market turnover. Ludwigskanal had the highest (86.1 per cent), Hypo-Bank the second highest share (60.0 per cent), while Austrian time series had percentages between 16.0 and 21.0 per cent and Frankfurt Taunusbahn 30.7 per cent. Percentages are high, but they show a clear order between market places. Most trading days in Vienna and Frankfurt saw price changes, probably with at least some turnover, while Augsburg stock exchange seem to have been inactive most of the time (see Table 5.10 and Figure 5.5).

Another proxy can add more details to the Augsburg picture. We know price supplements from Berlin, Hamburg, Leipzig and Augsburg. For Vienna and Frankfurt only the mere prices are delivered. Such price supplements can give a rank of turnover. They indicate for instance if a price was estimated, if it was an

Table 5.9   Listings

Series	Company	Listing in
1	Hypo-Bank	Frankfurt, Munich and Augsburg
2	Ludwigskanal	London, Frankfurt, Munich and Augsburg
3	Abg.-Mchn. Eis.	Munich and Augsburg
4	OeNB	Amsterdam, Augsburg, Berlin, Frankfurt, Hamburg, Munich, Leipzig and Vienna
6	Mailänder B.	Milan, Augsburg and Vienna
7	Pesther Eis.	Budapest and Vienna
9	Rhs./Lwh.Berb.	Milan, Paris, Augsburg, Frankfurt and Munich

Table 5.10   Percentage of prices unchanged from one day to another

	in %
Hypo-Bank	60.0
Ludwigskanal	86.1
OeNB	18.2
Nord-/Bochniabahn	17.3
Mailänder	21.0
Raaber/Gloggnitzer Bahn	16.0
Taunusbahn	30.7

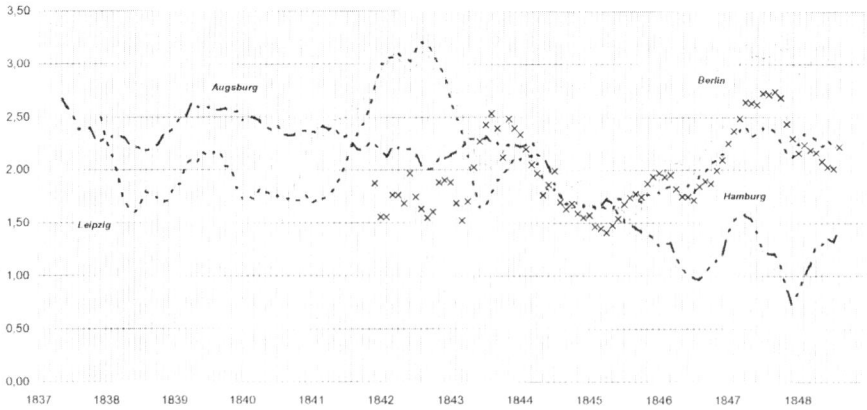

Figure 5.5   Stock market turnover proxies

asked or bid price or a price agreed upon. Nonparametric data like these are good for intertemporal comparison, but not for comparisons between different places. Augsburg daily prices were based on real turnover until mid 1844, but loss of market share already began earlier, since Augsburg did not manage to take part in the stock market boom like Berlin, Leipzig and Vienna. As a result Augsburg turnover decreased later on making Augsburg an inferior stock trading place. This was true in spite of Bavaria being a stock market pioneer in 1835/36 Germany with the first successful placement of railway stocks and two early 'jumbos' each of 5m fl: Ludwigseisenbahn from Nuremberg to Fürth resp. Ludwigskanal and Hypo-Bank. Between mid 1845 and the first months of 1847 Augsburg turnover fell most of the time, while Berlin, Hamburg and Leipzig turnovers had a sharp rise. This trend can be confirmed in general by literature.[26]

Hard facts on market turnover are very rare. In only a few cases do we know some figures from market reports, company books and records. Such a case is Hypo-Bank, Germany's first private bank run as a stock corporation.[27] According to the bank's stock register, turnover figures were pretty low, growing to a maximum of 687,000 fl (= 1.4m Mk) during the first half of 1843. This period of time had 125 trading days in Augsburg giving a theoretical turnover of 5500 fl (=11,000 Mk) per day. These figures probably differ from real ones, since on one hand Hypo-Bank stocks were also traded in Frankfurt and Munich, and there were also private transactions. On the other hand stocks often were not transferred in the company's stock register in the case of trading over the counter, and this portion might easily have grown over time. Divergence comes across comparing Hypo-Bank's transcription figures with its turnover proxies, showing quite different trends and levels especially in the years 1841 and since 1846, when Augsburg's stock exchange lost market shares, while ups and downs coincide more or less (see Figure 5.6).

The difference becomes evident when compared to the Viennese stocks. Market comments in 'Allgemeine Zeitung' mention state interventions at six days summing up to 4m fl (= 8m Mk), showing market turnover on these days amounting to almost 400,000 fl (= 800,000 Mk) per stock and day. This is a prominent sum even when considering that these days had especially high turnovers. In the case of two of the stocks, we know exact turnover figures (see Table 5.11).

These considerations show that market turnover in Frankfurt and Vienna (and probably also in Berlin, Leipzig and Hamburg) was probably high enough for certain market efficiency, but this was only a part of turnover in German stocks. In Frankfurt, Vienna and probably other big and traditional places, like Berlin and Hamburg, additional market places existed, either organized by the associations of local businessmen in their own rooms after market closed, on Sundays, holidays and hectic days ('Effectensocietät'), or for convenience and cost reasons as hedge exchanges mostly situated in coffeehouses open even to women. These unofficial market places seem to have had remarkable turnover. Besides the eight German

---

26 L. Lieb, *Die Entwicklung der Augsburger Effektenbörse (1816–1896)* (Augsburg, 1930).

27 The authors could copy the data from the original minutes of the board thanks to the company's then archivist and historian Dr Franziska Jungmann-Stadler.

Figure 5.6   Turnover in hypo-bank stocks

Table 5.11   Interventions of the Austrian state

Date	Mailänder Bahn	Pesther Eisenbahn
20.4.1847	363.6	—
21.4.1847	363.6	—
26.4.1847	712.7	200
28.4.1847	509.1	1680
30.4.1847	1672.7	1000
7.9.1847	800	600

Expenses in 100 000 Mk

stock exchanges having more or less regular trade in stocks, four more places had official stock exchanges with at least sporadic trade (Munich, Nuremberg, Bremen and Hanover. Königsberg stock exchange lay out of the confederation). Also some trade existed at a few additional places (Magdeburg, Brunswick, Halle, Mainz, Mannheim, Zwickau, Stettin, Essen, Düsseldorf, Elberfeld and Stuttgart). Some of them became official stock exchanges later on.[28]

In summary, turnover in German stocks was very likely high enough to guarantee certain market efficiency. This was especially true for Vienna and probably also for Frankfurt stock markets, whereas severe doubts remain in the case of Augsburg – maybe with the exception of the years 1837–44. In 1848 market turnover dropped sharply in Frankfurt and fell to almost nothing in Augsburg, while Vienna retained more of its former activity.

28 E. Marx, *Die Entwicklung der deutschen Provinzbörsen* (Vienna, 1913); D. Schell, 'Beiträge zur Geschichte der ehemaligen Handelsbörse zu Elberfeld', in *Zeitschrift des Bergischen Geschichtsvereins*, vol. 40, 1907.

Market Entry

Another important condition for market efficiency is free entrance to the market. Again Vienna and Frankfurt stock exchanges exceeded Augsburg, where access to the floor was only permitted to members of the local trade association ('Kaufleutestubengesellschaft'), while Vienna and Frankfurt exchanges were open to all male persons who were not bankrupt. Nevertheless private investors usually placed their orders with the help of local bankers or registered brokers. Pure distance was much more important than institutional differences. Regarding still long travel and transmission times, local market participants could keep in much better contact to stock markets: Rumours, written stock market reports and even stock exchange gazettes and daily newspapers' market reports reached them much faster and they always had the possibility to go spontaneously to market or send someone to do so. This was one of the reasons why stock exchanges in big cities like Vienna and Berlin developed much faster than those in smaller towns like Frankfurt and Augsburg (see Table 5.12).[29]

Table 5.12   Inhabitants 1840/41*

Vienna	340,000
Berlin	332,213
Hamburg	189,476
Frankfurt	66,200
Augsburg	37,000

* E. Lichtenberger, *Wien – Prag: ein Städtevergleich* (Vienna, 1993); W. Fischer, J. Krengel and J. Wietog (eds), *Sozialgeschichtliches Arbeitsbuch I* (Munich, 1982); N. Götz, 'Stadt und "Verstädterung" seit der Mitte des 19. Jahrhunderts', in G. Bott (ed.), *Leben und Arbeiten im Industriezeitalter* (Stuttgart, 1985).

Unhindered market access implies fair transaction costs. Compared to other markets, transactions in Germany were not at all expensive (see Table 5.13). This was especially true for commission paid to private and official brokers. Small orders in Germany cost only about half of Amsterdam or Paris orders, and only about 10 per cent of London orders, and even big orders were cheaper by 1/3 in Berlin than in Amsterdam or Paris, while expensive London orders cost three times more.[30] (London had no official commission list at that time. Schick is referring to usual prices showing that London brokers concentrated on big clients.)

Only bearer certificates are ideally transferable, but in those days most German stocks were registered. One of the main reasons of Berlin's success as a stock market was the fact that its railway stocks issued since 1840/44 were bearer papers. But also in the case of registered papers, market participants eased transfers. As an example heavily traded OeNB stocks were often registered under fictitious names, making

---

29 Gömmel, 'Effektenbörsen im 19. Jahrhundert'.
30 Schick, 'Handbuch'.

Table 5.13   Taxes and fees

% of par value	Brokerage	Courtage	Stamp tax	Ad valorem tax	Statal fee	Total	Witholding tax*
Augsburg	0.25–0.33	0.2				0.45–0.533	
Frankfurt	0.125–0.33	0.2				0.325–0.533	
Vienna	0.33–0.5	0.05				0.383–0.55	5%†
Berlin	0.125–0.33	0.1–0.2				0.225–0.533	
London		1	0.5	0.002–7.5	0.002–7.5	1.503–11.25•	
Paris		0.25	0.05			0.3	
Amsterdam	0.25–0.5	0.05–0.5				0.3–1	

* Percentage of dividends.
† In the case of OeNB, the company paid for the tax.
• Fees could be subject to individual arrangements.

transfers possible as if they were bearer stocks. Also fractional share certificates were traded instead of ordinary full OeNB stocks.

A stock's transferability is also influenced by its price, and early German stocks carried a high value. The least expensive stock was offered by Frankfurt-based Friedrich-Wilhelm-Nordbahn with a face value of 100 Tlr (= 300 Mk), while the most expensive was OeNB stock with a par value of 1 000 fl C.W. (= 2 000 Mk) (see Table 5.14). (For reasons of convenience the currency denomination is done in Mark (Mk), German currency 1873–1924: 3 Mk = 1 Taler (Tlr), 2 tlr = 3.5 south German guilder (fl sdt.W.), 1 Tlr = 1.5 Austrian guilder (fl Ö.W.). There was a (usually slight) difference between Austrian bank notes (fl W.W.) and full-bodied coins (fl C.W.), but it is not important in this context.) In most cases face value was only of theoretical interest, since stocks and interim certificates of newly founded companies only had to be paid in to certain extent until more money was needed by the company. And there was always the possibility to buy derivates (see below).

The high cost and lack of transferability of stocks were less important in Vienna and Frankfurt, because of widely used forward transactions. Corresponding to the decline of Augsburg turnover, there was no more forward trading after 1836. 'Allgemeine Zeitung' mentioned end-of-month prices of Taunusbahn almost every day in 1847 (forward dealings of less traded Rheinschanze/Ludwigshafen-Berberau and Friedrich-Wilhelm-Nordbahn are not given). Officially traded derivatives had a much greater variety than today, covering options and futures and all kinds of prolongations, straddles, options to double etc.[31] As a result the cost of stock was not such a problem as it seems from a theoretical standpoint.

_____
31 Schick, 'Handbuch'.

Table 5.14   Face value of stocks, 1836–1848

Series	Company	Face value	in Mk	Paid in 1836–48
10	Friedr.-Wilhelm-Nordbahn	100 Thlr	300	10–75%
11	Taunusbahn	250 fl sdt.W.	428.57	1840 100%
8	Pesther Eisenbahn	250 fl. C.M.	500	1848 50%
7	Raaber/Gloggnitzer Eisenbahn	400, since 4-2-1844	666.66/800	10–100%
6	Mailänder Bahn	500 fl W.W.	800	10–100%
1	Hypo-Bank	1 000 Lire	857.14	10–100%
2	Ludwigskanal	500 fl sdt.W.	857.14	100%
3	Augsburg-Münchener Eisenbahn	500 fl sdt.W.	857.14	10–100%
9	Rheinschanze/Ludwigshafen-Berberau	500 fl sdt.W.	857.14	10–90%
4	OeNB	1000 fl. C.M.	2000	**1841** 50%
5	Nordbahn/Bochnia-Bahn	1000 fl W.W.	<2000	100%

Market Interference

Market manipulations hinder efficiency and we know of extensive backing actions for several stocks included into this study. According to 'Allgemeine Zeitung', the Austrian government announced on 3 October 1845 that it would support falling stock market prices by 2m fl (= 4m Mk) but it spent a lot more money backing four railway stocks (Pesther, Raab/Glognitzer, Mailänder, Ödenburger). Market-known state interventions summed up to 10m fl (= 20m Mk) only between 9 November, 1846, and 30 April, 1847, and the state bought almost half of the companies' stock capital for round about 25m fl (= 50m Mk) until the year's end.[32] For several reasons these extensive interventions did not destroy market efficiency: Interventions only took place on the occasional day. Obviously markets neither believed in the state's will nor its potential to defend the announced support levels effectively, nor had they become suspicious about the quality of stocks in question. In this way stock market prices overran or underran support levels most of the time. Price changes' distribution did not change considerably, and especially the percentage of day-to-day unchanged prices did not alter.

---

32 H. Strach, 'Geschichte der Eisenbahnen Österreich-Ungarns von den Anfängen bis zum Jahre 1867', in *Geschichte des Eisenbahnwesens des österreichisch-ungarischen Monarchie*, vol. 1, I (Teschen, 1898).

In the case of Ludwigskanal, backing actions had much more effect. The project of this canal connecting the Main and Danube rivers was pushed by King Louis I of Bavaria, who was very sceptical about railways. Thus the Bavarian public was sceptical about the canal and the King asked Rothschild in Frankfurt to underwrite 75 per cent of the company's capital to place it in half of Europe within one year. The King had guaranteed a yearly dividend of 4 per cent in case the canal was finished by 30 July 1842. Market's scepticism turned out to be right. Although completion was delayed, guaranteed dividend was only paid for the second half of 1843 and the first half of 1844, because it was no longer appropriated by the Bavarian parliament since October 1844. Estimated construction costs were overrun by about 70 per cent,[33] but this did not trouble stock holders, because the Bavarian state had guaranteed to build the canal and sell it for 8.53m fl (=17.1m Mk) to the company. The state delivered the canal to the company on 3 July 1846. Parts of the canal had been opened already before with disappointing transportation figures.

The King's wish to own the company grew stronger under these circumstances. He had asked his government if it would make sense to buy up all canal stocks already in July 1839. A corresponding purchase order reached Rothschild at the latest in 1840.[34] Markets became aware of these operations pretty fast. Starting with a relatively normal chart, the percentage of unchanged Ludwigskanal prices rose sharply with the last quarter of the year 1841. Since September of that year only offer prices were quoted for many months. Those offer prices rose constantly since January 1844 after the completion of part of the canal (6 May 1843), when (probably at first overly optimistic) transportation figures were published periodically. This increase shows that selling pressure was not very high during this time. Market turnover was evident from September 1846 for the first time since 1841, but price charts had an unnatural smoothness certainly caused by Rothschild's interventions. Outstanding stock capital shrank from 10 to 8.53m fl sdt.W. (= 17.1 resp. 14.6m Mk) until the 1846 general meeting of stock holders. Mere offer prices were published again from February 1847 onwards. Rothschild continued to buy stocks during the second half of the year, but in 1848 even this demand stopped. It is likely that Rothschild continued his interventions later on for several years as the law concerning final nationalization was already enacted in 1852 under the new King Maximilian II.[35]

Stock market prices of Ludwigskanal were severely influenced by these interventions at least from mid 1840. There was no other demand, but selling pressure continued in contrast to Austrian railway stocks. As a result trading in Ludwigskanal stocks became inefficient, historical findings very much confirming the above mathematical ones. In the case of all other stocks investigated, there is no evidence for inefficiency through intervention.

This should also be true for other kinds of manipulations. People often complained about pointed rumour, bull or bear market syndicates and even fraud in newspapers, pamphlets and handbooks. As in today's market, rumours were rife according to

---

33 H. Gollwitzer, *Ludwig I. von Bayern* (1986, reprinted Munich, 1987).

34 Gollwitzer, 'Ludwig I.'.

35 A.J. Liebl, *Aufgeh'n wird die Erde in Rauch. Geschichte der ersten Privaten Eisenbahnen in Bayern* (Munich, 1985).

stock market reports, and many of them could have been pointed ones. On the other hand, bull or bear market syndicates were extremely seldom, since such confidential arrangements became manifest in the moment they were successful. To sum up, the degree of manipulations do not seem to have been important enough to reduce efficiency of the regarded markets severely. This was also true for most of the other premises for market efficiency:

- Information policy both of stock exchanges and of listed companies was not ideal, but it improved resulting in a somewhat sufficient level. Insider trading seems to have been a frequent phenomenon, but this is true for all stock markets until the 1980s. Velocity of information transaction in many cases gradually became fast enough during the time in question to enable arbitrage.
- Markets seem to have been broad enough in terms of variety of both market sides: stockholders and companies. Market turnover was sufficient until 1844 in Augsburg and until 1847 in Vienna, Berlin, Frankfurt and Leipzig. The year 1848 was probably inefficient at all market places.
- Market entry was free enough, especially if we have a look at transaction cost and even at transferability and value of stocks.
- Market interference seldom destroyed efficiency, the only exception being Ludwigskanal.

Discussion

During the first phase of German industrialization a substantial part of business investments were financed over stock markets. This is especially true of fast growing railway construction. This points to certain efficiency of stock exchanges, since such volumes cannot be raised without well functioning secondary markets. Usual measures of market efficiency do not work without mapping certain causalities, but necessary data are not available in this case. For this reason, this study uses time series of market prices directly with the help of measures of nonlinear dynamics without the assumption of such coherence. Mathematical findings were validated by economic findings according to Eugene Fama's Efficient Market Hypothesis with almost identical results. Including the year 1847 null hypothesis of market efficiency could not be rejected in the cases of Vienna and Frankfurt stock exchanges. Nevertheless certain nonlinearity could be found. Efficiency of Augsburg certainly shrank since mid 1844. Though this is also true for local blue chip Hypo-Bank, it is particularly relevant to Ludwigskanal which, since September 1841, owned the only clearly inefficient stock of the study. 1848, the year of revolutions, was inefficient for all markets investigated after its turbulent March, but the Vienna stock market best maintained its prior position. Coincidence of mathematical and economic findings show that measures of nonlinear dynamics proved its worth in this context. This is even true for Hurst exponent tending to be unpopular among physicists for its limited exactness.

CHAPTER 6

The Balkan Railways, International Capital and Banking from the End of the Nineteenth Century until the Outbreak of the First World War

Peter Hertner

Abbreviations Used in the Footnotes

ASI-BCI	Archivio Storico Banca Intesa, patrimonio Banca Commerciale Italiana, Milano
BA	Bundesarchiv, Berlin
BNP Paribas	BNP Paribas. Archives historiques, Paris
CAMT	Centre des Archives du Monde du Travail, Roubaix
GP	*Die Große Politik der Europäischen Kabinette 1871–1914. Sammlung der Diplomatischen Akten des Auswärtigen Amtes*, Berlin 1924 ff.
HADB	Historisches Archiv der Deutschen Bank, Frankfurt/Main
OestA, HHStA, MdÄ	Österreichisches Staatsarchiv, Wien: Haus-, Hof- und Staatsarchiv, Ministerium des Äußern
SG.AH	Société Générale. Archives Historiques, Paris

During the second half of the nineteenth century, railways, 'the very symbol of rapid progress',[1] increasingly became one of the vital instruments for the integration of nation states, multinational empires, and colonies throughout the entire world. They served as a strategic tool for the development of hitherto backward areas; they helped to penetrate regions far away from the political and economic centres and to open them up to the achievements of the 'civilized world'. 'Because railways can change spatial realities, they have been a favoured tool of empire builders.'[2]

Until the end of the 1860s, the main railway lines had been completed in Western, Southern and Central Europe.[3] In the European East, vast parts of the Russian

---

1 R. Fremdling, 'European railways 1825–2001. An overview', in *Jahrbuch für Wirtschaftsgeschichte*, 2003, p. 209.

2 R. Lee, 'Railways, space and imperialism', in G. Dinhobel, *Eisenbahn/Kultur. Railway/culture* (=Mitteilungen des Österreichischen Staatsarchivs, Sonderband 7) (Vienna, 2004), p. 91.

3 R.E. Cameron, *France and the economic development of Europe, 1800–1914* (New York, 1975, 1st ed. Princeton, N.J. 1961), pp. 204–320.

Empire had then still to be covered by a railway network. The Balkan peninsula, most of it still under Ottoman rule, also urgently needed, according to contemporary observers, this new way of communication and transport. It would provide economic development but also better and faster political and military control for the new states which had sprung up recently in this part of Europe, like Serbia, Montenegro or the Moldavian principalities, but also for the rulers in Constantinople trying to modernize the empire of the 'sick man of Europe'.

Baron Hirsch and the Oriental Railways, 1869–90

Already in the 1860s the Turkish government had granted railway concessions to foreign investors: one was situated in the Dobrudja region and was to link Cernavoda on the Danube River to Constanţa on the Black Sea – altogether just 64 kilometres, built and managed by British capital. When this region later became part of Romania the government at Bucharest bought the line from its British shareholders, in 1882.[4] The other one was to link Rustchuck (now Ruse), again on the Danube but farther upstream, to Varna which was to become the major Bulgarian port on the Black Sea. According to Rondo Cameron, it '... was a truly international enterprise, with French engineers, British contractors, Belgian materiel, and capital from all three as well as the Netherlands'.[5] This line had a length of 225 kilometres and was opened in 1867.[6] Neither of these lines really lived up to original expectations, i.e. to link West and East in a quicker and safer way – navigation on the Danube proved to be just too slow and complicated and loading from railways to ships and back again took too much time; thus the Mediterranean route from Marseilles or Brindisi to Constantinople remained the preferred one for travellers and exporters from Western Europe until the end of the 1880s.[7]

The idea of building a railway which would then connect 'the English Channel to the Persian Gulf' dates from the 1840s and 1850s. In 1855, during the Crimean War, the Sublime Porte suggested such a project to Western investors,[8] and, the following year, 'Palmerston, who opposed the idea of a Suez Canal, wrote that the real communication with India must be a railway to Constantinople, and from there through Asia Minor to the Persian Gulf'[9] – a Baghdad Railway *ante litteram*. Nothing came out of these or other ideas and initiatives, partly because the Ottoman Government showed no further interest in such projects.

---

4   R.M. Dimtschoff, *Das Eisenbahnwesen auf der Balkan-Halbinsel. Eine politisch-volkswirtschaftliche Studie* (Bamberg, 1894), pp. 5–8.

5   Cameron, *France*, p. 321.

6   Dimtschoff, *Eisenbahnwesen*, pp. 8–12.

7   W. Rechberger, 'Zur Geschichte der Orientbahnen. Ein Beitrag zur österreichisch-ungarischen Eisenbahnpolitik auf dem Balkan in den Jahren von 1852–1888,' unpublished Ph.D. thesis (Universität Wien, 1958), pp. 16–26.

8   Cameron, *France*, p. 320.

9   K. Grunwald, *Türkenhirsch. A study of Baron Maurice de Hirsch, entrepreneur and philanthropist* (Jerusalem, 1966), p. 29.

After it had been evicted from Germany in 1866 Austria became increasingly interested in its Balkan 'backyard' and thus presumably also in the big railway project.[10] 'In 1867, on the visit to Vienna of the Sultan Abdul Aziz and Grand Vizier Fuad Pasha, the Sultan was persuaded that such a railroad would help cement his Balkan dominions'.[11] Recommended by the Austrian Minister of Foreign Affairs von Beust, the Belgian firm Van der Elst & Cie. was granted a concession in 1868 to construct a railway through the Balkans to Constantinople. Behind Van der Elst & Cie. we find the Belgian financier Langrand-Dumonceau, who tried to form a Catholic financial group during the 1860s; he was engaged in the provision of finance to the Pope, but also in numerous railway speculations.[12] Langrand-Dumonceau's group collapsed a few months afterwards, it had not yet been able to collect all the capital needed for this big undertaking. By June 1869, the Ottoman government declared the provisional railway concession which it had granted to Van der Elst a year before to have become invalid.[13]

Who was to take Langrand-Dumonceau's place? It was a comparatively small private banker from Brussels, Baron Maurice de Hirsch – or Moritz von Hirsch, as he had been called in Bavaria, the country of origin of his family. He was born in Munich in 1831 as son to Joseph von Hirsch, banker to three kings of Bavaria and descendant of a family of Jewish *Hoffaktoren*. Apart from his personal ambitions and his remarkable capability as a financier Moritz von Hirsch became successful as an investment banker thanks to his close relations to the Bischoffsheim family, bankers in Brussels, Amsterdam, Antwerp, Paris and London after having left Mainz. This was one of the most important banking families in nineteenth-century Europe. Moritz von Hirsch married Clara Bischoffsheim in 1855, moved to Munich, and then again to Brussels about three years later, where together with his brother-in-law he founded Banque Bischoffsheim de Hirsch, a private banking house which twelve years later became one of the founders of Banque de Paris et des Pays-Bas. From 1871 he lived mostly in Paris.[14] According to Paul Emden the Bischoffsheims '... allowed him [Hirsch, P.H.] to use the organisation of the banking house of Bischoffsheim & Goldschmidt for his transactions, and at times they also left the management in his hands, but, a little afraid of his all too great spirit of enterprise and daring – others less favourably inclined occasionally thought him reckless – they did not take him into partnership'.[15]

---

10 In the early 1860s Austria had still favoured a line which would have run through Transylvania and the Carpathians down to the Danubian principalities – which would later become Romania – and from there to the Danube which then still formed the border with the Ottoman Empire (Rechberger, 'Zur Geschichte der Orientbahnen,' pp. 1–15).

11 Grunwald, *Türkenhirsch*, p. 30.

12 G. Jacquemyns, *Langrand-Dumonceau. Promoteur d'une puissance financière catholique*, vol. 4 (Brussels, 1964), pp. 234–8; cf. also Grunwald, *Türkenhirsch*, pp. 20–25, 30.

13 Dimtschoff, *Das Eisenbahnwesen*, p. 22; G. Jacquemyns, *Langrand-Dumonceau. Promoteur d'une puissance financière catholique*, vol. 4 (Brussels, 1965), pp. 66–7.

14 P.H. Emden, *Money powers of Europe in the nineteenth and twentieth centuries* (London, 1936), pp. 325–30; Grunwald, *Türkenhirsch*, pp. 9–27; E. Bussière, *Paribas 1872–1992. L'Europe et le monde* (Antwerp, 1992), pp. 21–2, 27.

15 Emden, *Money powers*, p. 320–21.

On 12 April 1869 Moritz von Hirsch signed a concession agreement with the Imperial Ottoman Government '... for the construction and operation of a railway network in European Turkey which was to connect Constantinople with Vienna ...'.[16] It is not quite clear if Hirsch entered into the previous agreement between the Sublime Porte and Langrand-Dumonceau or if he himself came to terms with Constantinople. At the beginning Hirsch seems to have desired a clear distinction between the construction of the network, a task he wanted to take up himself, and its operation, where he desired to involve the South-Austrian Railway, the well-known *Südbahn*, founded by the Rothschilds, which however withdrew its approval at the very last moment. The Austrian State Railways, despite its name a private firm which had been created by the Péreire brothers, also declined to participate.[17] Hirsch was therefore practically forced to found by himself, as an operating company, the Paris-based Compagnie Générale pour l'Exploitation des Chemins de Fer de la Turquie d'Europe in January 1870. Its principal shareholders were the Anglo-Austrian Bank in Vienna, the Société Générale, Paris[18] and the Banque Bischoffsheim de Hirsch in Brussels, as well as Moritz von Hirsch. 'Chairman and negotiator with the Turkish authorities on behalf of the new company'[19] was Paulin Talabot, 'the French ironmaster and railway magnate'.[20] Besides Baron Hirsch the directors of the construction company, Société Impériale des Chemins de Fer de la Turquie d'Europe, consisted mainly of representatives of the Anglo-Austrian Bank and of people who seem to have been close collaborators of Hirsch. 'Each of the companies was registered with a capital of 50 million francs of which one quarter was paid up.'[21]

The 1869 concession[22] provided for a network of about 2500 kilometres: the principal line was from Constantinople to the Austro-Hungarian border via Edirne – Plovdiv – Sofia – Nish – Pristina – Sarajevo to Sisak; there were four connecting branches: Edirne – Dedeagatch on the Aegean coast; Plovdiv – Burgas on the Black Sea; from Nish to the frontier with Serbia; Pristina – Salonica. '... the concession-holder was assured. (a) of an annual rental of 14,000 francs per completed kilometre, payable by the Ottoman government, for the entire period of 99 years, to be paid out of a state loan, and (b) an annual rental of 8000 francs per kilometre from the operator'.

---

16 Grunwald, *Türkenhirsch*, p. 28.

17 B. Gille, *Histoire de la maison Rothschild*, vol. 2 (Geneva, 1967), p. 526.

18 The Parisian Société Générale participated by subscribing a third of the original capital of 50 million francs but decided to take shares for a nominal amount of 8 million francs; the rest was to be offered to 'participants' who might be interested and particularly to the members of its Conseil d'Administration (SG.AH, minutes of the Conseil d'Administration, 329e séance du 11 Janvier 1870). As to the participation of the Anglo-Austrian Bank cf P.L. Cottrell, 'London financiers and Austria 1863–1875: the Anglo-Austrian Bank', in *Business History*, vol. 11, 1969, p. 117.

19 Grunwald, *Türkenhirsch*, p. 35.

20 Cameron, *France*, p. 96.

21 Grunwald, *Türkenhirsch*, p. 36.

22 Cf the handwritten copy of the *Convention de la concession* of 17 April 1869 and the printed copy of the *Convention principale d'exploitation* of the same date in: HADB, OR 530.

The Turkish government agreed to pay a higher subsidy for the construction cost of the line in the mountains of Bosnia.[23]

Particularly original was the solution found for financing this huge enterprise.[24] Hirsch became famous all over Europe for creating the so-called *Türkenlose*, '... an entirely novel type of Government loan: the 3 per cent Turkish Lottery Bonds, which carried a low rate of interest but were paid off by drawings every two months at a very high redemption price; they enjoyed great favour amongst small investors on the Continent, especially in France and in Germany, and continued to do so although as early as 1875 the Sublime Porte defaulted on the drawings, which were, however, resumed in 1881 (under the Decree of Mouharrem); payment of interest stopped in 1876'.[25]

There were, however, two substantial problems involved with these lottery bonds: First of all, this type of bond could not be officially quoted on either the Vienna, Paris or London stock exchanges. In Paris this was forbidden by a law dating from 1836, in Vienna stock-exchange regulations did not admit these bonds to official trading. An exception had been made before in the case of the Suez Canal lottery bonds, but then above all France and also Austria had showed a strong political interest in that specific item. The other fly in the ointment consisted of the way the six-monthly drawings of the lottery bonds were arranged: all those bonds not yet sold or even not yet issued participated in the drawings and fell automatically to Hirsch's company. Thus '... the chances of getting even a small prize were exceedingly remote for all save very large-scale investors',[26] and soon people started to talk of a case of 'organized theft'.[27] After much toing and froing between Hirsch and the Austrian government the *Türkenlose* were finally quoted on the Vienna Exchange on 27 June 1870. The French government had promised to follow immediately but in fact did not, and shortly afterwards the Second Empire broke down and France had more important problems to tackle.[28]

The first series of these bonds sold very well thanks to a well-organized publicity campaign and in spite of the outbreak of the Franco-Prussian War.[29] The second

---

23 Grunwald, *Türkenhirsch*, p. 34.

24 At the beginning ' ... the Anglo-Austrian provided the Balkan railway company with short-term bridging funds until there was a flow of capital available from the Bond issues' (Cottrell, 'London financiers', p. 117).

25 Emden, *Money powers*, p. 322; C. Clay, *Gold for the Sultan. Western bankers and Ottoman finance 1856–1881: a contribution to Ottoman and international financial history* (London and New York, 2000), p. 199, describes the solution adopted by de Hirsch with these lottery bonds in the following manner: '... to go over the heads of the great financial institutions, to issue the loan in a form designed not to appeal to well-informed bankers and their affluent or relatively affluent clients but to less sophisticated small investors who could not normally be tempted to subscribe to Ottoman *valeurs* at all'.

26 Clay, *Gold for the Sultan*, p. 199.

27 Rechberger, 'Zur Geschichte der Orientbahnen', pp. 78–9, 117.

28 *Ibid.*, pp. 102–23.

29 Cf the contract made between Hirsch and a syndicate of banks (among them Société Générale, Anglo-Austrian Bank, Oppenheim, Banque de Crédit et de Dépôt des Pays-Bas) on 23 Nov. 1869 for the sale of 750,000 'Türkenlose' (BNP Paribas, Archives Historiques,

series, issued in September 1872,[30] fell in a much more difficult period and only part of it could be sold; the remaining bonds had to be taken back by the syndicate of issuing banks.[31] When the Ottoman state suspended its payments for all debt services in 1875, the quotation of the *Türkenlose* fell from an original high of 180 to a low which fluctuated between 20 and 30. From 1882 drawings were again honoured, albeit only partially.[32] If we can believe the figures presented by Karl Morawitz, himself a banker and later on head of the Anglo-Austrian Bank, the profit made out of the entire business until Hirsch's retreat in 1890 should have been 160 to 170 million francs, a sum which Morawitz thinks to be a more or less fair reward for 'the enormous amount of labour, diligence and intelligence' applied by 'a small banker from Brussels' in such a hostile and difficult environment as that offered by 'a half-barbarian country, as was the case with the interior parts of Turkey still thirty years ago'.[33] Even George W.F. Hallgarten, whose judgement on Hirsch and his business practices is anything but lenient, sees in him the person who had helped to open the Balkans and to anticipate, as a private capitalist of an older type, modern economic imperialism.[34]

Obviously the construction and operation of this network needed sound finance and solid technology, but above all it required constant collaboration and backing from the Ottoman authorities. Given the unpredictable shape of politics at the Sultan's court this meant, to begin with, close contacts with the ruling elite. In the words of David Landes '... one may be sure that much influence with government was bought – tactfully, through gratuities and accomodations, and crudely, by bribes' – and Landes does not only refer to the well-known backward conditions on the shore of the Bosporus.[35] Hirsch had been lucky enough to get his concession when the 'Western-oriented Grand Vizier Ali Pasha' who favoured a railway link with Western Europe was governing the Ottoman Empire. He died in September 1871 and his successor Mahmud Nedim Pasha followed a completely different line, preferring rail connections with Russia via Romania to any direct link with Western Europe via Austria-Hungary. This thoroughly changed situation led to a revised concession

---

3\Cabet-1\192). The issuing took place between 15 and 17 March 1870 (SG.AH, minutes of the Conseil d'Administration, 337e séance du 1 Mars 1870).

30 Cf. the prospectus 'Empire ottoman. Emprunt à primes. Emission de 880,060 obligations à primes ... ' (27 August, 1872) (ibid.).

31 J. Bouvier, *Le Crédit Lyonnais de 1863 à 1882. Les années de formation d'une banque de depôts*, vol. 2 (Paris, 1961), pp. 690–91; Clay, *Gold for the Sultan*, pp. 202–3.

32 P. Dehn, 'Deutschland und die Orientbahnen', in *Jahrbuch für Gesetzgebung, Verwaltung und Volkswirtschaft im Deutschen Reich*, vol. 9, 1885, n° 2, p. 62.

33 C. Morawitz, *Die Türkei im Spiegel ihrer Finanzen. Nach dem französischen Original 'Les finances de la Turquie'* (Berlin, 1903), pp. 422–3.

34 G.W.F. Hallgarten, *Imperialismus vor 1914. Die soziologischen Grundlagen der Aussenpolitik europäischer Grossmächte vor dem Ersten Weltkrieg*, 2nd ed., vol. 1 (Munich, 1963), p. 245.

35 D.S. Landes, *Bankers and pashas. International finance and economic imperialism in Egypt* (London, 1958), p. 29, note 1). This goes with Grundwald's comment: 'It can be safely assumed that Hirsch had to pay his way in Turkey, as was customary' (Grunwald, *Türkenhirsch*, p. 52).

agreement with the Oriental Railway Company. Thus by a new contract in 1872 the overall length of the network was reduced to 1260 kilometres.[36]

Still, in 1872 construction was well under way, starting from Constantinople and from the Aegean coast. 387 kilometres were already in operation, '... 102 ready for operation and 661 under construction – altogether 1,150 kilometers'.[37] People who lived along the future track were rather sceptical when the first surveyors arrived: the Bulgarians feared that they would be recruited as forced labourers by the Ottoman authorities, the Turks thought that railways were 'too European' for their future lives; it was primarily the Greek traders who were enthusiastic when they considered their coming business chances.[38] In spite of ongoing construction work the connection to the West – through Bosnia or through Serbia – still remained to be made. By the end of 1872 part of the Bosnian line had been completed, but in 1876 the operating company gave it back to the Ottoman government, which so far had refused to connect it with the Austro-Hungarian network. 'After a few months of Ottoman operation, the line was abandoned.'[39]

By the end of 1874 or, if we are to believe Morawitz, in the course of 1875 1179 kilometres,[40] 'all the lines entrusted to Hirsch were completed, but not those which were to be built by the Turks. Thus the railway project meanwhile consisted of three isolated lines'.[41] Unfortunately, in October 1875 the Ottoman state suspended all its payments. In two decades it had borrowed 2.5 billion francs, of which more than nine tenths came from abroad.[42] Between 1869 and 1875 '... the nominal value of new borrowing exceeded the estimated revenues of the central government ...'.[43] Morawitz calculated that only about 10 per cent of this huge debt had been used for the building of new infrastructure, above all railways.[44] Six years later, in 1881, '... a contract was concluded between the Ottoman government and the representatives of its foreign and domestic creditors for the resumption of payments on Ottoman bonds. This agreement, called the Decree of Mouharrem (from the Turkish month in which it was drafted), instituted European control of a part of the imperial revenues'.[45]

Meanwhile, railway construction in the European part of the Ottoman Empire had come to a standstill, not least because of Anti-Turkish revolts in Bosnia and Bulgaria between 1875 and 1878 and, of course, also as a consequence of the Russo-Turkish War of 1877–78. The 1878 Congress of Berlin, in Article 10 of the agreement,

---

36 Morawitz, *Die Türkei*, pp. 416–17.

37 Grunwald, *Türkenhirsch*, p. 39.

38 Rechberger, 'Zur Geschichte der Orientbahnen', p. 124.

39 Grunwald, *Türkenhirsch*, p. 40.

40 Morawitz, *Die Türkei*, pp. 417–18.

41 Grunwald, *Türkenhirsch*, p. 41.

42 Morawitz, *Die Türkei*, p. 56; S. Pamuk, *The Ottoman Empire and European capitalism, 1820–1913. Trade, investment and production* (Cambridge, 1987), p. 75, table 45 for the year 1881.

43 Pamuk, *The Ottoman Empire*, p. 60.

44 Morawitz, *Die Türkei*, p. 56.

45 D.C. Blaisdell, 'European financial control in the Ottoman Empire. A study of the establishment, activities, and significance of the Administration of the Ottoman Public Debt', Ph.D. thesis Columbia University (New York, 1929), p. 1.

entrusted the new state of Bulgaria, as a successor of the Ottoman Empire within its new boundaries, with the task of providing for a railway link with Austria-Hungary.[46] Hirsch's Compagnie pour l'exploitation des chemins de fer de la Turquie d'Europe was explicitly mentioned in this paragraph. Also in 1878, Hirsch transferred the operating company from Paris to Vienna and replaced its French directors with Austro-Hungarian members.[47] Again according to Article 10 of the Berlin Treaty, Bulgaria '... had to guarantee 7,000 francs per kilometres each year to the company [Hirsch's operating company, P.H.] and was entitled to only half of the profit over and above this amount. This arrangement, which was hardly designed to make the railroads profitable, remained in force until Bulgaria nationalized the line during the 1908 crisis'.[48] Only four years later, in 1882, the delegates of Turkey, Bulgaria, Serbia and Austria-Hungary met in Vienna in a *conférence à quatre* and reached an agreement in March 1883 which provided for the construction of two missing railway links: one from Bellova via Sofia, Nish and Belgrad to Semlin in Hungary, the other from Nish to Vranje and from there to Skopje – Üsküb in Turkish – and thus to the line connecting Mitrovitza and Salonica.[49] The Ottoman Government, however, was not in a hurry to translate these decisions into action, particularly when Bulgaria occupied Eastern Rumelia, which formally was still an autonomous province of the Turkish Empire, and with it the railway lines as soon as they had been finished there in 1888.[50] The Sublime Porte wanted to react but did not have the means, not least because of European financial control of an important part of its income.

---

46 According to P.F. Sugar, 'Railroad construction and the development of the Balkan village in the last quarter of the 19th century', in R. Melville and H.-J. Schröder (eds), *Der Berliner Kongreß von 1878. Die Politik der Großmächte und die Probleme der Modernisierung in Südosteuropa in der zweiten Hälfte des 19. Jahrhunderts* (Wiesbaden, 1982), p. 495) ' ... the emphasis the continental powers (Germany and Austria-Hungary) placed on railroads at the Congress of Berlin was aimed at the displacement of the British and French from the Balkan markets'. This is all the more convincing since the lines built until the middle of the 1870s linked Mediterranean ports like Salonica or Dedeagatch or Black Sea ports like Varna with the interior parts of the Balkan peninsula without yet offering connections to Central Europe (see for instance Grunwald, *Türkenhirsch*, pp. 44–8; V. Paskaleva, 'Die Anfänge des deutschen wirtschaftlichen Einflusses auf dem Balkan und in der Türkei in den 60er und 70er Jahren des 19. Jahrhunderts', in R. Melville and H.-J. Schröder (eds), *Der Berliner Kongreß von 1878. Die Politik der Großmächte und die Probleme der Modernisierung in Südosteuropa in der zweiten Hälfte des 19. Jahrhunderts* (Wiesbaden, 1982), p. 512.

47 Morawitz, *Die Türkei*, p. 419; W.N. Medlicott, *The Congress of Berlin and after. A diplomatic history of the Near Eastern settlement 1878–1880*, 2nd ed. (London 1963), p. 411; Grunwald, *Türkenhirsch*, p. 46; G. Rhode, 'Der Berliner Kongress und Südosteuropa', in K.O. Frhr. v. Aretin (ed.), *Bismarcks Außenpolitik und der Berliner Kongreß* (Wiesbaden, 1978), pp. 107–29.

48 Sugar, 'Railroad construction and the development of the Balkan village', p. 492.

49 Rechberger, 'Zur Geschichte der Orientbahnen', pp. 195–208.

50 The sector between Bellova and Vakarell (47 kilometres), which was on Bulgarian territory but had been constructed by the Ottoman Bank and claimed by the Turkish government, was occupied by Bulgaria in July 1888. A few months later Bulgaria agreed to pay a yearly rent to the Ottoman government, or more exactly the Ottoman Bank (Dimtschoff, *Das Eisenbahnwesen*, pp. 77–80).

Thus Hirsch, probably weary of the eternal conflicts with Constantinople, reached a compromise in 1885 providing the Ottoman administration with an 'advance' of 23 million francs, to be paid out of means he had so far withheld because of alleged violations of the existing contract with the Ottoman side.[51]

Bulgaria had opted for a state-owned railway system in 1884 and it was the Bulgarian state that had constructed the last missing link which, after its inauguration in 1888, made through traffic possible from Vienna to Constantinople.[52] For the time being and despite its new state railway system Bulgaria did not touch the rights of the Oriental Railways in Eastern Rumelia, but it started to build a railway line running parallel to the Oriental Railways track in this province, thanks to a loan acquired through the Viennese Länderbank and the Nationalbank für Deutschland, Berlin, in 1892. Georg Siemens of Deutsche Bank might have preferred to sell the Eastern Rumelian part of the Oriental network to Bulgaria, but his partners in Vienna, and with them the Ottoman government, opposed such a solution. In order to find a *modus vivendi* favourable to his bank and to the Oriental Railways Siemens put pressure on Bulgaria by starting an action against its loans at the Berlin stock exchange. Thus in 1899 he succeeded in forcing Bulgaria to accept an agreement with the Betriebsgesellschaft of the Oriental Railways: the Betriebsgesellschaft would lower its tariffs, putting them on the same level as fixed by the Bulgarian state lines; at the same time it would from now on take over the management of a parallel railway line, of which 80 kilometres had already been constructed by the Bulgarian state in order to put pressure on the Oriental Railways.[53]

As a consequence of the Congress of Berlin, Serbia had also become formally independent in 1878. On this occasion it had gained some additional territory in the South, including Nish, from the Ottoman Empire. The well-known French banker – or better: speculator – Eugène Bontoux and the group he had formed around the Union Générale made a contract with the Serbian government in April 1881 providing for a loan of nominally 100 million francs from the Union Générale, the construction of a railway network in Serbia and the creation of an operating company. Bontoux and his group went bankrupt in January 1882 but the Serbian government managed to transfer the entire business to another Parisian bank, the Comptoir d'Escompte de Paris, which just carried it on.[54] By 1884 a line had been constructed which went from Semlin, on the border to Austria-Hungary, to Belgrad and from there to Nish. Two lines, one from Nish to the Bulgarian border, the other from Nish to

---

51 Morawitz, *Die Türkei*, pp. 420–21.

52 I. Simeonoff, 'Die Eisenbahnen und Eisenbahnpolitik in Bulgarien', Ph.D. thesis Universität Erlangen (Halle/Saale, 1909), pp. 37–40; S. Kumpf-Korfes, 'Die ökonomische Expansion des deutschen Finanzkapitals in Bulgarien vom Ende des 19. Jahrhunderts bis zum Ausbruch des Ersten Weltkrieges', in *Zeitschrift für Geschichtswissenschaft*, vol. 17, 1969, p. 1432.

53 F. Meinhard, 'Die Entwicklung der Balkanbahnen vom Jahre 1892 bis zum Jahre 1904', in *Archiv für Eisenbahnwesen*, vol. 28, 1905, pp. 1352–3; Simeonoff, 'Die Eisenbahnen', pp. 59–69; K. Helfferich, *Georg von Siemens. Ein Lebensbild aus Deutschlands großer Zeit*, 2nd ed., vol. 3 (Berlin, 1923), pp. 10–11; Kumpf-Korfes, 'Die ökonomische Expansion', pp. 1432–3; R.J. Crampton, *A concise history of Bulgaria*, 2nd ed. (Cambridge, 2005), pp. 121–2.

54 J. Bouvier, *Le krach de l'Union Générale (1878–1885)* (Paris, 1960), pp. 98–103.

Vranje where it met the Turkish network, were completed in 1886 and 1887. In the following year the missing piece on the Turkish side between Vranje and Skopje (Üsküb) was finished.[55] These two sections finally closed the gap between Occident and Orient and in this case it was the Imperial Ottoman Bank which had stepped in by founding in 1884, together with Paribas, the Société Générale, Bleichröder, the Frankfurt private banking house of Bethmann and the Comptoir National d'Escompte de Paris, a construction company with a nominal capital of 30 million francs. Within three years the two sections of 131 kilometres in total length had been built. The actual construction work had been done by the Régie générale des chemins de fer et des travaux publics of Count Vitali.[56] 'On 12 August 1888, almost twenty years after the signing of the original concession, the first train left Vienna for Constantinople.'[57] The distance covered amounted altogether to 1686 kilometres.[58] The line from Belgrade to Salonika had already been inaugurated in May the same year. The wife of Edouard Hentsch, a banker from Geneva who was president of the Comptoir d'Escompte de Paris between 1872 and 1889, has left us a vivid account of the pomp and circumstance attending the inauguration ceremonies.[59] *The Economist* wrote in its issue of 26 May 1888

> [...] The opening ceremony took place on the 19th May, when one train left Nisch and another Salonica in the morning, and met at the Turkish frontier, where the last piece of rail was laid. The reception of the European guests on Turkish territory as far as Salonica was most enthusiastic, both from the authorities and the population, and it prognosticates well for the future.[60]

Thus the story of the Orient Express could finally start – though in literature it began some decades later, as we know.

The Oriental network, once completed, was certainly a success of Western European finance and technology, but compared to what had been constructed before in Britain, France, Germany or even the Eastern parts of the Austro-Hungarian monarchy, it represented a second-rate solution. Already in 1872 the Ottoman government, not without ulterior motives, had accused Hirsch of having chosen the cheapest way for construction by, for instance, building wooden bridges instead of

---

55 P. Jordan, 'Die Entwicklung des Eisenbahnnetzes auf dem Gebiet des heutigen Jugoslawien (bis 1918)', in R. Plaschka, A.M. Drabek and B. Zaar (eds), *Eisenbahnbau und Kapitalinteressen in den Beziehungen der österreichischen mit den südslawischen Ländern* (Vienna, 1993), p. 24. Carl Fürstenberg, the famous banker and one of the heads of the Berliner Handelsgesellschaft, did not believe in the profitability of these Serbian lines in the near future and therefore refused to accept them as a security for his claims against the Serbian government, H. Fürstenberg (ed.), *Carl Fürstenberg. Die Lebensgeschichte eines deutschen Bankiers, 1870–1914* (Berlin, 1931), pp. 286–7.

56 A. Autheman, *La Banque impériale ottomane* (Paris, 1996), p. 106.

57 Grunwald, *Türkenhirsch*, p. 58.

58 Sugar, 'Railroad construction', p. 488.

59 R. Hentsch, *Hentsch. Banquiers à Genève et à Paris au XIXe siècle* (Brussels, 1996), pp. 195–9.

60 'The Economist', May 26, 1888, p. 669.

stone ones[61] (Rechberger, 1958, p. 145). A commission of foreign experts which inspected the Roumelian lines in 1874 found out that not all of the construction work had been really finished.[62] In order to save capital the track, as it was built, frequently avoided passing directly through nearby villages and towns. The result was 'railway stations without towns and towns without railway stations'.[63] 'Most of the major towns in both central and western Macedonia lay at a considerable distance from the railway line',[64] and the roads linking these towns to the railway stations were generally in a rather bad shape. Besides, neither the Ottoman Empire nor, one or two decades later, Bulgaria and Serbia managed to add sufficient branch networks to their main railway lines. As a result, apart from the three principal lines in Macedonia for instance, '... the survival of horse and mule caravans testifies to the limited impact of these [...] lines on the Macedonian economy'.[65] Furthermore, '[...] trains were slow and could not catch up with European standards'.[66] Decades later, around 1900, the speed even of express trains was still only half of what such trains achieved in Britain or France,[67] and this was certainly not only due to the difficulties of the ground in the Balkan hills and mountains but also to an inadequate substructure. Still, compared to the railways in the other parts of the Turkish Empire, the European network was ahead: 'In 1911, Ottoman railroads [...] in the Balkans contained 1,054 miles of track and carried 8 million passengers while those in Anatolia held 1,488 miles with 7 million passengers. By contrast, the 1,488 miles of track in the Arab provinces carried only 0.9 millions, a reflection of the scant population.'[68] The well-known Baedeker travel guide tried to dampen tourists' fears when it underlined in its 1914 edition for 'Constantinople and Asia Minor' that the trip to Constantinople would offer 'all sorts of comfort'. The 'Orient Express' which would subsequently become so famous was scheduled to do the journey from Budapest to Constantinople via Sofia four times a week. The one-way ticket for the 35-hour trip cost 171.30 francs. The ordinary fast train which ran daily needed 40½ hours for the same distance. In this case the first class-ticket amounted to 123.80 francs.[69] Almost forty years

---

61 Rechberger, 'Zur Geschichte der Orientbahnen', p. 145.

62 Österreichisches Staatsarchiv, Wien, Allgemeines Verwaltungsarchiv: k.k. Handelsministerium. Präsidium, Akte Nr. 1889 (31 October/10 November 1874).

63 Simeonoff, 'Die Eisenbahnen', p. 27.

64 B.C. Gounaris, *Steam over Macedonia, 1870–1912. Socio-economic change and the railway factor* (Boulder, Colorado, 1993), p. 53.

65 J.R. Lampe and M.R. Jackson, *Balkan economic history, 1550–1950. From imperial borderlands to developing nations* (Bloomington, 1982), p. 302.

66 Ibid., p. 65.

67 Thus the express trains from Constantinople to Sarambey (552 kilometres) achieved an average speed of 42 km/h compared with the best results in France of 93.5 km/h and in Britain of 87.7 km/h. The comparative Bulgarian figure was however only 35.3 km/h and the Greek one of 33.7 km/h still lower: W. Schulze, 'Die Fahrgeschwindigkeit der Schnellzüge auf den Haupteisenbahnen in Europa', in *Archiv für Eisenbahnwesen*, vol. 24, 1901, pp. 120–51, p. 142.

68 D. Quataert, *The Ottoman Empire, 1700–1922*, 2nd ed. (Cambridge, 2005), p. 123.

69 K. Baedeker, *Konstantinopel, Balkanstaaten, Kleinasien, Archipel, Cypern. Handbuch für Reisende*, 2nd ed. (Leipzig, 1914), pp. IX, 25.

before, in 1875, a German traveller going by train from Salonica to Mitrovitza in the Kosovo region needed no less than two days, with an obligatory overnight stop at Üsküb (Skopje), for this trip of about 365 kilometres. He spoke of this railway as 'so to speak an embryo, or at the most a child full of the best promises', since in those years links to Central Europe had not yet been constructed.[70]

On the other hand, as happened in practically all regions outside of Western and Central Europe and North America at least until 1914 – with Tsarist Russia being a partial exception – the construction of the Oriental Railways meant that investment goods were ordered in and delivered from the main industrial countries. To give but a few examples relating to our case: in 1881, the operating company of the Oriental Railways employed 105 locomotives, of which 14 came from Austrian producers, three came from France, 11 had been imported from Belgium and the same number from Britain. The remainder, 66 machines, had been delivered by German suppliers. By far the majority of the 2483 wagons also came from Germany, with a small number from Belgian and French suppliers.[71] By then also, most of the original 257 wooden bridges used by the Oriental Railways had been replaced by iron ones. Almost 90 per cent of the iron used for these constructions came from two large German suppliers, the rest from a Belgian one.[72] Construction of the track, bridges and station buildings had, at least in the Rumelian part between Bellova and Adrianople, been carried out 'exclusively by German engineers, technicians and auxiliary staff',[73] but there can be no doubt that indigenous labour had been used for all types of earthworks.[74]

As to the personnel employed, unfortunately it has not been possible so far to ferret out any reliable statistics on its size and structure. Jüttner, in his report on the Oriental Railways dating from 1881, underlined that the *Beamte*, i.e. the managing staff, consisted to a large extent of German or Austrian citizens, 'particularly in the construction department'.[75] 'As was the case with all foreign owned companies operating in the Empire, the overwhelming majority of the administrative staff, especially in the higher ranks, were Europeans.'[76] On the other hand, the 'native population is quite apt for the lower functions of the railway service and is therefore increasingly employed for that purpose'.[77] In 1905–1906, in the vilayet of Salonica

---

70 K. Braun-Wiesbaden, *Reise-Eindrücke aus dem Südosten*, vol. 3 (Stuttgart, 1878), pp. 211–12.

71 Jüttner, 'Die orientalischen Eisenbahnen', in *Archiv für Eisenbahnwesen*, vol. 5, 1882, pp. 209–11.

72 Ibid., pp. 203, 205.

73 Paskaleva, 'Die Anfänge', p. 514.

74 ' [...] workers and timber were provided locally. Everything else had to be imported, including the technical personnel', Y.N. Karkar, *Railway development in the Ottoman Empire, 1856–1914* (New York, Washington, Hollywood, 1972), p. 97.

75 This was quite different for instance in the case of the new Serbian state railways: the contract of January 1881 between the French Union Générale and the Serbian Government provided that the entire managing personnel had to be chosen 'as much as ever possible' from people of Serbian origin: 'Über den Bau und Betrieb der Serbischen Eisenbahn (Belgrad – Nisch – Wranja)', in *Archiv für Eisenbahnwesen*, vol. 4, 1881, p. 173.

76 Gounaris, *Steam over Macedonia*, p. 68.

77 Jüttner, 'Die orientalischen Eisenbahnen', p. 291.

alone, and not counting the personnel employed for service in the trains, there were about 2000 people working for the three railway companies which served this region.[78]

So far Hirsch, in spite of all the old and new problems he had to face with the Turks and the new Balkan states, with his shareholders and the holders of the *Türkenlose* as well as with the banks, had not given up. During the 1880s he increasingly tried to get rid of his huge empire. From spring 1882 Hirsch had probably started to negotiate with the Imperial Ottoman Bank. This institution had been founded in 1862–63 as a state bank by a Franco-British group. Until the First World War it was to be found 'everywhere' in the Turkish economy, dominating above all its commercial and financial relations with the outside world.[79] Thus 'the history of Ottoman banking is in large measure the history of the Ottoman Bank', as David Landes has pointed out.[80] The Ottoman Bank and its unknown partners from Vienna and Berlin – at least one of them can however be identified as having been the House of Bleichröder – did not reach agreement with Hirsch, since they believed that there were still too many unsolved problems between the Baron and the Ottoman Government which, had they taken over, they would have inherited.[81] In 1883–84 there were negotiations, without tangible results, between Hirsch and the Austrian State Railways, and in 1887 we can observe new talks between Hirsch and the Imperial Ottoman Bank, again to no avail.[82]

Finally, on 8 September 1888, Gerson von Bleichröder and Julius Schwabach as representatives of the House of Bleichröder, Adolf von Hansemann (Disconto-Gesellschaft) and Messieurs Heine and Berger from the Ottoman Bank met in Ostende to discuss an eventual takeover of Hirsch's Oriental Railways. Among other things they decided that a participation of Austro-Hungarian banks, and possibly also British partners, should be sought for, that the German and the French partners should have an equivalent amount of shares and that each national industry should profit from orders for railway supplies according to national quotas attributed to the banks. The Ottoman Bank would continue its talks with Hirsch. Capital requirements would amount to a total sum of 110 to 120 million francs. A necessary condition for a definitive offer of this group of banks to Baron Hirsch would be that he managed

---

78 M. Anastassiadou, *Salonique, 1830–1912. Une ville ottomane à l'âge des Réformes* (Leiden New York Cologne, 1997), p. 343.

79 J. Thobie, *Intérêts et impérialisme français dans l'empire ottoman (1895–1914)* (Paris, 1977), pp. 81–9, quote on p. 81; E. Eldem, 'The Imperial Ottoman Bank: actor or instrument of Ottoman modernization?', in K.P. Kostis (ed.), *Modern banking in the Balkans and West-European capital in the nineteenth and twentieth centuries* (Aldershot, 1999), pp. 50–60; for an informative description of its functions and structure see Clay, *Gold for the Sultan*, pp. 73–86.

80 D.S. Landes, *Bankers and pashas*, p. 62.

81 CAMT, Roubaix, 207 AQ 328: 'Note sur la question des chemins de fer turcs' [without date, but probably from 1882]. There are also traces of contacts established during the same year with the Austrian Credit-Anstalt but possibly they were only part of negotiations started by Hirsch with the entire Rothschild group, and in this case Bleichröder would have been included (ibid.). See also G. Schöllgen, *Imperialismus und Gleichgewicht. Deutschland, England und die orientalische Frage, 1871–1914*, 3rd ed. (München, 2000), pp. 38–9.

82 Ibid.

to conclude a satisfactory contract with the Ottoman Government.[83] Evidently nothing came out of this, since in a memo written a few weeks afterwards by one of the leading men of the Ottoman Bank we find the proposal that Bleichröder and the Disconto-Gesellschaft should be asked to wait for further studies on this question because in the meantime Deutsche Bank and its group had launched a *coup* by obtaining a concession for the Ismid – Ankara line, the future Anatolian Railway.[84]

Deutsche Bank had not, however, limited its initiatives to the Asiatic part of the Ottoman Empire. Already in April 1888 the head of its *Vorstand*, Georg Siemens, had asked the German Foreign Ministry if it had any politically motivated objections to make against their buying up shares of the Oriental Railways. It did not.[85] By the end of July, Deutsche Bank had started to become seriously interested in the company,[86] and two months later negotiations with Baron Hirsch concerning such a sale were initiated by Deutsche Bank with the help of its old ally Wiener Bankverein. Both banks, the German and the Austrian one, wanted to send experts to Paris to collect detailed information on the operating company belonging to Oriental Railways.[87] This operating company had officially moved its seat to Vienna already in 1879 but its administrative headquarters were still situated in Paris. Before things could advance further there was, however, an urgent need to improve the relationship between Hirsch and the Sublime Porte. Therefore already in the middle of the 1880s a group of independent arbitrators had been recruited;[88] another try was launched in 1888.[89] In both cases Georg Siemens had been involved as one of the persons who were asked to propose feasible candidates.

In October 1888 Siemens himself was looking for an expert with railway expertise, since Deutsche Bank had seemingly decided to buy a certain number of shares of the operating company of the Oriental Railways in spite of the fact that Hirsch was still also negotiating with the Austrian State Railway[90] which, contrary to its name, had been founded in 1855 as a private firm by Crédit Mobilier and remained under French control until the nationalization of its Hungarian network by the Hungarian government in 1891 and of its Austrian lines by the Austrian administration in 1909.[91]

---

83 Ibid.: 'Türkische Eisenbahnen. Conferenz in Ostende den 8. September 1888'; BA, R 901/11973, fol. 51–2: memo by the Undersecretary in the German Auswärtiges Amt, von Berchem, of 22 September, 1888. Cf. also F. Stern, *Gold and iron. Bismarck, Bleichröder, and the building of the German Empire* (London, 1977), p. 421.

84 CAMT, 207 AQ 328: Unsigned memo of 2 October 1888. For the history of the Anatolian concession cf. F. Seidenzahl, *100 Jahre Deutsche Bank* (Frankfurt, 1970), pp. 63–81; M. Pohl with A. Raab-Rebentisch, *Von Stambul nach Bagdad. Die Geschichte einer berühmten Eisenbahn* (Munich Zürich, 1999), pp. 22–33; B. Barth, *Die deutsche Hochfinanz und die Imperialismen. Banken und Außenpolitik vor 1914* (Stuttgart, 1995), pp. 76–9.

85 Stern, *Gold and iron*, pp. 420–22; Barth, *Die deutsche Hochfinanz*, p. 76.

86 HADB, OR 530: Joly (Wiener Bankverein) to G. Siemens (29/7/1888).

87 Ibid.: Joly to G. Siemens (2/10/1888).

88 Ibid.: Wiener Bankverein to G. Siemens (27/2 and 20/3/1885).

89 Ibid.: Hirsch to G. Siemens (20/71888).

90 HADB, OR 530: G. Siemens to Oberbaurat Jaedicke, Cologne (14/10/1888); ibid.: Joly to G. Siemens (9 and 21/11/1888).

91 Cameron, *France*, pp. 217–21.

The Austrian State Railway eventually dropped out of this race, possibly because of Bulgarian opposition to the sale of the Oriental Railway to an Austrian company.[92] When this decision became known Siemens cabled to Deutsche Bank from Paris on 9 April 1889: 'We will have to do this business.'[93] A few weeks later, in May, serious negotiations finally started between Hirsch and Siemens as well as Moriz Bauer of Wiener Bankverein.[94] These talks went on well into the spring of the following year. Quite early Ernest Cassel, the well-known financier based in London,[95] was involved as sort of a mediator since he had close connections to Hirsch as well as to Bischoffsheim & Goldschmidt.[96]

During all these months Siemens never lost interest in dealing with Hirsch since he considered this deal to be 'an extraordinarily remarkable one and one which fits well into the sphere of our business undertakings'.[97] By March 1890 Deutsche Bank and Wiener Bankverein sent their delegates to Paris and negotiations with Hirsch had almost come to an end. The question whether the two banks should ask the Ottoman Bank to participate in an eventual deal with Hirsch right from the beginning was raised,[98] and rejected presumably because the Turkish government, fearing an ultimate gain in influence by the Ottoman Bank, opposed it.[99] Moriz Bauer, in a letter to Georg Siemens of 26 March 1890, proposed to discuss with the Turkish government and with their colleagues of the Imperial Ottoman Bank 'the idea of a general trust company for Turkish railways'.[100] We shall see that this was exactly the thing which was to be realized shortly afterwards.

Finally on 17 April 1890 a group of banks, led by Deutsche and Wiener Bankverein, signed a contract at Brussels with Baron Hirsch through which they bought from him, for the moment, a quarter of the shares in the operating company (*Betriebsgesellschaft*) of the Oriental Railways,[101] at the same time obtaining an option for the remaining shares. Eventually this syndicate of banks acquired 88,000 shares out of a total of 100,000 representing the share capital of the *Betriebsgesellschaft,* i.e.

---

92 At least according to Barth, *Die deutsche Hochfinanz*, p. 81.

93 HADB, OR 531.

94 Ibid.: Hirsch to G. Siemens (9/5/1889); G. Siemens to Hirsch (17/5/1889).

95 Emden, *Money powers*, pp. 331–42; P. Thane, 'Financiers and the British state: the case of Sir Ernest Casse', in *Business History*, vol. 28, 1986, pp. 80–99.

96 HADB, OR 531, G. Siemens to Cassel (6/6/1889); Cassel to Siemens (8/12/1889).

97 Ibid.: G. Siemens to Moriz Bauer (Wiener Bankverein) (4/1/1890).

98 Ibid.: Telegram (24/2/1890) of Wallich and Raphael de Bauer (brother of the Viennese Moriz Bauer and director of the seat of Banque de Paris et des Pays-Bas at 'Brussels to Deutsche Bank or G. Siemens, cf.' Pirenne, 'Bauer (Raphaël, chevalier de)', in *Biographie Nationale, publiée par l'Académie Royale des Sciences, des Lettres et des Beaux-Arts de Belgique*, vol. 39 (Brussels, 1976), pp. 80–94; Bussière, *Paribas*, pp. 41, 43, 52; B. Koehler, *Ludwig Bamberger. Revolutionär und Bankier* (Stuttgart, 1999), pp. 158–61).

99   HADB, OR 531, G. Siemens to Moriz Bauer (31/3/1890).

100 Ibid.

101 BNP Paribas, 3\CABET-1\193; cf also Barth, *Die deutsche Hochfinanz*, p. 81; Schöllgen, *Imperialismus und Gleichgewicht*, p. 47.

all of those possessed by Hirsch himself, as well as all financial claims put forward by Hirsch *vis-à-vis* the Ottoman government.[102]

How was this important amount of capital to be managed? As we have seen above, it was Moriz Bauer who had, already in March, insisted with Georg Siemens on the creation of a 'trust company' as a viable solution for this problem. In mid-May he again urged Siemens, who was planning a trip to Switzerland, to consult personally on this matter with the heads of two important Swiss banks, Schweizerische Kreditanstalt (Crédit Suisse) in Zurich and Basler Bankverein, forerunner of the later Union Bank of Switzerland. The *trust company* which would eventually be established would immediately take over all the shares and financial claims bought from Hirsch. It could afterwards be charged with other securities but it should, as a next step, increase its equity capital in order to be able to issue bonds with a sufficient guarantee.[103]

This idea, developed by a banker like Bauer, contained the essence of what a well-known economist of those days, Robert Liefmann, called *Effektensubstitution*, i.e. the process by which securities of one company were substituted by those of another one. Fundamentally this was done for three reasons: (1) to achieve a better distribution of risk, since the newly created holding company would normally hold securities from more than one firm; (2) to enable the financing of companies which were not yet capable of placing their own securities in the capital market (for instance, because their plants were still in construction and could thus not yet yield a profit); and (3) to exercise control via such a holding without investing further capital.[104]

A New Financial Holding: Bank für Orientalische Eisenbahnen, Zurich

On 1 October 1890 the Bank für orientalische Eisenbahnen held its first general assembly. The founders consisted of a group of banks, mainly from Germany, Austria and Switzerland: Deutsche Bank, Wiener Bankverein, Dresdner Bank, Deutsche Vereinsbank, Württembergische Vereinsbank, Crédit Suisse, Basler Handelsbank, but also the Imperial Ottoman Bank.[105] To this company, according to Liefmann 'the oldest and most important financial holding established in Switzerland',[106] a capital of 50 million francs in ordinary shares was assigned of which, however, only 20 per cent had been paid in. Besides, there were also 13 million francs of preferential shares. A few weeks afterwards the company issued bonds for 63 million francs, the statutory upper limit corresponding exactly to nominal capital.[107] The first securities

---

102 Helfferich, *Georg von Siemens*, vol. 3, p. 9.

103 HADB, OR 532: Bauer to Siemens (14/5/1890).

104 R. Liefmann, *Beteiligungs- und Finanzierungsgesellschaften. Eine Studie über den modernen Kapitalismus und das Effektenwesen*, 2nd ed. (Jena, 1913), pp. 71–8.

105 F. Seidenzahl, 'Bank für Orientalische Eisenbahnen (Eine Finanzholding und ihr Portefeuille)', in Deutsche Bank (ed.), *Beiträge zu Wirtschafts- und Währungsfragen und zur Bankgeschichte*, nos. 1–20 (Mainz, 1984), pp. 15–6.

106 Liefmann, *Beteiligungs- und Finanzierungsgesellschaften*, p. 496.

107 *Erster Geschäftsbericht der Bank für orientalische Eisenbahnen in Zürich: 1. Oktober 1890 bis 30. Juni 1891*, Zürich 1891, pp. 8–10. For the financial development of B.O.E. see

taken over by the Bank für orientalische Eisenbahnen were of course the shares of the Betriebsgesellschaft, bought from Baron Hirsch: their nominal value was 44 million francs out of a total capital of 50 million.[108]

This type of financial holding was, at least for continental Europe, quite an innovation[109] and as such it might be compared to the appearance of the new 'universal banks' and their forerunners, the Belgian Société Générale and the French Crédit Mobilier, decades earlier. But why was Bank für orientalische Eisenbahnen (B.O.E.) founded in Switzerland? There were certainly advantages offered by the Swiss *Obligationenrecht* of 1881 which was less strict than the corresponding German law as far as the evaluation of participations or the legal responsibilities of the Board of Management (*Vorstand*) and the Administrative Council (*Verwaltungsrat*) were concerned. Swiss companies could buy their proper shares if they wished to do so and further capital increases were permitted before the preceding ones had been completely paid in. Bonds could be issued without any upper limit whereas in Germany this limit was formed by the amount of nominal capital – this was particularly important for financial holdings. Finally, taxes on securities were relatively low in Switzerland when compared to France or Germany.[110] There were also concrete political reasons for choosing Switzerland – or Belgium – as host countries. After the Franco-Prussian War of 1870–71 these two neutral countries, being the places where French and German capital could meet without being bothered by political motives, became the turntables for international investment – Belgium until 1914 and Switzerland well beyond. Even if Deutsche Bank and Wiener Bankverein had godfathered the Bank für orientalische Eisenbahnen it was legally a Swiss company and its day-to-day administration, particularly bookkeeping and correspondence, was, by special contract, handed over to Crédit Suisse, a rather close ally of Deutsche Bank, which also administered its funds.[111] The Swiss share in the *Orientbank* consortium amounted to only 6 per cent – the Austrian was 54 and the German 40 – but the influence of Crédit Suisse on this particular holding was 'surprisingly large'. Walter Adolf Jöhr, who has written an excellent history of

---

also W. Reibel, 'Die Gründung ausländischer Eisenbahn-Unternehmungen durch deutsche Banken', Ph.D. thesis Universität Köln (Düsseldorf, 1934), pp. 74–7.

108 Liefmann, *Beteiligungs- und Finanzierungsgesellschaften*, p. 496.

109 The first company of this type of financial holdings in Switzerland was the Schweizerische Eisenbahnbank, founded in 1879 (cf. H. Bauer, *Schweizerischer Bankverein 1872–1972* (Basel, 1972), pp. 67–71). For the role of this new type of company in the international electrical industry from 1895 onwards cf. P. Hertner, 'Les sociétés financières suisses et le développement de l'industrie électrique jusqu'à la Première Guerre Mondiale', in F. Cardot (ed.), *Un siècle d'électricité dans le monde* (Paris, 1987), pp. 341–55.

110 M. Jörgens, *Finanzielle Trustgesellschaften*, Ph.D. thesis Universität München (Stuttgart, 1902), pp. 73–5; K. Hafner, *Die schweizerischen Finanzierungsgesellschaften für elektrische Unternehmungen*, Ph.D. thesis Université de Fribourg (Geneva, 1912), pp. 30–31.

111 *Bericht des Verwaltungsrathes der Bank für Orientalische Eisenbahnen ... vom 5. September 1891*, Zürich 1891, p. 21.

this Zurich-based bank, sees one of the reasons for this fact in B.O.E. being sort of a 'neutral instance' between the various interest groups present in this holding.[112]

Georg Siemens, in a letter to Moriz Bauer written shortly after the foundation of B.O.E., underlined the problems awaiting the new owners of the Oriental Railways: according to Karl Schrader, a former railway manager, currently a member of the German Reichstag and also a member of the supervisory board of Deutsche Bank, who had done most of the negotiations with Hirsch,[113] the operating company of the Oriental Railways had suffered from contradictory interventions coming from its directors in Paris and in Constantinople. Unfortunately its relations with Bulgaria where its lines passed through were 'very bad', but its 'real enemies' were, according to Schrader, the Austrian and Hungarian railway companies, which showed no interest at all in favouring the traffic to Serbia and Bulgaria and wanted to divert it instead to Trieste and Fiume, nowadays Rijeka.[114] The growing self-assertiveness of the emerging Balkan states, Bulgaria first and Serbia later, was recognized very early by the leading staff of the railway company. Otto von Kühlmann, former manager with Hirsch's company and now director general of the Anatolian Railways, called the Bulgarians, in a letter of 23 October 1890 to Georg Siemens, 'impertinent people': 'They have 300 kilometers of railways in their country for which they have not paid anything and then they complain because they believe railway tariffs are too high.'[115] Herbert Feis observed the same problem with the eyes of a historian and with the benefit of hindsight, since he published his well-known book *Europe, the world's banker* only in 1930: '[...] As Serbia and Bulgaria made progress with their own railway system, as they repurchased other privately built railways within their territories, they resented the independence of the lines of the Oriental Railways within their borders. For that company was run from Vienna, had rate schedules and regulations outside of their control and its higher personnel was foreign. The company was accused, justly or otherwise, of subordinating the interests of the countries which it traversed to its own financial interests and to Austro-German economic interests and of making no effort to develop local resources and industry.'[116]

---

112 W.A. Jöhr, *Schweizerische Kreditanstalt 1856–1956. Hundert Jahre im Dienste der schweizerischen Volkswirtschaft* (Zurich, 1956), p. 189.

113 For Schrader's role cf. Seidenzahl, *100 Jahre Deutsche Bank*, pp. 154, 166 as well as the correspondence in HADB, OR 530.

114 HADB, OR 532: Siemens to Moriz Bauer (10/10/1890).

115 Ibid.: von Kühlmann to Siemens (23/10/1890). As a matter of fact, until 1891 when the Bulgarian and the Oriental tariffs were unified, the tariff of the *Betriebsgesellschaft* of the Oriental Railways was higher than the Bulgarian one, and particularly so for local passenger transport. It was also clearly higher than the tariffs of the Prussian State Railways, W.K. Weiß-Bartenstein, 'Bulgariens Verkehrspolitik und Verkehrswesen', in *Archiv für Eisenbahnwesen*, vol. 38, 1915, p. 1239.

116 H. Feis, *Europe, the world's banker, 1870–1914*, 1ˢᵗ ed. New Haven,1930 (Clifton, 1974), p. 298.

All these problems caused even some of Deutsche Bank's most reliable partners, for instance the leaders of Württembergische Vereinsbank in Stuttgart, to regard Siemens's engagement in the affair of Oriental Railways as a 'folly'.[117]

In parallel with its activities connected with the Oriental Railways, Deutsche Bank managed to get a concession for another railway line from the Sublime Porte in October 1890.[118] This one provided for 219 kilometres of a line running from Salonica to Monastir, today's Bitolj in the Republic of Macedonia, together with the claim to extend it to an Albanian port on the Adriatic Sea.[119] The motive for establishing such a new line might have been that by running it through Turkish Macedonia and extending the line eventually up into Serbia the Oriental Railways – which were supposed to manage this additional network too – would have been able to pass around Bulgaria which, at least for the moment, was considered to be the most difficult partner. In 1893 another concession was given to a group headed by the Ottoman Bank and by Banque de Paris et des Pays-Bas, with the Frankfurt private banking house Bethmann as a third partner.[120] This railway, called Chemin de fer Jonction Salonique-Constantinople, was supposed to run from Salonica eastward along the Aegean coast for 511 kilometres to Dedeagatch – today Alexandroupolis – where it would have joined the Oriental Railways network. The company started with a nominal capital of 15 million francs and the issue of 3 per cent bonds for an amount of 50 million francs.[121] This line and the Salonica-Monastir line proved to be particularly useful to the Turkish army which could, as soon as these links had been finished, send large amounts of troops at short notice from the capital and from Anatolia to the European provinces of the Ottoman Empire, particularly to ever-rebellious Macedonia.[122] The 'Constantinople Junction railway', wrote the British correspondent William Miller in 1898, '... enabled the Turks to strike hard and quickly at their foes.'[123]

---

117 O.K. Deutelmoser, *Kilian Steiner und die Württembergische Vereinsbank* (Ostfildern, 2003), p. 228, note 463.

118 The German Foreign Office supported the request made by Deutsche Bank and its group to the Turkish government but it declined any responsibility in case of political unrest (BA, R 901/11975, f. 35: memo by Undersecretary of State count Berchem, March 12, 1890).

119 Helfferich, *Georg von Siemens*, vol. 3, p. 50; Gounaris, *Steam over Macedonia*, pp. 51–3.

120 A. Autheman, *La Banque impériale ottomane*, pp. 128–29. Still in 1913, the Ottoman Bank owned 15 per cent of the capital of the Jonction railways (J. Thobie, 'Les choix financiers de l'"Ottomane" en Méditerranée orientale de 1856 à 1939', in *Banque et investissements en Méditerranée à l'époque contemporaine*. Actes du Colloque de Marseille, 4–5 Feb. 1982 (Marseille, 1985), p. 72, table no. 6). For the role of the Bethmann bank and the Bethmann family as a link between French and German banking cf. B. Barth, 'The financial history of the Anatolian and Baghdad railways, 1889–1914', in *Financial History Review*, vol. 5, 1998, pp. 120–21.

121 BNP Paribas, 6\DFOM-221\493: prospectus for the issue of 100,000 bonds for 500 francs each at 3 per cent interest (1893). Cf. also the detailed financial report of 12 February 1913 on this company, done by the research branch of Crédit Lyonnais (Archives Historiques du Crédit Agricole, Paris. Fonds Crédit Lyonnais, DEEF 24189).

122 Gounaris, *Steam over Macedonia*, pp. 55–8; Anastassiadou, *Salonique, 1830–1912*, pp. 175–6.

123 W. Miller, *Travels and politics in the Near East* (London, 1898), p. 363.

Judged from the annual reports and from the data on transports of passengers and merchandise the two decades between 1890 and 1909 were quite successful but, given the permanent unrest and the recurrent revolts in the European parts of the Ottoman Empire, traffic could of course not be compared to Western European standards. In 1903, for instance, there were violent revolts in Macedonia[124] and the Turkish Army sent about 200,000 men there to quell the uprising. The report of the operating company for 1903 describes concomitant Macedonian terrorism in the following way:

> Last year's Macedonian movement differed from all similar uprisings of earlier times in its utterly ruthless use of explosives. Frequent attempts were made to blow up our railway lines, fortunately mostly with only slight success [...]. Several atrocities were perpetrated with infernal machines against moving trains, and a number of passengers were killed or injured. [...][125]

Terrorist action of this kind became rather frequent in 1903–1904, as described here, and again in 1910–11. 'These incidents occurred overwhelmingly in Ottoman Macedonia and Thrace ...', and the French-controlled Jonction Salonique-Constantinople line was also among the preferred targets of terrorism.[126]

Already in 1895–96 B.O.E. enlarged its portfolio by acquiring ordinary and preferential shares of the Salonica-Monastir railway from Deutsche Bank. This purchase comprised 96.35 per cent of the entire nominal capital of that railway company.[127] Thus an appreciated service was certainly rendered to the financial status of Deutsche Bank, although from June 1894 the line up to Monastir had been finished and profited from a payment of 14,300 francs per kilometre per year from the Ottoman government, guaranteed by the tithes of the Sanjaks of Salonica and Monastir collected by the Administration of the Ottoman Public Debt.[128] After this purchase, B.O.E.'s portfolio did not change for a decade. Only in 1905–1906 did it decide to buy shares of the Anatolian Railway, for a nominal value of 7.5 million francs.[129] This was again a favour done to Deutsche Bank and its group, which had to finance the continuous needs of this railway.

On the other hand, Deutsche Bank and its group used B.O.E. for a compromise with the Imperial Ottoman Bank, concluded on 22 April 1905. It provided that each of the two partners would have to offer 25 per cent in any new business opened in

---

124 F. Adanir, *Die makedonische Frage. Ihre Entstehung und Entwicklung bis 1908* (Wiesbaden, 1979), pp. 160–99.

125 *Betriebsgesellschaft der Orientalischen Eisenbahnen. Vierundzwanzigste ordentliche Generalversammlung abgehalten in Wien am 31. Mai 1904: Betriebsjahr 1903*, Wien [1904], p. 3.

126 P. Mentzel, 'Accidents, sabotage, and terrorism: Work hazards on Ottoman railways', in C. Imber, K. Kiyotaki and R. Murphy (eds), *Frontiers of Ottoman Studies: State, province, and the West* (London, New York, 2005), pp. 229–31.

127 The company had also issued bonds for a nominal amount of 60 million francs (cf. *Bericht des Verwaltungsrathes der Bank für Orientalische Eisenbahnen ... vom 19. September 1896*, Zürich 1896, pp. 6, 12).

128 Ibid., p. 6.

129 The prize was 5.4 million francs (*Bericht des Verwaltungsrates der Bank für Orientalische Eisenbahnen ... vom 25. August 1906*, Zürich 1906, pp. 4–6, 14).

Turkey. On top of that the Ottoman Bank would receive 25 per cent of B.O.E.'s capital.[130] Such a move would have again alleviated Deutsche Bank's balance sheet and further internationalized B.O.E., and that would probably also have pleased Crédit Suisse. It does not seem that the Ottoman Bank ever took such a block, but in 1907 in any case one of the members of its Paris general committee joined B.O.E.'s Administrative Council.[131]

There was another regrouping of B.O.E.'s portfolio in 1906 when half of the stock of the operating company (*Betriebsgesellschaft der Orientalischen Eisenbahnen*) was sold, with the help of its banking group, on the stock exchanges of Zurich, Basel, Geneva, Berlin, Frankfurt and Vienna.[132] By the end of 1906 even 45,240 of these shares – out of an original stock of 88,904 owned by B.O.E. – had been sold. B.O.E. made a profit of 3.42 million francs out of this.[133] Having wound up this sale, and again during the financial year 1906–1907, B.O.E. bought 37.5 per cent of the shares of the Haidar-Pasha Harbour Company from the Anatolian Railways.[134] In this case too it had looked after the interests of Deutsche Bank and its group.

By the beginning of 1907 only 30 per cent of B.O.E.'s 50 million francs of nominal capital had been paid in. A general assembly then decided to set its nominal capital at 40 million francs, of which however 50 per cent had to be paid up. In the course of the same operation 50 million francs of 4-per cent bonds were converted into 30 million francs of 4.25-per cent bonds.[135] In 1908 B.O.E. took over 94 per cent of new shares issued by the Anatolian Railways – 63.5 million francs, of which it had to pay in just 10 per cent. Most of this was earmarked for irrigation works in the plains of Konya.[136]

As a result of the Young Turk Revolution, and one day before the Austro-Hungarian annexation of Bosnia-Hercegovina, in September 1908 Bulgaria declared its complete independence,[137] officially took over Eastern Roumelia and seized 310 kilometres of the Oriental Railways network. The seizure was motivated by a strike

---

130 The text is to be found in: HADB, P 7950. Cf also R. Poidevin, *Les relations économiques et financières entre la France et l'Allemagne de 1898 à 1914* (Paris, 1969), p. 274; Barth, *Die deutsche Hochfinanz*, p. 226.

131 *Bericht des Verwaltungsrates der Bank für Orientalische Eisenbahnen ... vom 17. September 1907,* Zürich 1907, p. 26.

132 Ibid., pp. 3–4.

133 HADB, OR 858: Frey to Gwinner (18/1/1907).

134 For the Haidar-Pasha Harbour Company cf. Barth, *Die deutsche Hochfinanz*, p. 125; Pohl, *Von Stambul nach Bagdad*, pp. 133–4.

135 *Bericht des Verwaltungsrates der Bank für Orientalische Eisenbahnen ... vom 17. September 1907,* Zürich 1907, pp. 14–16.

136 *Bericht des Verwaltungsrates der Bank für Orientalische Eisenbahnen ... vom 19. August 1908,* Zürich 1908, pp. 3–4; for the irrigation project in the Konya area cf. Pohl, *Von Stambul nach Bagdad*, pp. 109–10.

137 Cf. F. Ahmad, *The Young Turks. The Committee of Union and Progress in Turkish politics 1908–1914* (Oxford, 1969), p. 24.

of local railway staff[138] which had been fomented by the Bulgarians.[139] 'After the strike ended the [Bulgarian, P.H.] government declared its intention of retaining the line, asserting a willingness to indemnify the company, but not making clear where the necessary funds were to be found.'[140] In June 1909 the Turkish Government received compensation of 42 million francs from the Bulgarians which had been 'furnished by the Russian Government'.[141] The operating company of the Oriental Railways was then compensated by the Turkish Government with a sum of 21.5 million francs for the losses incurred in the course of this seizure. From then on its network was reduced to a length of 954 kilometres.[142] In 1910 the Anatolian Railways called another 10 per cent on their shares. B.O.E. met these needs by issuing another series of its 4.25-per cent bonds, for an amount of 7.5 million francs.[143]

The B.O.E. report for 1910/11 tells us that 'the company has been able to pay a dividend which has varied between 5.5 and 6.5 per cent during a considerable number of years'. 'Since one can expect an appropriate and stable return on our share capital also for the future our banks – which had already participated in the foundation of our institution – thought that this would be the moment for introducing the shares of the Bank für Orientalische Eisenbahnen on to the Swiss stock exchanges of Zurich, Basle and Geneva.'[144] In 1910 the seat of the operating company of the Oriental Railways was transferred from Vienna to Constantinople. It became a Turkish company, and one might suppose that this was a political move, motivated on one side by the growing nationalism in Turkey itself; the other reason will have to be found in the desire to keep the company out of the growing conflicts between Austria-Hungary and the new states which had sprung up in the Balkan area. At the same time the now Turkish company remained under the control of its German and Austro-Hungarian shareholders, particularly the B.O.E., and received considerable compensation payments from the Turkish and the Bulgarian governments.[145] The

---

138 GP, vol. 26/1, pp. 71–2, document n° 8951; memo of the undersecretary of state to the German Foreign Office, Stemrich, of 23 September 1908; OeStA, HHStA, MdÄ, AR, F 19, Karton 47, Fasz.3.

139 Weiß-Bartenstein, 'Bulgariens Verkehrspolitik', pp. 1233–4; Kumpf-Korfes, 'Die ökonomische Expansion', p. 1433.

140 Feis, *Europe, the world's banker*, p. 301. Cf also Crampton, *A concise history of Bulgaria*, p. 130.

141 Ibid.; W. Gutsche, *Monopole, Staat und Expansion vor 1914. Zum Funktionsmechanismus zwischen Industriemonopolen, Großbanken und Staatsorganen in der Außenpolitik des Deutschen Reiches 1897 bis Sommer 1914* (Berlin (DDR), 1986, p. 162.

142 BNP Paribas, 3\CABET-1\194: French translation of the minutes of the shareholders' meeting of the operating company of the Oriental Railways (15/121909); printed *Notice* on the Compagnie d'Exploitation, probably from 1923.

143 *Bericht des Verwaltungsrates der Bank für Orientalische Eisenbahnen ... vom 19. August 1910*, Zürich 1910, pp. 3–5.

144 *Einundzwanzigster Geschäftsbericht des Verwaltungsrates der Bank für Orientalische Eisenbahnen ... für die Geschäftsführung während des Zeitraumes vom 1. Juli 1910 bis 30. Juni 1911*, Zürich 1911, p. 3.

145 W. Gutsche, *Monopole, Staat und Expansion vor 1914. Zum Funktionsmechanismus zwischen Industriemonopolen, Großbanken und Staatsorganen in der Außenpolitik des Deutschen Reiches 1897 bis Sommer 1914* (Ost-Berlin, 1986), p. 163.

acquisition of almost 10,000 preference shares of the Mersina-Tarsus-Adana Railway in 1910 was financially not important at all, but was probably justified by the overall strategy of Deutsche Bank in this area.[146]

The Italo-Turkish War of 1911–12, but above all the two Balkan Wars of 1912/13, not only did much harm to general railway traffic, but also blocked the operations of the now Turkish *Compagnie d'Exploitations des Chemins de fer Orientaux*, particularly in those areas occupied by the Serb, Greek and Bulgarian armies. By the end of the Second Balkan War in the summer of 1913, due to huge territorial changes 466 kilometres of the Oriental network had remained on Turkish soil, 85 kilometres were now in Bulgaria, 77 kilometres in the new Greek areas and not less than 371 kilometres in Serbia's new territories.[147] Whereas the Greek government showed itself disposed to a possible compromise, both the Serbian and Bulgarian governments had occupied the lines of the Oriental Railways and operated them under their own responsibility. In the end a solution was found with Bulgaria, but the problems with Serbia became chronic. During the entire period between the end of the Balkan conflict and the outbreak of the First World War, the Serbian administration showed almost no signs of wanting to come to an agreement with the Compagnie d'Exploitation.[148] In April 1913, it accused the company of having, right from the beginning of the conflict, concentrated most of its wagons and locomotives at Salonica, thus depriving Serbia of all of its means of transport. Such a situation ought to be avoided in the future.[149] To most observers it seemed clear that Serbia wanted to integrate its part of the Oriental network into the Serbian state railway system.[150]

As we have already seen, both countries, Serbia and Bulgaria, were aiming at state railway systems. Both of them discouraged private investors, as the difficult relationship between newly founded Bulgaria and the Oriental Railways quite clearly demonstrated. Thus the Serbian attitude in 1913/14 is just another illustration of this general approach. From an economic point of view, of course Michael Palairet is convincing when he states that the policies of nationalizing foreign-owned railway companies by both countries '... merely burdened them with compensation payments which damaged their finances, and made it even more difficult to raise funds to build

---

146 Ibid., p. 4, 22.

147 W. Gutsche, 'Serbien in den Mitteleuropaplänen des deutschen Imperialismus am Vorabend des ersten Weltkrieges', in *Zeitschrift für Geschichtswissenschaft*, vol. 23, 1975, p. 41.

148 *Dreiundzwanzigster Geschäftsbericht des Verwaltungsrates der Bank für Orientalische Eisenbahnen ... vom 20. September 1913*, Zürich 1913, pp. 3–6; *Vierundzwanzigster Geschäftsbericht des Verwaltungsrates der Bank für Orientalische Eisenbahnen ... vom 5. November 1914*, Zürich 1914, pp. 3–5.

149 That is what the Serbian envoy to the Austro-Hungarian government said to the Austrian politician Joseph Maria Baernreither on 7 April, 1913, J.M. Baernreither, *Fragmente eines politischen Tagebuches. Die südslawische Frage und Österreich-Ungarn vor dem Weltkrieg*, ed. by J. Redlich (Berlin, 1928), p. 231.

150 Cf. the exchange of notes between the Serbian and the Austro-Hungarian Foreign Offices in: OeStA, HHStA, MdÄ, AR, F 19, Karton 47, Fasz. 1.

extension lines. ... [They] ... regarded the railway as a facility of the administration rather than as a provider of economic services'.[151]

The Austro-Hungarian Solution

Given the really difficult situation which prevailed in the entire Balkan peninsula during and after the two wars of 1912–13 it was quite a surprise when B.O.E. and Deutsche Bank managed, by the end of April 1913, to sell their shares in the Compagnie d'Exploitation to a syndicate of Austro-Hungarian banks.[152] B.O.E., in its annual report for 1913, explains quite clearly how it saw the matter: according to its view there was little hope that an easy and quick understanding could be reached with the successor states to the Ottoman Empire. There would be too many chances that line operations would remain disturbed for a rather long, in any case incalculable, period. Under these conditions it would be better to sell. The Salonica-Monastir shares would be given away at a fixed price, the shares of the operating company of the Oriental Railways at a fixed price plus a participation in eventual gains that might be realized in the future. The prices which would be paid now by the Austro-Hungarians were considered to be just adequate, not really corresponding to their intrinsic value. An additional participation in future profits was, as we have seen, guaranteed. It should furthermore be accepted that one could now enjoy '... the calm with which one might from now on observe the political events in the Balkan peninsula as materially no longer really engaged observers'.[153] In another letter Deutsche Bank underlined that this sale would enable them and their 'friends' to recuperate the capital invested in the European part of Turkey and to '[...] liquefy it in favour of our Asiatic railway enterprises, particularly the Baghdad railway'.[154]

The buying group was led by the Wiener Bankverein, not really a newcomer to this scenario, and furthermore comprised two other big Viennese banks, Anglo-

---

151 M. Palairet, *The Balkan economies, c. 1800–1914. Evolution without development* (Cambridge, 1997), p. 329.

152 Cf. for the correspondence on this matter which started in November 1912 and came to the desired agreement in April 1913: OeStA, HHStA, MdÄ, AR, F 23, Karton 105. For the German part cf. GP, vol. 37/2, pp. 713–15, documents n° 15118 and particularly n° 15119 (German ambassador at Vienna, von Tschirschky, to Chancellor von Bethmann Hollweg, 28 April 1913). A copy of the agreement between the two groups of banks of 16 April 1913 can be found in HADB, OR 1375. The negotiations between Deutsche Bank (von Gwinner) and B.O.E. (Frey) on the one side and the Viennese group, particularly Bodenkredit-Anstalt and Wiener Bankverein, on the other is in HADB, OR 614.

153 *Dreiundzwanzigster Geschäftsbericht ... vom 20. September 1913,* pp. 6–7 (quote on p. 7). Cf. also the arguments put forward in the meeting of the Council of Administration of B.O.E., held in Vienna on 16 April 1913 – the day of the agreement – where the sale was justified in the same way (HADB, OR 850).

154 Seidenzahl, *100 Jahre Deutsche Bank*, p. 233. – Arthur von Gwinner who was then the leading manager of Deutsche Bank underlines this point of view also in his memoirs, A. von Gwinner, *Lebenserinnerungen*, 2nd ed., ed. by M. Pohl (Frankfurt, 1992), p. 85.

Austrian Bank and Allgemeine Boden-Credit-Anstalt.[155] On the Hungarian side were Ungarische Allgemeine Creditbank, Pester Ungarische Commercial-Bank and Pester Erster Vaterländischer Sparcassa-Verein. Each of the two groups got exactly 50 per cent. 51,000 shares of the Compagnie d'Exploitation were on sale. Of these 45,000 came from B.O.E. and 6000 from Deutsche Bank itself. The price was fixed at 52.45 million francs, of which 17.5 millions were to be paid at a later date.[156] The Austro-Hungarian government, particularly its Minister of Foreign Affairs, Count Berchtold, showed great interest in this transaction and obliged the banking syndicate to take important decisions in this particular railway matter only after close consultation with the Government. The Administration was authorized to buy these shares at any moment and for a fair price, but the banks could also sell to the Government whenever they desired to do so.[157] One might suppose that Berchtold hoped to be able to put increasing pressure on the Serbian government once Austro-Hungarian banks had acquired control of this network. This proved to be a profound illusion, at least until the outbreak of the First World War in the following year changed everything. There were however contemporaries who recognized this problem, as one can read in *Der Oesterreichische Volkswirt*, an authoritative Viennese economic journal, of 3 May 1913: the author of this article was convinced that the transaction had not so much been in the interest of this group of Austro-Hungarian banks as driven by the Viennese Foreign Office. He criticized the deal particularly from a political point of view, since in his opinion it would embitter relations with the Balkan states.

---

155 The Governor of Bodenkreditanstalt, Rudolf Sieghart, claims in his memoirs a leading role in this sale. According to him the idea of this transfer had been devised by Felix Somary who had been working until 1909 as an assistant manager to Karl Morawitz, head of the Viennese Anglo-Austrian Bank, and had then left Vienna for Berlin, R. Sieghart, *Die letzten Jahrzehnte einer Großmacht. Menschen, Völker, Probleme des Habsburger-Reichs* (Berlin, 1932), p. 164. Somary confirms Sieghart in his own memoirs: '[...] The Oriental Railways were of no interest for their yearly dividend payments but for Austria they were of the highest political value after the Balkan War had ended. I took an option on the majority of its shares and sold it to the Austrian and the Hungarian Governments', F. Somary, *Erinnerungen aus meinem Leben* (Zurich, 1959), p. 98. Sieghart's version is confirmed in the *Tagesbericht* of 19 November 1912 written by a high official of the Viennese Foreign Ministry, Ippen, who says explicitly that the idea came originally from Felix Somary and that his initiative had been 'probably the first step' (HHStA, MdÄ, AR F 23, Karton 105). The proof that somehow Sieghart and Somary told the truth lies in the fact that Somary claimed 'the fee which has been promised to me' in a letter to Helfferich on 17 May 1913 and that Deutsche Bank informed him through a letter of 20 June 1913 that a sum of 100,000 francs would be remitted to his account (HADB, OR 614).

156 GP, vol. 37/II, pp. 714–15, document n° 15119. Cf. also D. Löding, 'Deutschlands und Österreich-Ungarns Balkanpolitik unter besonderer Berücksichtigung ihrer Wirtschaftsinteressen', Ph.D. thesis Universität Hamburg (Hamburg, 1969), pp. 52–9; Barth, *Die deutsche Hochfinanz*, p. 360; E. Kolm, *Die Ambitionen Österreich-Ungarns im Zeitalter des Hochimperialismus* (Frankfurt, 2001), pp. 232–3.

157 Cf. A. Kanitz-Wiesenburg, Wiener Bankverein, typescript preserved in the Historical Archives of BankAustria-Creditanstalt, Vienna [ca. 1936], part 3, pp. 123–4.

Either we live in peace with Serbia, and then we will not need the shares [of the Oriental Railways, P.H.]. If we are in conflict with that country, then – with or without the shares – power will decide, in the last instance bayonets.[158]

Other countries did not want to stay behind. Italy was particularly interested in the concession of a line joining Monastir with Valona or Durazzo on the Albanian coast, a concession which had originally been granted to Deutsche Bank when it received access to the Salonica-Monastir line.[159] Otto Joel, leading manager of the Banca Commerciale Italiana, sent a telegram to his friend Count Hutten-Czapski at Berlin in which he urged him to ask the German government for a conference with Austria-Hungary and Italy on these railway matters before the Paris conference on financial issues of the Balkan states started.[160] This was one of the reasons why Joel travelled a few days later to Vienna, where he secured consent from the Austro-Hungarian government, which seemed to agree.[161]

A few months later, in autumn 1913, an attempt was made to get even French and, to a lesser extent, Russian capital into the Oriental Railways business, possibly on a 50/50 basis with the Austro-Hungarians, because it was hoped that by this means Serbian opposition could eventually be mitigated. As a by-product, much-needed capital would flow from the ever-resourceful Paris capital market to Austria-Hungary.[162] The French Minister of Foreign Affairs, Pichon, in a discussion with the Russian ambassador to France, emphasized the right which, according to his interpretation, Serbia had to nationalize the Oriental Railways on its territory, but nevertheless pleaded for another solution to this conflict by 'internationalizing' the Oriental network.[163] From the end of the First Balkan War in April 1913, a so-called *syndicat d'initiative* had been formed by the well known French construction group Régie Générale de Chemins de Fer of Count Vitali and the Paris private bank Gunzburg, with Wilhelm von Adler, an ex-director of the Wiener Bankverein who had acquired an important position within the French Société Générale, as counsel.[164]

---

158 'Die Erwerbung der Orientalischen Eisenbahnaktien', in *Der Oesterreichische Volkswirt*, n° 31 of 3 May 1913.

159 PA, R 14349: Reports from the German ambassador in Rome, v. Flotow (17 and 18/5/1913).

160 Ibid.: text of the telegram from Joel, sent to the Auswärtiges Amt on 20/5/1913.

161 BI.BCI, PJ 13: Joel to Minister of Foreign Affairs di San Giuliano (31//1913); PA, R 14585: German ambassador in Vienna, v. Tschirschky to Auswärtiges Amt (28/6/1913).

162 Cf Löding, 'Deutschlands und Österreich-Ungarns Balkanpolitik', pp. 176–9; A. Ableitinger, 'Österreichische Versuche um Zugang zum Pariser Finanzmarkt vor 1914', in F. Kreissler (ed.), *Relations franco-autrichiennes 1870–1970. Actes du Colloque de Rouen 29 février–2 mars 1984* (Rouen, 1986).

163 Report of the Russian ambassador in Paris, Izvolski, to the Russian Minister of Foreign Affairs of 10/23 October 1913, in F. Stieve, *Der diplomatische Schriftwechsel Iswolskis 1911–1914. Aus den Geheimakten der Russischen Staatsarchive*, vol. 3 (Berlin, 1926), pp. 318–19.

164 According to information gathered by the German ambassador in Vienna, von Tschirschky, von Adler or – as the French called him – d'Adler was not a French citizen '... but in France he is considered to be a Frenchman. He lives in Paris, plays an important role in the French business world and enjoys at the same time the confidence of the Austrian business circles' (GP, vol. 37/2, p. 726, document n° 15131: von Tschirschky to Chancellor Bethmann

By November 1913 the French group had prepared a project which consisted of the creation of two operating companies, one for the Serbian and one for the Greek network. In each of them either the Serbians or the Greeks should get one third of nominal capital. Another third was reserved for French and another one for Austro-Hungarian capital. Both companies would be controlled by a financial holding or, as it was called, *une société de trust*, organized according to French law and based in Paris. Within the holding French and Austro-Hungarian capital would have equal shares and an equal number of representatives. Its president would be a Frenchman.[165]

The Société Générale, one of the big Parisian *banques de depots*, was asked to collaborate,[166] but this was a pure formality since Wilhelm von Adler, a close collaborator of this bank, had been one of the promoters of the project. At a later date the Greek and the Serbian governments would probably want to buy the networks situated on their soil. In this case the financial holding company would try to mobilize the necessary funds on the international, particularly the French, capital market by issuing its own bonds. The sum required would be altogether around 80 million francs.[167] Russia, which regarded Serbia as part of its zone of influence, would get a share in the French quota of the Serbian operating company.[168] Italy, again represented by Banca Commerciale's Otto Joel, tried to stay in this game too, but asked only for a subparticipation in the Austro-Hungarian quota. When the government in Vienna refused, the Italians wanted to ride on the French ticket.[169]

The Germans knew about the Franco-Austrian negotiations, and Deutsche Bank was not amused when it was informed that the Austro-Hungarian banking group would not want to hand them back the Eastern part of the Oriental network to which they felt entitled through the agreement of April 1913. The German side, and particularly Deutsche Bank, believed that the network in those European areas

---

Hollweg on 2 January 1914). B. Michel, Banques et banquiers en Autriche au début du 20e siècle (Paris, 1976), p. 247, tells us that the French ambassador at Vienne, Dumaine, called von Adler in 1913 a 'financier cosmopolite' and comments then: 'Cette étiquette un peu méprisante [...] ne nous apprend rien, sinon la méfiance des ambassadeurs pour les milieux financiers.' Already in January 1913 von Adler had proposed a joint venture composed of French and Austrian capital through the acquisition of the Western part of the Oriental Railway network. Such an initiative would ' ... increase the guarantees that for the line to Salonica [...] no tariff policy could be realized against Austria and that existing stipulations would be respected scrupulously' (W. von Adler to Sektionschef Ritter von Wimmer of the Austrian Ministry of Finance on 4 January 1913, in: OeStA, HHStA, MdÄ, AR F 23, Karton 105).

165 SG. AH, B 3180: 'proposition française pour la solution des questions de chemins de fer dans les nouveaux territoires serbes et grecs' (21/11/13).

166 Ibid.: draft of a letter by Régie Générale de Chemins de Fer and the private banking house Gunzburg to Société Générale of 25 Nov. 1913.

167 Ibid.: 'Note sur la société financière à créer' of 6 January 1914.

168 The Russian ambassador in Paris, Izvolski, to the Russian Minister of Foreign Affairs on 23 November/6 December 1913 (Stieve, *Der diplomatische Schriftwechsel Iswolskis*, vol. 3, pp. 373–4).

169 HHStA, MdÄ, AR F 23, K 105: telegram of the Austro-Hungarian ambassador at Rome, von Merey (20/12/1913) and draft of the answer to von Merey (24/12/1913); HADB, OR 614: Frey (Crédit Suisse) to Helfferich (Deutsche Bank) on 2 March 1914; Helfferich to Frey on 7 March 1914.

which after the Second Balkan War still belonged to the Ottoman Empire – more than 400 kilometres – would in the meantime have become a valuable complement to the lines built through German initiative in the Asiatic part of the Empire.[170] The German government was equally against 'a total elimination of German influence on the Oriental Railways'.[171] Already at the end of January 1914 the Secretary of State and head of the Auswärtiges Amt von Jagow had declared to the Italian ambassador at Berlin, Bollati, that Germany was against the internationalization project and that it was making all sorts of efforts in order to make the Franco-Austrian compromise fail.[172] The Serbian government on the other hand, which still preferred the eventual nationalization of the Oriental network in Serbia to the Franco-Austrian project of internationalization, tried to gain time.[173] On 16 May 1914 – two and a half months before the outbreak of the First World War – *The Economist* wrote: 'After five months of useless negotiations [between Serbia and Austria-Hungary, P.H.] the question of the Orient Railways has reached a critical point, which almost excludes all hope of a satisfactory arrangement.'[174]

In the end, nothing came of the Franco-Austrian project.[175] Instead, an additional agreement was made between the German-Swiss group which had sold the 51,000 shares in the spring of 1913 and their Austro-Hungarian counterparts: the shares bought by the banks from Vienna and Budapest were to be blocked for a period of ten years and an ensuing sale to foreign buyers could be vetoed by the Viennese government.[176] This was not only a result of pressure exercised by the German government and Deutsche Bank and its group but was also due to diverging opinions

---

170 And this particularly since, as a result of the Second Balkan War, Adrianople/Edirne – and together with it a larger part of former European Turkey – had been retained by the Turks (GP, vol. 37/2, pp. 728–31: memo by Deutsche Bank director Helfferich of 23 December 1913).

171 Ibid., pp. 739–40, document n° 15139: von Jagow, Secretary of State of the German Foreign Office, to the German ambassador in Vienna, von Tschirschky, on 23 February 1914. On 10 March 1914, von Jagow told the Austrian politician Baernreither that it would be 'politically totally incomprehensible' if Austria opened the Oriental Railways to French and Russian capital (Baernreither, *Fragmente eines politischen Tagebuchs*, p. 302).

172 Ministero degli Affari Esteri, Roma. Archivio Storico-Diplomatico, Serie Politica (1908–1914), Pacco 746: Telegramma in arrivo n. 825 of 29 January 1914.

173 Cf. the correspondence between the Austro-Hungarian Legation in Belgrade and the Ministry of Foreign Affairs in Vienna between January and April 1914 in: OeStA, HHStA, MdÄ, AR, F 19, Karton 47, Fasz. 1. – Cf also in SG AH, B 3180: 'Note' of 30 April 1914 ('[...] du côté serbe, la négociation relative aux Chemins de Fer orientaux a été menée avec une lenteur particulière et avec l'intention visible de n'accepter l'internationalisation que si tout espoir devait être abandonné de voir le Gouvernement Austro-Hongrois agréer la formule du rachat').

174 *The Economist*, May 16, 1914, p. 1127.

175 For an excellent description of this project and its development cf. Michel, *Banques et banquiers en Autriche*, pp. 276–9.

176 GP, vol. 37/2, pp. 744–5, document n° 15142: *Aide-mémoire* sent by the German Undersecretary of State in the Foreign Office Zimmermann to the Austro-Hungarian Embassy in Berlin on 9 March 1914.

within the Austro-Hungarian government, where particularly the Hungarian Prime Minister Tisza was opposed to the internationalization project.[177]

A Few Concluding Remarks

Much more could be said on the entire topic, for instance about plans made since 1908 between France, Italy, Russia and Serbia to construct a railway line from the Danube to the Adriatic Sea or about Austrian plans to build a railway across the Sanjak of Novi Pazar.

For the moment one can only conclude that the case study presented in this chapter started with a rather bold but nevertheless traditional banker like Hirsch. It then switched over to a quite advanced form of late nineteenth-century capitalism, the finance company, embodied in the Zurich-based Bank für Orientalische Eisenbahnen – but also applied in the above-described Franco-Austrian internationalization project of 1913/14. Even this more elaborate system, however, fell victim to the new national states which had grown up in the Balkans as heirs to the Ottoman Empire (and later to the Habsburg one), for whom state railway systems became sort of a status symbol – as state-owned airlines were later to do.

One might conclude by saying that capitalism's irresistible march could well be interrupted and then delayed in some parts of Europe even by second-rate wars and conflicts and by relatively small states. If bankers in Berlin, Vienna, Zurich, Milan or Paris had ever forgotten this possibility, they were thoroughly reminded of it when and if they looked to the European South-East between the 1870s and 1914.

---

177 OeStA, HHStA, MdÄ, AR, F 23, Karton 105: Berchtold to Tisza on 7 August 1913 (draft of a letter).

CHAPTER 7

Modern Communication:
The Information Network of
N.M. Rothschild & Sons in
Nineteenth-Century Europe

Rainer Liedtke

In times in which online databases, news channels with live quotations from international stock exchanges and, of course, Google, are literally at the fingertips of practically everybody in the Western World, we are used to having any information at our immediate disposal. Due to the overwhelming quantity of facts and figures, today selection is the key to a successful information management. In the nineteenth century, however, the sheer availability of information stood in the foreground, and the circle of people who had access to information from beyond their immediate locality was very small. Apart from governments, rulers and merchants, it included in particular bankers. These depended, especially if they operated internationally, on a precise knowledge of economic and political developments as a vital precondition for doing business.

To obtain information, bankers could either read newspapers, or they could resort to a rather more reliable, more precise and quicker source, the reports of agents. For the purposes of this investigation an 'agent' is someone who is conducting a task, most often a business or an assignment for a banker. Two different groups of agents can be discerned, which were partially overlapping: business partners from another location with their own firm who traded with the banker but also furnished him with general information on the one hand, and individuals who were employed by the banker to represent his interests in a foreign location. The latter were acting exclusively on behalf of that banker.

In the following I would like to outline how a merchant bank built up a network of agents (of both kinds) in the nineteenth century, how this network operated and how it transformed over time, in other words, how it modernized. I am particularly interested in the relation between the banker on the one hand and the agent on the other. For this purpose I have researched the agents' network of the London merchant bankers N.M. Rothschild & Sons between the Napoleonic Wars and the 1880s.[1] Rothschilds was founded as a bank in London in 1809 and it was closely connected to four other Rothschild houses on the continent: Meyer Amschel Rothschild & Söhne in Frankfurt, operating from the late eighteenth century to 1901; de Rothschild

---

1 The following analysis is a summary of my study: *N.M. Rothschild & Sons: Die Kommunikation im Bankenwesen im Europa des 19. Jahrhunderts* (Cologne, 2006).

Frères & Cie in Paris, 1810 until today – although under a different name and with another structure; S.M von Rothschild & Söhne in Vienna, 1821–1938 and C.M. von Rothschild in Naples, 1821–61.[2] Except for Frankfurt, these establishments had each been founded by one of the five sons of Meyer Amschel Rothschild, a coin dealer from Frankfurt who in the late eighteenth century had commenced a highly successful banking business in his home town. After his death in 1812, his oldest son Amschel Meyer took over the Frankfurt house.[3] These houses co-operated very intensely and also shared agents, but in the following I am focusing largely on the London house. I have primarily researched the agents on the European continent, although N.M. Rothschild also had representatives in South and North America and Asia.[4] My research has borrowed some ideas and concept from network analysis as it is undertaken in the social sciences, although it does not claim to conduct a fully fledged analysis of that kind.[5]

How should one imagine the Rothschild agents' network? There was a 'foundation period', which lasted from the final phase of the Napoleonic Wars until the early restoration period and focused on the Netherlands and Flanders and some port cities of the North and Baltic Seas. In particular Amsterdam, Antwerp, Rotterdam and Hamburg were important posts for agents during this time. There are two reasons for that. First, this area was economically highly important at the time, but it declined soon after. Second, at the end of the allied struggle against Napoleonic France, the Rothschilds undertook an extensive operation of buying up gold on the continent, minting it into coinage appropriate for continental use and supplied British troops on the Iberian peninsula with it.[6] This was the economic way in which the London

---

2   The most comprehensive historical account of the Rothschild bank and family to date is N. Ferguson, *The World's Banker. The History of the House of Rothschild* (London, 1998).

3   See A. Elon, *Founder. Meyer Amschel Rothschild and his Times* (New York, 1996) for an essayistic, yet mostly accurate historical account of the life of the 'First Rothschild'.

4   The best known Rothschild agent in North America was August Belmont, a clerk from the Frankfurt house, who was sent to New York in 1837 and made a meteoric rise to become one of the richest Americans and an influential politician in the Democratic Party. See I. Katz, *August Belmont. A Political Biography* (New York, London, 1968).

5   For a succinct summary of some principles of network analysis see T. Schweizer, 'Einführung', in T. Schweizer (ed.), *Netzwerkanalyse. Ethnologische Perspektiven* (Berlin, 1988), pp. 1–11. For examples of adaptations of network analysis for historical studies see J.F. Padgett and C.K. Ansell (eds), 'Robust Action and the Rise of the Medici, 1400– 1434', in *American Journal of Sociology*, vol. 98, 1993, pp. 1259–1319; U. Brunnbauer and K. Kaser (eds), *Vom Nutzen der Verwandten. Soziale Netzwerke in Bulgarien* (19. und 20. Jahrhundert) (Vienna Cologne Weimar, 2001); J. Herres and M. Neuhaus, *Politische Netzwerke durch Briefkommunikation. Briefkultur der politischen Oppositionsbewegungen und frühen Arbeiterbewegungen im 19. Jahrhundert* (Berlin, 2002); F. Edelmayer, *Söldner und Pensionäre: Das Netzwerk Philipps II. im Heiligen Römischen Reich* (Munich, 2002); G. Russel and C. Tuite (eds), *Romantic Sociability. Social Networks and Literary Culture in Britain 1770–1840* (Cambridge, 2002); M.B. Rose, *Firms, Networks and Business Values. The British and American Cotton Industries since 1750* (Cambridge, 2000).

6   H.H. Kaplan, *Nathan Mayer Rothschild and the Creation of a Dynasty: The Critical Years 1806–1816* (Stanford, 2006) covers this period with a strong focus on financial history but without paying much attention to the agents.

house grew but it also gave it political clout, and the North Sea ports were the theatre of action.

The heyday of the communication network lasted from the 1820s to the early 1850s. It was expanded tremendously and reached far into southern and eastern Europe, with emphasis on the northern Italian cities and also Austrian Triest, southern France, the German traffic and trading hubs of Cologne, Leipzig and Berlin; Madrid and Lisbon in the southwest up to the easternmost outposts Riga and St. Petersburg and many cities in between. Overseas agents established themselves in particular in South America and the south of North America.

Finally there was a period from the later 1850s to the late 1870s, which mark the end of my research period, in which the density of the network shrunk again somewhat. This had to do primarily with the advent of the electric telegraph and news agencies. Many contacts which were previously essential for supplying London with stock exchange rates were now expandable. Plus there was also a specific reason related to the Rothschild firm: three of the five founding brothers – the heads of the houses in Frankfurt, Vienna and Naples – died in the year 1855. Although this did not affect the London house directly, since Nathan Rothschild had already passed away in 1836, it brought changes in the structure of the business.

What can be said about the structure of this network? It was very obviously not formed according to a master plan. Neither was it haphazard, but it was continuously altered to adjust to the changing economic and political conditions. Network analysis would characterize the Rothschild network as extremely asymmetric, because the bank N.M. Rothschild and nothing but the bank was at its centre. Graphically the network could be drawn like a wheel, with the Rothschilds being at the hub and having contact to all other members. Among each other, the agents occasionally had contacts but usually not. Therefore some of the spokes of the wheel would need to be connected but it would be far away from being round.

People were the essence of the network. The extent to which the London Rothschild received useful information depended in large part on the quality of their agents. How did one become an agent and what qualifications did these people need? With regard to the first type of agents, the business partners, there was first a regular business correspondence and mutual trust built up. Then such individuals were, if need be, also used to communicate political intelligence or draw up scenarios of how particular markets or stock exchanges would develop in the future. Far more interesting from an analytical point of view is the second type of agent, those who were directly in the Rothschild employ. Very often these were individuals who had been clerks for a number of years in one of the Rothschild houses and were therefore regarded as trustworthy. They were then sent to establish themselves in locations which the Rothschilds deemed important enough to have their own representation. By far the most important quality of every agent was loyalty. If it became apparent that an agent also supplied competitors with information, he was very quickly cut loose.

Far less important was that an agent knew the language of his adopted country. Many agents threw themselves into linguistically very cold waters and survived, at least initially, only with the help of a translator. The Rothschilds usually put more emphasis on the general business skills of their selected confidants and that they were able to move smoothly in society, since a good deal of the information they had to acquire came through formal or informal social contacts. Lucrative new business ventures could be gained in particular in noble circles – very often identical with political power – where etiquette was an important prerequisite for admission. It was not all that important for an agent to have specific knowledge of trading in certain goods or dealing with stocks which were common in his designated location. Many agents' letters are full of descriptions of new markets or complicated stock exchange deals, claiming that the representatives were slowly beginning to understand how things worked. This was on the job training without the employers being able to exercise any real control over their representatives, which required a particularly large amount of trust.

How extensive was this communication network? In the Rothschild Archive, there are 143 holdings called 'Agents Correspondence'. Approximately 100 of these were primarily business partners and three to four dozens were agents in the truer sense of the word. The majority of these people were German or British, occasionally Germans who had immigrated to Great Britain. Sometimes agents took over the nationality of their place of work. After all, Mayer Amschel Rothschild & Söhne was a German company, and the Frankfurt house had a large amount of clerks who were also posted around to serve in other houses.

How about ethnicity as selection criteria? Anthropologists say that ethnicity has a great influence on how we judge other people's trustworthiness. That is how they explain the continuing success of tightly knit business networks of, for example, Muslim-Arab merchants in East India in the nineteenth and twentieth centuries and of course the centuries' old predominance of Jews in European finance. Given the high proportion of Jews in European finance in the nineteenth century and given that the Rothschilds never wavered in their commitment to their own Jewishness and put great emphasis on supporting Jewish causes, one would expect that the network consisted predominantly of Jews. Certainly it would have been easy to find qualified and trustworthy Jewish agents for all or at least most locations in Europe. However, during the entire period of investigation, less than 40 per cent of all the agents were Jews. Given the high proportion of Jews in European finance, that figure is particularly low. There is a reason for that which almost suggests that the directors of N.M. Rothschild had read some management literature or they have foreseen some of the classical sociological theories of the twentieth century with remarkable clarity.

An information network which operates in a multi-ethnic world can only be successful if it is not based on one ethnicity. Why? Members of a particularly defined group only obtain a certain kind, quantity and quality of information. Within an information network, so called 'strong ties', such as kinship, ethnicity or close friendship limit the information floating around in the network. The more 'weak ties' someone has to others, the greater is the variety of information he or she obtains. The theory of 'weak ties' has been formulated by the American sociologist Mark Granovetter in the 1970s and the Rothschild network proves its validity.[7] One can compare it to a party in which all the guests are from the same social background

---

7   M. Granovetter, 'The Strength of Weak Ties', in *American Journal of Sociology*, vol. 78, 1973, pp. 1360–80.

and the same field of occupation. Topics for discussion would be as limited as the quantity of information exchanged.

This does not mean, however, that there were no strong ties in the Rothschild information network. In particular a fair number of agents were related to the Rothschild family, usually in a minor way and later in their careers, but apart from that the network was formed in a way a consultant of the twenty-first century would recommend it. It was a comparatively loose and predominantly uniplex network of relations. Uniplex means that not all the participants in the network knew each other and that between pairs of actors usually only one relationship existed, a business one. The opposite would have been a multiplex network in which there were strings of parallel relations between the individual actors. It can be argued that this structure of the net, and in particular its openness with regard to ethnicity, was an important condition for its success.

What kind of relationship existed between the Rothschilds and their agents? Probably the dominant characteristic here was that the Rothschilds generally gave agents a lot of room to manoeuvre. They were not expected to slavishly follow orders but to judge for themselves how best to serve the interests of the bank. After all they knew local circumstances and markets better than the principals in London. Agents were constantly moving to explore new business opportunities and the letters to London are full of suggestions for innovative ventures. Frequently, agents also contradicted or at least partially corrected Rothschild orders and opinions, if they judged that local conditions merited a different approach. Conflicts were very infrequent, given the number of agents and the scale of the operations. If, as happened occasionally, agents were attacked by the Rothschilds, they seldom complained openly about having been mistreated in their letters to London. Replies and defences were worded very carefully. For all agents it was paramount that the relationship was not permanently damaged. Overall, the network functioned without any major flaws and it was remarkably stable, since agents usually stayed with the Rothschilds for very long periods, often their lifetime.

This contradicts a postulation of network theory, which says that a uniplex information network with a comparatively low level of social control among the individual members usually sees plenty of trouble, since actors are not emphasizing conformity and are not seeking compromises. Therefore such a network would be potentially more unstable than a multiplex network in which actors were more interested in keeping up good relations. But the Rothschild network was extremely stable and also stable for generations. Why? It seems that the decisive reason for that was that all the agents had an overwhelming interest to maintain good relations to the most important banking dynasty of their times.

This becomes even more understandable if we ask how agents were actually paid. Many were not paid at all, or only received allowances out of which they also had to pay their expenses. I have not been able to find a contract between the Rothschilds and an agent which would specify any terms. Occasionally an agent was asking for an allowance to be topped up, mostly in order to be able to afford more representative lodgings or more generous hospitality for business clients. Generally agents traded for their own account and participated in business deals the Rothschilds conducted, and that is how they made their money. They used the infrastructure at their disposal and in particular the prestige a connection to the Rothschilds carried. Obviously that was fine with the Rothschilds, as long as the 'agency costs' were kept low.[8] That does not only mean direct expenditure for agents but means in particular money that the Rothschilds could lose if their agents were working primarily with their own financial well-being in mind. This was and is a perennial problem of all business representations. If one regards, for example, the various European trading companies, such as the Dutch East India Company, they were constantly complaining of enormous agency costs, since they could not control the agents in far-away places appropriately. The Rothschilds complained about this only very rarely.

④ The Rothschilds had a large and well-functioning information network at their disposal. Was that the reason for their enormous business success in the nineteenth century? If one follows some of the myriad myths that exist about the Rothschilds that was certainly the case. They were the best-informed people in Europe and had spies at all relevant European ministries and courts. They used top-notch and secretive transmission techniques, such as carrier pigeons or had the most daring captains of canal boats in their employ, who carried vital messages through the worst storms, so that the Rothschilds could make a killing at the stock exchange. Finally, an extremely efficient courier system at the exclusive disposal of Rothschilds is cited to explain an information advantage.

However, all these explanations, conjured up by contemporaries as well as by historians and publicists until the present day, have little or no basis in reality. The Rothschilds were well informed, but normally they did not receive information earlier than everybody else.

The Rothschilds did use carrier pigeons and had their own canal boats, but they were not the only ones and that did not necessarily give them the edge over competitors. This can clearly be ascertained from an investigation of the Rothschild family correspondence, i.e. the letters which were exchanged between the directors of the various houses on an almost daily basis. They contain numerous complaints that a courier arrived later than that of a competitor or that everybody in town had information while Rothschilds did not. At the same time, the Rothschilds and their agents were careful about investing money in expensive couriers and for at least 80 per cent of their letters they used the normal postal services or also couriers of other people.

And when it comes to the issue of receiving information faster than other people, one has to ask, which other people? In the first quarter of the nineteenth century, for example, the London Rothschilds were certainly better informed than the British government about political events on the continent. But that was hardly surprising given the chaotic organization of the King's/Queen's Messenger Service, which was overhauled only in the mid-1820s. Until then on average merely 34 Messengers crossed the channel per year.[9]

The advent of the electric telegraph was seen with suspicion by the Rothschilds and several offers in the 1850s by Julius Reuter, the pioneering news agency

---

8   For a good historical example of agency costs that went out of control see: A.M. Carlos and N. Stephen, 'Agency Problems in Early Chartered Companies. The Case of the Hudson's Bay Company', in *Journal of Economic History*, vol. 50, 1990, pp. 853–75.

9   See V. Wheeler-Holohan, *The History of the King's Messengers* (London, 1935).

proprietor, to supply the bank with exclusive news were rejected.[10] The Rothschilds were not keen on modernizing their information network in a technical sense, since speed was not the key to being well informed but rather the precision, the reliability and most importantly the exclusiveness of the information.

How was that achieved? First of all, Rothschild agents were, not least through their connection to the leading banking dynasty, regarded as high powered information brokers at European courts and ministries. Those individuals in powerful positions who gave information to agents also received some from them and thus became part of the network on a lower level. The quality of the agents and their connections was decisive for the quality of the information. But that alone cannot explain the strength of the information network. For that we have to look beyond the agents and focus on the Rothschild family, which was firmly entrenched in four, if we include Naples, five European countries. The Rothschild houses in London, Paris and Vienna were located in political and commercial centres. Frankfurt was an important European trading and finance spot. Everywhere family members received direct information from the highest political levels. Salomon von Rothschild in Vienna, for example, was a constant visitor to Prince Metternich and shared the information he gained from him very readily with his brothers and nephews. In my opinion, it is this internal information network, in conjunction with a well-oiled and high powered group of agents, which guaranteed the Rothschilds the sort of information they could utilize to their best advantage for their business ventures. In other words, the most important agents of the Rothschilds were other Rothschilds. Between both networks strong synergy effects existed.

The family information network has not been researched extensively until now, because until the 1850s the Rothschilds used almost exclusively *Judendeutsch*, a kind of German written in Hebrew characters, in their correspondence. In particular in hand-written form, this is very difficult to penetrate. These highly informative private letters which reveal how this financial empire functioned, demonstrate that a combination of hard work, excellent connections and sometimes pure luck was responsible for the Rothschild success. However, the very existence of these letters in a Jewish script prompted not only contemporaries but also historians later on to claim that the Rothschilds used a 'secret language' to communicate important decisions. In reality all Jewish business competitors of the time were easily able to read such letters, and also the offices responsible for intercepting mail in many European states had specialists who were well trained to comprehend Hebrew script.[11] This fact is all the more frustrating for the modern historian.[12]

---

10 D. Read, *The History of Reuters* (Oxford, second ed. 1999), pp. 17–18.

11 F. Stix, 'Zur Geschichte und Organisation der Wiener Geheimen Ziffernkanzlei. Von ihren Anfängen bis zum Jahre 1848', in *Mitteilungen des Österreichischen Instituts für Geschichtsforschung*, vol. 51, 1937, pp. 131–60.

12 The Rothschild Archive is currently undertaking a major transcription and translation project to make these letters available for researchers' use.

PART III
Modernization of Banking in Sweden, the Netherlands, and Greece

The Emergence of Joint-Stock Companies during the Industrial Breakthrough in Sweden

Oskar Broberg

In this chapter the joint-stock company is regarded as a decisive organizational innovation of the nineteenth century. Through the joint-stock company productive assets were made more impersonal and the importance of financial markets rose. The financial markets channelled resources to the new expanding sectors of the industrialized economy. Thus, the joint-stock company reinforced a Schumpeterian process of creative destruction which was a vital feature of the modernization process.

Modernization is a complex concept. In the present context modernization is broadly understood as the transformation from a traditional, rural, agrarian society to a secular, urban, industrial society. To be more specific, one aspect of this transformation is highlighted in the chapter – the increased importance of impersonal property relations. It is argued that impersonal property relations, manifested in the joint-stock company, furthered the industrialization process, which in turn reinforced a broader process of modernization. Two aspects of the joint-stock company are seen as particularly important – firstly, the division of ownership into transferable shares and secondly, the concept of limited liability. In the chapter 'joint-stock company' and 'corporation' will be used interchangeably, both refer to a firm with limited liability and ownership divided into shares.

During the past 30 years institutional theorists have given a more nuanced version of the picture, inherited from earlier neoclassical theory, of firms as profit maximizing abstractions. New institutional theory has shown how the actions of firms are influenced by the surrounding institutional framework, for example through the form of economic organization chosen by firms.[1] The institutional framework – in this context the legislation on joint-stock companies – and its process of change therefore becomes of central importance in understanding the modernization of society.

What importance has earlier research attached to Swedish incorporation? The first generation of economic historians – writing in the 1940s – mentioned the joint-stock company in passing, but did not emphasize its importance for the industrialization process.[2] This picture dominated the field for a long time. In his 1996 article Gustafsson argues that Heckscher, Gårdlund and Montgomery had been

---

1   T. Eggertsson, *Economic behavior and institutions* (Cambridge, 1990).

2   See E. Heckscher, *Svenskt arbete och liv* (Stockholm, 1941); T. Gårdlund, *Industrialismens Samhälle* (Stockholm, 1942); and A. Montgomery, *Industrialismens genombrott i Sverige* (Stockholm, 1947).

too focused on the 1870s. Instead, Gustafsson argues, it was during the late 1890s that the Swedish growth accelerated and consequently that it was the period around the turn of the century that ought to be labelled the 'industrial breakthrough' of Sweden. Gustafsson writes that 'during this phase modern business organization – reaping the benefits of economies of scale and integration – as well as joint-stock companies and developed banking also saw the light'.[3] Both Magnusson and Schön shares Gustafsson's view, in their respective textbooks on Swedish economic development. Schön is most explicit, linking the joint-stock company to the modernization of the Swedish financial market. Schön argues that this was of great importance for the rise of large industries from 1890s onwards.[4]

The object of this study is to re-examine this issue from two perspectives: on the one hand to review the research on the incorporation of Swedish business, on the other hand to add new empirical data to the discussion. Briefly, the questions at issue are: (1) How did the legal framework change during the emergence of joint-stock companies? (2) When did joint-stock companies become the dominating form of business organization in Sweden? (3) How does Sweden fit into a European perspective, with regard to the development of joint-stock companies?

The paper starts with a theoretical discussion of some central concepts for the study of joint-stock companies. The second part describes joint-stock company formation during the nineteenth century, internationally and in Sweden, with the focus on the institutional framework. In the third part of the chapter research on Swedish joint-stock companies is reviewed. In the fourth part I present new data on incorporation in Sweden. Finally there are conclusions.

II

As a point of departure for this inquiry into business incorporation in Sweden a contractual approach will be presented. Starting with Berle & Means and Ronald Coase a new approach to the issue of business organization emerged in the 1930s. As Berle & Means notes the first decades of the twentieth century were not only a time of organizational change, but also the time when American society as whole transformed its relation to private property. Berle & Means denote this change as the breakthrough for the 'corporate system' – a process propelled by the financial system:

> It was apparent to any thoughtful observer that the American corporation had ceased to be a private business device and had become an institution. In 1928, when the project was launched, the financial machinery was developing so rapidly as to indicate that we were in the throes of a revolution in our institution of private property.[5]

---

3   B. Gustafsson, 'The industrial revolution in Sweden', in M. Teich, B. Gustafsson and R. Porter (eds), *The industrial revolution in national context : Europe and the USA*, (New York, 1996), p. 216.

4   L. Magnusson, *Sveriges ekonomiska historia* (Stockholm, 1997); L. Schön, *En modern svensk ekonomisk historia. Tillväxt och omvandling under två sekel* (Stockholm, 2000).

5   A.A. Berle and G. Means, *The Modern Corporation and Private Property* (New York, 1932), p. V.

Berle and Means concluded that the growth of the size of the corporation, which could be well explained by the industrialization process, gave rise to important challenges in business organization. The problem, they argued, was that the sheer size of modern corporations drove a wedge between owners and managers with the result that 'professional corporate managers tend to be agents out of control'. Later this problem was formulated as the problem of agency costs.

A few years later Coase raised the fundamental question why firms existed at all? His answer was that the costs of coordination – later named transaction costs – determine the extent to which firms are formed. This answer put the focus on the relation between market participants and the costs associated with transactions.[6] Taken together these two contributions gave birth to the notion of looking at business from a contractual point of view, arguing that it is worthwhile to look upon a firm as a set of contracts. The driving force behind the establishment of these contracts is that of coping with transaction and agency costs. This view was formalized by Jensen and Meckling in their 1976 article.[7] Following this tradition Eggertsson discusses the different forms of economic organization and discerns the pros and cons of each type.

Both proprietorships and partnerships are characterized by small agency problems because the residual claimants and the ultimate decision makers are the same. This is particularly important in economic activities where monitoring is difficult and the long run result depends heavily on output quality – for example in care-intensive activities. On the other hand this close relation between ownership and control creates potential problems which may hamper the firm's level of investment. Firstly, the horizon problem arises due to the fact that an owner's preferred consumption pattern may not be in line with the investment needs of the company. Secondly, a low level of investment may also be the result of risk-averse strategy due to the diversification problem, which arises because a large share of the owner's both physical and human wealth is invested in the firm. To some extent the problems of horizon and diversification can better be dealt with in a partnership than in a proprietorship. In a partnership it is easier to raise capital in order to achieve economies of scale. However, the risk that capital-intensive investments that are profitable by the market criterion never come about in proprietorships and partnerships still remains.

In a closed corporation, where residual claimants enjoy limited liability, the risk of under-investment is partly solved. Individuals can invest the amount that they are willing to risk, but not more, in a venture by buying shares in the corporation. The arising agency problem is restrained mainly by the fact that the entrepreneur and the people investing in the firm are socially related individuals.

Finally, in the open corporation the full potential of impersonal ownership is let loose. Only the open corporation has the capacity of raising capital on the capital market. This is made possible through the use of limited liability. The use of the capital market creates a continuous market evaluation of the firm which encourages managers to undertake risky, but profitable, investments. The capital

---

6   R. Coase, 'The Nature of the Firm', in *Economica*, vol. 4, 1937.

7   M.C. Jensen and W.H. Meckling, 'Theory of the Firm: Managerial Behavior, Agency Costs and Ownership Structure', in *Journal of Financial Economics*, vol. 3, 1976.

market also opens up the door to entrepreneurs who are neither rich themselves nor know investors personally. At the same time the agency problems are greatest in an open corporation, since the owners and the managers are distinctly separated. It is therefore vital for an open corporation to find strategies to cope with these problems. Firstly, contractual devices are developed to constrain opportunist behaviour. These can be controlling, such as auditing committees and budget restrictions, or more positive incentive programmes, where compensation to managers is linked to the corporation's performance. Secondly, competition in various forms can help to constrain opportunist behaviour. The capital market's continuous market evaluation puts pressure on managers to prioritize the firm's performance. If managers fail to do so the firm will face problems in raising capital, and consequently the threat of being taken over by competitors increases. Furthermore the competition on the job market for business managers also puts pressure in the same direction. The contractual devices and the competitive forces work jointly to reduce agency problems in the open corporation. Eggertsson points out distinctly the theoretical advantage of the open corporation compared to the other forms of economic organization that has been mentioned:

The relative advantage of this form of organization lies in the structure of residual claims, which encourages large-scale risky investments. The common stocks of the open corporation, the least restricted residual claims in general use, minimize the potential conflict between *utility maximization by owners* (shareholdes) and maximization of the *market value of the firm*.[8]

Obviously transaction costs are not the only factor determining which form of organization entrepreneurs choose; for example, the role of state intervention in the form of taxes and subsidies is important. However, Eggertsson's conclusion is that even in a *laissez-faire* economy different forms of economic organization would prevail.

Two things stand out as important in relation to modernization. Firstly, the advantage of raising capital and undertaking risky investments should encourage the development of corporations in a period of industrialization. With a Schumpeterian interpretation of the contractual approach this would imply that the unique contractual devices of the corporation let loose the 'gales of creative destruction'. In other words, corporations *further* modernization. Secondly, the emergence of the corporation as the dominating form of business organization strengthens the institution of impersonal property relations. This would imply that corporations *are* modernization. In short, incorporation and modernization are interdependent processes reinforcing each other through the rise of an industrialized economy.

III

The fully fledged joint-stock company, with limited liability, enters history as a legal entity from the mid nineteenth century. However the pre-history stretches back several hundred years. Usually the beginning of joint-stock companies is associated

---

8　Eggertson, *Economic behavior and institutions*, p. 183.

with the formation of English and Dutch merchant companies in the sixteenth century – which in turn had its roots in earlier federations of merchants such as the English 'Merchants of the Staple'. An important driving force behind the new form of organization was the new commercial possibilities which necessitated that venture capital could be raised on a larger scale and for longer periods of time than before.[9] From the beginning the most important aspect of the royal charters were the right to sue and be sued, in other words that the company was a legal entity. Shares in the successful companies were also traded. Limited liability was not encoded in law until the nineteenth century, but in practice small shareholders enjoyed limited liability since it would be too cumbersome to sue each shareholder individually.[10] This important feature of merchant companies was also true for smaller countries. In Denmark, for example, merchant companies with royal charter were set up after the Dutch model.[11]

Before the first joint-stock company law, royal charters, granted for each company, constituted the institutional framework. These charters were usually connected with the power of the state, such as the granting of trade monopolies, and the joint-stock companies were not considered as an alternative for business in general. At the end of the eighteenth century this began to change. However, in the beginning of the nineteenth century the view still dominated that the use of limited liability needed to be restricted to public utility companies, for example the building and maintaining of turnpikes and canals.[12]

In contrast with Europe, where incorporation followed national borders, the incorporation of American business followed state borders. In general the United States was in the forefront of corporate legislation. It was the states of New York and Massachusetts that paved the way in general corporation legislation during the first decades of the nineteenth century. By 1840 general incorporation legislation was in place in most states of the United States.[13]

Scepticism towards joint-stock companies endured for a long time. The nineteenth century developed into a long institutional tug-of-war which ran parallel with the industrialization process in most European countries. The first European legislation of importance was the French 'Code de Commerce' from 1807. This was not a joint-stock law in the proper sense, but more general legislation on the organization of business. Another important prerequisite for coming events was the English upheaval of the Bubble Act in 1825. In Holland the first joint-stock law was passed in 1838.

9   C.P. Kindleberger, *A Financial History of Western Europe* (London, 1984).

10   G. Todd, 'Some Aspects of Joint Stock Companies 1844–1900', in *Economic History Review*, vol. 4, 1932.

11   J. Rendboe, 'De to forste danske aktieselskabslove af 1917 og 1930 – var de påvirket af intressegrupper?', in *Erhvervshistorisk Årbog 1998–98* (Århus, 1999).

12   O. Handlin and M.F. Handlin, 'Origins of the American Business Corporation', in *Journal of Economic History*, vol. 5, 1945. See also P. Cottrell, *Industrial Finance 1830–1914* (London, 1980).

13   R.E. Seavoy, *The Origins of the American Business Corporation 1784–1855* (London, 1982).

The Dutch kept the royal charter but stayed true to its liberal tradition and kept the regulation short, leaving much room for individual design of the articles.[14]

Contrary to the gradual process up until the 1850s, events took a sharp turn in England with the new legislation of 1855 and 1862. The Companies Act of 1862 marked the consolidation of joint-stock company legislation, when incorporation became a matter of registration instead of royal charter. Furthermore limited liability was secured in law. These events in England also changed the situation in France, strengthening the forces pushing for economic liberalization, and in 1867 a modern joint-stock company law came into place. In Germany joint-stock companies were rare before the *Miteigentümergesetz* in 1851. This law was followed by a more modern company law in 1870, which really marked the beginning of incorporation in Germany.[15]

Several semi-peripheral countries soon followed in the footsteps of France and Germany. During the 1870s and 1880s joint-stock legislation was passed in Belgium (1873), Hungary (1875), Switzerland (1881), Italy (1883), Spain (1885) and Portugal (1888). In Scandinavia both Denmark and Norway held onto a liberal interpretation of the old legislation – as an effect the first complete joint-stock company legislation was passed in Norway in 1910 and in Denmark in 1917. However, in both countries joint-stock companies were well established during the latter half of the nineteenth century. In Finland the first law was passed in 1864, based on charter. The legislation was then modernized in the 1890s.[16]

As has been shown, legislation on joint-stock companies followed in most Western European countries during the second half of the nineteenth century. The laws differed in detail due to the diversity of institutional landscapes, but looking at this process in a historical perspective the similarities on central issues seem more important. The most salient features seem to be the establishment of: the corporation as a legal entity, the right to use limited liability, ownership through transferable shares, the definition of the corporation's bodies and the fact that the new legislation made it easier than before to start a joint-stock company.

The starting point for a history of Swedish joint-stock companies is debatable. From the legal point of view the passing of the new legislation of 1848 would be a natural start, but there were several companies which started well before 1848 which operated more or less as joint-stock companies. In his doctoral thesis Johan Hagströmer collected what was known about these companies.[17] Hagströmer found 38 companies, chartered between 1607 and 1842. An overall trend was the dominance of projects with high risks, such as trans-continental merchant companies during the seventeenth and eighteenth centuries, and capital intensive projects such as canal

---

14 E. Bergelmer, *Redogörelse för det viktigaste af den utländska lagstiftningen om aktiebolag* (Stockholm, 1907). See also Handlin, 'Origins of the American Business Corporation'.

15 C.E. Freedeman, *Joint-Stock Enterprise in France 1807–1867* (Chapel Hill, 1979). See also Cottrell, *Industrial Finance 1830–1914*, and Kindleberger, *A Financial History of Western Europe*.

16 See Bergelmer, *Redogörelse för det viktigaste af den utländska lagstiftningen om aktiebolag*, Freedeman, *Joint-Stock Enterprise in France 1807–1867*, and Rendboe, 'De to forste danske aktieselskabslove af 1917 og 1930'.

17 J. Hagströmer, *Om aktiebolag enligt svensk rätt* (Stockholm, 1872).

companies in the first half of the nineteenth century. The state had a prominent role in the formation of these early companies since the charters were often complemented with monopolies of different kinds. Limited liability was not explicit in the articles of association, but Hagströmer argues that limited liability was implicit in many cases. To his list of companies Hagströmer also adds some twenty or thirty companies formed in the nineteenth century which were not chartered by the goverment but had limited liability written into their articles of association. Carl-Axel Nilsson argues that these companies' legal status was unsure and that their situation was brought into the debate on the new legislation:

> The creation of the law of 1848 must be considered against the background of the position of the unchartered corporations. Their legal right to limit liability of the shareholders was unclear and that seems to have created problems for the courts. The law came into being to remedy this uncertainty and to establish clearly the conditions under which the limited liability functioned.[18]

At the Riksdag of 1844–45 a motion was proposed by W.F. Dalman for new legislation on joint-stock companies. The motion was a reproduction of the French regulations for 'sociétés anonymes'. After minor changes during the legislative process the motion resulted in the joint-stock company law of 1848. The law stated that all joint-stock companies were to be chartered by the government and in return the principle of limited liability was legally established. In order to aquire this status the company's capital was to be divided into shares and the company had to register at the local court. The court, in turn, was obliged to announce the articles of the company in public papers. Compared with its successors the law was not particularly detailed, but gave considerable room for the founders to design the articles of assocation according to their will – it was, for example, up to the founders to decide whether the company would issue bearer shares or inscribed shares. In the law of 1848 there was included a right for the state to grant or refuse the chartering of companies on the ground of public benefit. This was a legacy from the old suspicion of joint-stock companies. In practice, though, this was not enforced.[19] As Nilsson writes:

> The conclusion is that the State, in accordance with the law of 1848, certainly had the option of testing in each separate case whether the benefits of the law should be given to a company organization, but this right was exploited to only a very limited extent. The procedure became largely a matter of registration.[20]

The law of 1848 remained more or less the same for almost fifty years. Only two minor changes came about – in 1879 it became required that also the members of the board should be registered with the court and in 1887 a law was passed that transfered this registration to a special register dealing with all types of companies.[21]

---

18 C.-A. Nilsson, 'Business incorporations in Sweden 1849–1896', in *Economy and History*, vol. 2, 1959, p. 40.

19 Hagströmer, *Om aktiebolag enligt svensk rätt*. See also A. Koersner, *Om aktiebok, inregistrering av aktier och aktieförvärvsrätt* (Stockholm, 1929).

20 Nilsson, 'Business incorporations in Sweden 1849–1896', p. 43.

21 S.O. Arlebäck, *Från ägarmakt under ansvar till företagsledarmakt u p a* (Lund, 1995).

During the 1880s a commission was set up to analyse the need for a new joint-stock company law. The legislative process was influenced by the contemporary international debates and the law of 1895 marked the transition from the system of chartering to a system of registration. From 1 January 1897 all joint-stock companies had to register at the newly established department of patents and registration (PRV). This meant that the issue of becoming a joint-stock company was no longer the potential public benefits but rather the legality of the articles of association. This shift opened the door to more detailed regulation.[22] One example was the question of capital requirements, which had not been addressed in 1848 – but created quite some debate during the legislative process in the 1890s. In the end the decision was that minimum capital was to be set at 5,000 kronor and shares could be issued at nominal values at a minimum of 10 kronor per share. If, however, the company's capital exceeded 10,000 kronor then the minimum nominal value of the shares was set at 50 kronor.[23]

Despite the more detailed regulations, the procedure of starting a joint-stock company was made easier. When the law was made more detailed the articles of association did not need to be as specific as before. In contractual terms there were economies of scale in moving more details from each company to the standard form of company which all companies had to comply with under the new law. In retrospect the law of 1895 seems to be the point at which the Swedish legislation on joint-stock companies reaches its modern form. The succeeding changes in 1910, 1944 and 1975 were not distinguished by radical initiatives but rather concentrated on technical details.[24]

In 1905 a commission was set up to analyse the possible need for changes in the law of 1895. The commission made a thorough investigation of the different laws in European countries. The commission's general conclusion was that there was no need for wholly new legislation, but that the Swedish legislation lagged behind with regard to companies' duty to disclose information, and that the protection of minorities in the Swedish legislation needed to be strengthened. In the public debate some criticism was heard. Fear was raised that the commission had gone too far in the protection of minorities, leading to an oppression of the majority.[25] However, the commission's report formed the basis for the government bill of 1910 on a new joint-stock company law. Due to the increase in technical details the result was that the new law was almost doubled in size. This trend continued in 1944 (see Table 8.1).

During the 1920s and 30s there was an ongoing international adjustment of company law, spurred by the changing conditions of the industrialized economies. The use of joint-stock companies had spread throughout the economy, and the industrialization process was favouring increasingly bigger companies. This led to

---

22 Arlebäck, *Från ägarmakt under ansvar till företagsledarmakt u p a*.

23 Gårdlund, *Industrialismens Samhälle*. See also S. Skarstedt, *Allmänna aktiebolagslagen* (Stockholm, 1930).

24 J. Macey, *Svensk aktiebolagsrätt i omvandling – en rättsekonomisk analys* (Stockholm, 1993).

25 Affärsvärlden, *Den nya aktiebolagslagen* (Stockholm, 1908).

Table 8.1   The increasing size of the joint-stock legislation in Sweden

Year	Total number of sections
1848	15
1895	81
1910	141
1944	228

Source: Arlebäck, Från ägarmakt under ansvar till företagsledarmakt u p a, pp. 37, 43.

new legislation on joint-stock companies, in Holland 1928, England 1929, Denmark 1930, Switzerland 1936 and Germany 1937.[26] In Sweden the need for similar adjustments was highlighted by the crash of Ivar Kreuger's financial empire in 1932. In the aftermath of this crisis a commission was appointed in 1933 to a revision of joint-stock company law. Once again the duty of disclosure was at the centre of attention. It was argued that, due to Kreuger's ability to manipulate the information flow, Swedish financial markets had been duped into taking much greater risks than were perceived or desired. The commission's conclusion was that regulations were needed in new areas. In the bill that was presented in 1941 there was included detailed regulation on consolidated financial statements, fusions and how responsibilities were to be divided between a company's different governing bodies. In the end the law of 1944 did not include anything fundamentally new, but it was nevertheless a very extensive and detailed revision of the earlier law.[27]

To conclude, during the nineteenth century joint-stock legislation was passed in most Western European countries, including the US. There were national differences, but these were more at the level of details. The Swedish case was representative. The joint-stock law of 1848 was the first step and the joint-stock law of 1895 marked the transition to a modern corporate type of legislation.

IV

Research on the development of joint-stock companies in Sweden started with Hagströmer's dissertation in 1872. This was also the first contribution from a legal point of view, one which has been followed later by several other studies of the relevant legislation. These findings have been described in the previous section of this chapter. I will now turn to the economic research that has been done on the founding of joint-stock companies.

It has been has been pointed out that joint-stock companies, up until the 1890s, were mainly founded to establish limited liability for their owners. According to this view it was not until the turn of the century that the aspect of capital raising became

---

26 Statens Offentliga Utredningar, SoU 1941:9 Lagberedningens förslag till lag om AB (Stockholm, 1941).

27 Arlebäck, Från ägarmakt under ansvar till företagsledarmakt u p a. See also Affärsvärlden, Den nya aktiebolagslagen (Stockholm, 1941) pp. 25–6.

a vital issue in the founding of joint-stock companies in Sweden.[28] This view is shared by Carl-Axel Nilsson, who has produced the most comprehensive study of the founding of joint-stock companies in Sweden in the latter half of the nineteenth century. His data on incorporation show a marked increase from 1865 to 1874 and then a stagnating phase until the 1890s. During the whole period, 1849–96, industry was the dominant sector, accounting for roughly 60 per cent of the total number of incorporations. During the first ten years textiles were the largest subgroup in industry. The rest of the period was dominated by incorporation in the metal and lumber industries. The communication and transport sector accounted for roughly 20 per cent and the remaining 20 per cent consisted mainly of incorporation in trade and service. Though thorough, Nilsson's study is based only on the number of incorporations and not on the amount of capital raised.[29]

Jörberg studied the distribution of ownership in Swedish industry 1872–1912. Depending on which variable is chosen the dominance for joint-stock companies, over proprietor and partnerships, varies from the 1870s to the 1900s. Even in the 1870s the joint-stock companies dominated output. By the 1880s a majority of the employees in industry worked for a joint-stock company and during the first years of the new century more than 50 per cent of industrial establishments were joint-stock companies. Jörberg concludes that it was the boom of the 1870s that marked the real breakthrough of the corporate form in Swedish industry.[30]

Wohlin collected data on incorporation during the period 1894–1904 and demonstrated a strong correlation between the numbers of companies founded and the state of the market. Wohlin states that the number of incorporations was larger than in earlier decades and also that incorporation took place in smaller industries, where joint-stock companies had not been created before. The 1890s is usually viewed as the decade of industrial breakthrough in Sweden. Several researchers draw attention to the parallel surge in the formation of joint-stock companies. It is argued that an industrial breakthrough is propelled by expanding financial capitalism, which in turn needs the institution of the joint-stock company to function.[31]

The scope of this chapter is from the 1840s to the 1930s. For the later part of this period, after 1904, there is no comprehensive study of the size of incorporation. Dahmén has studied the industrial development of the interwar years, but he does not distinguish joint-stock companies from other firms.[32]

The bulk of earlier research on the incorporation of Swedish business has been centred on industry. As Andersson-Skog points outs a focus on the production process has characterized research in economics and economic-history since the 1930s.

28 Gårdlund, *Industrialismens Samhälle*, and Schön, *En modern svensk ekonomisk historia.*

29 Nilsson, 'Business incorporations in Sweden 1849–1896'.

30 L. Jörberg, *Growth and Fluctuations* (Stockholm, 1961).

31 See for example J. Glete, *Ägande och industriell omvandling* (Stockholm, 1987) and J. Jörnmark, *Skogen, staten och kapitalisterna* (Lund, 2004).

32 E. Dahmén, *Svensk industriell företagarverksamhet. Kausalanalys av den industriella utvecklingen 1919–1939* (Stockholm, 1950).

Andersson-Skog argues that this has led to other perspectives being neglected, for example, issues related to distribution.[33]

To sum up, earlier research has clearly shown that incorporation in Swedish industry took off during the decades after the legislation of 1848 and at the end of the century joint-stock companies dominated as the organizational form in industry. However, other areas of economic activity are much less studied. This is especially true for the first decades of the twentieth century, and there are reasons to believe that these sectors were also an important aspect of the Swedish modernization process.

V

In order to shed new light on the incorporation process a series has been constructed of the foundation of joint-stock companies from 1850 to 1938. The data has been collected from various sources, all of which are based on either official records or official statistical compilations. For the period 1850–81 the work of Van der Hagen and Cederschiöld has been used – a putting together of the charters that the government granted to all new corporations.[34] For the period 1882–93 official statistics have been used.[35] For the period 1894–1912 the archives of the Department of Patents and Registration have been used.[36] As mentioned before the legislation of 1895 obliged all joint-stock companies to register with PRV, which makes it possible to construct a series of all corporations founded each year. Beginning in 1913 the official statistics were modernized and for the period 1913–38 official statistics have once again been used.[37]

The series includes year of start, amount of share-capital and a division into four categories by type of corporation. The year of start refers to either when the company was registered by the government (1850–93 and 1913–38) or when the articles of association were approved (1894–1912). This is of course a defect, but working with PRV's register shows that it is of minor importance. The four categories that have been used are Industry, Transport, Trade and Other – the last category includes companies such as finance, real estate and service.

The series does not include new issues of shares, because this data is not available before 1895. New issues are naturally important in order to understand the full potential of the 'corporate system', especially for open corporations where new issues are often used in phases of expansion or reconstruction. For example in the late 1920s, new issues of shares in existing companies were an important part

33 L. Andersson-Skog, 'Omvandlingens sekel' in L. Andersson-Skog and O. Krantz (eds), *Omvandlingens sekel. Perspektiv på ekonomi och samhälle i 1900-talets Sverige* (Lund, 2002), p. 27.

34 A.L. Van der Hagen and S. Cederschiöld, *Svenska Aktiebolag med begränsad ansvarighet 1848–1881* (Stockholm, 1882).

35 Bidrag till Sveriges Officiella Statistik (BiSos), Kungl. Maj:ts Befallningshafvandes Femårsberättelser 1881–1895, serie H [Official Statistics].

36 Riksarkivet [The National Archives of Sweden], Stockholm: Patent- och Registreringsverket [henceforth PRV]; Bolagsbyrån, DIAA.

37 Statistisk Årsbok 1913–40 [Statistical Yearbook].

of Ivar Kreuger's strategy. The role of new issues, in the period 1895–1938, will be investigated in a follow-up study.

From the data available it is not possible to determine whether incorporations originate from newly created firms or whether the firms had existed as partner/ proprietorship before. The focus of this chapter is, however, on the incorporation process as such – not on measuring overall business activity. Furthermore, the incorporation of already existing firms was usually done in connection with other changes in the firms' structure – such as reconstructions or expansions.[38]

Figure 8.1 shows the number of incorporations each year for the whole period investigated. Six periods can be distinguished. It is clear that the legislation of 1848 did not immediately result in widespread incorporation and the first period, 1850–64, may be characterized as a slow beginning. During the second period, 1865–74, incorporation gained speed. Most likely this was due to a combination of the fact that the corporate form had become better known and of the boom in the early 1870s. The third period, 1875–95, was characterized by a stagnating number of incorporations and an even falling number during the recession years of the late 1870s. During the fourth period, 1896–1912, incorporation was surging. In 1894 183 joint-stock companies were founded, compared with 814 in 1907 and 886 in 1911. This increase coincided with the expansion of the Swedish economy known as the 'industrial breakthrough'. After the peak in 1911 incorporations fell back. The fifth period, 1912–21, may be characterized as a turbulent time. It is not a daring interpretation that this turbulence was a consequence of the overall economic climate. In the long perspective the period 1910–20 and the first years of the 1920s were the most turbulent times of the whole twentieth century. The sixth period, 1922–38, displays an interesting pattern. The Swedish interwar years are usually depicted as turbulent times, as in most other countries. Despite this, the number of incorporations remained surprisingly stable at around 1000 per year. In the deep depression of 1921–22 there were even more incorporations than there had been during the first 30 years, 1849–79, put together. Later in this chapter I will present other data that will help to interpret this pattern.

The data presented in Figure 8.1 can only reveal a crude pattern. Though this is clearly of importance to the questions at issue, it is necessary to disaggregate the series. In Table 8.2 the incorporations from 1850 to 1938 are presented for each category, as a percentage of the total number of incorporations (n). It is clear that industry dominated the incorporations during the first four periods. The transport sector achieved its largest share of incorporations during the second and third periods. This seems reasonable, taking into account that both railway transport and shipping were expanding rapidly during these decades. Incorporation in trading progressed during the nineteenth century, but the big surge began in 1913 and almost half of all incorporations thereafter originated from trade.

One important issue in this chapter is the connection between incorporation and the role of the financial markets in the modernization process. Given this approach it is of course vital not only to study the number of joint-stock companies founded, but also the amount of capital subscribed. Figure 8.2 shows the amount of subscribed

---

38 Nilsson, 'Business incorporations in Sweden 1849–1896'.

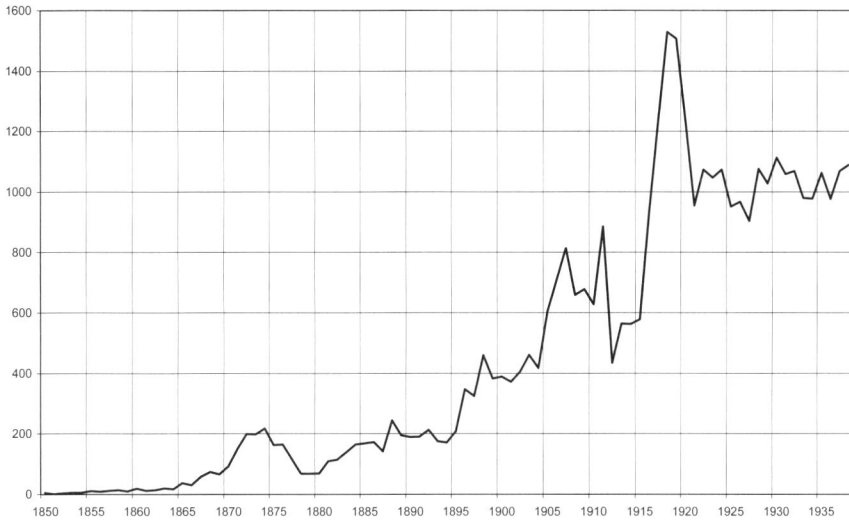

Source: Van der Hagen and Cederschiöld, *Svenska Aktiebolag med begränsad ansvarighet 1848–1881*. BiSos, 'Kungl. Maj:ts Befallningshafvandes Femårsberättelser 1881–1895'. Statistisk Årsbok. Patent- och Registreringsverket, 'Bolagsbyrån'. Data included in appendix.

Figure 8.1   Number of joint-stock companies founded each year, 1850–1938

Table 8.2   The distribution of incorporation 1850–1938, divided in four categories (%)

Year	Industry	Transport	Trade	Other	n
1850–1859	71	10	1	18	78
1860–1869	53	9	20	18	347
1870–1879	52	19	16	14	1438
1880–1889	52	16	10	22	1516
1890–1899	57	13	12	16	2660
1900–1909	52	8	19	21	5510
1910–1919	32	7	45	16	8857
1920–1929	29	5	51	16	10321
1930–1938	30	4	49	17	9397

Source: See Figure 8.1.

share-capital in the joint-stock companies founded, from 1850 to 1938. Figures 8.1 and 8.2 are in accordance with each other with respect to the general trends. Firstly, there is a peak in the 1870s. Secondly, there is an increase in subscribed capital from 1895 and onward. Thirdly there is a boom in 1918, followed by the bust of the early 1920s. In 1918 the total subscribed capital amounted to 597 million SEK.

However, there are some important differences between the two series. Firstly the differences between each year are greater in share capital than in the number of incorporations. This would imply that the founding of joint-stock companies was dependent on the state of the market. When this was good it was possible to attract larger amounts of capital and in a recession companies started with relatively less capital. In some cases single incorporations influenced the series significantly. The most obvious example was during the boom of 1907, when the subscribed share-capital was composed to 50 per cent by the merger of the leading sugar producers in Sweden. Likewise, in the 1850s and 1860s there was little incorporation in the 'Other' category, except for three major incorporations in the financial sector – two insurance companies and one bank. In 1870–71 the transport sector reached its peak, attracting 37 per cent of all new capital. The years following were, on the other hand, completely dominated by industry. Between 1873 and 1877 industry attracted 82 per cent of all new capital.

The other big difference between Figures 8.1 and 8.2 has to do with the depression of the 1920s. From the peak in 1918 the amount of subscribed capital fell back to about the same level as before the boom. Since the number of incorporations did not fall as much, this would imply that the average start-up company was smaller in the 1920s than during the decades before. This assumption is confirmed by Table 8.3, showing the average start-up capital 1850–1938. For each period in Table 8.3 the total amount of subscribed capital is added up and divided by the number of incorporations. This figure is then adjusted by a Consumer Price Index. The result is a steadily downwards trend during the entire period.

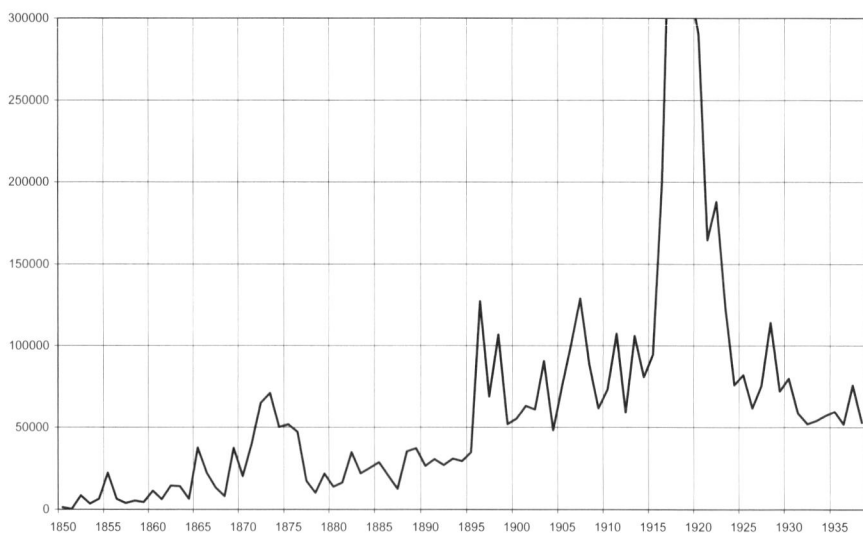

Figure 8.2   Total amount of subscribed capital in new joint-stock companies 1850–1938 (Thousand SEK)

Table 8.3   The average start-up capital 1850–1938 (inflation adjusted, Thousand SEK)

Year	Thousand SEK
1850–1859	1063
1860–1869	719
1870–1979	295
1880–1989	204
1890–1899	241
1900–1909	188
1910–1919	148
1920–1929	60
1930–1938	37

Source: See Figure 8.1.

Schumpeter argues that structural transformation is driven by the realization of entrepreneurial ideas, and that entrepreneurs gain access to a society's resources through credit creation.[39] The process of credit creation is generally dominated by the leading participants on the financial market. In Sweden the financial system has been dominated by the commercial banking sector. This was even more pronounced during the 'industrial breakthrough', from the 1890s onward, as the joint-stock banks expanded rapidly.[40] As stated earlier in the paper the industrialization process may be viewed as an important part of a broader modernization process. Therefore, to further understand the role of the joint-stock company in the modernization process it is important to investigate the link between incorporation and financial markets. To address this question two systems of measures have been constructed.

Firstly, the scale of incorporation was established by comparing the amount of capital raised by newly founded joint-stock companies with the Gross Domestic Product (GDP). Since both capital and GDP can be assumed to adjust to inflation, current prices were used for both. The result is a time-series of subscribed capital as a percentage of GDP.

In Figure 8.3 it is possible to discern a similar, although more pronounced, pattern as before. Swedish incorporation was intense from the mid-1860s to the late-1870s, before entering a slower phase up to 1895. During the years from 1895 until 1920 new joint-stock companies attracted unsurpassed levels of capital – reaching levels above 5 per cent of GDP. During the crisis of the early 1920s the ratio dropped below 1 per cent and continued to fall even more in the 1930s. The data presented so far has demonstrated that the period usually referred to as the 'industrial breakthrough' coincided with an unprecedented expansion of joint-stock companies.

---

39 J. Schumpeter, *The theory of economic development* (1911, reprinted Cambridge, 1934).

40 A. Ögren, *Empirical Studies in Money, Credit and Banking. The Swedish Credit Market in Transition under the Silver and Gold Standards 1834–1913* (Stockholm, 2003).

Figure 8.3   Subscribed capital relative to gross domestic product in Sweden, 1850–1938 (%)

Source: See Figure 8.1.

Secondly, the role of commercial banks in the credit-creation process was investigated by constructing a measure of their lending. The banks' lending against collateral in shares was compared to GDP in order to assess the role of joint-stock companies in the credit-creation process. The data for this comparison was collected from the official bank statistics.[41] Before 1870 banks rarely used shares as collateral. During the 1870s and 1880s lending against shares made up 1 to 2 per cent of GDP. From the beginning of the 1890s to the end of the First World War the proportion rose steadily, peaking at fully 20 per cent in 1918. The statistics were changed during the period and it is only from 1912 that the statistics include the banks' total lending. Before 1912 current accounts are not included in the statistics. This means that the figures up to 1911 are somewhat underestimated. However, the overall trend is unaffected by this change. During the interwar years the proportion once again fell back as the commercial banks struggled hard to consolidate their positions and in the latter half of the 1930s lending against shares, once again, constituted less than 5 per cent of GDP.

---

41   Sammandrag af enskilda bankernas qvartalsuppgifter 1866–1912. For the years 1913–38 Sveriges Officiella Statistik, Statistiska Meddelanden, Serie E, Uppgifter om bankerna has been used.

VI

The purpose of this chapter has been to re-examine the role of joint-stock companies in Swedish economic history. The emergence of joint-stock companies is seen as an important step in the process of modernization because this institution furthered impersonal property relations, which in turn promoted the transformation of the Swedish economy during the last decades of the nineteenth and the first decades of the twentieth century.

The development of a modern corporate legislation has been described. Internationally, the United States quickly took the lead in this process during the first decades of the nineteenth century. England's shift in the 1850s marked the beginning of a new era in Europe. Despite differences in detail, virtually all Western European countries had adopted the essentials of modern corporate legislation by the turn of the century – limited liability and impersonal ownership through shares. Sweden fits well into this international context. The first Swedish joint-stock law was passed in 1848, but the prehistory stretches all the way back to the merchant companies of the seventeenth century. A new law was passed in 1895, marking the transition from a system based on royal charter to a modern system based on registration. As a consequence of the changing conditions brought about by industrialization, major revisions in the joint-stock company law were enacted in 1910 and 1944. The development of a Swedish corporate legislation illustrates how institutional changes are often lengthy historical processes.

Earlier research in the history of Swedish incorporation has mainly been focused on the nineteenth century. This has been a quite natural delimitation since the focus has been mostly on industry. According to this research the breakthrough of the corporate system may be dated to the 1870s and the 1890s. Accordingly Swedish industry was dominated by firms organized as joint-stock companies around the turn of the century. However, my time-series of incorporations stretching from 1850 to 1938 slightly changes this picture. During the first decades of the twentieth century incorporation gained speed among trading firms, and from 1910 and onward incorporation in trade dominated the picture both in number of incorporations and subscribed capital. Furthermore the average size of all newly founded corporations fell sharply during the first decades of the twentieth century, implying that the corporate form was no longer reserved for large industrial firms but that it had become more widespread in the economy. This is important in a modernization context since it emphasizes the importance of sectors in the economy other than industry.

Berle & Means argued that the institution of private property changed in the US during the first decades of the twentieth century, due to the increasing importance of the 'corporate system'. This transformation, they argued, was propelled by the 'financial machinery'. This line of thought goes well with a Schumpeterian understanding of structural transformation, that is, structural transformation driven by entrepreneurial ideas financed through credit creation. Earlier research has maintained that the formation of joint-stock companies during the latter half of the nineteenth century was mainly driven by an urge to achieve limited liability, and that it was from the 1890s that the question of raising capital rose in importance. In this chapter it has been shown that from 1895 there was a sharp increase in the total amount of capital in newly founded joint-stock companies. During the period 1895–1920 the levels were unprecedented even as a percentage of GDP. This increase coincided with the modernization of the financial system in Sweden. For example, the new stock exchange made it easier for open corporations to attract capital. At the same time the commercial banks expanded and made it easier also for closed corporations to attract capital through lending against shares as collateral. In other words, this chapter would support the notion that the issue of raising capital became more important from the incorporation perspective after 1895. At the same time, however, the spreading of the corporate form led to a sharp increase in closed, relative to open, corporations. Studying the stock exchange will not reveal the capital-raising issues of the closed corporations. A different path, interesting but unfortunately beyond the scope of the chapter, would be to pursue the study of the commercial banks' lending against shares.

To conclude, views on the importance of incorporation have varied among researchers. I would argue that the incorporation of Swedish business was essential to the structural transformation that Swedish industry underwent around the turn of the last century. Furthermore I would argue that the emergence of a 'corporate system', with its strengthening of impersonal property relations, is an important feature in the modernization of Sweden.

Sources

Riksarkivet [the National Archives of Sweden]

Patent- och Registreringsverket, Bolagsbyrån, DIAA [The Department of Patents and Registration].

Statistical Sources

Bidrag till Sveriges Officiella Statistik (BiSos), Kungl. Maj:ts
Befallningshafvandes
Femårsberättelser 1881–1895, serie H [Official Statistics].
Sammandrag af enskilda bankernas qvartalsuppgifter 1866–1912 [Summary of
    Bank Reports]
Statistisk Årsbok (1913–1940) [Statistical Yearbook]
Sveriges Officiella Statistik (1913–1938), Statistiska Meddelanden, serie E,
    Uppgifter om bankerna [Summary of Bank Reports].
Sveriges Officiella Statistik (2000), Statistiska Meddelanden, serie PR, Priser och
    Konsumtion, [Official Statistics].

Appendix to Chapter 8

| | GDP | CPI | Number of incorporations | | | | | | Subscribed Capital (Thousand SEK) | | | | |
	current prices, MSEK	1914 = 100	Industry	Transport	Trade	Other	Total		Industry	Transport	Trade	Other	Total
1849	505	66.7	1	3	0	2	6	1849	900	391	0	94	1385
1850	520	66.5	2	1	0	2	5	1850	1238	27	3	60	1328
1851	535	67.8	1	0	0	0	1	1851	230	0	0	0	230
1852	543	70.0	2	1	0	1	4	1852	990	7500	0	81	8571
1853	570	72.2	5	1	0	0	6	1853	3489	15	0	0	3504
1854	645	77.2	6	0	0	0	6	1854	6496	0	0	0	6496
1855	735	82.8	6	0	2	3	11	1855	4640	2445	0	15198	22283
1856	834	91.3	8	0	0	1	9	1856	6210	0	0	210	6420
1857	880	91.5	7	0	0	5	12	1857	3200	0	0	590	3790
1858	802	81.9	8	3	0	3	14	1858	2270	2920	0	125	5315
1859	788	77.1	10	0	0	0	10	1859	4455	0	0	0	4455
1860	826	80.6	16	1	0	2	19	1860	9838	1500	0	22	11360
1861	866	83.9	11	0	0	1	12	1861	6108	0	0	75	6183
1862	859	86.2	8	3	0	3	14	1862	6313	5980	0	2163	14456
1863	896	81.9	8	4	0	8	20	1863	3582	3335	0	7244	14161
1864	894	78.4	8	0	0	9	17	1864	5395	0	0	991	6386
1865	893	78.3	22	8	1	6	37	1865	14545	22428	200	563	37736
1866	883	80.8	18	4	2	6	30	1866	11759	440	60	10127	22386
1867	917	85.9	35	0	14	9	58	1867	9327	0	401	3590	13318
1868	889	88.8	32	7	27	8	74	1868	6851	472	345	465	8133
1869	940	83.7	26	4	27	9	66	1869	4365	7140	1355	24632	37492
1870	993	80.2	38	9	35	11	93	1870	14036	2497	241	3507	20281
1871	1,046	82.3	69	41	27	14	151	1871	11808	20150	131	8044	40133
1872	1,213	85.6	86	40	37	36	199	1872	33431	18475	3571	9682	65159
1873	1,379	92.4	118	33	24	23	198	1873	57176	9870	266	3863	71175
1874	1,482	95.7	135	34	26	22	217	1874	34862	9709	1287	4302	50160
1875	1,442	95.1	88	33	22	20	163	1875	39758	9281	649	2130	51818
1876	1,515	95.4	80	26	31	27	164	1876	34368	10126	969	1795	47258
1877	1,480	94.9	66	15	12	24	117	1877	15252	1308	113	727	17400
1878	1,348	88.7	29	20	11	8	68	1878	5358	2768	295	1661	10082
1879	1,304	83.2	34	17	5	12	68	1879	18568	1524	100	1660	21852
1880	1,359	87.5	26	18	12	13	69	1880	9252	3849	129	614	13844
1881	1,429	89.7	50	25	9	25	109	1881	11879	2356	150	1996	16381
1882	1,427	87.3	46	28	10	30	114	1882	n.a	n.a	n.a	n.a	34907
1883	1,480	86.8	67	21	15	36	139	1883	n.a	n.a	n.a	n.a	21987
1884	1,439	83.6	62	28	22	52	164	1884	n.a	n.a	n.a	n.a	25302
1885	1,441	79.7	92	30	16	30	168	1885	n.a	n.a	n.a	n.a	28796
1886	1,343	75.8	84	25	32	31	172	1886	n.a	n.a	n.a	n.a	20683
1887	1,299	73.1	91	11	10	30	142	1887	n.a	n.a	n.a	n.a	12561
1888	1,371	75.7	154	29	19	42	244	1888	n.a	n.a	n.a	n.a	35475
1889	1,470	79.1	117	24	14	40	195	1889	n.a	n.a	n.a	n.a	37383
1890	1,513	80.8	115	23	20	31	189	1890	n.a	n.a	n.a	n.a	26622
1891	1,587	83.3	110	28	28	24	190	1891	21694	10569	230	1500	30692
1892	1,625	81.8	107	26	33	47	213	1892	19879	5145	883	2964	27076

Year	C1	C2	C3	C4	C5	C6	C7	C8	C9	C10	C11	C12
1893	30953	3181	962	4884	27402	175	n.a.	n.a.	n.a.	n.a.	78.5	1,609
1894	29514	3925	233	8090	22874	171	n.a.	n.a.	n.a.	n.a.	74.5	1,608
1895	34912	3218	737	4857	28130	208	n.a.	n.a.	n.a.	n.a.	75.9	1,692
1896	127221	40998	3564	11529	71130	347	68	39	45	195	75.3	1,786
1897	69022	11974	1751	18400	36897	324	46	36	46	196	77.7	1,941
1898	106894	24406	5746	15353	61389	460	71	62	52	275	81.4	2,104
1899	52000	10635	4827	10250	26288	383	71	56	54	202	85.0	2,266
1900	55367	10494	4193	6877	33803	389	73	60	51	205	86.0	2,327
1901	63321	14617	4897	7922	35885	372	65	59	43	205	83.9	2,285
1902	61091	11303	7466	4071	38251	405	73	67	41	224	84.6	2,293
1903	90670	22753	6043	7819	54055	461	80	83	34	264	86.0	2,439
1904	48240	6817	5496	5713	30214	418	72	67	49	230	85.0	2,498
1905	75749	20209	10212	7522	37806	605	123	124	54	304	86.8	2,557
1906	100788	24088	7926	11076	57698	709	161	145	41	362	88.6	2,877
1907	128821	51960	7947	7638	61276	814	175	148	56	435	93.2	3,151
1908	88613	28128	12901	4479	43105	659	155	152	40	312	94.6	3,111
1909	61839	21772	8852	3947	27268	678	160	165	30	323	93.7	3,099
1910	73433	16723	7374	6636	42700	628	142	170	35	281	93.7	3,349
1911	107443	40161	15611	4019	47652	886	212	223	56	395	96.5	3,420
1912	59340	11860	4538	2104	40838	435	80	123	31	201	98.5	3,651
1913	106015	9702	44407	9827	42079	564	91	254	39	180	98.8	3,971
1914	80991	11063	41997	3159	24772	563	80	300	26	157	100.0	3,970
1915	94630	7151	51055	21427	14997	578	75	299	59	145	115.0	4,589
1916	200712	12649	73494	62205	52364	935	106	481	111	237	130.0	5,745
1917	413206	66035	177696	26055	143420	1232	192	613	76	351	164.0	6,691
1918	597632	155298	228086	41836	172412	1529	226	760	90	453	232.0	8,910
1919	321407	48655	133240	20917	118595	1507	175	787	70	475	268.0	11,174
1920	290247	84200	92646	16777	96624	1243	179	571	50	443	269.0	12,409
1921	164532	12733	68491	5665	77643	955	133	496	36	290	231.0	9,395
1922	187924	93120	46446	8313	40045	1074	120	600	57	297	187.0	8,088
1923	122779	29030	46133	7143	40473	1047	125	550	68	304	174.0	7,733
1924	76101	9054	29711	15096	22240	1074	117	622	62	273	174.0	8,054
1925	82186	29583	23703	8066	20834	952	147	524	39	242	177.0	8,226
1926	61897	7241	27604	2932	24120	968	165	519	39	245	171.0	8,391
1927	75632	10468	25443	3707	36014	904	150	470	32	252	169.0	8,446
1928	114111	8077	38880	3917	63237	1076	246	461	35	334	170.0	8,747
1929	72283	17615	25721	5264	23683	1028	278	436	50	264	168.0	9,202
1930	79982	9622	31532	3446	35382	1113	234	501	44	334	163.0	9,181
1931	58677	8144	33852	2021	14660	1059	199	497	51	312	158.0	8,504
1932	52120	5720	21536	2243	22621	1069	146	560	30	333	155.0	7,906
1933	54142	5558	25971	7738	14875	980	169	488	38	285	151.0	8,060
1934	57175	6160	30473	1532	19010	978	161	460	27	330	152.0	8,776
1935	59750	8349	24307	1399	25695	1063	181	502	42	338	155.0	9,449
1936	51956	6677	19864	3101	22314	977	163	498	37	279	157.0	10,038
1937	75867	8413	39173	2207	26074	1069	166	568	45	290	161.0	11,028
1938	52905	6838	26877	2412	16778	1089	189	554	29	317	165.0	11,487

CHAPTER 9

The Modernization of a Dutch Commercial Bank: The Twentsche Bank, 1858–1931

Douwe C.J. van der Werf

Between 1858 and 1931 Twentsche Bank (DTB) underwent a process of modernization.[1] In this period it developed from a banker in Enschede, a city in the Dutch textile area called 'Twente', into one of the major financial institutions of Amsterdam. As well as growing in size, it also took on new tasks: financial payments, credit, securities, and new issues, to mention only the most prominent. The leading figure at the bank in this period was Willem Blijdenstein.[2] He turned it into a major bank. Second in importance was Adam Roelvink.[3] He ensured that it remained a major bank.

Willem and Benjamin Willem Blijdenstein Jr in Enschede and London

Willem Blijdenstein started his career in 1856, at the age of sixteen under his father, Benjamin Willem Blijdenstein Jr (Benjamin), a banker in Enschede.[4] To further his ambition to work in London, then the financial capital of the world, he took an apprenticeship with a company in Rotterdam: the firm did considerable business in London, giving Willem an opportunity to learn the English language.

His father flooded him with questions about their business dealings. It soon became clear that they were involved in bill jobbing, in issuing bills of exchange (commercial promises of payment) purely to make money, which was a grave matter in those days.[5] Because of the reputation the company had as a consequence acquired,

---

1   Twentsche Bank (1840–1964) merged with Nederlandsche Handel-Maatschappij (1824–1964) in 1964 to form Algemene Bank Nederland. In the same year Rotterdamsche Bank (1863–1964) merged with Amsterdamsche Bank (1871–1964) to form Amsterdam-Rotterdam Bank. Algemene Bank Nederland and Amsterdam-Rotterdam Bank merged in 1990 to form ABN AMRO Bank. Compare: D.C.J. van der Werf, 'The two Dutch bank mergers of 1964: the creations of Algemene Bank Nederland and Amsterdam-Rotterdam Bank', in *Financial History Review*, vol. 6, 1999, pp. 67–84. For a general introduction to the history of ABN AMRO Bank, see J. de Vries, W. Vroom and T. de Graaf (eds), *Wereldwijd bankieren ABN AMRO 1824–1999* (Amsterdam, 1999).

2   Benjamin Willem Blijdenstein (Enschede 1839–Hilversum 1914), generally referred to as Willem. This convention is adopted here to avoid confusion.

3   Adam Roelvink (Zutphen 1856–Oploo 1927).

4   Dr Benjamin Willem Blijdenstein Junior (Enschede 1811–66). Founder of Twentsche Bank. This name is abbreviated here to Benjamin.

5   Bills of exchange were used as payment for goods. The issuing of bills to raise cash was known as bill jobbing, or kiting.

a month later Willem returned to Enschede. This was probably in retrospect a shrewd decision, since within a few months the firm had suspended payments.

Benjamin then sent Willem to a Dutch firm in London. Benjamin wanted to know everything about this butter company, since he was dealing with their bills of exchange. The firm bought butter in Deventer and paid with bills via the financial firm of S.H. van Groningen in Deventer, some of which ended up in Benjamin's hands. Benjamin soon discovered that the firm was borrowing money at 15 per cent interest. He thought this was a bad sign, since it was a high rate, and realized it implied that the butter merchants were unable to obtain credit under normal terms. What became of the firm is not known.[6]

Willem worked in London both to gain experience and to keep an eye on his father's business contacts. Meanwhile, Benjamin sent him bills of exchange to trade in London, from which he gradually built up his own business. These activities originated with Benjamin's ambition, but Willem also had his own reasons for going to London. He wanted independence, to have his own business; nothing seemed worse to him than to remain in Enschede and 'dissipate his energy and resilience' as he explained. It was time to leave.[7]

In 1858 he opened an office in London (see Figure 9.1). He was nineteen years old. The business flourished. In 1860 half the growth in the bank's gross profit came from London, and half from Enschede. A major part of their business involved the sale of Amsterdam bills. English traders needed these to pay Dutch firms. This system of using bills of exchange as a means of payment was regulated by the companies themselves. They received bills as payment and sent bills to their own suppliers. They bought and sold bills from traders like Benjamin and Willem, who made their living from trading in Dutch bills in London. It was therefore vital for them to keep abreast of the financial reliability of those who issued bills and traded in them. This is evident from Benjamin's advice to Willem to keep his eye open while in Rotterdam and London, but also from the eight business principles Benjamin gave to Willem on how to conduct business, and how to present his affairs (the last three items) (see Figures 9.2 and 9.3):

- Be solid. Do not focus on the potential profit, but on the solidity.
- Collect information. Try to find out whether a trader is careful, whether he works hard.
- Work cheaply. Aim for a low margin and a high turnover.

---

6   Most of the archives cited here form part of the Twentsche Bank (DTB) archive, preserved at Historisch Centrum Overijssel (HCO) in Zwolle, the Netherlands. Items from this archive are listed as HCO, DTB, inventory number, with a description. Here: HCO, DTB, inv. no. 3095, letters from Benjamin to Willem, 12 June 1857, 14 June 1857, 22 June 1857, 24 June 1857, 6 Nov. 1857, 13 Nov. 1857, 14 Nov. 1857, 24 Nov. 1857, 13 Dec. 1857. Idem, inv. no. 3095, letter from Benjamin to Luttenberg, 14 June 1857, not sent. Idem, inv. no. 3136, Notes by Willem on the early years of Twentsche Bankvereeniging, marking the 50th anniversary in 1911. Various items cited here are held at ABN AMRO Bank's Historisch Archief, abbreviated as AAHA, inv. no. with a further description.

7   HCO, DTB, inv. no. 3111, deliberations by Willem, written in 1859/60 and 1861.

Figure 9.1   The first offices of the Twentsche Bank in Enschede, around 1870. Standing in front of the building is managing partner Jan Herman Wennink

– Concentrate on Twente. Do business with people and companies you know.
– Take occasional chances, do not be too careful, try new things.
– Build a sound reputation. Ensure that you have enough cash available in case of a crisis.
– Be visible. Make sure your business contacts see you.
– Protect your name. Create an impression of thrift and caution, buy ordinary wines, for example, not expensive ones.

The Blijdensteins' objective was to raise confidence in their bills, so that traders would buy from them as confidently as they did from Hope.[8]

Amsterdam

Soon after setting up their London office Benjamin realized that he would have to open a branch in Amsterdam to sell London bills. However, he did not have the capital for this, and no personnel to run the business there. Moreover there was a danger that his reputation might suffer if his associates considered that he was expanding too fast by branching out of Enschede. But Amsterdam beckoned,

---

8   Idem, inv. no. 3095, 14 Sept. 1859, 21 Sept. 1859, 24 Sept. 1859, 1 Oct. 1859, 2 Oct. 1859, 11 Oct. 1859, 4 Feb. 1860, 28 Mar. 1860, 11 Aug. 1860, 17 Nov. 1860, 19 Mar. 1861, 18 Sept. 1861, 3 Oct. 1861, 28 Oct. 1861.

Figure 9.2   Benjamin and Willem, London, *c*.1860–1866

since Willem found that he could ask between 6 and 7 per cent interest from major industrial producers, which he reported to be the going rate (he mentioned no companies by name). For deposit accounts the rate was 4 per cent, leaving a margin of 2 per cent for the banker. Deposits were a new area of business for him in 1859. To enter this business he needed the trust of private customers. This was not feasible while the firm remained a one-man company run by Benjamin, since the business needed to be transparent. It was necessary therefore to form a public limited company, whose affairs could be examined by shareholders and the public. This would draw large sums of money at 5 per cent interest. However, the firm established in Amsterdam in 1861 was not a public limited company, but a limited partnership or commanditaire vennootschap (CV) called Twentsche Bankvereeniging (TBV). This was a company in which textile manufacturers in Twente were able to invest capital in the form of limited guarantees; thus not in cash. The attraction for these companies was that they could obtain loans on their guarantees at advantageous rates. Liability, meanwhile, rested in the first place with Benjamin and thereafter with the limited partners. Willem took on joint responsibility in 1862. We do not know why Benjamin and Willem preferred the form of a limited partnership, but an indication is perhaps that some years later, in 1869, Willem declined an uncertain

Figure 9.3   London office, *c*.1910

appointment as director of a public limited company in favour of a position as an independent partner.[9]

The Amsterdam business grew rapidly. This was at a time of momentous change in trade with the Dutch East Indies. In the 1850s the Nederlandsche Handel-Maatschappij lost its official monopoly on colonial trade. This was part of the liberalization of international commerce.[10] Textile manufacturers were now able to export cotton to Java themselves, and Willem and Benjamin were able to supply the financial services they needed.[11]

Within a year of opening in Amsterdam a precarious situation developed from which the Blijdensteins only just managed to extricate themselves. This was linked to the great fire of Enschede in 1862, in which 80 per cent of the city was

---

9   Idem, inv. no. 3085, circular dated 1 Aug. 1862. Idem, inv. no. 3095, 10 Feb. 1859, June 1859. Idem, inv. no. 3111, note by Willem, 5 Aug. 1859. Idem, inv. no. 2581, letter from Willem to Rotterdamsche Bank, 5 Feb. 1869.

10   J. Luiten van Zanden and A. van Riel, *Nederland 1780–1914, staat, instituties en economische ontwikkeling* (The Hague, 2000), pp. 231, 260. For a general description of the financial sector in Amsterdam in this period see J. Jonker, *Merchants, Bankers, Middlemen, The Amsterdam money market during the first half of the 19th century* (Amsterdam, 1996).

11   J.A. Boot, *De Twentsche Katoennijverheid 1830–1873* (Amsterdam, 1935), p. 247.

destroyed in a matter of hours and most of the textile factories were lost.[12] After the fire it proved difficult to place textile manufacturers' bills since they had lost their perceived creditworthiness. Benjamin felt that the manufacturers would be able to bear the losses, since they were well insured. Nevertheless, things almost went badly wrong when they found themselves unable to offload the bills and ran out of money for withdrawals. Apart from the various temporary solutions that saw them through the crisis (they sought support everywhere), they instituted a structural change by attracting limited-liability capital from financiers rather than industrial companies, which both increased their liability and raised the amount of cash at their disposal. Moreover, they also invited these investors to open deposit accounts at high interest (7 per cent in 1869), and later also a share in profits.[13]

After Benjamin's death in 1866, the focus of the bank's business remained in Twente; Willem anticipated that the textile industry would expand and so opened a branch in Almelo. Like the Amsterdam office, here too a textile magnate stood surety.[14]

Reorganization in 1870

To expand the business further, for which capital was required, Willem reorganized the bank, in a process that began in 1870 and was to take several years. In a new development, he was now officially severally liable, bringing in capital to cover the capital of the other partners.[15] Another new development was the appointment of supervisory directors. This was not necessary for a limited partnership, but was considered a prudent move. The active partners appointed these directors themselves, selecting prominent personalities who were not necessarily participants in the company. They were passive supervisors (had they been active they would also have been severally liable).[16] To serve as supervisory directors Willem invited Carel Frederik Wilhelm Wiggers van Kerchem, a former president of Javasche Bank; Julius Pinner, an expert on credit societies, and C.H. Stork, a lawyer and attorney in Almelo.[17] They were required to approve new severally liable partners and directors, as well as the annual accounts.[18]

---

12 L.A. Stroink, *Stad en land van Twente* (Amsterdam, 1974), p. 476. HCO, DTB, inv. no. 3095, 9 May 1862, 13 May 1862.

13 Idem, inv. no. 3095, 11 May 1862, 11 July 1863, 5 Aug. 1864. Idem, inv. no. 2581, letter from Willem to an uncle, 22 Nov. 1866.

14 Idem, inv. no. 2581, letter from Willem to D. Jordaan, 31 Dec. 1867. Surety was provided by H.J. van Heek, Wed. A. Ledeboer (sister of H.J. van Heek), and Abraham Ledeboer.

15 The three severally liable partners were Willem, his mother and J.H. Wennink. Wennink was the cashier at the Enschede office. Willem represented his mother and J.H. Wennink. Idem, inv. no. 499, statutes of Twentsche Bankvereeniging of 1 Jan. 1871.

16 E.G.J. Tilman, *Over commanditaire vennootschappen bij wijze van aandelen* (Leiden, 1860), pp. 40–42.

17 Carel Frederik Wilhelm Wiggers van Kerchem (1825–88), Julius Pinner (d. Amsterdam 1882), C.H. Stork (1820–1905).

18 Including the opening of new branches, fixing the percentage of profits awarded to the new partners in consultation with the joint partners, and supervising the managing partners.

As part of the reorganization, the limited partnerships were made negotiable (enabling gains to be realized), by allowing the partners to exchange their participation for registered shares which could then be transferred.[19] A new innovation was the issuing of dividends, with the limited partners as principal beneficiaries of a fixed minimum dividend, followed by a fixed minimum for the severally liable partner. If profits were sufficiently high the amounts paid out could be significant: part would be shared with the limited partners, but if earnings were exceptional the severally liable partner would have sole rights to the remainder.

The reorganization was a success, attracting large amounts of capital and deposits. Although much of the capital could be withdrawn at short notice, the company shored up its foundations by fixing part of the capital for a five-year term. This meant that liquidity remained a problem, even though partners now deposited their investment rather than simply providing surety.[20]

Part of the reorganization also involved the creation of Credietvereeniging (CRV). This was a bank within TBV, founded in 1871 to be able to provide credit without affecting the bank's dividend as a result of possible losses. Borrowers had to provide a guarantee, and a reserve was established so that it would not be necessary to draw on the guarantee immediately. Several leading businessmen were appointed to Credietvereeniging to assess credit applications.[21]

To overcome the difficulty of finding senior managers, Willem developed the concept of participating and financially responsible managers with a broad freedom within the company (based on the example of London financial firms).[22] Willem preferred the new organization (still a limited partnership) to a public limited company in which, as he saw it, directors received a fixed amount and took a small share of the profits. Under such a construction directors would have been more interested in their private business than in their work. This, according to Willem, was why public companies tended to make poor profits.[23]

The Paris Branch

The reorganization proved a success, capital grew (sixfold after 1870 in three years), but a downturn in the economy caused problems when the dividend fell from 11 per cent in 1870 to eight in 1871, and to six in 1873. Willem resolved this by taking over a bank in Paris in 1875, Léon et Dreher; the bank's anticipated dividend rose

---

19 AAHA, library, Memorie van toelichting bij het jaarverslag van de TBV over 1872.

20 AAHA, library, cf the 1870 TBV annual report (commissarissen section, p. 4). HCO, DTB, inv. no. 2582, letter from Willem, 29 July 1871. Idem, inv. no. 2185, letter from Willem to Tadama, 31 July 1871.

21 Idem, inv. no. 2467, minutes of the Commissie van Admissie, 30 April 1873. Idem, inv. no. 2461, statutes of Twentsche Bank-Vereeniging Credietvereeniging, 1873.

22 Idem, inv. no. 7, minutes of the general meeting in 1877. Idem, inv. no. 2581, letter from Willem to D.B. Jordaan, 7 May July 1869.

23 Idem, inv. no. 2581, letter from Willem to D.B. Jordaan, March 1870. AAHA, library, TBV report on 1871, p. 12.

Figure 9.4   Head office, Amsterdam, Spuistraat, *c*.1910

so substantially as a result that he could now afford to confine his involvements to businesses offering moderate risk at adequate profits.[24]

This continued for several years, until in 1883 the Paris bank incurred heavy losses on the stock market. Willem, who held principal liability, suffered a personal loss of half a million guilders (almost five million euros in current terms). This and other setbacks in this period left Willem owing a substantial amount to his bank. As a result he was no longer able to cover his financial liability to his limited partners. His solution was to share the liability, the control and the profits in the business with his four joint directors. In 1887 he transferred half his reserve funds and fixed capital investments, and henceforth they shared the senior management of the firm. Yet while this was true in theory, the reality was different. At the request of the supervisory directors Willem was given a veto on decisions he felt were not in the bank's interests, and he kept the right to appoint his own successor.[25]

---

24 AAHA, library, TBV report on 1875.

25 The other directors were A.J. Brink (London), Helmich Ledeboer (Almelo), Adam Roelvink and Jan Berent Roelvink (with Willem in Amsterdam). HCO, DTB, inv. no. 369, minutes of the meeting of the board of supervisory directors (hereafter abbreviated as RVC), 10 July 1886, 4 Dec. 1886, 23 Dec. 1886, 22 Jan. 1887 (resolution adopted), 26 Mar. 1887

Willem's Sons and Successors

In the 1890s Willem's sons entered the bank.[26] Or more correctly, perhaps, he brought them into the bank. Mr Willem (as he was known in the family) was the eldest: Willem's heir apparent. He had been forced to study, under threat of otherwise being sent to work on a plantation on Java. When he failed to pass the first stage of his Law degree there appeared to be no place for him in the bank. Dropping his studies was not an option, however, since Willem did not employ people at the bank who were unable to finish what they had started. Mr Willem persevered and eventually graduated in 1893.

He subsequently received enormous praise for his work at the bank in Enschede. While working in London he married Lida van Heek. As a result he was able, through his father-in-law, to take a major financial stake in his father's bank in London.[27] His father wanted him to take over the business, and advised him not to remain in the background, but to take initiatives and search for new sources of profit.

Growth and Expansion of the Bank

In the late 1890s the bank increased its capital in expectation of new business anticipated from the growing American economy. This was the last occasion on which limited capital was acquired. Business did indeed grow, profits began to flow and the personal incomes of the partners rose. They invested their savings in the bank, and over the years their capital became just as significant as that invested by the limited partners (see Figure 9.5). And when the 1887 partners left the bank (because of age or death), their capital was paid out and replaced by sums from the remaining partners, or by investments by new partners. Gradually, therefore, the capital was accumulated by the Blijdenstein sons, since they were the new partners: Mr Willem in 1905, Theek in 1909 and John in 1911.[28]

(resolution ratified). Idem, inv. no. 17, minutes of the annual general meeting of limited partners, 30 April 1887.

26 Mr Willem (b. 1867), John (b. 1872), Theek (b. 1874) and Louis (b. 1878). Two other sons, both named Herman, died young, one at the age of seven, the other at 26. The three daughters (Francine, Henriette and Maria) played no role in the bank's affairs. Louis remained at the bank until 1916, after which he moved into fruit farming.

27 His father-in-law was G.J. van Heek (Enschede 1837-Enschede 1915), partner at Van Heek & Co and Fa. G.J. van Heek & Zn. He served as a TBV supervisory director 1884–1912. HCO, DTB, inv. no. 3140, letters from Willem to Mr Willem, 25 July 1888, Nov. 1888, 29 Jan. 1889, 16 May 1894. Idem, inv. no. 3146, letters from Mr Willem to Lida, 25 Jan. 1896; letter from Mr Willem to Van Heek, 30 Jan. 1896.

28 Idem, inv. no. 52, TBV annual report for 1910. Idem, inv. no. 372, RVC, 20 Dec. 1912. Cf statues of 1910 and 1911: Idem, inv. no. 384, RVC, 23 July 1910 and 8 Oct. 1910, and on the partnership contract, art. 15: idem, inv. no. 370, RVC, 9 July 1898.

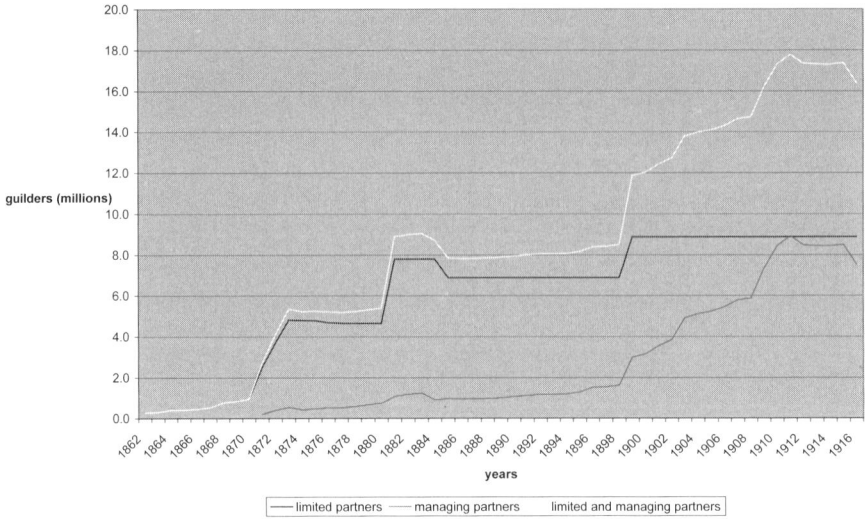

Figure 9.5   Capital formation at Twentsche Bank, 1862–1916

Adam Roelvink's 1906 Plan

Apart from growing profits and capital accumulation at the bank, the years of expansion also led to an increasing demand for credit and issues. Adam Roelvink indicated the necessary adjustments that would be needed for this. He had worked at the bank since 1874. He began at the age of seventeen, entering the Enschede office directly upon leaving school, and subsequently moving on to the head office in Amsterdam, where in 1884 he became one of the directors. He was the ideal person, and the only man at the bank with the skills to focus on activities at the stock exchange. These skills were significant: he had to be able to act firmly, to deal courteously with others and to have a sound general background, to be capable and have experience. Some even thought him more effective at the stock exchange than Willem himself: he knew the business and the people (see Figures 9.6 and 9.7).[29]

In 1906 Adam proposed a plan to reorganize the bank to enable it to expand its involvement in issues. This required a significant increase in capital. The bank would also need to become independent of Willem, who was by now 67 and such a dominant figure that no one could replace him. As a result, the bank would become a public limited company, leaving Willem in control, and recompensed by the transfer of his bank. The limited partners would become the shareholders. Willem only agreed to the change if the limited partners became the owners instead of him and if all other aspects of the company remained unchanged. He wished to retain control with his sons, and he felt that Mr Willem was ready to take over the reins. But Adam

---

29 Idem, inv. no. 369, RVC, 10 May 1884, 7 June 1884.

Figure 9.6   Willem Blijdenstein (1839–1914), by Jan Pieter Veth, oil on canvas, 1908/1909

Figure 9.7   Adam Roelvink (1856–1927), artist unknown, oil on canvas, on the occasion of his retirement as managing partner in 1916

argued that the public limited company needed to be free to choose its own directors, and considered it a vote of no confidence to have to remain subservient to Willem's sons. From then on his motivation was one of simple self interest, and 'the sentiment disappeared'.

Unlike Willem, the supervisory directors supported Adam's plans. They wanted the bank to develop on all fronts, including issues, and so they refused to support the accession of Willem's sons. They wanted Adam to be president-director and Mr Willem his deputy. But Willem had the final say, and since Adam's plan contradicted his own vision for the bank, the transfer to a public limited company remained a taboo subject for years.[30]

Willem's Appointed Heir

A few years later, when Willem realized that he would not be able to direct the bank for much longer, he decided to arrange his succession. Apart from making his sons members of the board of partners (the governing body), he also asked Theek to join the board of the head office, and to prevent the board becoming too large he tried to dislodge Jan Berent Roelvink. This was Adam's elder brother who, together with Willem, Mr Willem and Adam, formed the head office board. Willem argued that Jan Berent had intimated an unwillingness to help train Mr Willem, and was perhaps less than capable.[31] Indeed he even recommended Jan Berent for a post at Nederlandsche Bank, when Adam would have been the perfect choice. But Adam defended Jan Berent through thick and thin. He provided an essential contribution, as a highly personable man and sat, for example, on Amsterdam's municipal council – which would have been impossible for a Blijdenstein, according to Mr Willem.

This was a crucial moment for the bank. At this point Willem considered removing Adam as well as Jan Berent, but decided against doing so since Adam's skills were vital to the bank's success. Willem realized at the same time that his sons had been waiting too long to be able to take on the leadership. He therefore felt obliged to retain sole control as the managing director as long as his sons remained disinclined to take up the reins. He felt they were failing in their duty by remaining in the background, whether it was due to lack of confidence or misplaced deference.[32]

---

30 Idem, inv. no. 568, letter from managing partners to limited partners, 30 Dec. 1916. Idem, inv. no. 567, Nota van den Heer B.W. Blydenstein van 28 juni 1906; Aan de Commissie, gevormd overeenkomstig besluit der vergadering van Commissarissen der Twentsche Bankvereeniging van 7 Juli 1906, Maart 1907; letters from Adam to Willem, 16 April 1907, 29 April 1907, 12 July 1907, 23 July 1907. Letters from Willem to Adam, 27 April 1907, 3 July 1907; RVC, 27 July 1907; letter from Willem to the supervisory directors 31 July 1907.

31 In 1903 Willem proposed appointing Mr Willem as his successor in Rotterdam. This was prevented when key supervisory directors and joint partners in Amsterdam dissuaded him.

32 Idem, inv. no. 384, letter from Willem to A.J. Brink, February 1909. Idem, inv. no. 3132, letter from Willem to the supervisory directors, 17 May 1898. Letter from Willem to Jan Roelvink, May 1908. Letters from Adam to Mr Willem, 7 April 1909, 21 April 1909, 11 May 1909. Letter from Willem to Adam and Jan, 20 Oct. 1909. Letter from Mr Willem to Willem, 22 Oct. 1909. Letter from Willem to Adam, 30 Dec. 1909. Idem, inv. no. 3143, letter from

Six months later, in 1911, he made way for Mr Willem, then 43, as director and owner of the bank; he wished to prevent the need for change in the board of directors in the event of his death, so that for the outside world the situation remained stable. His capital therefore remained in the bank (his heirs were compensated with an increased profit guarantee). At the same time, Adam, rather than Mr Willem, was placed in control of the bank. Mr Willem (and Adam) did however retain a veto on decisions of the partners. The management of the Amsterdam head office now fell to Adam, Mr Willem and Theek. In the end, Jan Berent Roelvink had been replaced after all.[33]

Other Banks

Twentsche Bankvereeniging (TBV) was one of a group of commercial banks that experienced phenomenal growth in this period. Rotterdamsche Bankvereeniging (Robaver) grew especially fast, but TBV did not follow Robaver's strategy for rapid growth by investing large sums in industrial and commercial companies. This was because the Blijdenstein family was unable to cover the required extra (limited-liability) capital, so that the bank eventually reached an impasse (see Figures 9.8 and 9.9).

While the existing situation was certainly in the Blijdenstein family's interest, reforms were clearly required if TBV was to remain a major bank in the Netherlands. Without changes, for example, Adam was unable to expand the underwriting business. In Adam's most pessimistic assessment, TBV's capital (compared to its credits and loans) was only half that of Robaver and Amsterdamsche Bank. For the actual banking business of providing credit and issues, TBV had insufficient capital. Moreover, Adam felt that TBV was unable to choose its own directors, a direct criticism of the policies of the Blijdenstein sons, who were in fact the directors.

That was Adam's opinion. But Mr Willem was happy to continue without underwriting, while Willem wanted TBV to simply remain a large healthy bank without having to be second only to Nederlandsche Bank and Nederlandsche Handel-Maatschappij. The supervisory directors thought differently. They

---

Willem to Mr Willem, 23 Oct. 1909. J.G. van Maarseveen, *Briefwisseling van Nicolaas Gerard Pierson 1839–1909* (Amsterdam, 1993), vol. III, p. 529. Letter from B.W. Blijdenstein to N.G. Pierson, 4 Mar. 1909. Jan was the second candidate in 1892 when the secretary of Nederlandsche Bank's term expired. The first was the current secretary, J.G.N. de Hoop Scheffer. He was to remain in office. The contacts between Willem and N.G. Pierson were known to Adam Roelvink (cf HCO, DTB, inv. no. 3132, letter from Adam to Mr Willem, 21 April 1909) .

33 Idem, inv. no. 3143, letters from Willem to the supervisory directors, 19 May 1910 and from June 1910, the agreement of Dec. 1908, and Willem's proposal attached to the minutes of the supervisory directors board of 25 June 1910, 23 July 1910, 8 Oct. 1910 and 21 Jan. 1911. Idem, inv. no. 498, letter from Willem to the supervisory directors, June 1910. Idem, inv. no. 384, contracts between the partners are kept with the minutes of the RVC, 20 May 1910, 23 July 1910 and 8 Oct. 1910, 21 Jan. 1911.

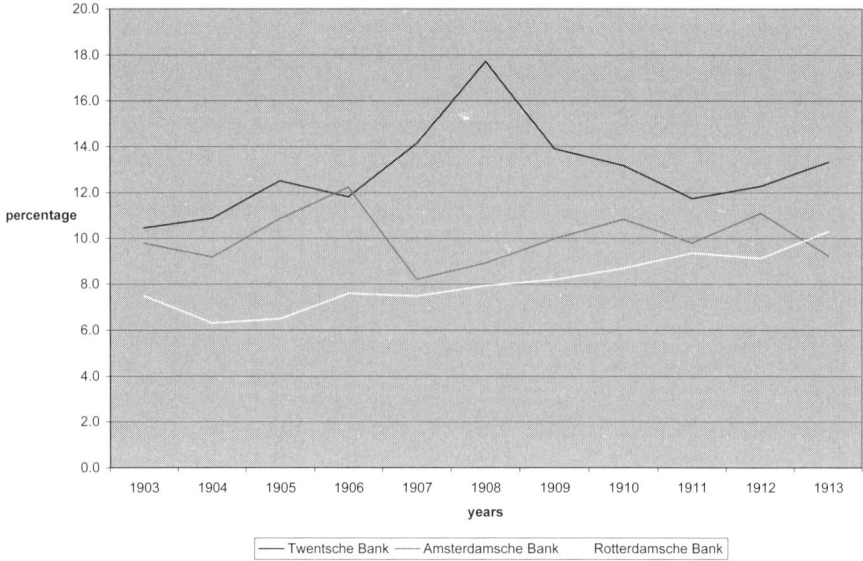

Figure 9.8   Profitability of the three banks, 1903–1913

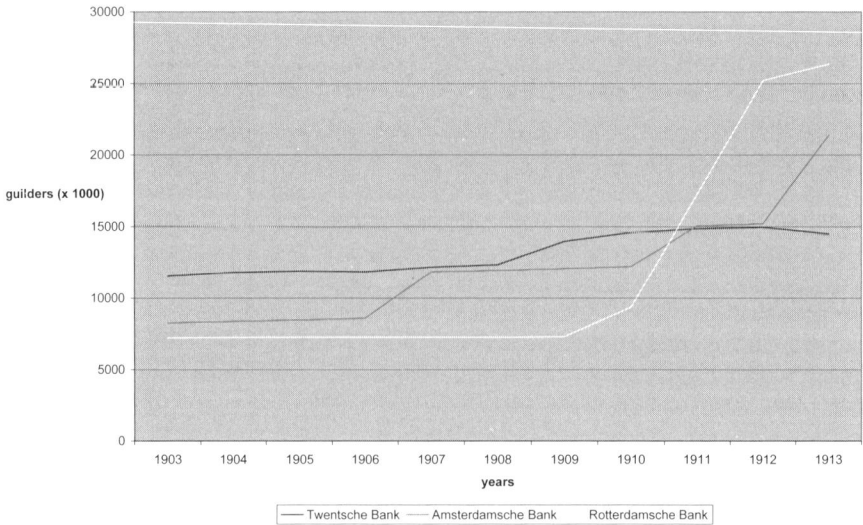

Figure 9.9   Capital and reserve of the three banks, 1903–1913

wanted the bank to keep up with developments. Mr Willem allowed himself to be persuaded and Willem invited the limited partners to prepare a plan.[34]

This plan (devised by Adam) did not turn the bank entirely into a public limited company: the Blijdensteins continued to supply binding recommendations for the supervisory directors and the directors, and were required to approve the statutes. Moreover, the supervisory directors were not able to dismiss the directors.[35]

Formation of a Public Limited Company in 1916

For Adam, the negotiations were made considerably easier in 1914 when Willem died at the age of 75, since his sons made fewer demands than their father had. He advised that a new board of directors be formed of the three Blijdensteins and his own son-in-law, J.M. Telders. Adam no longer wished to serve as a director, given his age (he was 59) and domestic situation.[36] He was however prepared to provide leadership as a delegated supervisory director. The limited partners benefited from the change in Adam's plan: they were awarded a larger percentage of the profits. This formed the basis for the bank's metamorphosis in December 1916 into a public limited company: Twentsche Bank (DTB). With this the capital was increased with the sole purpose of acquiring two banks in Rotterdam and The Hague.

It seems remarkable that the bank did not raise capital to provide more credit, or to increase its involvement in underwriting. Presumably this was because the quality of the capital improved, since it was no longer withdrawable, and capital was probably freed up in London since the bank planned to reduce its involvement there. Perhaps it was also apparent that capital would become available from the transfer of the bank's German offices.[37]

---

34 Idem, inv. no. 359, meetings of 27 April 1912 and 26 April 1913. The next year J.H. ter Kuile noted that the dividend was particularly low (7 %, while the previous year it was 6.75 %), at a rate of 145 % this gives a profit of 4.5 to 4.75 %. Amsterdamsche Bank raised its divided in the same year from 9.5 to 11%. Idem, inv. no. 567, letter from Adam to Willem 23 Oct. 1913, p. 13. Idem, inv. no. 568, RVC, 3 Jan. 1914. Idem, inv. no. 372, RVC, 19 Jan. 1913, 3 Jan. 1914, 17 Jan. 1914.

35 Idem, inv. no. 568, letter from Willem to Mr Willem, 14 Feb. 1914; Idem, inv. no. 3164, undated manuscript by Willem.

36 Henceforth the directors were appointed by the shareholders on binding advice of the supervisory directors. Supervisory directors were also appointed by the shareholders on binding advice of the supervisory directors. Delegated supervisory directors had the same powers as a director (Statuten van de Twentsche Bank NV, article 11 and 12). J.M. Telders had been introduced to TBV by Mr Willem some years earlier to keep Adam at the bank (Telders had worked at Hollandsche IJzeren Spoorweg- Maatschappij). HCO, DTB, inv. no. 567, letters from Adam to Mr Willem dated 2 Sept. 1913, 12 Sept. 1913; idem, inv. no. 567, letters from Mr Willem to Adam dated 5 Sept. 1913, 16 Oct. 1913.

37 This involves Wissel- en Effectenbank in Rotterdam, and Bank voor Effecten- en Wisselzaken in The Hague. Idem, inv. no. 568, letter from John to Mr Willem, 25 July 1916. Idem, inv. no. 568, memo from limited partners regarding the establishment of Twentsche Bank, 30 December 1916.

Compulsory Sale of German Branches

For the DTB's banks in the German border region the conflict between the great powers in the First World War was not without consequences. These formed part of the bank's Twente network in Gronau (founded 1890), Rheine (founded 1893) and Münster (founded 1898).[38]

Dutch foreign trade came under increasing pressure at this time as a result of the war between Britain and Germany, particularly as a result of British attempts to blockade traffic to Germany. This included banking facilities.[39] The pressure increased in October 1917 when the US declared that all companies with offices in enemy territory would be treated as allies of the enemy. They had to surrender their holdings in those countries and had to apply to the American authorities for permission to continue doing business in the US. While DTB had no offices in the US it did hold deposits which would, without this permission, have been placed under American control. Indeed, in mid-November, France blacklisted any Dutch bankers who refused to sever their banking links with Germany.[40] DTB was therefore compelled to divest itself of its German banks.

An attractive offer was received in late 1917 from Disconto-Gesellschaft AG of Berlin, and the three German offices were sold.[41] 'Due to current circumstances', the DTB annual report explained. The shares of the three banks were exchanged for shares in Disconto-Gesellschaft, in addition to which Disconto-Gesellschaft paid 450,000 marks for the goodwill.[42] Whether the deal was advantageous or not, the 450,000 marks, payable a year after peace was concluded, had by then lost their value, with the collapse of the German currency.[43] On the date of sale, the sum had been equivalent to 157,000 guilders; on the date of payment it was barely 25,000 guilders.[44] Clearly, Disconto-Gesellschaft had counted on a further decline in the currency's value, which had already set in (from 57.73 in 1914 to 36.53 in 1917). That is precisely what happened, although matters could have been even worse since the value plunged to 0.005 in 1923.

---

38 These were Gronauer Bankverein Ledeboer ter Horst & Co, Rheiner Bankverein Ledeboer, Driessen & Co and Westdeutsche Vereinsbank, Kommanditgesellschaft auf Aktien, ter Horst & Co.

39 C. A. van Manen, *De Nederlandsche Overzee Trustmaatschappij*, vol. 3 (Amsterdam, 1935), p. 302.

40 Idem, vol. 4, p. 147–9.

41 HCO, DTB, inv. no. 373, RVC, 25 Oct. 1917, 25 Nov. 1917, 8 Dec. 1917.

42 Idem, inv. no. 373, CVT, 25 Oct. 1917; 22 Nov. 1917.

43 Idem, inv. no. 1157, letter from Disconto-Gesellschaft to DTB, 11 Jan. 1918.

44 The rate of exchange of the German on 29 Nov. 1917 was 34.85 (per 100), on 11 May 1920 this was 5.55. The date 11 May 1920 was the date the war ended (11 Nov. 1918, Compiègne), to which an additional six months was added with (according to a letter from Disconto-Gesellschaft to DTB, 11 Jan. 1918).

Unrest in the Provinces

After reorganizing the bank as a public limited company, Twentsche Bank quickly developed a provincial network, making up the backlog which had resulted from its lack of capital.

The expanding network took the form mainly of participations in key provincial banks. A delicate issue soon arose, in the form of liability for the creditors of these banks. This was the result of these banks doing business in DTB's name (in order to beat off competition from the local branches of the other major banks). DTB was forced to accept this liability, although not officially, so that in the event of a financial collapse they would have to take liability on a case by case basis. The bank's legal advisors pointed out the dangers of this half measure; they argued that the new acquisitions should be turned into branches. Provincial directors, who now exercised considerable freedom, would then have to follow DTB guidelines. But the Blijdensteins were reluctant. They considered the controls adequate and felt no need for a major change. Indeed, according to John, too much central control from Amsterdam created a lack of flexibility, reducing the sense of responsibility and enterprise in the provincial banks.

DTB's participations were further defended with the argument that each bank's own capital was liable. At least this was the case if a bank collapsed, and would be a strong incentive for its joint owners. Nevertheless, taking control before disaster struck might also have its merits. Either way, DTB realized the risks it had taken on by acquiring these banks and attempted to resolve the problem by transferring large credits to its own Credietvereeniging which took two thirds of the risk to the provincial banks' third. By 1918 the provincial banks (including Twente) accounted for half of DTB's loans: a substantial proportion.[45]

Changes at the Top

When John became ill in 1918, and it was apparent that he would not recover quickly, E.D. van Walree took over his position. He was an experienced banker originally from Nederlandse Handel-Maatschappij, and took on the job for a five-year term.[46] When John returned (in 1920), Mr Willem decided to retire from the business. He was in his early fifties, but had lost all interest in the bank since it had become a public limited company. He felt the weight of the moral responsibility more than the previous financial liability. And he had been obliged to show his face in public

---

45 HCO, DTB, inv. no. 373, RVC 08 Dec. 1917. Idem, inv. no. 386, memo from John regarding a discussion of the board of supervisory directors on 6 Dec. 1918. HCO, DTB, inv. no. 373. This memo was appended to the minutes of the meeting of supervisory directors of 6 Dec. 1918.

46 E.D. van Walree (Brummen 1871–Baarn 1950). See F.A. Dankers, 'Emile David van Walree, consul en bankdirecteur', in J. Charité (ed.), *Biografisch Woordenboek voor Nederland*, vol. 3 (The Hague, 1989), pp. 647–8. HCO, DTB, inv. no. 373, RVC 29 and 30 Mar. 1920. Idem, inv. no. 392, minutes of the meeting of DTB directors, 9 July 1923.

far more, which he disliked doing. He decided to move to the country and withdraw entirely once a new director had been found.

At the same time, Adam Roelvink drew attention to the lack of controls over the provincial banks, where major losses were being incurred. His criticisms were aimed at John. Adam wanted the acquisitions of provincial banks to stop, and to turn the focus on their reorganization into DTB branches under the bank's full control and responsibility. He also demanded that the board of directors be reorganized, since three Blijdensteins out of five directors was too many. It resulted in a split between the three Blijdensteins against the two other directors and the delegated supervisory director (Adam himself).

The supervisory directors presented a compromise solution: John was given a year to show that his approach to the provincial banks was correct, and Adam was appeased by an expansion of the board of directors. In fact the latter never occurred since the proposed additional director withdrew at the last minute.[47] After his trial year, John received the approval of the supervisory directors for his policies relating to the provincial banks. He then tried to persuade the supervisory directors to choose between Adam Roelvink and himself. They refused, however, after which John decided in due course to leave the bank. By that time Mr Willem had already retired as a result of ill health. Two prominent figures in the bank were subsequently appointed to the board. This was apparently a temporary measure since their directorships were for a limited period, and since one was 69 and the other 65. It seems the bank was unable to attract any other capable candidates.[48]

Acquisition by Amsterdamsche Bank

In 1923 the director of Amsterdamsche Bank, A.J. van Hengel, proposed working together with DTB, which needed capital. DTB soon realized that there was little advantage for its shareholders in this collaboration, indeed they would quickly lose influence. Even though DTB had an initial advantage in having six directors while Amsterdamsche Bank only had four, after a few years the scales would have tipped in favour of Amsterdamsche Bank since DTB's board was due to be reduced to three, two of whom were older than 65.[49] In the supervisory directors' board the DTB

---

47 The candidate was A.R. Zimmerman (Amsterdam 1869–Velp 1939). See J. Bosmans, 'Alfred Rudolph Zimmerman', in J. Charité (ed.), *Biografisch woordenboek van Nederland*, vol. 1 (The Hague, 1979), pp. 678–9.

48 HCO, DTB, inv. no. 390, letter from Mr Willem Blijdenstein to the directors of DTB, 8 July 1920. Idem, minutes of the directors, 10 Aug. 1920, 11 Aug. 1920. Adam Roelvink was delegated with director's powers (see idem, inv. no. 390, John's memo of December 1920). Idem, inv. no. 390, discussions of the special committee of 6 Dec. 1920, 23 Dec. 1920. Idem, inv. no. 390, letter from D.W. Stork to the directors, 28 Dec. 1920; Idem, inv. no. 390, part of the minutes of the board meeting of 24 Dec. 1920 and 5 Jan. 1921; RVC 28 Jan. 1921. Idem, inv. no. 391, discussion of the special committee, 27 Jan. 1922. Idem, inv. no. 391, letter from John to D.W. Stork, 11 Feb. 1922; letter from D.W. Stork to John, 13 Feb. 1922.

49 These were P. Bredius (Amsterdam 1857–1931), J.G. Schlencker (1853–1928) and J.M. Telders (Amsterdam 1880–Bad Reichenhall 1937).

group would have been a minority immediately. It took DTB's supervisory directors just ninety minutes to reject the proposal. The plan was aborted. Interestingly, Van Hengel had not intended a merger, which might have produced certain savings, but a collaborative arrangement to rival Robaver which led the Dutch banking world in both business and capital. Apart from this impression held by DTB's directors, they would surely have realized that this was a veiled attempt by Van Hengel to take DTB over, rather than collaborate or merge.[50]

Reorganization of Provincial Banks, Credietvereeniging and London

In 1924 Adam Roelvink retired as supervisory director. He had worked at the bank for 43 years and had served as a delegate supervisory director, a supervisory director and general advisor a further ten years. He preferred to let his fiftieth anniversary pass unmarked, formally and informally. D.W. Stork, chairman of the supervisory directors nevertheless wrote him a letter noting Adam's key contribution, the transformation of the bank into a public limited company, adapting it to the changes taking place in the Dutch banking world. Adam Roelvink died in 1927.

Adam's insight into the bank's business is evident from at least three aspects of the reorganization designed to bring the bank into line with rest of the Dutch banking world. First, his vision of the organization of the provincial banks which he wanted to turn into fully-fledged branches under DTB's complete control and responsibility. In 1917–24 these banks had caused significant losses, and the prognosis was not good. Optimism returned, however, and in 1927 they were doing well. More profits were expected in 1928. But competition from other provincial banks grew, since they could boast the ultimate responsibility of their parent company. As a result, people increasingly preferred to entrust their savings and deposits to rival banks than to DTB's.

DTB, which in practice did carry liability by taking responsibility for major losses, and appointing directors and supervisory directors, therefore failed to profit from the advantages simply because it refused to declare its liability officially. In the end DTB had no choice and profits were high, so the bank was able to take on the financial risk. In 1930 the provincial banks were turned into local branches.[51] Adam had been vindicated.

In the 1920s, Credietvereeniging (CRV), the bank's 1871 showpiece, came under increasing pressure as its reserves were eroded. This resulted in a negative image of the vulnerability of published reserves. Borrowers realized they ran the risk of being held liable and feared they would soon have to share in the losses if the reserves melted away. A number of borrowers moved to other banks. It was impossible

---

50 HCO, inv. no. 392, secret minutes of the meeting of the supervisory directors, 1923.

51 HCO, DTB, inv. no. 390, Adam Roelvink's memo of September 1920. See DTB annual report of 1919. Idem, inv. no. 386, memo from the directors of DTB, written by Director G. Warning and Deputy Director A.E. Meijer, to the supervisory directors, attached to the minutes of 24 Jan. 1930. DTB annual report for 1930. Idem, inv. no. 1580, Bijzondere regeling voor de bijkantoren van het Westelijke rayon; Algemeene regeling voor de bijkantoren van De Twentsche Bank NV te Amsterdam.

to dissolve CRV at that time, however, since the bank needed the guarantee fund (otherwise it would have had to issue shares).

In fact Adam had proposed winding CRV up twenty years before, in 1906, because of the advantages for TBV, and because Amsterdamsche Bank and Incasso-Bank both seemed to function without special reserves for credit facilities. The country's other credit societies had by then also largely disappeared. Adam had withdrawn his proposal to wind up CRV, which had been Willem's baby, in order not to jeopardize his plan to turn TBV into a public limited company.

In 1927 the situation was different. There was no need to raise additional capital, since the directors considered the bank held sufficient capital; CRV was dissolved.

An additional reason for dissolving CRV was that credit applicants did not wish to expose themselves to their colleagues and competitors on the CRV applications committee. An announcement of an application was enough for a firm's rivals in any given sector. By turning the application committee into a credit committee the power of decision was replaced by an advisory function. The committee was no longer mentioned to lenders.[52] This did not remove the fear of rival companies learning of an application for credit. This was still a real factor in the 1960s.[53]

The committee's continued existence helped ensure a healthy flow of credit, since it enabled the bank to stay in touch with leading representatives of the principal industrial sectors. This allowed the bank to obtain information, and the committee itself was an important channel of contact with the industrial world.[54]

Finally, the London office: Adam had already recommended in 1906 that London was no longer relevant to TBV. Its business had nothing to do with the bank's business in the Netherlands. It specialized in floater business. Floaters are national or local government debts (such as Treasury bills) at fixed interest. Floaters change in value as the interest rate rises or falls. It is in this, and in the margin of interest rates, that the advantage of these transactions lies. This is working with interest rates on a huge scale. Adam had resigned himself to the situation as long as Willem remained in charge of TBV, but intimated that once Willem had gone he would no longer be willing to carry the responsibility. He was not the only one who wished to close the London office. Some of the supervisory directors, and Jan Berent Roelvink agreed with him. Neither was the bank's involvement supported by John's joint partners in London (who wished to continue), especially Willie Ledeboer, who noted that '[...] in his opinion business should be engaged in to make a profit, but in his view John worked far too much for honour. The result was a large turnover, a major increase in costs, but without adequate returns'.[55]

---

52 HCO, DTB, inv. no. 567, Schets-plan voor de overgang van de Commanditaire Vennootschap in eene Naamlooze Vennootschap door Adam Roelvink, 15 March 1906. Idem, inv. no. 372, RVC, 19 Jan. 1913, 3 Jan. 1914, 17 Jan. 1914. Idem, inv. no. 2470, Commissie van Admissie, 26 April 1901. Idem, inv. no. 43, report on Amsterdam, for 1906. Idem, inv. no. 2060, memo of July 1927 from the directors to Commissie van Admissie, p. 4, 8 and 9.

53 From an interview with Jhr G.C. Six, former secretary of the board of directors and board of supervisory directors of Twentsche Bank.

54 HCO, DTB, inv. no. 408, board of directors, 26 Nov. 1926.

55 Idem, inv. no. 371, RVC, 15 Feb. 1907.

Floater dealings disappeared with the collapse of the Gold standard in September 1931: the devaluation of Sterling cut the bank's holdings in London by an immediate 1.8 million guilders, with a further loss of half a million guilders due to arbitration losses.[56] These were significant amounts in view of DTB's gross profits for that year of 11 million guilders. DTB's directors finally realized the irrelevance of the bank's involvement in London, since the London office's activities bore no relation to the rest of the bank's business in the Netherlands, yet still carried risks. Floater dealings were therefore placed on the back burner and DTB withdrew most of its capital from London. Although DTB's partners also left London, the office continued to function on a reduced scale, in order to preserve the bank's image. Once again a former vision of Adam's (articulated 25 years earlier) was realized.

Summary

Successive waves of modernization took place at Twentsche Bank in the years 1858–1931. It is possible to break these down into periods. Confining the discussion to the main changes, the following series emerges, with reasons and principal circumstances (see Table 9.1). Various general economic circumstances provided opportunities, while others restricted the bank. In the main, until 1917 positive influences tended to dominate: in this period time was mostly on the bank's side. This means that there was usually room to expand. Some major political events can be identified, such as the shift in trade with the Dutch East Indies which enabled textile manufacturers to export directly and therefore led to a need for financial services. The sale of DTB's German offices in 1917 also had a political background.

Most remarkable of all are the motives based on personality. For example, Willem, who longed for independence and realized his dream by going to London, and later also founded a limited partnership rather than a public limited company. At the same time he managed to shape the limited partnership so that it benefited from many of the advantages of a public limited company by, for example, establishing a board of supervisory directors and making shares negotiable. Yet these remained temporary stopgaps. As long as the bank was a limited partnership it was unable to attract sufficient capital to expand. Evidence shows that TBV would have remained a family bank, falling out of the race with Amsterdamsche Bank and Robaver (later also Nederlandsche Handel-Maatschappij) if Adam Roelvink had not intervened to push through the bank's reorganization into a public limited company.

Many questions remain regarding, for example, what motivated Willem. It is interesting to note that Willem, who appears so rational, lost all sense of perspective in his attempts to ensure that his sons would and could succeed him. It is known (from his notes) that John for one did not relish the idea, while Mr Willem, who would never have said as much, felt like a fish out of water at the bank, especially after it had become a public limited company. The three sons were reluctant to take over control. Yet perhaps there is a rational explanation after all. There was a scarcity

---

56 Idem, inv. no. 415, board of directors, 23 Sept. 1931, 25 Sept. 1931, 28 Sept. 1931. Idem, inv. no. 376, RVC 26 May 1932.

Table 9.1   Modernizations at Twentsche Bank, 1858–1931

Date	Modernization	Reason	Principal circumstances
1858	Establishment in London	Benjamin wants to expand and control the business. Willem wants his own business, and to be independent. He wants to leave home.	Benjamin and Willem recognize an opportunity in the inefficient trade in bills between London and Holland.
1861	Establishment in Amsterdam	Benjamin wishes to expand the business.	Political circumstances: liberalization of international commerce led to a shift in exports from NHM to textile manufacturers. High margins make lending to the textile industry attractive.*
1870	Reorganization of limited partnership.	Willem wishes to expand business.	Economic upturn.
1871	Foundation of Credietvereeniging.	To protect the business against losses.	Economic upturn.
1875	Acquisition of Paris bank.	Dividend guarantee for limited partners.	Economic downturn.
1885	Start of share issue business.	Availability of suitable staff.	Development of share issuing business in the Netherlands.
1887	New group of partners besides Willem.	Maintenance of cover for limited partners, after losses in Paris in 1883.	
1916	Change from limited partnership to public limited company.	Insufficient capital in the family to keep up with growing business. Influence of Adam Roelvink.	Economic upturn.
1917	Sale of offices in Germany.	Anglo-American ban on trade with Germany.	Political circumstances: First World War.
1920	Reorganization of board of directors.	Conflict in existing board.	Economic downturn.
1927	Dissolution of Credietvereeniging.	Loss of business.	Competition in sector.

Date	Modernization	Reason	Principal circumstances
1930	Reorganization of provincial banks.	Loss of business.	Competition in sector.
1931	Restriction of business in London.	Risks in London, lack of purpose of involvement in London for general bank business.	Economic downturn, devaluation of Sterling in 1931.

* It is unclear when credit was first provided to industrial companies from the acquired deposits. However, it was taking place in 1859, and again in 1863, when the transactions involved discounts by TBV aided by acquired deposits.

of skilled banking personnel. Maybe this is how Willem viewed his sons: there was no one else available. This lack of qualified bankers is apparent from the influence of Adam Roelvink and the successive attempts to attract Zimmerman, mayor of Rotterdam, to the post of director (which eventually failed). It is also apparent from the sources.[57]

A final personal factor was John's illness in 1919. This led to Van Walree's appointment as a deputy director, and a loss of influence of the Blijdensteins on the board. If John had not fallen ill, the new configuration would presumably have taken longer to develop.

The three final modernizations, the reorganization of the provincial banks, dissolving Credietvereeniging and scaling down the London office, were more or less forced on the bank, which had continued to employ outmoded practices and needed to catch up with changing circumstances in the banking world.

---

57 J. de Vries, *Herinneringen en dagboek van Ernst Heldring (1871–1954)* (Groningen, 1970).

Appendix

Table 9.2   Capital formation at Twentsche Bank, 1862–1916 (in millions of guilders)

Date	Limited Partners	Managing Partners Capital	Managing Partners Reserve	Managing Partners Capital and Reserve	Managing Partners and Limited Partners
1862	0.3				0.3
1863	0.3				0.3
1864	0.4				0.4
1865	0.4				0.4
1866	0.5				0.5
1867	0.5				0.5
1868	0.8				0.8
1869	0.8				0.8
1870	1.0				1.0
1871	2.5	0.2		0.2	2.7
1872	3.7	0.4		0.4	4.1
1873	4.8	0.4	0.1	0.5	5.4
1874	4.8	0.3	0.2	0.4	5.2
1875	4.8	0.3	0.2	0.5	5.2
1876	4.7	0.3	0.2	0.5	5.2
1877	4.7	0.2	0.3	0.5	5.2
1878	4.6	0.2	0.4	0.6	5.2
1879	4.6	0.3	0.4	0.7	5.3
1880	4.6	0.3	0.5	0.7	5.4
1881	7.8	0.3	0.8	1.1	8.9
1882	7.8	0.3	0.9	1.2	9.0
1883	7.8	0.3	1.0	1.3	9.1
1884	7.8	0.3	0.6	0.9	8.7
1885	6.9	0.3	0.6	1.0	7.8
1886	6.9	0.3	0.6	1.0	7.8
1887	6.9	0.3	0.6	1.0	7.8
1888	6.9	0.3	0.7	1.0	7.8
1889	6.9	0.3	0.7	1.0	7.9
1890	6.9	0.3	0.8	1.1	7.9

Date	Limited Partners	Managing Partners Capital	Managing Partners Reserve	Managing Partners Capital and Reserve	Managing Partners and Limited Partners
1891	6.9	0.3	0.8	1.1	8.0
1892	6.9	0.3	0.9	1.2	8.1
1893	6.9	0.3	0.9	1.2	8.1
1894	6.9	0.3	0.9	1.2	8.1
1895	6.9	0.3	1.0	1.3	8.2
1896	6.9	0.6	1.0	1.5	8.4
1897	6.9	0.6	1.0	1.5	8.4
1898	6.9	0.6	1.1	1.6	8.5
1899	8.9	1.4	1.6	3.0	11.9
1900	8.9	1.5	1.7	3.2	12.0
1901	8.9	1.8	1.8	3.5	12.4
1902	8.9	1.9	1.9	3.9	12.7
1903	8.9	2.9	2.0	4.9	13.8
1904	8.9	3.1	2.0	5.1	14.0
1905	8.9	3.2	2.0	5.2	14.1
1906	8.9	3.3	2.1	5.4	14.3
1907	8.9	3.6	2.2	5.8	14.7
1908	8.9	3.5	2.3	5.9	14.7
1909	8.9	4.2	3.2	7.3	16.2
1910	8.9	5.0	3.4	8.4	17.3
1911	8.9	5.2	3.7	8.9	17.8
1912	8.9	4.6	3.9	8.5	17.3
1913	8.9	4.5	4.0	8.4	17.3
1914	8.9	4.3	4.1	8.4	17.3
1915	8.9	4.3	4.2	8.5	17.4
1916	8.9	3.9	3.6	7.5	16.4

Source: Annual reports of Twentsche Bank.

Table 9.3   Profitability, capital and reserve of Twentsche Bank (DTB), Amsterdamsche Bank (AB) and Rotterdamsche Bank (RB), 1903–1913, in guilders (x 1,000) and percentage

Date	Capital and Reserve (guilders x 1,000)			Net Profit (guilders x 1,000)			Profitability (percentage)		
	DTB	AB	RB	DTB	AB	RB	DTB	AB	RB
1903	11537	8265	7225	1207	810	541	10.5	9.8	7.5
1904	11795	8365	7240	1284	768	456	10.9	9.2	6.3
1905	11890	8465	7250	1487	920	471	12.5	10.9	6.5
1906	11840	8590	7260	1398	1051	551	11.8	12.2	7.6
1907	12169	11840	7270	1719	972	544	14.1	8.2	7.5
1908	12338	11940	7270	2186	1064	577	17.7	8.9	7.9
1909	13975	12065	7300	1943	1206	598	13.9	10.0	8.2
1910	14585	12215	9360	1922	1323	813	13.2	10.8	8.7
1911	14862	15055	17250	1745	1477	1615	11.7	9.8	9.4
1912	14966	15205	25209	1837	1688	2304	12.3	11.1	9.1
1913	14509	21395	26350	1932	1975	2715	13.3	9.2	10.3

Source: Historisch Centrum Overijssel (HCO) in Zwolle, the Netherlands, Twentsche Bank archive, inv. no. 566.

CHAPTER 10

Success and Failure of Modernization in Post-War Greek Banking: The Case of Ergasias Bank

Margarita Dritsas

Introduction

Banking modernization has historically been a long-standing process in the national development agenda, highlighting the fact that the banking sector like a sort of barometer reacted to the impact of all crises, economic and political. Modernization, when applied, was the result of processes of emulation, competition and institutional specialization within the banking sector, on the one hand, and of government regulation on the other.

As Greece expanded in the second half, and more particularly during the last quarter of the nineteenth century and was opened to foreign capital markets, new banks were founded with foreign capital resources, and new types of banking were introduced. The Bank of Athens, representing French capital interests introduced to Greece the pattern of 'banque d'affaires' or universal banking. It was founded in the 1890's and in a country changing fast, it became the main competitor for the biggest national credit institution, the National Bank of Greece. It fostered many large infrastructure projects as well as industries and maintained the role of investment bank until it merged in 1952 with its antagonist, the NBG. This period also saw monetary modernization with Greece joining the Latin Monetary Union and later attempting to adopt the gold standard and instead resorting to the system of forced circulation, ending with a default on foreign payments and the imposition of international financial control (1898). In 1910, the country opted for the gold exchange standard and a relative stability lasted until 1917, when Greece entered the War. During this period, smaller banks had proliferated, benefiting from free trade policies and monetary stability. Peaceful development however was interrupted, and as war expenditure soared the public debt was inflated and banks were once again found in turmoil.

A second more comprehensive phase of banking modernization occurred in the interwar years, when the discussion about the chronic deficiencies of the Greek economy came to a head after the tragic loss of Asia Minor in 1922. The reform incubated for several years was effected this time under the influence of the League of Nations and British banking policy. Temporary stabilization was brought about with the help of large public loans advanced to Greece by foreign banks under the aegis of the League of Nations. Management of the loans was entrusted to the National Bank, which still maintained the issuing monopoly in addition to having launched new operations in the Greek market. A large public debt, high inflation, chronic budget deficits had meanwhile created an explosive situation necessitating another emergency loan (1925). Problems it was estimated, could be solved if the country acquired a central bank and the drachma joined the gold standard. The policy was not restricted to Greece but was imposed on most other Central and South Eastern European countries. While until then, banks operated according to the main foundation law of the NBG, in 1927 a new law foresaw the creation of two state-run institutions, the Bank of Greece and the National Mortgage Bank. As a result, the National Bank of Greece lost the issuing privilege to the Central Bank, some of its other functions went to the mortgage bank, and rural credit was assumed by a third bank, the Agricultural Bank in 1929. There was a period of difficulty in the relations between NBG and the new Central Bank arising from an initial phase of competition between the two institutions. Furthermore, the collapse of a series of smaller financial companies in the wake of the economic crisis, precipitated the first comprehensive Bank Act in 1931 (Law 5076/1931). The new law regulated the operation of all banks and joint-stock companies. It described in detail which organizations qualified as banks; it fixed minimum capital requirements for the foundation of a bank; it outlined the obligation of banks to maintain liquid funds to a proportion of 12 per cent of their total drachmae deposits, at the Bank of Greece. The law also forbade banks to carry out commercial or industrial activities and fixed credit limits. With few changes, this law remained in force until the 1970s. The Greek banking system continued to be characterized by a high degree of concentration.

A third period of modernization started during the post-Second World War reconstruction era, but reached its full momentum much later during the mid 1970s and lasted until the late 1980s. A new institutional framework was introduced and new banks emerged, based on different ideas of banking and allowing the application of many innovations to the Greek banking system, including a new bank.

What follows is concerned with this last phase of changes. After giving a rough outline of the background on which new elements were grafted, the main features of a new bank founded during this period, will be used to illustrate better the points made.

The Background which made Modernization Necessary

Unlike earlier phases of modernization, the post-war process was not only comprehensive but followed a different direction than previous attempts, i.e. it introduced increasing deregulation of banking and allowed the foundation of new types of banks.

The period between the end of the Second World War – in essence after 1949 and the end of the Civil War – was dominated by the reconstruction effort of a country utterly ruined and impoverished by the hostilities. The economy was in shambles and governments strove to restore monetary stability, on the one hand, and to bring production up to the pre-war levels, on the other. Capital requirements were formidable and shortages just as dramatic. New control agencies emerged as early as in 1946, such as the Currency Committee, which became the central mechanism for the control of economic policy. A 50 per cent devaluation of the drachma in 1953 was accompanied by a reduction in interest rates, whilst a certain liberalization occurred in price and import controls. Exports, as a result grew and together with emigrant and merchant marine remittances were considered the main sources of currency, but new legislation was also introduced to attract foreign capital (E.L.2687/1953). A new law regulated banking (Emergency Law 1665/1951) by introducing entry barriers, stipulating that any creation of a new bank was subject to a permit granted by the currency committee, while strict control was also exercised by the Bank of Greece on credit and deposit limits. It was clear that economic policy emanated from the Central Bank and its appendage, the currency committee. This was concurrent with the dominant view among state officials that central planning was the solution and that the total of credit demand for the whole economy should be considered, according to a set of uniform criteria, subject to capital availability.[1] The new laws of the 1950s, if anything, accentuated the high degree of concentration, which had since the interwar characterized the banking system on the whole. The process was furthermore strengthened when four of the main banks merged. Immediately after monetary stabilization (devaluation of the drachma) in 1953, the Bank of Athens was absorbed by the National Bank of Greece (NBG), whereas five years later, the Ionian Bank merged with Laiki (Popular) Bank in 1958.[2] The creation of larger banks accentuated the role of commercial banking in the economy and in 1954, the Currency Committee allowed banks to use their funds to finance industry and trade. The mergers and a rise in interest rates led to an increase of private deposits and savings (which had been decimated during and after the war),[3] but credit policies in contrast remained conservative.[4]

Central planning and strict control was the mark not only of banking but industry too, pertaining on the whole to the private sector. Chronic weaknesses of the secondary sector had their corollary in a contradictory and insufficient state industrial policy, which was generally inserted in the framework of import substitution and autarchy. Industrialization was still seen as one of the central goals of modernization and national development, but in the absence of sufficient motivation from private investment, the State stepped in to ensure its recovery and progress. Accordingly, new institutions emerged to design and coordinate the necessary policies and special incentives were introduced (Law 4171/1961). Alongside conventional banks, special state-run credit organizations were founded to cover the needs of industry and the already budding tourist development (OXOA, OBA, etc).[5] It was natural that competition would arise between commercial banks and those credit institutions run by the state. Commercial banks followed suit by founding specialized subsidiaries. An investment bank was founded in 1962 by the Commerical Bank of Greece,

---

1   *Trapeza Hellados, Ta prota Peninta Chronia* (Bank of Greece, The first fifty years) (Athens, 1977), p. 428.

2   Fifteen years later, the new bank would be acquired by Emporiki Bank.

3   Interest rate on deposits was increased from 7 to 10 per cent, in order for savings to flow back to the banks.

4   This policy facilitated the operation of alternative financial networks.

5   The Organization for the Financing of Economic Development – OXOA (1954) and the Organization of Industrial Development – OBA (1960) eventually merged in 1964 to form a state-run investment organization.

while in 1963, the National Bank established its own subsidiary ETEBA. The two large privately owned banks could now freely hold stocks of customer companies, and through the control of industrial and other large firms, they gradually formed important business groups.

Despite the impressive rate of development after 1956 when GDP rose by about 6.2 per cent annually until 1967, central control over banking was maintained. Bank deposits increased spectacularly (Zetrides 1973) but their character did not change, i.e. they remained short-term. The new law also intervened to regulate the supply of credit by 'convincing' commercial banks to advance 30 per cent of their disposable capital as long-term loans, which would mostly be channelled to industry and to the public sector. Quantitative and qualitative control of advances was still entrusted to a special department of the currency committee (Central department of bank advances follow-up). The promotion of long-term lending was also based on a policy of differential interest rates between deposits and advances, and depending on the quality of collateral of customer firms. These measures represented a shy and cautious attempt at modernization but on the whole, fell short in their more general goal to lead to a competitive economy. This first period of post-war Greek development closed tragically with a military coup and a seven-year dictatorial regime. The process of modernization, which had appeared to set in motion hesitant changes and a certain restructuring of the economy was interrupted abruptly, and the banking reform was postponed until the return to democracy in 1974.

The preconditions established until 1966, nevertheless, the impetus gathered by the promise of accession to the EEC after the signing of the special agreement in 1961, and the more general situation in Europe allowed the Greek economy to continue its course during the early dictatorship years. Soon, however, serious problems would appear as the economy shifted towards consumption. Although demand expanded there was little adjustment of the institutional framework to the new needs. Construction and building industry became the steam engine of the economy benefiting from an unprecedented extension of credit and by tax benefits. At the same time, mass tourism was energetically encouraged and emigration was strengthened.

Commercial banking discovered consumer lending, and tried to solve the shortage of foreign resources by accepting deposits in foreign currencies of Greeks residing and working abroad. It also extended the opening of current accounts only to face an immediate problem from the plethora of bounced cheques which led instead to the introduction of more bureaux gathering intelligence on customers.[6] High inflation ensued in 1973 and the advent of the first oil crisis, the situation also being aggravated because of the collapse of monetary stability (ensured until then by participation in the Bretton Woods System). The impact was disastrous for the Greek economy, prompting the author of a Bank of Greece report to confirm: 'The economic policy of the dictatorship not only reversed the monetary balance but led to a general recession. At the same time, it interrupted progress towards restructuring the Greek economy.'[7]

---

6   Until then, only big banks like the NBG or Comm. Bank had such facilities which they had introduced during the interwar years.

7   *Trapeza Hellados*, p. 628.

The banking system reacted to the crisis by contracting credit, and leaving the space open to foreign banks, which had meanwhile proliferated, succeeding in capturing a growing share of the Greek market. It is worth noting that until 1964 two foreign banks operated in Greece but between 1964 and 1972 five more were added. They controlled 7.4 per cent of deposits and 9.4 per cent of credit but their share was steadily increasing. Two years later, there were 12 foreign banks controlling 11 per cent of total credit advances. Despite a certain 'balkanization' or fragmentation of their share caused by the increase in their numbers, their profits remained impressive. In 1973, their average ratio profit/capital was 26.5 per cent compared with 6.4 per cent only for Greek banks.[8] Foreign banks had continued to prosper even after the collapse of the dictatorship and in 1976, they owned 35 branches across the country, concentrating 15.4 per cent of all advances and 12.5 per cent of all deposits.[9] This performance compared with the corresponding figures for 1966 (2.5 per cent and 2 per cent respectively) was to a large extent due to the inertia in the Greek banking system and the failure of modernizing efforts.

The 1970s

Despite adverse international economic conditions the return to political normalcy in Greece generated an unprecedented feeling of euphoria and relegated to a lower priority the importance of economic shocks. Relative economic recovery occurred after 1975, while negotiations resumed for full accession of Greece to the EEC.[10] Between 1974 and 1979 OECD reports ranked Greece second after Japan in terms of labour productivity growth.[11] A wind of modernization blew across the country and this is well documented among other indicators in the rise of GDP from $1870 in 1973 to $4164 in 1980.[12] With regard to the banking system, in 1975 there were 22 commercial banks operating in Greece and eight credit organizations. Of the banks, ten were Greek and twelve were branches of foreign banks (of them six were American, one British, one Canadian, one French, one Dutch and one Iranian). The National Bank of Greece continued to be the biggest financial institution of the country with a substantial part of its assets owned by the state. Agricultural Bank was state-run, while there were two mortgage banks and three investment banks. The list was completed by the existence of two specialized organizations, the Caisse d'Epargne and the Post Office Savings Bank.

The post-dictatorship period marked a clear break with the autocratic past and signalled important institutional changes both in politics and the economy, not always,

---

8   This analysis is included in a memorandum for the foundation of Trapeza Ergasias in November 1974.

9   K. Kostis, *Collaboration and Competition: Seventy Years of the Union of Greek Banks* (Athens, 1997), p. 201.

10 Negotiations had been interrupted during the dictatorship years and full accession was only effected in 1981.

11 Cf. G. Alogoskoufis, 'Greece, the two faces of Janus: Institutions, Policy Regimes and Macroeconomic Performance', in *Economic Policy*, April 1995, pp. 149–91.

12 *Trapeza Hellados*, p. 721.

however, free of contradictions. While there was extensive political liberalization, state intervention in the economy, which had been a standard feature in Greece since the inter-war period, was stepped up. Investment and growth rates recovered and inflation was checked. After 1979, however, a gradual downtrend started, becoming more obvious by the second oil crisis in 1982, and was sustained by higher public deficits and debts (increased expenditure for defence, on the one hand, and extensive nationalization of ailing private firms, on the other). The state sector of the economy was given a further boost producing a crowding-out effect for the private sector of the economy – especially industry – which became even less competitive. Many firms already living on borrowed time, came to the brink of bankruptcy and banks and other special agencies were called to salvage them.[13] Furthermore, governments could no longer postpone satisfying long suppressed popular demands for income redistribution, and curtailment of unemployment. Amidst such difficulties, which would otherwise have produced a drastic change in policy, Greece became a full member of the EEC (1981). Accession, which had been high on the agenda of political desiderata, resulted in trade liberalization and massive transfer of resources from Brussels, which, in addition to introducing distortions in various economic sectors (e.g. agriculture), concealed for some time yet the real and serious economic problems.[14] Hesitant attempts at stabilization started rather late (by the PASOK Socialist in 1985, and by the Conservative New Democracy governments in 1991 and 1992) and were allowed to be truncated, while the country continued to rely on significant EEC transfers.[15] Even after, despite accession to the monetary union, Greece remained one of the less wealthy and problematic European partners.

In the post-dictatorship period, three elements continued to stand out in the banking system: concentration, centralization of power and inefficient state control. By 1970, banking policy was fully regulated by the state through the monetary committee and the Central Bank. Furthermore, the 'nationalization' of the two major banks, the National Bank of Greece and the Commercial Bank of Greece accentuated the inefficiency and bureaucratic character of the system, making the major credit institutions rather sluggish state accessories. Already in 1972, 90 per cent of all banking was effected through the two giants. Indeed, at the end of 1972, the Big Five (NBG, CBG, Ionian-People's Bank, Credit Bank and General Bank) controlled 97.5 per cent of banking assets, 91.3 per cent of deposits, and 89.6 per cent of credit.[16] Almost 73 per cent of deposits with the commercial banks were private, having

---

13 In 1983, the Organization for the Reconstruction of Ailing Enterprises was founded, taking over private firms in order to turn them around, sell them or close them down.

14 Opinions on the degree of liberalization differ. A. Giannitsis, *Accession into the EEC and the Effects on Industry and Trade*, Foundation of Mediterranean Studies (Athens, 1988) (in Greek), argues that average nominal protection rate was reduced from 45 per cent to 35 per cent between 1975 and 1985, while Alogoskoufis, 'Greece', and L. Katseli, 'Structural Adjustment of the Greek Economy', in C. Bliss and J. de Macedo (eds), *Unity with Diversity in the European Economy: The Community's Southern Frontier* (Cambridge, 1990), maintain that effective protection hardly declined and the impact on Greece's economic performance was small, thanks to the long transition periods enjoyed by Greece.

15 Alogoskoufis, 'Greece', p. 157.

16 A. Zitridis, *The Banking System in Greece* (Athens, 1973), pp. 25–6, 28–33.

grown substantially since 1956. Commercial banks controlled almost 45 per cent of total credit, 81 per cent of which could be described as short-term. Equally important was the concentration in the network of branches

Central planning and control of credit was a result of political will but also went parallel to the primitive state of the capital market, especially the stock exchange. The long history of distrust between the citizens of Greece and state authorities, inefficient policies and repeated economic crises had fostered a particular mentality: Investment was channelled rather to real estate acquisitions, speculation on foreign exchange and on gold, even hoarding, but not so much on stock transactions.[17] The number of quoted enterprises was still very small and big firms could always find capital from the big banks with which they had forged long and solid network ties. Interest rates continued to be regulated centrally by the monetary committee, which also obliged commercial banks to deposit, free of interest, part of their deposits and their foreign currency reserves with the central bank. Despite the existence of several banks, essential differentiation of institutions was very weak and antagonism among banks remained limited. The central bank was not commonly used as a lender of banks, the use of a checkbook was not widespread, current accounts absorbed only 33 per cent of the total money supply. Long-term lending to industry became compulsory for the banks and eventually reached 35 per cent of total credit. Of their total deposits, 33 per cent had to be channelled to industry. Detailed and complicated administrative procedures were imposed on commercial banks and led to the latter's increasing bureaucratization. Competition was restricted to technical improvements and methods of transactions (e.g. mobile banking in the provinces introduced by the CBG, till system of service, savings booklets, etc. It became standard procedure for the governors of the big state banks to be appointed by the government and they were invariably political figures with little, or often no, managerial qualifications. This had negative consequences for continuity of policy, planning, and rationality in decision making. At the same time, powerful business groups had emerged, as a number of smaller banks, insurance firms, industries, tourist enterprises, shipyards and shipping enterprises were now controlled (through investment subsidiaries) by the National Bank of Greece (NBG) and by its competitor, the Commercial Bank of Greece (CBG).

By the mid-1970s, the system had become overburdened with serious problems. Commercial banking had become an oligopoly, if not in fact a monopoly, given the size of the largest bank, the NBG. When the Commercial Bank of Greece was nationalized, the system reached an apogee of centralization, bureaucratization and inefficiency. Among European countries, Greece also had the largest concentration rate. Compared with Italy, Portugal, Austria, Ireland, Holland, Belgium, Sweden, Norway, Finland, Denmark and Spain, Greece had in 1974 the smallest number of national commercial banks, the biggest number of foreign banks and the smallest number of commercial banks in relation to the total number of national and foreign

---

17 Between 1973 and 1978, land values had increased fourfold, gold value tripled. Stocks lost up to 8 per cent. Cf. A. Nicolopoulos, *Memorandum on the Capital Market*, June 1978. Ergasias Archives, File: Foundation-Correspondence.

credit institutions.[18] Furthermore, the gigantism of NBG was proportional neither to the volume of deposits nor to economic growth.

Meanwhile, interesting changes were occurring in the landscape of foreign banking, where relatively fewer constrains were imposed and where actors had proliferated.[19] By 1972, the number of foreign banks had risen to seven – there were only two by 1964 – and their share of the market although barely 7.4 per cent of deposits and 9.4 per cent of credit was growing. In 1974, there were already twelve institutions, controlling altogether 11 per cent of total credit, but causing a fragmentation of their portion of the market. They nevertheless extracted important profits as shown by five American banks in 1973, which marked average rates of net income/capital at 26.5 per cent, against 6.4 per cent of Greek banks.[20] A consensus, naturally, emerged among decision makers that institutional modernization was indispensable.

Ergasias Bank S.A.

Looking at the creation of a new bank, Ergasias S.A., founded in 1975 allows us to highlight the most important features of the reform and its limits. The foundation took place against a background of strong forces of preservation, and its founders sought to exploit the liberalization promoted by the new legislation. At the same time, it became a modernizing agent of the Greek banking system by introducing new features in terms of structure and culture of a credit institution. It also embarked on introducing and consolidating, for the first time in Greece, what could be described as 'niche' banking, having internalized the important changes that had occurred in Greek society.

It was in an environment of high bank concentration, low differentiation and low specialization and of a great vacuum created in private banking that Ergasias Bank was founded in 1975, the first new bank in Greece since 1937.[21] Its emergence coincided with the desire for general liberalization and gave a practical expression to the move for specialization of the financial system. Its foundation carried out neither by one of the leading credit institutions, nor by any one or any group of

---

18 K. Kapsaskis, *Commercial Banks in Greece – 1974*, Memorandum in Greek, October 1974. Estimates were based on data published by the Bankers Almanac 1973/74. Ergasias Archives, Foundation Correspondence.

19 In 1972, seven foreign banks operated in Greece, all of which were American: American Express had settled in Greece already in the 1920s. First National City Bank of New York was established in 1964. Chase Manhattan Bank, Bank of America, Bank of Nova Scotia, First National Bank of Chicago and Continental Illinois National Bank settled between 1968 and 1971, at the height, that is, of the military dictatorship.

20 Ergobank, *Memorandum for its foundation*, November 1974. Ergasias Archives, Foundation Correspondence. Percentage refers to ratio net income before taxes/as percentage of equity.

21 In 1937, the Army Fund Bank S.A. (Trapeza metochikou tameiou stratou) was founded and marked the increasing importance of the army in Greece, during the years of the Metaxas dictatorship (1936–41). It was renamed General Bank of Greece in 1965, at a time of political instability and of limited liberalization.

prominent businessmen, signalled a turning point of sociological importance in Greek entrepreneurship. Big banks and big business had little incentive for similar ventures. They were content with the ties they had forged among them over the years and the networks, which they had formed and which attenuated any dysfunction caused by the oligopoly structure. The leading banks had turned their attention rather to investment banking and continued to finance the secure needs of old and big firms. Although many of these firms had turned over part of their business to foreign banks, and although the share of NBG's market (in terms of deposits) had considerably decreased between 1970 and 1973, the status quo was not seriously threatened.

Ergasias Bank was created by, and for, the rather marginal, even traditional, but particularly dynamic in the case of Greece, *petit-bourgeois* sector. It took the initiative of an astute middle class bank executive who realized the new potential and succeeded to rally the support of small entrepreneurs and capitalists. The post-war economy's impressive growth rates had encouraged the proliferation mainly of small- and medium-sized business firms. SMEs were beginning to be considered important for the Greek economy but were marginal in terms of their ability to communicate to form a collective consciousness and do business with formal credit organizations, relying mostly on informal lending networks. A multitude of self-employed professionals, increasing numbers of civil servants and white-collar workers completed the panorama of post-war middle class (*petit-bourgeois*) Greece. All of these were to become the backbone of the new bank's clientele. Many of these features may be considered less modern than what has so far been the norm in modernization perspectives; however, as a concept modernization has an ideal type value, when inserted in the framework of the particular conditions of each case considered. In this case, the new bank introduced several innovations, in addition to using in a new way and new combination various structures and agents of the Greek society and economy to produce a more effective and efficient institution.

Ergasias Bank as a special bank was conceived by Constantinos Kapsaskis, the son of a shopkeeper from the island of Zante, who started his career in 1942, at the age of 19, as a bank employee with the well established and quite innovative for the time Commercial Bank of Greece. He soon realized how sluggish and antiquated Greek banking was by comparison to the English system, which he had the opportunity to get familiarized with through CBG's branch offices in London. He tried to suggest reforms, which, however, did not meet with the approval of S. Andreadis, managing director and biggest shareholder of the bank. Kapsaskis resigned from the CBG and was employed by Hambros bank in London, where as he confessed later, he understood the rationale and the scope of real banking. With new experience under his belt, and already planning his return to Greece, he started working for American Express, which had branches in Athens and Thessaloniki, and where his European experience was appreciated. It was the period of the great expansion of American banks in Europe, the advent of crucial changes in the structure and style of management and human resources in the use of modern technology and in the overall post-war mentalities and ethics in business and banking. Once back in Greece (1961) as deputy manager of the Athens branch of American Express, Kapsaskis assessed the changes brought about in post-war Greek society. As representative of a foreign bank and familiar with the Greek system and culture he opened a new branch in

Piraeus and chose old colleagues from the CBG days to work closely with as well as partners from other foreign banks. They recruited the branch personnel by devising new tests of general knowledge, which were later used for recruitment in Ergasias Bank. The Piraeus branch was a success and Kapsaskis started working with the idea of diffusing it to the rest of Greece. Because Greek law did not allow foreign banks to have branches in the provinces, he came up with the idea of a Greek bank in which American Express and as many of its clients as they wished would participate. He communicated his idea about a new bank to his superiors in the USA but instead of an approval, he was transferred to New York with jurisdiction over France, Italy and Greece.[22] As he later declared, he now advised against the plan, and it is possible that Kapsaskis was trying to dissociate himself from US policy. When in 1974 the tables turned and the military regime collapsed, this original plan was definitely shelved. A new challenge became the creation of a modern Greek bank able to introduce innovations and make profits. The green light for Ergasias Bank was given. Kapsaskis estimated that inertia was a powerful force in old institutions, and that any reaction from the banking establishment would not be threatening. Besides, the new bank decided to tread cautiously and was not expected to break the banking oligopoly, while politicians and economists were skeptical about the impact of Greek mentality and culture.[23] In a memorandum Kapsaskis wrote in 1974 introducing the idea of Trapeza Ergasias, he stressed the importance of institutional sensitivity to the needs of the economy, to the problems and the aspirations of development agents in all economic sectors. He advocated abolition of oligopolies, autonomy for previously merged banks (i.e. the smaller banks absorbed by the two big ones). He suggested that collaboration was necessary between NBG and the Chambers of Commerce, of Industry and of Technology in order to create specialized banks covering the needs of neglected sectors like export trade, small industry, public works, local infrastructure, and shipping. His schema also included other modern institutions such as leasing and factoring companies, inter-bank money market mechanisms, commercial paper operations and finance companies.

The pattern on which Ergasias Bank was fashioned drew its principles from the Morgan Bank, Lloyds and Credit Suisse. It was conceived as a classic commercial bank, specialized in business with the Arab world and the Middle East, on the one hand, and, most importantly, the neglected sector of small- and medium-sized Greek enterprises (SMEs), on the other. It should be noted that within the larger European Community, Greece was (and still is) considered as a platform to promote relations

---

22 Greece was under military rule then.

23 In February 1975 a formal application for approving the statutes of the new bank was made. An assessment prepared by the Bank of Greece stated that 'the addition of new banks in the Greek system is purposeful and desirable, on the condition that the new unit would make profits, be independent and attenuate the existing banking monopoly'. The positive opinion was based on various estimates about anticipated performance measured (a) in terms of volume of deposits during the following five years, (b) in terms of expenses (lower than for other banks) and (c) in terms of the difference between credit and debit interest levels (ecart). Although the estimates arrived at by the Bank of Greece were almost 30 per cent lower than those by the candidate bank, the overall picture was optimistic. *Ergobank Archives*, Correspondence, Foundation 1 April 1975.

with the South, especially the Arab countries in Africa and the Middle East. The bank would not only advance loans to Greek SMEs, but would act as a general consultant to them so that they would give up traditional management techniques and become more productive. Kapsaskis also drew his precedent from history, on the one hand, from inter-war USA when after the Depression, the American Government had created a new institution, the 'Small Business Administration'. The second precedent, on the other hand, came from England, when in 1945, the Bank of England and six more banks created the Finance Corporation for Industry. In a way, the new Greek institution, as a hybrid between a savings bank and a finance organization, was the 1970s Greek version and response to the need of reform, fit for a small country, but equally ambitious with its earlier counterparts.

In all these respects, the bank represented an innovation of the system, it was created neither by the big banks nor by entrepreneurs, but by a group of bank managers. This, in itself, was a major deviation from the usual pattern of business activity in Greece, and, indeed, elsewhere too. In terms of its capital structure it was a completely new type of bank bearing no resemblance to the other Greek banks, state or privately controlled, since it was a small wide-based joint-stock company. Its statutes included the names of 1822 shareholders, among them businessmen, employees, pensioners, housewives, banking executives of whom none held more that 3 per cent of total capital. The decision for this condition was based on research previously carried out about conditions in the Greek capital market, especially the stock exchange. The latter's prestige was low, stockholders representing a negligible 1 per cent of the population, against about 20 per cent in the rest of Europe. There was, therefore, a reservoir of capital holders to be mobilized by systematic campaigning and the promise of quick and high profits by the new bank.[24] The idea met with much distrust, indifference or scorn, but a core of serious investors was eventually converted to the concept of the new bank and also accepted the principle of a wide capital base.[25] Among the founding members, who became outside directors of the board there were industrialists, shipowners, and other entrepreneurs, Kapsaskis, himself, and a university professor. Each could secure the support of a few tens of other shareholders, who eventually also became customers of the new institution. Several constraints were nevertheless introduced, so that control remained with the initial directors and the principle of representing the SME sector. The iron rule was that no one shareholder would control more than 3 per cent of total capital. This resulted in a type of management, on the one hand, much less dependent on the potential power of large shareholders and, on the other, in greater rationality and reliability. In fact, it gave full power to small capitalists. The initial distrust soon

---

24 Legislation was already favourable because return on stocks was not taxed as were dividends per shareholder up to 60,000 drs.

25 The standard comment was that 'Greeks were not ready for such new ideas' referring mainly to the wide base of the capital structure. Later, suspicion grew wondering who was hiding behind the group of four and the over one thousand shareholders registered. Cf. K.S. Kapsaskis, *Anamniseis 15 chronon syn-Ergasias* (Cooperation memoirs of the past 15 years) (Athens, 1991).

changed and with time sufficient resources were secured (start-up capital reached 800 million drachmas). No shareholder controlled more than 5 per cent of capital.

The novelty of a wide-base joint-stock firm, however, took some time to consolidate. Nor was it easy for a new culture to neutralize traditional mentalities and business practices. For a period of three years, between 1982 and 1985, there was a serious threat of the bank's structure disintegrating into a traditional type of firm with only a few large shareholders having full control. It took much more than time to stave off threats. On the one hand, the unwavering determination of the inside directors who were determined to safeguard their creation, was crucial in mobilizing the rest of the shareholders. Satisfactory results by the bank over an uninterrupted period of seven years kept ownership content. An enviable international reputation as a foremost institution, which adhered to a particular 'banking ethos' also provided support for the defenders of this type of bank and style of management.

The new institution introduced innovations in many areas, especially with regard to human capital. A number of Greeks at home and abroad became officers in the bank having previously held executive positions in foreign banks and/or having maintained their contacts with bankers outside Greece. Their experience allowed them to concentrate on issues of efficient organization and to modernize the decision-making process. Drawing resources from the Commercial Bank of Greece and American Express – both reputed for their successful combination of traditional and modern methods and techniques – was important for building the new bank culture. The rest of the personnel were recruited on the basis of a test devised to assess their general knowledge level, and on interviews – procedures that is, which were yet hardly used in Greek banking. One of the greater concerns of the founders and the initial group of employees (around forty) was training and education and one of their first actions became to start an on-the-job training programme where older colleagues were teaching recently recruited ones. Education included a two-month induction course both on teaching how to deal with formal banking operations (over the counter and behind the scenes) and to give advice about how to internalize the specific new culture/ethic, which the bank wished to instill. More advanced courses were followed by managers. Employees became a sort of advertisement for promoting quality of service and strengthening the social profile of the bank. During the whole of its autonomous life, the bank avoided a very strict division of labour, opting for a 'universal' style of functions. This made its labour force versatile and, at the same time, reduced considerably running costs. Emphasis was also put on relations with the customers. Twenty years later, one of its directors still found it necessary to insist that 'legally a bank belonged to its shareholders but ethically, it belonged to the depositors who were more numerous, entrusted more of their money to the bank and were the innocent agent in any credit institution'. Another motto, often repeated, was that for a smooth operation, there should be 'harmony and respect in the relations among shareholders, clients and employees'. Emphasis was put on as great as possible accessibility for the public.[26] Top managers and directors claimed

---

26 *Oikonomikos Tachydromos*, Special Issue on Business Ethics, 20 June 1996. These positive opinions should be contrasted and perhaps somewhat watered down if one considers that in other respects, the bank followed a rather traditional behaviour, e.g. with regard to

they were always available to listen to suggestions (also complaints) by the lower and younger employees. The principles of the new culture found expression in the slogan 'the Bank with Open Doors'. Unlike in the old, big Greek banks, despite the hierarchical structure, greater initiative was given to lower rank managers who made recommendations and took decisions for loans and other operations in their local jurisdiction, usually after gaining experience in various departments. Lending policy was strictly designed and loans were without exception approved on the basis only of sound criteria of performance, reliability and sufficient collateral. Applications and petitions were initiated at the branch level. Personal connections seemed to count much less than in the old and bigger banks.

Even the architecture of branch offices was designed to display these fundamental principles, justifying the assumption that symbols are equally important for diffusing and consolidating a particular culture. Art pieces collected by the bank also conveyed similar messages. Symbolism was complemented by a tangible remuneration policy, which included regular bonuses for performance, and avoiding unionization.

Ergasias Bank also minimized advertising expenses and emphasized instead the introduction of modern technology. Accounting was modelled on patterns used by foreign banks, and computerized. Ergodata, a computer firm aspiring to become what Olivetti was for Italy, and to expand abroad, was an early subsidiary of the bank. It acted as representative of Siemens mainframes with the purpose of manufacturing similar products in Greece. Furthermore, it undertook to install and service information systems planning to extend its scope to establishing a distribution network for such systems. Ergasias Bank was among the first Greek banks to operate a full 'On Line Real Time' system which contributed further to reducing transaction costs, and was the only Greek bank to prepare financial statements in accordance with international accounting standards.[27] This functioned like indirect advertising, since its performance could be easily and automatically compared with that of other international banks. As a small bank, it considered it less burdensome to create separate companies for many of the new lines of products it offered. Factoring, for example, operations on securities, leasing and many other services were therefore, promoted and carried out by internal departments.

The bank eventually became a catalyst for the cultural modernization of the whole Greek banking system, but although other banks were created since, none was based on similar principles. Nor did any of them mark the financial success of Ergasias. Many other banks, nevertheless, emulated many of the new policies, especially with regard to personnel structure, training and the launching of new products.

The twenty-five year record of Ergasias Bank showed a very successful course with the bank becoming the fifth largest in the country, surpassing not only other new banks but some of the oldest ones too. In 1997 it owned a network of 116 technologically modern branches, 2300 trained staff and no surplus manpower, which reduced considerably its functional cost. All along, it made profits and succeeded quickly to occupy third position in the list of commercial banks, behind NBG and

---

recruiting women, the number of whom remained reduced throughout the Kapsaskis years, or in its strict, rather hostile policy vis-à-vis trade union activity among employees.'

27 Capital Intelligence, *Bank Report, Ergobank*, September 1994.

CBG. Two sub-periods may be discerned in its history, before it eventually merged with Eurobank in 2000. The years 1975–82 were particularly good and allowed the bank to consolidate its position in the Greek system. It could also be considered as the 'heroic period' when the struggle concerned the protection of the sovereignty and integrity of the institution encapsulated in its original structure (wide-based share-ownership, democratic management), on the one hand, and the new culture (bank ethic), on the other. Its financial position became enviable and invited threats by potential raiders in 1982 and 1985, which however, failed. After that the bank felt safe and was free to show more dynamism, illustrated by a continuous growth through to the 1990s. Its 2628 shareholders of 1976 had become 22,500 in 1990. Its manpower had risen from 245 in 1976 to 1450 in 1990. Equally impressive was the value of its shares going from 1000 drs. in 1975 to 8000 in 1990. If dividends and interest were included, its value was worth 176,614 drs., an impressive achievement, indeed. It took fifteen years to complete its first phase of expansion by establishing 61 branches nationally and one representative in London. During this time, branches opened at a rate of 4.13/year. Since 1985 Ergasias was first among sixty banks in the West, in terms of productivity/performance. Among the five major Greek banks, it also marked the highest rate of profitability. According to *The Banker* in 1989, its profitability was the highest for a national bank (61.7 per cent) in Europe. Comparatively, the best Italian bank among 111 had a rate of 44.8 per cent, and the best among 11 English banks was 41.7 per cent. It seems that this position was attained not only by diversifying and introducing new products and services, but also by maintaining general expenses low. Both of these processes differentiated Ergasias Bank from the rest of the Greek credit institutions. Such expenses were estimated in 1990, at 45 per cent of revenue, compared with an average of 75 per cent for the other Greek commercial banks.[28] Within the same time span, Ergasias founded four subsidiary enterprises: ErgoInvestment S.A. was founded as early as 1977 as a wide-based joint-stock company with 7400 shareholders, in which Ergasias owned 39 per cent of its capital. Thirteen years later, 'Proodos Hellenic Investment S.A.' was also founded together with Baring Securities of London and 65 per cent of its capital was imported from abroad. Ergasias' share was 10 per cent. Concurrent with the bank's interest in information technology was, as already mentioned, the foundation of Ergodata. Another two subsidiaries operated in the securities market and insurance services. The latter was in cooperation with the German insurance firm Allianz A.G.

The year 1989 may be considered a turning point. Although progress and growth continued, the bank started to feel the competition from other bigger institutions and more general banking liberalization. The pace of change was slowing down but the initial momentum was still holding strong.

In 1994, a report published by Capital Intelligence gave this bank full marks as to its performance measured in terms of running expenses, which were kept low; of strong fee and commission generating business which was rising; of sound finance with high levels of profitability. There was a major weakness, however: Although the fifth largest bank in Greece, it was still relatively small, controlling only about 4 per

---

28 Kapsaskis, *Anamniseis*, p. 14.

cent of the market, and its share capital was unprotected against hostile raiders. For the next five years, Ergasias continued to figure among the top 25 banks in the world, in terms of soundness and profitability. In 1996, its performance (profits) was 10.5 times better than for the rest of the commercial banks in Greece but also in the rest of Europe. It came 10th in terms of best profit on capital (63.96 per cent) and 23rd in terms of best profit on assets (4.29 per cent). According to another assessment by *The Banker* of the 1000 world's largest banks Ergasias was among the top fifteen, in terms of profits on equity/capital-RoE, and among the twenty-five largest, in terms of return on assets-Roa. It also fared better than the four other Greek banks, which were also included in the list:

Date	ROE	ROA	Capital
1991	11th	16th	818th ($171mill.)
1992	13th	21st	862nd ($165 mill)
1993	11th	17th	849th ($181 mill)
1994	14th	23rd	809th ($225 mill)
1995	10th	–	762nd ($273 mill)
1998			($892 mill)

Source: *The Banker*, July issue of years 1992–96.

Its success appeared more impressive if compared with the performance of the other four major Greek banks as shown below:

1991

1. Ergobank	11th	16th	818th
2. Com. B.of G.	13th	34th	390th
3. Credit Bank	23rd	45th	613th
4. Nat. B. of G.	49th	418th	253th
5. Ionian B. of G.	110th	369th	907th

1992

1. Ergobank	13th	21st	862nd
2. Credit Bank	26th	59th	658th
3. Com B. of G.	127th	149th	387th
4. Ionian B. of G.	475th	693rd	287th
5. Nat. B. of G.	475th	693rd	287th

1993

1. Ergobank	11th	17th	849th
2. Credit Bank	18th	81st	706th
3. Com. B. of G.	231st	293rd	358th
4. Ionian B. of G.	437th	417th	641st
5. Nat. B. of G.	475th	693rd	287th

1994

1. Ergobank	14th	23rd	809th
2. Credit Bank	25th	92nd	547th
3. Nat. B.of G.	196th	616th	279th
4. Com. B. of G.	254th	265th	367th
5. Ionian B. of G.	334th	399th	634th

1995

1. Ergobank	10th	762nd
2. Credit Bank	20th	441st
3. Nat. B. of G.	131st	246th
4. Ionian B. of G.	478th	638th
5. Com. B. of G.	519th	377th

Source: The Banker, op. cit.

The impressive performance made pressures for a possible merger more intense. In 1999, at the time of negotiations with Eurobank, Ergasias, still occupied 21st (51.21 per cent) and 24th place (4.63 per cent) respectively on the list of the top 25 banks of the world. But, it was no longer the only Greek bank on the list, since the much larger and older Commercial Bank of Greece also figured in it.

From 1992 onwards, Ergobank began to realize that its future as an autonomous small bank might not be guaranteed. European integration necessitated the operation of much larger credit institutions, which would be in a position to organize better the new market conditions. New strategies and coalitions on the level of capital resources needed to be designed with similar banks. The governors of the bank considered that such strategies would allow further development of Greek banking in order to sustain the pressure of foreign capital and maintain a national presence. Greek banking needed to form large units with high diversification of services and products, and for this a powerful capital position and a constant presence (direct or indirect) anywhere in Europe was necessary. It was a strategy of survival, a compromise towards achieving economies of scale and competitive products, and still maintaining the familiar pattern which had taken so much energy to consolidate. Ergasias decided to invest in enterprises with complementary scope in order to gain a strong position in retail banking, an area its people knew well and where big European banks were dominant. Its role would be to operate on a regional market level, since it had a well structured network, trained personnel, good relations with customers, a sound portfolio and good management and leadership.

The logic of merging with another institution, however, which might not have been wholeheartedly endorsed by its founder, C. Kapsaskis whose physical demise in 1995 deprived the bank of much of its originality, prevailed (after a hostile take-over bid), showing perhaps eloquently the limits of modernization. In 1999, Ergasias Bank lost its autonomy succumbing to Consolidated Eurofinance Holding. This was the parent organization of another private bank, EFG Eurobank, where John Latsis, a ship-owner, was a majority shareholder. The company had risen to be the third largest private banking group in Greece. The merger between Ergasias and Eurobank was a foregone conclusion and was completed in 2000. A foreign organization, Deutsche Bank, now controlled 10 per cent of share capital.

No assessment or historical judgement on the merger is possible yet. Only hypotheses may be advanced. Did Ergasias Bank succumb to the common ailment of short life, which most firms in Greece – modern or traditional – have exhibited over the last century? It is true that most of the founding inner circle of managers were now close or past the retirement age; a new leadership capable of carrying forward innovative schemes and a daring comprehensive plan for the future had not emerged. Did the bank lose its direction? Comments that the bank suffered from its low profile in the financial market and that contrary to its initial phase of development, it had increasingly tended towards conservatism seem to suggest a possible regression. Ergasias bank has also been slower than its competitors to expand into retail banking and to follow its clientele abroad (into the Balkans).[29] Was a merger the natural or best outcome for the shareholders? Five years after the merger the tension between the old 'bank ethic' and the new directives still exists, but the tendency is towards neutralization of any osmosis process. The wide-base structure has not survived while management is entrusted to numerous MBA executives (with impressive qualifications if less versatile than the old guard). Any assessment of the merger should in any way take into consideration Eurobank's very different structure, culture and performance, all of which lie outside the scope of the present chapter. What emerges as a structural feature of the new era, which will determine yet another version of banking modernization, is the increased internationalization of the Greek economy and the banking sector, which is exerting pressure and may lead to painful adjustments. While the top corporate sector could now draw financial resources in Europe, competition by other Greek banks for the middle market controlled until the 1990s by Ergasias caused the latter to retreat. On the other hand, it also seems that the new culture was still quite young and not sufficiently strong to create a solid base for sustainable change.

---

29 Salomon Smith Barney, Global Equity Research, Greece, 19 August 1999, p. 5.

Conclusion

The history of Ergasias bank S.A. during its twenty-five years of autonomous life shows that the process of post-war modernization of the Greek banking system depended on much more than institutional and economic changes brought about by legislation and by integration of Greece into Europe. The latter provided an initial stimulus and an environment exerting pressure; other factors, however, have been equally important. Individual and group commitment inspired by particular mentalities – in this case formed outside Greece – should not be underestimated. While very often in economic and business history, the importance of structure and macroeconomic variables is underlined, the story of this bank shows that culture may at least be as important. It could safely be argued that the close fit between the scope and the physiognomy of Ergasias and the nature of post-war Greek society and economy enhanced the possibilities of survival and success. Simple commodity production and small- and medium-sized firms (SMEs) coexisted with large capitalist organizations, but remained marginal in terms of special banking institutions. Ergasias, to a large extent, enhanced communication and integration of such firms; it also benefited by focusing on the middle corporate market. It drew strength from professionals and generally the middle classes, reflected also on its share-ownership, capital structure and its employees. Approaching the marginal part of Greek business was the 'niche' which Ergobank successfully conquered. Later, retail banking was added on to this core element, without, however, ever reaching spectacular levels of development. On the other hand, the particularly functional culture encapsulated in the 'bank ethic' which dominated day-to-day operations and internal relations, contributed both to reducing running expenses and enhancing the profile of a 'friendly' bank, thus also sustaining success. On the liability side, the story showed that from the mid-1990s, as the Greek economy and production system became integrated more effectively in European capitalism and Greek units started to grow, Ergasias could no longer stand on its own and maintain impressive results.[30] The consequent reorientation towards more conservative patterns of operation and the strong clash of a young culture with the forces of internationalization suggest that the modernization hypothesis should be pursued further.[31]

---

30 Salomon Smith Barney, *Global*. The cover of the report had a photograph of a chess game entitled *Ergobank Checkmate*.

31 Other material used for this chapter includes: A.F. Freris, *The Greek Economy in the Twentieth Century* (London 1986); N. Mouzelis, *Modern Greece, Facets of Underdevelopment* (London, 1978); P. Kazakos, *Anamesa se Kratos kai Agora. Oikonomia kai oikonomiki politiki sti metapolemiki Hellada 1944–2000* (Between State and Market. Economy and Economic Policy in post-war Greece 1944–2000) (Athens, 2001).

Ergasias Archives Sources: Foundation Correspondence, Statutes, Correspondence 1975–2000, Press Reports, Financial Services, Board of Directors Minutes, Auditors Reports, Annual Statements, General Topics and Information Topics, Circulars, Textbooks on various operations used for training and education.

Ergasias Archives Reports: Capital Intelligence, *Bank Report*, Sep. 1994 and Nov. 1996, Moodys Investors Service, *Analysis*, May 2000, IBCA, *Report* EB:12/94:5, Merrill Lynch, Pierce, Fenner & Smith Inc., *Greece*, 30 Oct. 1995, Bank Watch, *Banking Company Profile*, July 22, 1996, Salomon Smith Barney, *Global Equity Research, Banks*, 19 Aug. 1999.

Appendix

Table 10.1   Ergasias (Ergobank) bank performance, 1991–1998

Date	ROE	ROA	Capital
1991	11th	16th	818th ($171mill.)
1992	13th	21st	862nd ($165 mill)
1993	11th	17th	849th ($181 mill)
1994	14th	23rd	809th ($225 mill)
1995	10th	–	762nd ($273 mill)
1998			($892 mill)

Source: *The Banker*, July issue of years 1992–96.

Table 10.2   Performance of the five major Greek banks

1991

1. Ergobank	11th	16th	818th
2. Com. B. of G.	13th	34th	390th
3. Credit Brank	23rd	45th	613th
4. Nat. B. of G.	49th	418th	253th
5. Ionian B. of G.	110th	369th	907th

1992

1. Ergobank	13th	21st	862nd
2. Credit Bank	26th	59th	658th
3. Com B. of G.	127th	149th	387th
4. Ionian B. of G.	475th	693rd	287th
5. Nat. B. of G.	475th	693rd	287th

1993

1. Ergobank	11th	17th	849th
2. Credit Bank	18th	81st	706th
3. Com. B. of G.	231st	293rd	358th
4. Ionian B. of G.	437th	417th	641st
5. Nat. B. of G.	475th	693rd	287th

1994

1. Ergobank	14th	23rd	809th
2. Credit Bank	25th	92nd	547th
3. Nat. B.of G.	196th	616th	279th
4. Com. B. of G.	254th	265th	367th
5. Ionian B. of G.	334th	399th	634th

1995

1. Ergobank	10th	762nd
2. Credit Bank	20th	441st
3. Nat. B. of G.	131st	246th
4. Ionian B. of G.	478th	638th
5. Com. B. of G.	519th	377th

Source: The Banker, op. cit.

Table 10.3   Commercial banking network of branches, 1972

Banks	Athens-Piraeus	Provinces	Total Country
Nat. Bank of Greece	86	195	281
Comm. Bank of Gr.	56	128	184
Ionian	36	59	95
Credit Bank	14	24	38
General Bank	20	11	31
Total Big Five	212	417	629
Other Gr. Banks	11	2	13
Foreign Banks	17	4	21
Total All Banks	240	423	663

Source: A. Zitridis (1973), *The Banking System of Greece*, Athens. p. 26 and own calculations.

PART IV
The Evolution of Modern Banking in the Far East

Patriotic Banking and the Modernization of China: The Banque industrielle de Chine, 1900–1922[1]

Frank H.H. King

Abbreviations Used

B&CC	British and Chinese Corporation
BI	Banque de l'Indochine
BIC	Banque industrielle de Chine
CCR	Chinese Central Railways
DAB	Deutsch-Asiatische Bank
f	folio
FO	Foreign Office, United Kingdom, papers in the Public Record Office, Kew, London
PS	Pekin [sic] Syndicate

I

Following China's defeat after the Boxer Uprising of 1900 and the subsequent financially crippling Boxer indemnity, the 'Powers', determined to assist in the modernization of China, sought ways to control and finance development despite their undermining of that country's creditworthiness. Initially the solution seemed to rest with the traditional search for concessions, a solution which, seen in the aftermath of the division of Africa, threatened China's sovereignty and was countered not only by the national Rights Recovery movement but also by the effective opposition of local gentry. The Powers were perforce left with the opportunity of finance alone, which, to be practical, had to be (i) coordinated and (ii) exclusive. To be effective the Powers had to set up a complex of agreements and companies which would satisfy the ambitions of the several nations involved and, at the same time, control China's

---

1   This chapter contains extracts from an essay written for the Vienna Conference and is part of my longer study of the Pekin [sic] Syndicate, a project administered by the Centre of Asian Studies, University of Hong Kong. For this particular chapter I have benefited from discussion and correspondence with Nobutaka Shinonaga. My work in various Paris archives was facilitated by the expert assistance of Ms Lindsay Bates, then working on her research degree with Marie Claire Bergère in the University of Paris. I also wish to express appreciation for permission to use the archives of the Ministry of Foreign Affairs, Paris, and for assistance from Margaret Lee in the Group Archives, The Hongkong and Shanghai Banking Corporation Ltd, Hong Kong (now transferred to Group Archives, HSBC Holdings, plc, in London).

access to overseas funds. In China, however, the need to finance current expenditures was an overall priority; overseas, multi-national financial interests challenged the arrangements approved by foreign ministries; furthermore, those interests left out of the agreements and those who disagreed with their terms were free to challenge, indeed undermine, arrangements carefully worked out.[2]

The consequent international groups, themselves composed of national consortia, attempted to control China's foreign borrowing by preventing non-consortia banks from presenting rival opportunities. Not only did this strategy fail, but elements in the French Foreign Ministry, personified by Philippe Berthelot, while acknowledging France's full participation in the various international arrangements, considered this was insufficient to make a *national* statement. They faulted France's consortium member, the Banque de l'Indochine [BI], for lack of independent initiative. Despite the strong opposition of the French banking community, a set of unusual circumstances permitted a rogue group of financiers, headed by André Victor, to obtain capital funds and in 1913 establish a nominally joint Sino-French venture, the Banque industrielle de Chine [BIC].

The project was flawed from the beginning. In 1908 Victor's group had obtained control of the British-incorporated Pekin Syndicate; this in itself threatened the precarious international balance. The Syndicate was liquid; Victor lent the funds to China, which in turn used them to finance its share in the proposed Banque industrielle. At the same time pressure from industrial groups was successful in confining the international consortia to financial loans, subsequently blurring the distinction between financial and industrial loans through uncontrolled use of supplier's credits and by the negotiation of project loans which included payment for unspecified purposes up-front; the related projects were then set aside. Prominent in approving such transactions was the Banque industrielle.

By 1919 the apparent success of this bank had encouraged its development as a *banque de dépôts*; funds were sought particularly from French, including missionaries, resident in China; banknotes were issued, and offices of the bank established in world financial centres. But in the year of its most optimistic report rumours were circulating of its dangerous illiquidity and of unsound banking practices, including trading with little regard to its capital base and speculation arising from the short-lived, high gold price of silver. The Banque industrielle collapsed, creating a political scandal which threatened French prestige in China, affected France's handling of the Boxer Indemnity payments and the terms of remission and placed the Pekin Syndicate bank back into British control, forcing the establishment of a successor bank with a smaller capital and less ambitious political objectives. The China Consortium, now officially recognized by the participating Powers, regained control, but at a time when China's shattered creditworthiness prevented further loans for modernization in a period of political turmoil.

---

2   The background material is taken mainly from my *The Hongkong Bank in the Period of Imperialism and War, 1895–1918* (Cambridge, 1988), being Vol. II of *The History of the Hongkong and Shanghai Banking Corporation*. See especially Part 2, 'The Hongkong Bank as Merchant Bank, 1895–1914'. Further references to the history will be cited as King, *The History* ..., followed by the volume number.

The problem, one might argue, was the absence of any recognized international overhead organization within which to operate. There was neither a European Union nor an International Bank for Reconstruction and Development. Those sincerely interested in China's modernization, while not travelling jets, were at least dashing between capitals on the Golden Arrow and other luxury trains, negotiating basic agreements, patching up subsequent disagreements, arguing their case with Foreign Ministries and anxious industrial groups while domestic Chinese finances degenerated. The attempt of the Banque industrielle to cut through was ill-conceived, unsuccessful and, in the end, corrupt. The bank neither enhanced France's national role in China nor advanced the modernization of China.

The demand for a bank owned and staffed by one's own nationals had two basic origins, neither of them conceived by practical bankers. At its most simplistic the demand appeared obvious just as stated: it was surely self-apparent that the French, for example, would (or perhaps ought to) wish to be able to deal with a French bank. This view might be supplemented by an apparently unrelated thought, namely that the idea of imperialism could be avoided by establishing such a bank as a 'joint venture' with the Chinese. That this might be in conflict with the original purpose was a proposition minimized by the fact the Chinese were unprepared to insist management follow sound banking practices.

For the French imperialist, the history of France in China was one of frustration. A major factor was in the lack of competitiveness of French industrial products minimizing the impact which, for example, the limited financial successes of the Russo-Chinese Bank or more general diplomatic negotiations might have had on France's overall China policy.[3] Imperialists, however, sought a scapegoat; within France they condemned what they deemed the conservative (or worse) policy of the established French bank in the East, the Banque de l'Indochine; elsewhere they saw their China policy weakened by a tendency to subordinate France to policies designed in Britain, including adherence to consortium policy and coordination even with a German banking group. There were similar complaints in Britain. The undisputed success of the Pekin Syndicate in obtaining (in 1898) vast mineral concessions in Shansi and Honan provinces was not followed by success in exploitation; hard-won railway concessions, for example the Shanghai-Nanking route, were not, even when brought through to completion, met with the same enthusiasm in the bond market as among potential contractors or in the Foreign Office.[4]

A significant French reaction was based on the premise that the national interest rested on a policy of furthering the industrial development of China by France and

---

3   *The Russo-Chinese Bank*, Birmingham Slavonic Monographs No. 2 (Birmingham, 1977). For comments on France's export difficulties in China see, for example, Robert Lee, *France and the Exploitation of China, 1885–1901* (Hong Kong and London, 1989). There is also commentary in Nobutaka Shinonaga, 'La formation de la Banque industrielle de Chine et son ecroulement – un defi des frères Berthelot', a doctoral thesis, University of Paris VIII (May 1988), a copy of which he very kindly sent to me.

4   An outline history of the Pekin Syndicate is provided in King, 'Joint Venture in China: the Experience of the Pekin Syndicate, 1897–1961, in *Business and Economic History*, second series, vol. 19, 1990, pp. 113–22. Further references to the history of the PS and related companies may be found in King, *The History* …, pp. 302–3, 330–36, and *passim*.

that failure to achieve this required not a change of policy but the improvement of the system, thus suggesting a search for the defective parts. This necessitated ignoring the basic but apparently incurable problem of non-competitiveness and focusing on scapegoats of which the Banque de l'Indochine proved, for some, the most ready to hand.

Basically the charge against the BI was that it was conservative, interested mainly in exchange, and not prepared to lead in the development of French industry in China. But the Berthelot-type criticism went beyond this and, in doing so, made the inevitable comparison with Britain. For example, Shinonaga summarizes the over-all comparison thus: the British had (i) the Hongkong and Shanghai Banking Corporation (now a wholly-owned subsidiary of HSBC Holdings, plc) for finance, (ii) the British and Chinese Corporation (B&CC) for research, investigation etc, and (iii) Pauling and Co. for execution. As for the French, they had the ineffective Banque de l'Indochine for (i), the Syndicat des constructeurs et industriels for (iii), and, lacking in his view a suitable (ii), Berthelot projected his Sino-French bank.[5]

The comparison however is fatally flawed. The British situation appeared static because of the ineffectiveness of rivals, not because of British official policy. From time to time the Legation and Foreign Office encouraged competition with the B&CC and the Hongkong Bank from such diverse interests as, for example, Pauling and Co., Sassoons, Pritchard Morgan, and others – but, of course, only *before* the Chinese had made their own selection. Once they had, officials supported the Chinese choice.[6]

Not only is the comparison flawed, but Berthelot's concept of nationalistic banking was also unsound. A comparison of the BIC with the Sino-American Bank of Commerce is instructive. Both were initiated by officials without banking experience, both were motivated by nationalist sentiments – the need for 'x' country's merchants to have access to 'their own' bank, one which would supposedly be sympathetic to them as fellow nationals; furthermore, both banks were founded with unrealistic expectations regarding Chinese cooperation with or in the bank. As for the French/British banking comparison, when Berthelot had his BIC it in any case developed along different and speculative lines. While it is true that the French remained incorporated under French law whereas the American joint venture subjected itself to Chinese jurisdiction, the end was the same – excessive lending to the Chinese government with inadequate security, consequent loss of capital, and eventual failure.[7]

---

5   'La Formation ...', pp. 39–40.

6   King, *The History* ..., II, 245. This subject is covered by E.W. Edwards in (i) 'The Origins of British Financial Co-operation with France in China, 1903-6', *English Historical Review* 86: 286–317 (1971) and (ii) 'British Policy in China 1913–1914; Rivalry with France in the Yangtze Valley', *Journal of Oriental Studies* 40: 20–36 (1977) and references cited therein, esp. p. 300, n. 35.

7   The history of the Chinese-American Bank of Commerce is the subject of a study by Noel H. Pugach, University of New Mexico. The comments here are based on his published paper, 'Keeping an Idea Alive: the Establishment of a Sino-American Bank', in *Business History* Review, vol. 56, Summer 1982, pp. 267–93, but he has since published his *Same bed, different dreams, a history of the Chinese American Bank of Commerce, 1919–1937* (Centre of Asian Studies, University of Hong Kong, 1997).

Indeed, merchants ideally sought a bank which both treated them fairly and had available the facilities they required. The Hongkong Bank, for example, prided itself on serving all communities. Banking nationalists had trouble reminding their fellow-citizens that the Hongkong Bank was in some sense 'alien'. A French diplomat, writing of the French-financed Russo-Chinese Bank, considered that the French business world as a whole preferred to deal with the British banks in North China, 'where they were sure of finding a very different welcome from that which awaited them at the Russo-Chinese'.[8] In Tsingtau German merchants urged the Hongkong Bank to establish an agency there in competition with the Deutsch-Asiastische Bank, while the DAB complained in general of German merchants who remained loyal to the Hongkong Bank.[9] With a French-speaking chief manager (F. de Bovis, 1891–93), up to four German directors, and offices in Lyon and Hamburg, Saigon and Haiphong, the Hongkong Bank could offer services which met the very needs which the nationalists claimed their citizens required through an agency of a French or German bank.

In banking as in other China activities, the French policy of exclusion was unwise. If banks are more wisely founded on banking principles, then a comparison of two rival exchange banks, one 'British', the Hongkong Bank, and the other French, the Banque de l'Indochine, would be appropriate.[10] Indeed, the Hongkong Bank was noted by European imperialists as a model in the execution of an imperial policy; in a sense Berthelot's complaint was that the French bank failed in this particular. But Berthelot was neither the first nor the last Frenchman to misunderstand British institutions.

The Hongkong Bank's success as a bank depended, in fact, on the eventual absolute independence of its management and on its Head Office location in the East. Imitators never appreciated the significance of the first and noted but failed to duplicate the latter, the concept of policy and decision making in the East. The French BIC and the German Deutsch-Asiatische Bank [DAB] saw the advantages to having a local committee or, in the latter bank, the 'head office' in the East, but the power lay not in Shanghai or Peking but in Europe, that is, with the Board of Directors in Paris or Berlin. Furthermore, since the Hongkong Bank had been incorporated in Hong Kong, a territory which, with China, remained on a virtual silver standard during the relevant period, its accounts were denominated in a silver unit of account, the Hong Kong dollar, and its financial fortune was therefore less affected by the secular decline in the gold price of silver.

Sitting in the Quai d'Orsay, reflecting on his China experience, Berthelot had a vision. China the limitless market was for him China the limitless opportunity for French industrial investment frustrated by the lack of French determination and vision; among the guilty, the direction of the Banque de l'Indochine. There is no evidence to

---

8   Quoted in Quested, *The Russo-Chinese Bank*, p. 37.

9   For Tsingtau, see King, *The History*, vol. 2, pp. 33–3g.

10   In addition to the work of M. Meuleau, *Des pionniers en Extrême-Orient. Histoire de la Banque de l'Inochine (1875–1975)* (Paris, 1990), see Y. Gonjo, 'La banque coloniale et l'Etat: la Banque de l'Indochine devant l'interventionnisme (1917–1931)', in *Le Mouvement social*, vol. 142, 1988, pp. 45–74; his history of the bank, now in Japanese (Hurans teikokushugi to ajia ... French imperialism in Asia ... 1985), is being published in French.

support this charge. St. Simon, the latter's chairman, summarized Berthelot's 1905 attempt to block expansion of the BI in favour of a new 'Banque Franco-Chinoise' as characterized by 'l'esprit boutiquier et peu intelligent'.[11] Simon's judgement was sound but would have no effect on a French visionary seeking '*la gloire*'.

Foreign banks, however, needed a source of funds beyond the deposits of expatriate firms and their employees or of the determined savings-bank patron, be he Chinese or foreign. The note issue has been cited as one such source; some have criticized it as an example of unbridled imperialism. On the contrary, the note issue served a useful function, given the confusion of coinage in China; acceptance of foreign banknotes was entirely discretionary since they were not legal tender; but with the exception of Kwangtung – where Hong Kong-issued notes were current – they circulated mainly in the treaty ports.[12] As a source of funds they were limited by the authorized size of the bank's fiduciary issue; expansion of the note issue was not in itself a source of funds beyond this point. Banknotes, however, created a problem of their own: they became a matter which the national government of the bank concerned could not ignore. Should the bank fail, its prestige no longer mattered, but, whatever the legal position, that of its government was endangered. In the British case, the Treasury considered banknotes as a private business affair, but even then the public aspects could not be ignored and, when the Oriental Bank failed in Ceylon in 1884, the colonial government stepped in to redeem their banknotes; in consequence increasingly stringent requirements limited both the profitability of the notes and the danger of their being dishonoured.[13] The Banque de l'Indochine had withdrawn its own China issue by 1908. French officials of the Berthelot persuasion seemed, however, to see the notes as a certificate of the French presence and positively encouraged their issue; with the BIC in difficulties in 1921–22, however, BIC banknotes were passing at a 30 per cent discount; this, whatever the legal position, immediately involved the French Government and its 'prestige' in Asia.[14]

The exchange banks had an advantage over Chinese depositories. First, their regulations provided for greater security and secondly, they were foreign, that is, they were covered by extraterritorial agreements and therefore not subject to the demands of Chinese officials. This made them the preferred depositories of Chinese merchants and officials in cases where security was ranked more important than a high rate of interest. Here, perhaps, an exchange bank could appeal to fellow-countrymen; certainly French official funds would be deposited in a French bank, etc, but there is evidence, not surprising in view of the support the idea of a BIC had received from the French Catholic hierarchy in China, that the BIC sought French missionary funds wherever they might be – thus giving the BIC a China-wide clientele with China-wide implications for French prestige. When the BIC solicited funds from afar, the prospective depositor could not himself keep in touch with events on the China coast; he had to take the bank on trust, and his assessment of the BIC would

---

11   St. Simon to Ph. Berthelot, 21 December 1905, in MAE (NS), Chine, vol. 403, folio 208, and quoted in Shinonaga, 'La Formation . . .', p. 48.

12   King, *The History*, vol. 3, pp. 61–5, 246–7.

13   King, *The History*, vol. 1, p. 375.

14   *The Times*, 6 July 1921, pp. 11f.

have been influenced by its claims to furthering the French role. Hence, whether the French authorities wished it or not, their prestige would be at stake, just as much as with banknotes, should anything undermine the bank's credit.

During the first decade of the twentieth century, at a time when Boxer Indemnity funds and loan-interest funds were being paid into government accounts, it seemed to some a matter of national disgrace if such funds had to be deposited in a bank of some other nationality; hence one reason for the development of small national institutions or extensions of existing banks in this period. Little if any economic benefit resulted; operations could easily have been carried on through the existing major exchange banks.

These notes have so far omitted consideration of the Chinese banks. During the negotiations for the 1911 Hukuang Railways Loan, Charles Addis remarked on the absence of a Chinese bank from the syndicate and compared the situation with Japan, noting that the idea of issuing a Japanese loan in London without the participation of the Yokohama Specie Bank was unthinkable. Certainly it was not 'imperialism' *per se* which was responsible. The Bank of China developed into a major competitor on the foreign-exchange markets during the late 1920s to mid 1930s; there was Chinese loan participation in the early 1930s.

As the Hongkong Bank proved successful, so it had many rivals claiming to be modelled on its statutes and practices. This is true in a limited sense of the Banque de l'Indochine and of the Yokohama Specie Bank. But the comparison is in reality superficial; the comparison may only be a matter of formal courtesy. However, the Imperial Bank of China, founded in 1897 under the sponsorship of Shen Hsuan-huai and with Andrew W. Maitland, retired as the Hongkong Bank's Tientsin agent, as manager of the Shanghai head office under Chinese managing directors, was indeed influenced by the Hongkong Bank while developing in essence as a purely Chinese joint-stock operation. Its potential was recognized, and it is mentioned in relation to the 1905, 5 per cent Honan Railway (Taokow-Chinghua) Loan.[15] In the case of the 1905, Shanghai Nanking Railway Loan, a provision called for the use of the Imperial Bank by the British and Chinese Corporation [B&CC] to facilitate the movement of funds in places where the Hongkong Bank had no office.[16] And there are other miscellaneous references to Chinese foreign-style banks, suggesting that the foreign bankers were not opposed to bringing Chinese institutions into the syndicates but that the institutions themselves lacked status, management, and facilities. This situation differed markedly from that in Japan, but that difference was real and recognized. Even in the early 1920s after the wartime growth of the Chinese modern banking system, a Chinese participation in the new Consortium would at least initially have been mainly 'face-saving' but, in any case, such participation proved politically impractical.

At the time of the 1911 Revolution, therefore, the foreign banks would appear to have reached an *impasse* as far as further expansion in China went, their contacts still restricted both geographically and by the intermediation of the compradore. Surplus

---

15   King, *The History* …, vol. 2, p. 348.

16   The text is found in J.V.A. MacMurray (ed.), *Treaties and Agreements with and concerning China, 1894–1919* (New York, 1921), vol. 1, pp. 387–402.

funds were lent to the native banks and to merchants for on-lending to producers of export products, but without supervision of production at source even these uses of funds seemed to have their limits. Meanwhile the potential of the modern Chinese banking system remained undeveloped. Similarly their role in financing major projects, that is, in participating in the expected 'modernization' of China, was similarly frustrated by a complex of factors, political, economic, and practical.

There was, however, one possible development – the creation of joint-venture banks which, with Chinese managers on board, could bridge the cultural gap and, with European know-how, undertake international banking with both the foreign and Chinese sectors. At least that would be the theoretical potential. If such a bank were, however, to become involved in government finance, the risks could be dramatic. Those with a visionary view of China refused to accept this 'calumny'. And it was the restless (or visionary) French who achieved the dubious honour of establishing in 1913 the joint venture Banque industrielle de Chine.

II

The founding of the Banque industrielle de Chine was unexpected. Berthelot's fixation regarding a Sino-French bank was well known, but equally well-known was the virtually unanimous opposition of the major French banking institutions and the hostility of the Banque de l'Indochine and of those connected with it. Furthermore, it was obvious that in 1913 the Chinese government did not have the funds available for investment in a joint enterprise. As for the French government, it was apparently fully committed to 'consortium' policy and cooperation in China with Britain and Germany. There would appear, therefore, to have been no role for a new bank to play, even were it financed.

That the BIC was founded and did find a role, however dubious, requires an explanation, bearing in mind the background comments outlined in the first section of this essay.

If the exchange banking system provided the routine of trade and minor investment finance, thus underlying the basic economic relations between China and the European countries, there was also a more vexed history of development finance, Chinese government borrowing, and concessions which, it was popularly supposed, threatened the integrity of the Empire. The bulk of the resulting financing had been on a sound financial basis, consequent on the Imperial Government's concern regarding foreign borrowing and to the role of the Foreign Inspectorate of Customs, specifically Sir Robert Hart, in providing the necessary security for the foreign loans on a totally controlled basis and in accord with Imperial policy. However, there were also grandiose schemes which from time to time threatened to bypass the controls, with the ultimate potential consequence of undermining China's political integrity. These typically included multiple concessions, the creation of a government bank with the right to issue fiduciary notes, and crippling rates of interest – *inter alia*, there was R. Montgomery Martin's proposed Imperial Bank of China in 1864, the proposals made in 1887 by 'Count' Eugène de Mickiewicz, and the schemes planned by C. di Rudiní and Angelo Luzzat[t]i with Ma Chien-chung in the mid-1890s.[17] As these last mentioned were the unlikely but remote ancestors of the BIC, their evolution will be considered further below.

The late 1890s has been referred to as the period of the Battle for Concessions; the period from 1911 to 1914 might similarly be termed the Battle for Control of Finance. China's defeat in the first Sino-Japanese War climaxed a period of borrowing for internal and external military threats, but in amounts for which the amortization appeared under control. The indemnity loans, however, exhausted China's general creditworthiness and foreign promoters were accordingly not in a strong position to take immediate advantage of those clauses of the 1895 peace treaty which gave greater economic scope to foreign investment. Furthermore, the lack of general credit placed the focus not only on lending for investment but on control of that investment, since repayment had to be linked with the success of the project being financed. This reinforced the search for 'concessions', which would provide the concessionaire a broad range of semi-political controls; these, by their nature, are exclusive and tend, it was firmly believed, to lead to imports from the country whose nationals control the concession. This national element was exaggerated by the need for 'latecomers' in China to negotiate successfully against entrenched foreign interests, for example, the British Jardine, Matheson & Co.

In reacting to this situation the Chinese, who in the finalizing of any public deal worked only through the relevant legation, sought assurance that the company or syndicate they were negotiating with had in fact the support of the Legation. For the British Legation this became a delicate task since they had no authorized basis for choosing between one or another of their competing nationals – other than the approval of the Chinese, who might, however, approve more than one; in the face of coordinated efforts from European industrial missions sponsored or encouraged by their governments, the British Legation could only hope that British interests would somehow combine and come to China with an already united front. In a sense, therefore, the jointure of Jardine, Matheson and Co. and the Hongkong Bank as founding sponsors of the British & Chinese Corporation seemed on first announcement to solve the British problem; it failed however in its purpose, first because it was not all-inclusive, secondly because the Hongkong Bank was the sole banking member of the company, and thirdly because the shareholders, having but a small stake in the company, did not accept that their interest in China had then to be exclusively through the B&CC.

One important independent competitor was in fact the Pekin Syndicate. Reference has been made to the comprehensive 'dreams' of di Rudiní/Luzzatti/Ma. In 1896 a

---

17   King, *The History* ..., vol. 1, pp. 530, 556. Angelo Luzzati came from a Turin family, but he allowed (encouraged?) his name to be spelt 'Luzzatti', suggesting a relationship, in fact non-existent, with the then Treasury Minister, Luigi Luzzatti of Venice, a prominent economist and political figure. For the Rudiní, Luzzat[t]i, Ma schemes, see King, 'The Founding of the Pekin Syndicate, 1897–1900: I. the Anglo-Italian Syndicate', presented at the Association for Asian Studies, Western/Southwestern Conference, Austin, Texas, Oct. 12–13, 1990; for Robert Montgomery Martin, see King, *Survey our Empire! Robert Montgomery Martin, 1801(?)–1868: a Bio-bibliography* (Hong Kong, 1979), pp. 193–8.

sensible observer might well have voted their efforts 'least likely to succeed'. Italy was not interested in China and its available capital was limited. Luzzatti had earlier tried to interest his fellow countrymen in a modest (but risky) Siamese investment but in the end had turned to the Rothschilds and to company promoters in Britain. Once again he took this course and, with virtually the same capitalists who had sponsored his Gold Fields of Siam Ltd a decade earlier, he successfully obtained the flotation of the Pekin Syndicate.[18] He returned to China and successfully negotiated vast mineral concessions in Shansi and Honan provinces, obtaining the endorsement of the Tsungli Yamen and the active support of Viceroy Li Hung-chang – who was, most probably, a shareholder. The normal course for such 'exploration' companies was to promote separate operating companies for each concession or mining area, but the terms imposed by China forbade any alienation. Hence special 'Shansi' shares, designed to finance exploitation of both concessions and to pay dividends from the specific profits from them, were issued in 1900, on the eve of the Boxer Uprising. The issue was, not surprisingly, unsuccessful; the shares were largely taken up by the underwriters, including, significantly, French and other continental finance houses.[19]

The defeat of the Boxers did not herald the break-up of China. Indeed, the foreign powers, having exacted indemnity and possessing various mining and railway concessions, encouraged the creation of an executive central regime on the nation state concept. The resulting central authority would, it was expected, uphold the concessions and other treaty rights granted, assert the status of China, and consequently prevent its break-up by frustrated (whether legitimately so or not) Powers. In the next decade, however, foreign concessionaires discovered that in mining the local political situation was paramount; concessions could not be enforced by the central government in the interior of China. In consequence such concessions were either developed only marginally or were redeemed by the Chinese in accord with the popular advocacy of Rights Recovery. In the case of the Pekin Syndicate, its railway from Taokow to Chinghua in connection with its Honan mines was sold to the imperial government for £800,000, which sum had been lent to the government by the Syndicate for 30 years at 87.5 and 5 per cent. Management was to be retained until repayment had been completed.[20] Although the PS was authorized to sell the consequent bonds to the public, it did not do so at that time; the interest, its directors thought, would be useful. As for the Shansi concession, the PS was advised by the Legation that in view of strong local opposition and the inability of

---

18   For the story of Luzzatti and the Siamese concessions, see King, 'Angelo Luzzatti and Early Mining Concessions in Siam, 1885–1891', in *Proceedings of the 4th International Conference on Thai Studies* (Institute of Southeast Asian Studies, Kunming, China, 1990), vol. 1, 102–10. There is a revised and updated version in [New Mexico Military Institute,] *Faculty Symposia Lecture Series, 1989–1990* (Roswell, New Mexico, 1991), pp. 103–15. The PRO file on Gold Fields of Siam, Ltd, is BT 31/4132/26628; see also articles in the *Mining Journal* (18 May 1888 and 20 Dec. 1890).

19   The Companies House, London, files on the Pekin Syndicate have been consulted.

20   For a useful comment on the economic and political reasoning behind China's agreement to this loan, see Ralph W. Huenemann, *The Dragon and the Iron Horse, the Economics of Railroads in China, 1876–1937* (Cambridge, Mass, 1984), p. 72.

the Manchu government to enforce the edicts of the central government, it should negotiate a redemption; the final sum agreed in 1908 was approximately £350,000 – considerably less than had been invested. The Honan concession was retained.

At the turn of the century the Pekin Syndicate had an authorized capital of £1.54 million, of which a total of £906,359 had been issued and was fully paid up. Any pretence of its being jointly Italian and British had been abandoned. Furthermore, the PS had negotiated railway concessions and had presented a British position independent of the B&CC. The solution in 1904 was to join these together with certain B&CC rights into a new company, the Central Chinese Railways [CCR], closely allied to the B&CC and with a board representing both companies. The Pekin Syndicate's Chairman, (Sir) Carl Mayer, had been nominated to the Hongkong Bank's London Committee, thus further coordinating the British side – to the extent of its still limited membership.[21]

This development was in itself helpful from the British point of view, but it did not solve the scramble for concessions and the Dutch auction of control provisions which the Powers saw as undermining their efforts to develop China. In an effort to curtail the ability of the Chinese to manage barbarians by setting them against each other, the British and French, encouraged by their respective foreign ministries and in the first move of what would be termed the *entente cordiale*, extended the scope of the CCR by including French and Belgian interests. The British Group, which included such companies as the B&CC, the Pekin Syndicate and the Yangtze Valley Co., and also the voting rights of the Belgian companies, had equal votes with the French Group; the British chairman also had a casting vote. Thus what was seen by French commentators as straightforward domination by the B&CC was in fact a complex structure, hanging on a single vote.

Parallel to this development was, as the French saw it, 'une banque pour le financement' – the Hongkong and Shanghai Bank.[22] But this, for two reasons, was in fact another weak point in the British structure: the Hongkong Bank (i) was the sole banking representative in the British group (until 1912) and (ii) was tied by a varied series of arrangements with foreign banks interested in the Far East, including the Banque de l'Indochine. As this structure became more formal and, indeed, more lasting, the term 'China Consortium' came to be applied to what was also referred to as the Four Power Groups (Britain, France, Germany and the United States), the Six Power Groups (with the addition of Russia and Japan) and finally, for the key 1913 Reorganization Loan, the Five Power Groups (with the omission of the U.S. after March 1913). The non-British groups were led respectively by the bank most interested in China, the BI, the DAB, the Yokohama Specie Bank, and the International Banking Corporation – this last becoming a wholly-owned subsidiary of the First National Bank of New York. However, the term 'China Consortium', while reasonable, should not be confused with the post-war, government-controlled consortium; pre-war the arrangements which brought the groups together, while approved by governments, were in the private sector and not reinforced by treaty. And here again the British position was weakened by the lone position of the Hongkong

---

21   King, *The History*, vol. 2, pp. 28 and 302–3.
22   Shinonaga, 'La Formation', p. 39.

Bank; in France the BI, although with broader support, did not represent all relevant French interests. The DAB and the Yokohama Specie Bank could discipline their markets; the American group was, on the other hand, not all that interested.

The purpose of the Groups was, as noted, ostensibly to prevent international rivalries from minimizing the level of control exercised on the construction of railways (or other objectives), thereby endangering of the viability of the project itself. However, negotiations never proceeded smoothly, and as China's central authorities began to reassert the country's international position, the foreign negotiators realized that the Chinese were in a position to demand a virtually free hand; they would accept financing only. There was in consequence a breakdown in relations between the consortium banks and industrial syndicates interested in China, the latter beginning to search for less dramatic means of financing their China projects, in some cases simply using supplier's credits.

As the Groups were losing control of the industrial-loan situation, the Chinese Revolution of 1911 brought to power a regime which was in constant need of finance. For this there were potentially no limits and, indeed, no obvious revenue sources for repayment – unless foreign intrusion were accepted and the principles of Rights Recovery virtually reversed. The Groups attempted to maintain a responsible position, but they were undermined by the determination of the Chinese government to obtain the necessary funds, if possible without onerous political conditions, and by the willingness of non-consortium or Group institutions to circumvent their own government's policy of giving the consortium institutions their sole, if temporary, support. If this situation were not sufficiently complex, there could be a further crisis if a joint-venture bank could find financing for China, one which would operate with the tacit approval of the European government and the support of a China arguing that such a bank was in fact 'Chinese' – the crisis came with the establishment of the Banque industrielle de Chine.

There is, however, still a gap in the exposition – between 1908 and 1913. To rectify the story we must return to the Pekin Syndicate, left with its Honan Concession and with its finances sound and, most important, liquid.

In 1910 a requisition from a group of continental shareholders called for a special meeting of the Pekin Syndicate; their object, to replace the Board of Directors. They were forestalled; the Board resigned, and the group, eventually dominated by the French speculator and banker Charles Victor of the Société auxiliaire de crédit, a man who had twice been convicted of fraud (November 1906 and June 1909), took control.[23] On December 1, 1912, Charles Victor, with his associate André Berthelot, came on the Board of the PS. André was the brother of Philippe Berthelot, then 'sous-directeur' on the Asia desk of France's Ministry of Foreign Affairs. That Victor had been able to engineer this coup was at least partly the result of the narrow holding of shares resulting from the unsuccessful Shansi issue of 1900; as Victor drove up the Syndicate's share prices to more than double their previous level, so reluctant British and institutional underwriting holders had sold.[24]

---

23   As reported in *Le Reflet* (27 Oct. 1912), found in the Fontainebleau archives of the Ministry of Economic Affairs.

24   Report in the Fontainebleau archives, B 31297, No. 4.

The success of Victor's speculations was sufficient to shake the Consortium. The Pekin Syndicate was a part of the British Group in the British/French CCR. Both the Pekin Syndicate and the B&CC had the right to nominate directors to the Board, but on condition that, for example, directors nominated by the board of the PS would receive the approval of the B&CC. The PS, however, had become French-controlled but remained a part of the British Group. Had the Pekin Syndicate's representatives on the Board of the CCR resigned in consequence of the resignation of their own parent board – as they most certainly should have done in normal business practice – either the new PS board would have nominated replacements acceptable to the B&CC or there would have been a lack of quorum; the CCR would have been unable to function. The CCR board assumed, not without reason, that the nominees might well be unacceptable, that is, would be unfriendly to British aspirations and/or to the principles of cooperation assumed in the consortium.

Despite the objections of the new PS board, the directors from the old PS board indicated that, for the reasons stated, they would not resign from the board of the CCR until the new PS board had nominated directors acceptable to the B&CC, that is, British nationals not connected with rival syndicates. The PS board submitted a list and asked the CCR directors to choose; this was considered 'invidious' and an *impasse* was reached.[25] Then the threatened lack of quorum occurred in any case; a B&CC-nominated director of the CCR died.

The B&CC, being in the control of the Hongkong Bank and Jardine Matheson, were wholly committed to the consortium principle for dealings with China. They were particularly concerned with the potential of any new set of PS-nominated directors; they recognized that the British Group would most probably not vote as a block, and the CCR would have left effective British control. Since Victor's group was not bound by the conventions of the China consortium, in which the CCR/B&CC were key influences, the whole structure put together so carefully with Foreign Office endorsement by the Hongkong Bank's then junior London manager, Charles Addis, appeared to be crumbling.

Over a period of some four years the Pekin Syndicate and the B&CC attempted to field a list of mutually acceptable directors to represent the British group on the CCR. In June 1913 the CCR recognized that the Pekin Syndicate's participation in the BIC was 'likely to affect the Agreement (of 1905) with the British Group', but the CCR's subsequent efforts to have the agreement annulled were blocked by the PS, which would do nothing until their nominees were admitted to the CCR board. In 1914 there was a trade-off; the old PS nominees resigned and each side agreed to accept the other's nominees to the Board, thus recreating a quorum.[26] At the same time the Foreign Office argued as to whether the Pekin Syndicate remained a British company entitled to British Legation and consular support in China.

---

25   Correspondence between the Secretary, PS, and the Secretary, B&CC in a file dated between 14 June 1910 and 15 May 1914 found in the B&CC files with Matheson and Co., London.

26   From a summary history of the CCR found in the B&CC files with Matheson and Co., London.

All this manoeuvring weakened the position of the China consortium, but it was only a first step. There were those both in France and in China's French community who still advocated a Sino-French industrial bank; their diverse but equally impractical plans would come together at just the time when an imperialist visionary, Philippe Berthelot, was in charge of China affairs while his brother André administered and another Frenchman, Charles Victor, controlled the funds of the Pekin Syndicate; coincidentally, it was a time when the Chinese government was most in need of funds. This was a deadly combination – and a successful one.

The final impetus for the new bank came from the French Settlement in Tientsin. The banker involved was A.-J. Pernotte, manager of the Tientsin branch of the Banque de l'Indochine; he had been in China since 1903 and had risen rapidly in the bank's hierarchy.[27] With Elie Bouchard and the German Wilhelm Pape he had access to the highest officers of Yuan Shih-k'ai's [Yuan Shikai's] government and the final plans for what would be the Banque industrielle de Chine were developed in 1912/13 in a fashion to surprise completely the Hongkong Bank, the British Legation, and indeed most observers in China and Europe. As late as 28 March 1913, for example, Addis's associate Murray Stewart was sending to the Foreign Office a copy of a communication 'confidentially received', giving some particulars of the agreement *said* to have been concluded in Peking between the French syndicate and the Chinese Government.[28]

III

Major loans could take years to negotiate; the projects they were intended to finance would take longer. The cumbersome process was acceptable to the members of the national groups if only because the sums involved were large and because the alternative to international cooperation appeared unsatisfactory. This line of reasoning was, however, less than acceptable to smaller industrial firms seeking immediate markets or to minor speculators, loan promoters, and other 'in-and-out' operators who sought immediate returns. But the governments, in so far as their writ was effective, were committed to the consortium, to their national groups. In Peking, however, the pressure on British Legation officers mounted, as first one industrial agent and then another sought official support for their negotiations with the Chinese.

British policy was in conflict with itself. There was a strong tradition against supporting a monopoly, now reinforced by the opinion, urged by Sir John Jordan, the British Minister in Peking, that the exclusive support policy was increasingly untenable in the face of competition by foreign firms within China seeking to undertake projects outside the scope of the consortium. If Chinese commitments were to be recognized by the Legation, contractors, etc, had eventually to be approved by one or another of the foreign legations, and the British Minister therefore came

---

27   For Pernotte's own story see A.-J. Pernotte, *Pourquoi et comment fut fondée la Banque industrielle de Chine* (Paris, 1922).

28   FO 371/1623, f. 43. Jordan's despatch of 5 December 1913, still contained inaccuracies. Ibid., f. 152.

under unacceptable pressure from his countrymen – including the representatives of Pauling and Co. To counter the monopoly criticism, the Foreign Office in December 1912 successfully pressured the Hongkong Bank to broaden its one-bank British group, but key China players were still excluded. In 1913 the Foreign Office had eventually to give way on two fronts: (i) restricting its consortium monopoly support to financial government loans on a one by one basis – thus promising support for the consortium only for the first in the series of proposed reorganization loans, and (ii) freeing the Legation to support non-consortium British companies in their negotiations for industrial loans.[29]

Sir Charles Addis argued strongly against both these moves. The arguments in favour of the consortium have been stated; the arguments against 'freeing' industrial loans were based partly on the danger of over-extension of credit and the consequent threat to Chinese sovereignty this could cause and partly on the problem of identifying what was 'industrial' and what was at least partly 'financial'. However, it was the threat of the Banque industrielle which forced the British hand and led to Addis's reluctant concurrence, although it is clear that as other governments had yielded to pressure, the British Foreign Office would have been unable to hold to their understanding with Addis.[30]

Ironically, the early loan operations of the BIC would prove the validity of Addis's arguments. The BIC's 1914 Pukow Loan would be a classic example of a financial advance disguised as an industrial project, whether or not all the promoters were initially aware of what was in fact happening. It would also be a classic example of Chinese evasion. In response to a direct query from the representatives of the Five Groups, i.e. the consortium, the Chinese Minister of Finance, Hsiung Hsi-ling, responded vigorously, '... the industrial loan under discussion concluded by the Government with the Sino-French Bank [i.e. the BIC] is purely for industrial development, and positively will not be used for administration expenses in contravention of the Reorganisation Loan Agreement'.[31]

The Chinese officials responsible for supporting the Sino-French – the Chinese name for the BIC was 'Chung-Fa shih-ye yin-hang', i.e. 'Sino-French Industrial Bank' – banking project were in no doubt as to what they expected. Here would be a bank with Chinese capital, though borrowed abroad, and representation on a board of directors able to finance the government without the necessity of negotiating with the Powers or the need to accept politically unpopular control measures.[32] That any banking venture should be acceptable to both parties on such a basis may seem incredible, but there is an explanation: both sides had different objectives the contradictory nature of which they disregarded, assuming that their own particular

29   Addis's summary of the consortium position and the correspondence with the Foreign Office and Lord Grey is found in PP.MS. 14/342.

30   Ibid. See also, esp. Grey to Addis, 2 September 1913 and Addis to Grey, 6 September 1913.

31   The exchange is found in FO 371/1623, dated 10 and 15 Nov. 1913.

32   The Chinese arguments for the BIC were presented to the National Assembly by the Chinese Minister of Finance, Hsiung Hsi-ling, on 30 Jan. 1913 and are quoted in Shinonaga, 'La Formation', pp. 53–5, on the basis of the report in MAE (NS), Chine, vol. 406, f. 69–71, in the Archives of the Foreign Ministry.

view would prevail. Thus for the Chinese, the BIC would be a source of uncontrolled funds; for the French the alleged inactivity of the Banque de l'Indochine would be circumvented, French economic influence would be extended, and the close relations with the host government would result in profitable industrial concessions which would further enhance French prestige. France would at last take its rightful place in China. Not surprisingly the Chinese objectives were more nearly realized.

One could argue that France was already heavily involved in financing China, first through the French group in the consortium and, secondly, through French direct and indirect (through the Pekin Syndicate) involvement in the CCR, which, after all, still held unfulfilled railway projects north of the Yangtze. This is without consideration of France's activities in Yunnan and with the Yunnan Syndicate or its financial role in the Russo-Chinese Bank or its successor, the Russo-Asiatic Bank. (The Russo-Chinese Bank was properly considered a tool of Russian political imperialism and, as such, had little influence after Russia's defeat in the Russo-Japanese War. However, French banking interests remained involved in its successor at least until 1917.)[33] But French imperialist thinking differentiated between participation as a nation and as part of a commercial company; thus its role in various British-based syndicates, and especially in the CCR, did not satisfy. Nor did its equivocal role in the Russian banks meet the need for French political participation; indeed, quite the contrary. France, the Colonial Party maintained, should have a presence in China as a nation and at all levels. There had to be a French bank leading where the Banque de l'Indochine had failed to tread.

The arrogance thus expressed was based partly on a lack of understanding of banking and risk factors, partly on a line of thought which was politically oriented and which did not fully consider the problem of sources of funds, creditworthiness, and eventual redemption of credits. But even as a political project, the new bank would be flawed; it could exercise control neither of its officers in China nor of its Chinese partners.

To be fair, this lack of understanding was also found on the British side. Sir John Jordan believed that the BI was involved and therefore did not take into account that the BIC could become a *banque de dépôts*, and his early reaction to news of the BIC was that 'British contractors and manufacturers should be invited to enter into some similar combination with the view of meeting French competition for industrial projects in this country'.[34] What he understood by the term 'similar combination' is not stated, but then Jordan was an admirer neither of the consortium nor of Sir Charles Addis's policies. Fortunately Addis had sufficient influence to curb any tendency to excess in the Foreign Office.

All this was, of course, obvious to the major financial houses in Paris, including the Banque de l'Indochine, whose chairman, St Simon, had long before countered Berthelot's arguments. The atmosphere was hostile; the Banque de l'Indochine would not be reconciled to the concept of an industrial bank and refused to cooperate. The BIC was nevertheless established.

---

33   Quested, *The Russo-Chinese Bank*, pp. 61–3.
34   Jordan to Grey, 5 Dec. 1913, in FO 371/1623, f. 152.

The Chinese contributed nothing to the BIC's Fr45 million initial capital (= £1.8 million). Their share of the initial one-third of the capital was actually advanced by the Pekin Syndicate against Chinese treasury bills; additionally the PS also subscribed to a further one-third of the 3000 founders' shares in its own name and in 1913 also held 15,350 ordinary shares, or 18.2 per cent of the capital, the second-largest shareholder (after the PS-financed Chinese government participation).[35] Furthermore, PS shareholders were offered BIC shares on advantageous terms. The promoters had milked a participant in the consortium to challenge the consortium; there was nothing either the British or the French could do to counter these developments. Indeed, Victor claimed, surely without evidence, that the PS had 'un contrat de Banque industrielle avec le gouvernement chinois, signé par l'Italien Luzzatti avec l'appui de Lord Rothschild'.[36] A comprehensive bank was indeed part of the di Rudiní/Luzzatti/Ma original scheme, but there is no official record of any such formal agreement with China – in the absence of which, if there proved to have been some arrangement, it would have no standing. It is also true that Lord Rothschild and Li Hung-chang were in communication with each other regarding the Pekin Syndicate's concessions and that the broad scope of the PS's articles of association would have permitted virtually any activity, including a bank. Victor's claim would, however, appear to be pure fantasy designed to permit the allocation of the PS's funds for his banking venture with a minimum of argument.

But although France officially remained committed to the consortium arrangements, at least for financial loans, the history as recounted by Shinonaga, Marc Meuleau, and others confirms that at key points, key officials either supported or did not oppose the progress of the Banque industrielle de Chine. For example, the CCR in responding to Foreign Office criticism made the specific charge that French officials in Peking were assisting negotiations between the embryo BIC and the Chinese government even before the agreement to omit industrial loans from the control of the consortium.[37] From time to time Philippe Berthelot intervened from the Quay d'Orsay, facilitating the activities of the bank or attempting to delay its exposure.[38] The BIC, however, insisted it was a private bank without government connections; its actions, the BIC claimed, were dictated by the hostile attitude of the Hongkong Bank and the British Legation.[39]

Sir Charles Addis considered that the establishment of the BIC violated the spirit of the Six-Power Groups and the Foreign Office protested.[40] As for the Banque de l'Indochine, it was approached by the BIC but resisted temptation. The BI board had to weigh the forces working on them: on the one hand there was the official French policy, the scepticism of the major French financial institutions, and the positive (and

---

35   *Money Market Review* (27 December 1913), p. 789.

36   Quoted in Shinonaga, 'La Formation', p. 56.

37   CCR to FO, 18 February 1914, FO 371/1937, f. 410. The letter also refers to the large cash advances made by the French to the Chinese government.

38   Report in *The Times* (9 August 1923).

39   See, for example, Pernotte to the PS, 30 March 1914, in FO 371/1941, f. 137.

40   Addis to E.G. Hillier in Peking, 3 April 1913, in Addis Private Letters, HSBC Holdings, plc, group archives.

tested) advantages of the consortium carried on in the context of the bank's existing exchange and lending policies in China; on the other hand there was the pressure of the Berthelot faction, the promise of high returns on virtually limitless China investment, and the growth of other China business which would naturally follow. Much depended on one's analysis of the BIC's management, its political connections, and the validity of its approach. The Pukow Loan was a deciding factor: the loan contained unsupervised finance for the Chinese government, the project was judged unsuitable, and it was a foretaste of the future. The Banque de l'Indochine opted for its traditions and the two French banks would remain hostile throughout.[41]

But all this was of no avail to the Pekin Syndicate; at least until 1920 its affairs and those of the Banque industrielle de Chine were inextricably interwoven with cross-linked boards of directors. The control of the Pekin Syndicate had given the Victor/Berthelot group the funds they needed to circumvent the opposition of the major banking houses in Paris. The impact of these developments on international China finance was, it is true, muted by the impact of the World War. (The Europe-based banks' inability to lend opened China to unilateral action by Japanese banks, especially from 1917.) Nevertheless the BIC was hyper-active and the pattern of its activities, leading to its eventual collapse, was evident, even as the Banque de l'Indochine had decided, early in its history.

The BIC's success in obtaining initial capital now had to be matched by raising funds to enable the French to fulfil French and Chinese expectations. The first major project was, as noted above, the financing of the development of Pukow, a port on the Yangtze lying at the southern end of the German/British railway from Tientsin. The BIC was to manage the public issue of the agreed Fcs150 million, 50 year, 5 per cent Industrial Gold Loan of 1914. This was quickly followed by the signing of an agreement for a Fcs600 million, 50 year, 5 per cent Ching-Yü (i.e.Yamchow [Qinzhou]-Chungking [Chongqing]) Railway Loan.[42] The latter had long been a French dream, but the former was actually in the British sphere of influence and seen by many as a direct challenge. Interestingly, Sir Charles Addis took a relatively benign view of the Pukow loan – at least, he commented, a development project was being undertaken; better by the French than not at all.

Neither of the BIC-managed loans led to actual development projects, but advances against the loan did provide funds for Yuan Shih-kai's government, funds which the Chinese did not have to account for to foreign consortium supervisors! The Foreign Office reported, for example, that the BIC had contracted to pay the Chinese government £4 million as an advance on the railway loan, adding that this might explain why the Chinese were not interested in further advances from the consortium.[43] Indeed the 1914 Industrial Loan could be faulted further; as an industrial loan its security was inadequate and the port itself had already been sufficiently developed. As early as May 1914 the Foreign Office had received copies of the *Journal des Débats* discussing the 'scandal' relative to the method of floating

---

41   Cf Meuleau, *Des pionniers*, pp. 252–71.

42   The texts of these two loans and related agreements are found in MacMurray, *Treaties and Agreements*, vol. 1, pp. 1055–66 and 1099–107.

43   FO 371/1933/F19853, ff. 231–32 (1914).

the loan, the *Journal* assuming as a matter of course that the loan's real purpose was to provide funds to the Chinese government and putting any reference to 'industrial' in quotes![44] Furthermore, such operations were shown to have been an important initial source of income to the BIC, taking a loan at 84 or Fr420 and selling to the public at Fr471.25.[45] But so sensitive had British opinion become that, even under these much-criticized circumstances, the CCR, as involved in the Tientsin-Pukow railway, had to respond to severe criticism from the Foreign Office on the grounds that only their supineness had permitted the French to obtain the contract. The CCR found such hysterical criticism not difficult to rebut.[46]

There were attempts, presumably inspired by the British directors of the PS, to have the Pukow Port project transferred to the PS, thus recognizing the significance of the British claims to priority in the Yangtze Valley, but the BIC refused.[47] Certainly the activities of the PS were now being scrutinized in Britain, as its role in financing the BIC was at last understood and its British status under review; this may have been inhibiting, even for the Victor/Berthelot group. However, the PS had become illiquid. In order to improve the Syndicate's position its board of directors in 1914 ordered the sale of bonds of the 1905 Loan at 87.5; the declared purpose was to finance projects in China to the relative advantage of the Syndicate.[48] The timing was poor and once again the Pekin Syndicate's fortunes were dimmed at just the moment it was successfully negotiating a joint mining venture with rival Chinese claimants in Honan.[49]

As the Banque industrielle de Chine lacked the cooperation of the Banque de l'Indochine, it took to itself the additional role of a *banque de dépôts*. The Banque de l'Indochine had to watch the BIC take an ever-increasing portion of French China business, although the major increase in the BIC's assets occurred in 1919 during the postwar China trade boom. At that time the BIC had twenty-two branches, including ten in China, three in Indo-China, and others in Japan, Paris, Antwerp, London and New York. Not surprisingly, the end-fiscal 1919 accounts, presented in the immediate aftermath of an increase in capital, suggest a large note issue, probably in the order of Fr140 million at a time when total liabilities, including shareholders' funds, were approximately Fr1 billion.[50] Perhaps the most remarkable item, however, is 'current and deposit accounts' of Fr675.7 million, an increase of Fr502 million in a single

---

44   FO 371/1937, ff. 452–4.

45   Ibid.

46   Exchange in FO 371/1937, ff. 396–97 and esp. CCR to FO, 18 Feb. 1914, ibid., ff. 410–1.

47   *The Times* (27 April 1914), p. 20b. In a letter from the Agent-General of the BIC, it was also asserted that the BIC's Peking concessions were valid and that there were no German interests.

48   Notice from the PS Board in *The Times* (7 Feb. 1914), p. 16e.

49   A copy of the loan announcement with closing date of 10 February 1914 is found in FO 371/1657, f. 51. The Pekin Syndicate's bankers were Lloyds.

50   The Hongkong Bank's total China issue at the time was HK$35 million (including Hong Kong). The actual BIC circulation is not stated because it is included in an item in the accounts entitled 'Loan accounts and creditors accounts'. *The Times* (26 July 1920), p. 22a–b.

year! Even if, as claimed, one-half of this were on a long-term or required-notice basis, the situation was dangerous – especially to the Pekin Syndicate. A glance at the BIC's assets shows investments and loans at Fr543 million, indicating a high degree of illiquidity, especially given the large sums advanced to the Chinese government and especially in view of the recent nature of the increased deposits bought in at interest rates reaching 17 per cent per annum.[51] André Berthelot as chairman presented his report in a context of total optimism: 'You can rely on us, Gentlemen, to prosecute this task with the perseverance, the energy, and the perfect indifference to malevolent criticisms ... .'[52]

But the reality was otherwise. In 1923 a French court ruled that the alleged Fr16.24 million profits shown in the 1919 accounts were fictitious; there had in fact been a deficit of Fr2.86 million. Indeed the court ruled that since 1913 the BIC had increased its business disproportionately to its resources.[53] If the two 1914 loans were *de facto* 'financial', the funds were advanced to the Chinese government at interest (as in the case of the Pekin Syndicate's 1905 Loan), helping in turn to finance the bank's several poorly researched loans to the private sector.

Jordan had reported as early as 1914 that the BIC's ability to find funds seemed inexhaustible but that the bank was 'none too sound'.[54] The Direction du Mouvement général des fonds had warned of the poor quality of the bank's portfolio in April 1917.[55] The subsequent collapse of the bank would appear on one level to have been caused by a combination of lack of confidence – it proved difficult to continue to buy-in funds at high cost and on-lend them to the Chinese government with no prospect of repayment at a time when there were no visible signs of development – over-extension during the postwar trade boom, and dealing during a most volatile period both in commodities and on the exchanges with the spectacular immediate postwar rise and then collapse in the gold price of silver. The real story, however, is more complex, with corruption, bribery, misrepresentation and incompetence an integral cause of the bank's downfall.

Charles Victor was bankrupt by early 1914 and had thus been eliminated early in the BIC's history, Pernotte would serve a prison term, André Berthelot resigned from presidency of the bank and from control of the Pekin Syndicate, in the latter case after exceeding his authority and undermining its financial position, and the unrepentant Philippe Berthelot was suspended from office, his name, in some circles, discredited.[56]

At some cost, the Banque de l'Indochine had been vindicated and a new consortium policy, now formally adopted by treaty, had been put into place without the participation of the BIC which was, in any case, on the verge of collapse. When

51   Meuleau, *Des pionniers*, pp. 261–71.

52   *The Times* (26 July 1920), p. 22a–b.

53   *The Times* (9 Aug. 1923).

54   Jordan papers, FO 350/11, ff. 53–56 and *passim*.

55   J.-N. Jeanneney, 'L'affaire de la Banque industrielle de Chine', in *Revue Historique*, vol. 253, 1975, pp. 377–416, esp. pp. 382–3.

56   Ibid., pp. 410–12. Berthelot's resignation was reported in *The Times* (27 Dec. 1921), p. 8c. The saga of Ph. Berthelot is continued in ibid. (17 March 1922), p. 11a and until the arrest of Pernotte, reported in ibid. (25 Feb. 1922), p. 12f.

the BIC's operations were suspended, part of the losses was met, in a series of controversial decisions, by the Pekin Syndicate. In 1920, for example, the PS held 17,208 ordinary shares and 391 founders' shares in the BIC costing £159,951, on which there was an unpaid liability of £93,612. In addition the PS had current and deposit account with the BIC in Europe and China totalling a sum of approximately £280,500. In a memorandum to the Foreign Office, the PS's British chairman commented, 'Thus it will be seen that the French policy was to use the monies of the Pekin Syndicate for the purposes of the Banque industrielle de Chine'.[57]

The Pekin Syndicate nevertheless remained solvent, in part because French legislation eliminated the requirement that subscribers be required to meet the unpaid balance of their partially paid-up shares. And although the Chinese government did not pay in its third of the capital, the Pekin Syndicate was absolved of further responsibility in this aspect of the problem.[58] The affair permitted the British directors to push through an arrangement for a predominantly British board; the Pekin Syndicate had returned, the Foreign Office noted, to its British allegiance.[59] Thereafter its role was confined to its subordinate participation in the CCR, the spasmodic development of its Honan concession, and the performance of certain additional tasks assigned by the Chinese Government during the Second Sino-Japanese War.

In the immediate post-World War I period, as noted previously, it was the turn of the United States to attempt 'patriotic banking' and consequently to experience loan defaults and failures. With idealism run wild, the American promoters of the Chinese American Bank of Commerce determined to incorporate under Chinese law and avoid the stigma (and safety) of possessing foreign extraterritorial privileges. The consequences of this Quixotic determination enabled Noel Pugach, author of the bank's history, to entitle his study 'Same bed, different dreams'.[60] Meanwhile, the Banque industrielle de Chine had remained active virtually to the eve of the exposé; in 1919 it joined seven other foreign banks in China to participate in the $500,000 Repatriation Loan to the Chinese government on the security of the salt revenues. The loan's purpose was to finance the forced repatriation of German citizens from China, but the Germans were back in time to witness the reopening of their Deutsch-Asiatische Bank even as the Banque industrielle disappeared, transferring its business to another equally superfluous but less ambitious French bank.[61]

---

57   Memo undated but early 1921 and found in FO 371/8021. The complex charges and counter-charges relative to the PS and BIC in 1920/21 are beyond the scope of this essay.

58   Report in *The Times* (21 July, 1922), p. 9c.

59   For the impact on PS shares, see *Money Market Review* 121: 43, p. 643 (9 July and 3 Dec. 1921). An increase in share prices occurred on the news that the BIC might reorganize, see *Investors' Chronicle and Money Market Review* (7 July 1922), p. 10, but the gain was lost by 15 July, see p. 74.

60   N. Pugach, '*Same bed, different dreams*'.

61   The irony of this coincidence was widely noted. See, e.g. *The Times* (1 July 1921), p. 15a–b. The 1919 loan is listed in China-Securities, Container 010, black ring-binder, in the A.N. Young papers, Hoover Institution Archives, Stanford, California, quoted in King, *The History*, vol. 3, p. 12.

Both the collapse of the BIC itself and the manner of that collapse had a serious impact on the credibility of the French in China.[62] Sino-French relations, themselves, were soured by arguments over calculations relative to the Boxer Indemnity.[63] For, at a time when the other Powers were considering remission, France had to pay off the debts of the BIC. Visionary banking had not furthered France's position in China, and, just as the French bank had obtained initial capital from the British-registered Pekin Syndicate, so now the French sought to pay back the bank's debts from Chinese funds obtained in excess of damages received during the Boxer Uprising so many years before.

The modernization of China fell victim to the dreams of ill-informed imperialists, inexperienced in banking. Intelligent men blinded by their own visions and speculators incompetent in sound banking had joined together to undermine the positive though unrealistic efforts which leading governments and financial institutions were attempting in China. They distorted the record of European banking in China. Their legacy was frustration.

---

62   A useful summary of the impact of the bank's collapse is found in notes contributed to London's *Morning Post* (4 July 1921), by B. Lenox Simpson; clipping found in FO 371/6589, f. 55.

63   This subject is covered in two memos with enclosures from Lord Hardinge to Marquess Curzon, Paris, 25 October and 22 November 1922, in FO 371/8021 [? illegible on copy], ff. 21–2, 48–9. See also, *The Times* (10 July 1922), p. 10c. My own summary, 'Nothing but bad', is found in *Modern Asian Studies*, 40.3 (July 2006), pp. 663–90.

CHAPTER 12

Two Centuries of Apex Banking: The State Bank of India and the Evolution of Modern Banking in India

Abhik Ray

The Temples of Greece, believed to be the first banks in the world, held deposits of cash and also undertook remittance business.[1] The priests turned the charge to good account and lent out at high interest the gold and silver deposited with them. The *Travels of Anacharsis in Greece* records that the money lent on trade could be as high as 30 per cent.[2]

At about the same time in distant India, though the legal rate of interest charged by the *shresthi*[3] was 15 per cent per annum, rates varied not according to the nature of the transaction but in relation to the particular caste to which the borrower belonged.[4] According to Vasishtha, the rates of interest were as follows:

Brahmanas (Priests) – 24 per cent per annum
Kshatriyas (Warriors) – 36 per cent per annum
Vaishyas (Merchants) – 48 per cent per annum
Sudras (Workingmen) – 60 per cent per annum

The *Arthashastra*[5] also refers to the high rates of interest prevailing then, varying between 15 (for secured loans) and 60 per cent (for unsecured loans). When the advance was considered to be quite risky, the rate of interest could even go up to as high as 240 per cent.

---

1   H.T. Prinsep, 'Note on the principle of banking in its application to the condition of things in India' in Papers presented for the use of the proprietors of the Bank of Bengal agreeably to a resolution at their special general meeting held on 25 February 1837 (Calcutta, 1837), p. 46.

2   C.N. Cooke, *The Rise, Progress and Present Condition of Banking in India* (Calcutta, 1863), p. 5.

3   Buddhist *Jatakas* or birth stories refer to the indigenous banker as *shresthi* in the fifth and sixth centuries B.C. Later, the indigenous bankers came to be known also as *shroffs, sahukars, banians, chettiars, mahajans, khatris, dubashes* and *seths.*

4   The institution of caste peculiar to India is perhaps the most vital principle of Hinduism, and has dominated Indian social life, manners, morals and even thought.

5   Kautilya or Chanakya, the able minister of Chandragupta Maurya, 'the first strictly historical person' to be referred to as an Indian emperor, wrote it as a treatise on statecraft. It also dealt with the management of the royal treasury and the means of raising revenue.

The Indian banker was a glorified moneylender, who unlike the traditional *Kabuliwallah* (Afghan moneylender) either received deposits or dealt in *hundis*,[6] or both. Although *hundis* find no mention in Buddhist literature, big merchants issued letters of credit and mention is made of 'signet rings being used as deposit or security, of wife and children pledged or sold for debt and of IOUs or debt-sheets'.

The celebrated lawgiver Manu, who wrote about indigenous banking in the first few centuries of the Christian era in his monumental classic *The Laws of Manu*, devoted a special section to 'Deposits and Pledges', indicating that deposit banking in some form must have been introduced by then. Advising people to make deposits with bankers of good repute, Manu wrote, 'A sensible man should make a deposit (only) with a person of (good) family, of good conduct, well acquainted with the law, veracious, wealthy and honourable (Arya)'.[7] The best definitions of a modern banker will perhaps find it difficult to improve on Manu's requirements for a good banker.

During Mogul rule, the indigenous bankers played an important part in financing the country's trade by means of credit instruments.[8] It was also then that these bankers gained prominence as they began carrying out numerous functions of the state – serving as officers of Royal Mints and also advancing large sums of money to the Royal Treasury in times of need. The power and influence of these *shroffs* was acknowledged even by Mughal Emperors. No emperor would ever send the *khelat* (robe of honour) to the Bengal nawab without sending one to Jagat Seth, the eminent banker of Murshidabad.[9]

When the Europeans came to India, an extensive network of Indian banking houses connecting important towns and trading marts covered the entire subcontinent. Equipped with a network of *kothis* or agencies extending to the far corners of the country, the *shroffs* could gather information expeditiously, keep track of changes in domestic channels of trade and finance and adapt themselves accordingly. They lent money to other bankers, landlords and princes, financed the cultivation and

---

6   The *hundi*, an inland bill of exchange in Indian language, was a written order, usually unconditional, made by one person on another for the payment, on demand (*darshani*) or after a specified time (*muddati* or usance) of a certain sum of money to a person named therein. The rules for presentation, acceptance, endorsement or dishonour could be much more complicated than those for European-style bills of exchange. See A.K. Bagchi, *The Evolution of the State Bank of India,* vol. 2, *The Era of the Presidency Banks, 1876–1920* (New Delhi, 1997), ch. 6, pp. 141–2.

7   'The Laws of Manu', trans. G. Buhler, in *Sacred Books of the East* (1886), vol. XXV, p. 286.

8   According to J.B. Tavernier, the French traveller, who paid five visits to India between 1640 and 1665, trade in India in the seventeenth century was financed partly in cash and partly by bills drawn on Surat and payable in two months. See J.B. Tavernier, *Travels in India*, trans. V. Ball, ed. W. Crooke (Oxford, 1925).

9   Rev. James Long, *Selections from unpublished records of Government for the years 1748 to 1767*, vol. I (Calcutta, 1886). For details on Jagat Seth see J.H. Little, *The House of Jagat Seth* (Calcutta, 1967). Described as the 'Rothschild of India' by Edmund Burke, the banking house would consider it beneath their 'dignity' to lend below Rs 100,000 – a colossal sum in those days. See D. Tripathi, *The Oxford History of Indian Business* (New Delhi, 2004), ch. 3, p. 38.

movement of commodities and during wars even the movement of armies. It was these indigenous bankers who financed the European merchants initially. Early nineteenth-century paintings of James Moffat, the famous British engraver, who came to India, show the moneylenders of Calcutta lending to a *sahib*[10] or *hundis* being discounted in 1810 at 36 per cent – when the normal rate, i.e. the rate at which bills of small traders were discounted by *shroffs*, was about 12 per cent.

Soon, however, the European merchants formed agency houses and took upon themselves the business of banking in addition to their commercial and trading activities. Apart from their inability to make use of the indigenous banking system for long, the European merchants also needed a safe place to deposit the capital they had steadily been accumulating. The agency houses accepted deposits, lent money to merchants, shipowners, ship managers, planters and governments and generally helped finance external trade. In 1770, the first western-style bank, the Bank of Hindostan, was set up in Calcutta by Alexander and Co., one of the leading agency houses of Bengal. It was the first bank to introduce paper money in India, with notes ranging from 4 to 1000 Sicca Rupees.[11] The circulation of its notes was confined entirely to Calcutta and its immediate neighbourhood, the government having refused to allow their reception into the collectors' treasuries in the *mofussil*. Some more banks set up by the managing agency houses in Calcutta and other presidency towns appeared soon after. Their base of operations consisted of deposits from European civil and military servants, the capital subscribed by the principals and the loans given to them by their Indian *banians* (in Calcutta), guarantee brokers (in Bombay) and *dubashes* (in Madras).[12]

In none of these private banks was the liability of the shareholders limited to the value of their shares. Nor could they be considered proper joint-stock banks, as most of the capital was owned by a few individuals and the banks were also managed by only a few. They were in law and in fact extended partnerships, which succumbed during the commercial crisis of 1830–33.

In the meantime, the wars unleashed by the Marquis of Wellesley, Governor General of India between 1798 and 1805, against Tipu Sultan and the Marathas and the continuous demand of the East India Company for a regular tribute from Indian tax revenues had placed the East India Company's Government in Bengal under severe financial strain. Raising loans from private sources had become increasingly difficult and more costly for the government. Large-scale borrowings had by then

---

10 An Arabic word originally meaning 'a companion' was used as a title all over India while referring to a European. It was also affixed to the name of a European and sometimes used as a specific title both among Hindus and Muslims.

11 The term 'sicca' was applied to newly coined rupees, which were at a premium over those worn out by use. The Sicca Rupee was abolished soon after the introduction of the Company's Rupee in 1835 to bring about uniformity of coinage over British India.

12 For a history of the agency houses operating in India see H. Furber, *John Company at Work* (Cambridge, 1951) and A. Tripathi, *Trade and Finance in the Bengal Presidency, 1793–1833* (Calcutta, 1956).

already resulted in heavy discounts on government treasury bills, a steep rise in rates of interest and an acute shortage of specie.[13]

> At the beginning of the century the European mercantile community was small, and consequently when the Government wished to raise large sums of money for the wars they were constantly engaged, they were obliged to look chiefly to the native mercantile community for the money required. The mode of raising money in those days was by the issue of what were called Treasury Bills, and these bills, in consequence sometimes of a scarcity of coin and more frequently of a combination among the native bankers, could not be cashed, except at a heavy discount.[14]

A plan for a semi-government bank for Bengal with a strong mercantile element was thus formulated in 1801 by Henry St. George Tucker, the Accountant General of the Government of Bengal, for stabilizing rates of interest and mobilizing credit so as to support both the public credit of the Company's Government in Bengal and the private credit of the merchants of Calcutta. According to Tucker, 'the establishment of a bank, besides securing many commercial advantages, would prevent depreciation of the Government bills, by introducing a new customer into the market, who would always be provided with a store of specie'. The government-sponsored bank in Bengal was set up as the Bank of Calcutta (the earliest progenitor of State Bank of India) on 2 June 1806. When the Court of Directors granted it a charter in 1808, it was redesignated as the Bank of Bengal and opened for business on 2 January 1809.

The establishment of the Bank of Bengal marked the advent of modern, limited-liability, joint-stock banking in India. So was the associated innovation in banking, viz. the decision to allow the Bank of Bengal to issue notes, which would be accepted for the payment of public revenues in government treasuries throughout Bengal and Bihar. The notes generally circulated, however, within the environs of Calcutta and were mainly used for effecting large transactions.[15] Issuance of notes was not to exceed four times the cash in hand and four times its capital.

As business in India expanded and as British rule extended to other parts of India, need was felt for the creation of similar banks in Bombay and Madras, the two other major centres of British rule and commerce in India. Thus were set up the Bank of Bombay (15 April 1840) and the Bank of Madras (1 July 1843), on lines similar to the Bank of Bengal. These three banks formed the highest tier of the apex banking system working within the borders of British India, including Burma and the so-

---

13 Twelve per cent treasury notes in 1801 were being sold at a discount of 3 or 4 per cent. Moreover, since much of the revenue was paid in gold coin, which was then at a discount of 6 to 7 per cent, the government lost in the conversion from gold to silver. See J.W. Kaye, *The Life and Correspondence of Henry St. George Tucker* (London, 1854), pp. 104–6.

14 Report of the Bombay Bank Commission (1869) in J.B. Brunyate, *An Account of the Presidency Banks* (Calcutta, 1900), p. 1.

15 According to Holt Mackenzie, Secretary to the Government, the notes of the Bank of Bengal bore a small premium, so great was the public confidence in the bank. See A.K. Bagchi, *The Evolution of the State Bank of India, The Roots, 1806–1876*, Part I, The Early Years, 1806–1860 (Bombay, 1987), ch. 7, p. 182.

called Native States. They were also, for all practical purposes, the most important government bankers within the territories concerned.

The right of note issue[16] granted to the three banks was very valuable, as it meant an accretion to the capital of the banks – a capital on which the proprietors did not have to pay any interest. The concept of deposit banking was also an innovation, because the practice of accepting money for safe keeping (and in some cases, even investment on behalf of the clients) by the indigenous bankers had not spread as a general habit in most parts of India. Till the abolition of the right of note issue of the three banks by the Paper Currency Act of 1861, these notes together with the capital formed the main investible resources of the banks.

The three banks were governed by charters, which were renewed from time to time. Besides providing for a share capital in which the government were also part owners, the charter among other matters stipulated the business which the bank could do and also imposed certain restrictions on it. Business was initially confined to discounting bills of exchange or other negotiable private securities, keeping cash accounts and receiving deposits and issuing and circulating cash notes. Deposits initially were in the nature of current-account deposits only, on which the banks did not have to pay any interest.[17] Restrictions on quantum of loans, period of accommodation and rates of interest were also laid down.[18] The security for such loans was public securities, commonly called Company's paper, bullion, treasure, plate, jewels or goods 'not of a perishable nature'. Loans against goods like opium, indigo, salt, woollens, cotton, cotton piecegoods, mule twist, silk goods and later tea, sugar, coal, jute, etc. were granted as cash credits and were either pledged or hypothecated to the bank. Loans against the security of illiquid assets such as land or buildings as well as shares and debentures were however forbidden. Loans could be granted so long as the cash in possession of the bank was at least one-third the value of notes and other claims payable on demand.

Indians were the principal borrowers against deposit of Company's paper, while the business of discounts on private as well as salary bills was almost the exclusive

---

16 Every private bank established in Bengal till then issuing notes had failed. The Union Bank founded in 1829 as an Indo-European enterprise was the only exception. Its notes were of course not received in government treasuries. Yet it met with considerable support from the mercantile community principally because unlike the Bank of Bengal it allowed interest on deposits. Unwise speculations in exchange operations and enormous investments in indigo eventually led to its collapse during the commercial crisis of 1847. See Bagchi, *The Evolution of the State Bank of India, The Roots*, part I, ch. 8 and B. Kling, *Partner in Empire: Dwarkanath Tagore and the Age of Enterprise in Eastern India* (Berkeley, 1976).

17 It was only in 1884 that the Bank of Bengal introduced the interest-bearing deposit scheme, viz. fixed deposits. The Banks of Bombay and Madras soon followed suit. Within three years, private deposits in the Bank of Bengal overtook public (government) deposits, moving further ahead with the introduction of the savings bank scheme in 1902. See A.K. Bagchi, *The Presidency Banks and the Indian Economy, 1876–1914* (Calcutta, 1989), ch. 3.

18 Loans were restricted to Rs. 100,000, period of accommodation confined to three months and interest limited to a maximum of 12 per cent. See Charter of the Bank of Bengal granted by the Governor General in Council at Fort William in Bengal on the 2nd of January 1809 (Calcutta, 1815).

monopoly of individual Europeans and their partnership firms. But the principal function of the three banks, as far as the government was concerned, was to help the latter raise loans from time to time, lend money directly to finance wars, famines, etc. and also provide a degree of stability to the prices of government securities.

Investment in government securities was the chosen preference of the banks, at least initially.[19] As loans to trade and industry increased over the years, the huge difference between loans and investments came down. In the days of the Imperial Bank of India loans and advances of the bank frequently exceeded its investments.[20]

The passing of the Paper Currency Act of 1861 and the decision to abolish the right of the Banks of Bengal, Bombay and Madras to issue notes led to a major change in the conditions of their operation. With the Government of India assuming from 1 March 1862 the sole power of issuing paper currency in British India, the three banks were soon made bankers to the government and initially entrusted with the task of management and circulation of the new currency. Moreover, the government undertook to lodge its treasury balances at all *mofussil* centres with the three banks at places where they would open branches. The banks embarked on frantic expansion and by 1876 their branches covered most of the major ports and many of the inland trade centres in India. The three banks and their successor, the Imperial Bank of India, continued to be bankers to the government till the creation of the Reserve Bank of India, the country's central bank, in 1935.

In May 1876 the Banks of Bengal, Bombay and Madras were brought under a common statute – the Presidency Banks Act – to have them governed by similar rules, subject the custody of government balances to stringent limits and strictly define the securities admissible and the terms on which loans and discounts could be granted. The government ceased to be proprietors but held the right of supervision. Much of this was occasioned by the failure of the Bank of Bombay in 1867, when corrupt mercantile directors and secretaries, gullible or negligent government directors and a complaisant government ensured the bank's entanglement in unfortunate speculations during the American Civil War.[21] A new Bank of Bombay emerged in its place soon after.

While the three banks were accorded a privileged status by virtue of their exclusive relationship with the government, they were at the same time compelled to accept certain restrictions on their activities. Principal among these was their rigid exclusion from engaging in any foreign-exchange business. Not only was such business considered risky for these banks, as they held government funds, it was also feared that these banks enjoying government patronage would offer unfair competition to the exchange banks mostly registered in the UK, which had

---

19 Up to 1822, for instance, the Bank of Bengal had invested Rs 6,000,000 in government securities in comparison to about Rs. 850,000 locked up in discounting salary, government and private bills. It was in such investments that the bank derived its main profits.

20 A. Ray, *The Evolution of the State Bank of India,* vol. 3, *The Era of the Imperial Bank of India, 1921–1955* (New Delhi, 2003), chs 2, 3 and 6.

21 For details see Bagchi, *The Evolution of the State Bank of India, The Roots,* part II, chs 25 and 26.

arrived in India by about the 1860s.[22] The British exchange banks were eventually to monopolize till well into the twentieth century the foreign-exchange business connected with the subcontinent's overseas trade and the remittance of large sums of money as tribute to London to cover the so-called 'Home Charges'.[23]

The exchange banks not only enjoyed an advantage over the Banks of Bengal, Bombay and Madras in being able to deal in foreign exchange; they also had greater manoeuvrability in the financing of internal trade, much of it linked to overseas trade. Unlike the three banks, the exchange banks were not bound by limits imposed on advances granted by them or the types of securities against which loans could be given.

With the arrival of the exchange banks, the three banks, which had till then been presiding over the banking system at its apex in the presidency towns of Calcutta, Bombay and Madras, were relegated to the role of intermediaries. In extending working capital finance to the exchange banks, the three banks of course indirectly financed overseas trade.

The presidency banks also remained at the apex of the domestic Indian money market. Besides financing Indian traders[24] within the provisions of the charter, they had also to deal with Indian bankers or *shroffs* who carried on their traditional business of discounting *hundis* and financing trade, manufactures (including artisanal) and agriculture. Other Indian banks, which performed more direct banking functions such as lending to traders, were also financed by the presidency banks.

The last quarter of the nineteenth century and the period after World War I saw a rapid commercialization of India. Quick expansion of India's railway network, conversion of subsistence crops into cash crops as a result of the emergence of new

---

22 Among the early exchange banks to arrive in India were the British banks of Chartered Bank of India, Australia and China, the Hong Kong and Shanghai Banking Corporation and the National and Grindlays Bank. The non-British banks included the Comptoir D'Escompte de Paris and Yokohama Specie Bank. See in this regard C. Mackenzie, *Realms of Silver: One hundred years of Banking in the East* (London, 1954) and F.H.H. King, *The History of the Hongkong and Shanghai Banking Corporation, Vol. I, The Hongkong Bank in Late Imperial China, 1864–1902: On an Even Keel* (Cambridge, 1954). The National and Grindlays Bank, also an exchange bank, was founded as the Calcutta City Banking Corporation in 1863 and incorporated in London in 1866 as the National Bank of India. See G. Tyson, *100 years of Banking in Asia and Africa* (London, 1963).

23 A.K. Bagchi, 'Introduction: Money, Banking and Finance in India since Early Medieval Times', in A.K. Bagchi (ed.), *Money & Credit in Indian History: From Early Medieval Times* (New Delhi, 2002), pp. ix–xli. While the annual surplus extracted from India and Burma was between £21.4 million and £28.9 million in 1870s, it rose to between £52.9 million and £65.3 million on the eve of World War I. See also A.K. Bagchi, *Perilous Passage: Mankind and the Global Ascendancy of Capital* (Delhi, 2006), ch. 17, p. 241. Only for a brief while in 1923 was the Imperial Bank employed to remit funds to London by purchasing bills from the exchange banks in India, which could be either discounted or held until maturity at the disposal of the Secretary of State. See Ray, *The Evolution of the State Bank of India*, vol.3, ch. 2, pp. 108–9.

24 With classes of admissible securities, periods for which loans or discounts could be granted and a minimum limit (Rs 10,000 in the case of Bank of Bengal in 1845) for opening a cash credit account in the presidency banks, only the affluent among Indians could avail of loans. Dwarkanath Tagore, 'the Prince among Indian merchants', for instance, borrowed Rs 60,000 from the Bank of Bengal in 1817 on deposit of securities of the East India Company.

irrigation networks and the transformation of large areas of the eastern Terais, hills of Assam and the Nilgiris under tea and coffee plantation into regions of estate agriculture par excellence caused a six-fold increase in India's overseas trade. The presidency banks were both beneficiaries and promoters of this commercialization process as they became involved in the financing of trading, manufacturing and mining activities of the subcontinent. While the Banks of Bengal and Bombay were involved principally in the financing of modern large manufacturing and mining industries (cotton, jute, sugar, tea, coal, etc.), the Bank of Madras went into the financing of small-scale industries in a way rarely attempted before.

In 1921, the three presidency banks with their 70 branches were merged to form an all-India bank, the Imperial Bank of India. But this creation was preceded by years of deliberations on the need for a state bank for India.[25] The scepticism of the Indian legislators about the efficacy of the arrangement was countered by the 'profound conviction' that the new bank would extend banking facilities, render the money resources of India more accessible to the country's trade and commerce and emerge as 'a really national institution'. The directors and shareholders of the three presidency banks thus pooled their resources and organizations with the hope that their united strength would 'consolidate the government connection' and help the new bank 'rule supreme in the banking world of India'. What eventually emerged was a 'half-way house' combining the functions of a commercial bank and a quasi-central bank.[26]

In order to ensure the spread of banking facilities throughout India and Burma 'at the quickest possible rate', the Imperial Bank succeeded in opening 100 new branches within the first five years of its existence, in accordance with an agreement with the Government.[27] Within a short while the bank emerged as the spearhead of banking development in India, and as the exclusive banker to the government earned an exceptional cachet in that sort of business. The new bank became the custodian of Government bonds and performed the treasury work of the Government free of charge by receiving all Government dues from the public, on which the Government drew for its disbursements. It also managed the public debt of the Government of India, provided the machinery for the issue of Government bonds, acted as a bankers' bank with the leading banks in India including the exchange banks, keeping a portion of their cash balances on deposit with it, and provided remittance facilities to the other banks and to the public at rates controlled by the Government. In 1935 the Imperial Bank ceased to be bankers to the government and became instead agent of the Reserve Bank for the transaction of government business at centres at which the central bank was not established. But it continued, among many other functions, to maintain currency chests and small coin depots and operate the remittance scheme for other banks and the public on terms stipulated by the Reserve Bank.

---

25 J.M. Keynes, 'Indian Currency and Finance', reprinted in *The Collected Writings of John Maynard Keynes*, vol. I (London, 1971). For deliberations in the Indian Legislative Council on the issue see Bagchi, *The Evolution of the State Bank of India*, vol. 2, ch. 19.

26 See Ray, *The Evolution of the State Bank of India*, vol. 3, ch. 1.

27 For details of the first branch expansion programme undertaken by the Imperial Bank see ibid., ch. 1, pp. 47–53.

The establishment of the Reserve Bank simultaneously saw important amendments being made to the constitution of the Imperial Bank, converting it into a purely commercial bank. The earlier restrictions were removed and the bank was permitted to undertake foreign-exchange business as well as executor and trustee business for the first time.

The period prior to the establishment of the Reserve Bank had witnessed extreme seasonal fluctuations in the Imperial Bank's bank rate. These fluctuations were, however, inevitable in an unsound monetary system in which banking and currency reserves stood separated and the government exercised direct control over currency in general and note issue in particular. The Imperial Bank nevertheless succeeded in bringing about a transformation in the Indian money market rates. The differential in the money market rates between Madras and the other two presidency towns of Bombay and Calcutta which was so evident in the days of the presidency banks was removed.[28] The expansion of emergency paper currency in terms of the Paper Currency Amendment Act, 1923 reduced the sharp fluctuations in money rates which used to occur throughout the year earlier on account of the seasonal swing of business. Interest rates fell at most places where the Imperial Bank opened offices, removing the old monopoly rates of the existing banks. Moreover, easy access to government funds coupled with the implicit or explicit official backing which the bank like its predecessors the presidency banks enjoyed enabled it to lend at a lower rate than the so-called bazaar rates. The remittance facilities provided by the bank through a large network of offices also considerably helped in the integration of the country's money market and reduced the seasonal and regional variations in money rates.

An innovative array of offices – branches, sub-branches, treasury pay offices, pay offices, sub-pay offices and outstations – unknown perhaps anywhere else in the world ensured the movement of goods and produce from the producing to the consuming centres as well as ports.

The three presidency banks and the Imperial Bank did not rest content with merely lending support to trade and industry. Customer service became a watchword for them all through. Even as early as 1889, a European officer was made to apologize to an Indian *baboo*[29] for alleged rudeness. The Imperial Bank also took particular care in retaining and expanding its business connections by offering constituents 'every reasonable facility' in the transaction of their business so that the 'best banking service obtainable in India' could be rendered to them.[30] 'Prompt, courteous and helpful attention' to constituents and a 'proper spirit of service' among all members of the bank's staff came to be insisted upon.

---

28 See *Banking and Monetary Statistics of India* (Bombay, 1954), section 8, p. 690, Table 1. While the bank rates of the Bank of Bengal and Bank of Bombay were more or less identical, the Bank of Madras rate was usually higher.

29 Like Master or Mr, it is a term of respect attached to a name in India. In the days of the Raj, the word often came to signify 'a native clerk who writes English'. See H. Yule and A.C. Burnell, *Hobson-Jobson: A Glossary of Colloquial Anglo-Indian Words and Phrases, and of Kindred Terms, Etymological, Historical, Geographical and Discursive* (Calcutta, 1903), p. 44.

30 For details see Ray, *The Evolution of the State Bank of India*, vol. 3, ch. 3, pp. 276–8.

Rarely did the presidency banks and the Imperial Bank depart from the tenets of sound banking (barring the unfortunate collapse of the Bank of Bombay). Without entering into rate-cutting wars, branches were enjoined to do everything possible to expand business connections. The adherence to rules at times even did not spare the high and mighty like Governor General William Bentinck.[31]

Scottish banking practices formed the backbone of the rules and regulations framed for the bank. A deftly-compiled book of instructions, the record of procedure and system of checks and periodical circular instructions enabled the functionaries of the presidency banks and the Imperial Bank to meticulously observe systems and procedures laid down from time to time. The system of audit and inspection, for instance, in place since the nineteenth century, ensured accounting efficiency and integrity.[32] Many of these systems were later to be adopted by the Reserve Bank of India for adherence by all scheduled banks in India.

It was essentially the soundness of business principles that saw the Imperial Bank being entrusted during World War II with the task of conducting banking affairs in Burma as agent of the Reserve Bank. A few years later, it was the Imperial Bank again which came to be vested with the task of conducting business in Pakistan for a while, after the Reserve Bank had ceased to be bankers to the Government of Pakistan.

Notwithstanding the inherent strength of the Imperial Bank and the commanding heights it had attained in the spheres of business, administration and efficiency, neither the Imperial Bank nor the other Indian commercial banks largely concentrated in the monetized and commercialized regions of the country had really succeeded in bringing banking to the vast majority of India's rural masses. The less developed 'subsistence' regions stood generally neglected, and credit in these areas was not only difficult to obtain but also very costly. The All India Rural Credit Survey Committee constituted by the Reserve Bank in 1951 to facilitate formulation of a long-term policy for rural credit found that the private creditor, i.e. the professional moneylender, the agriculturist moneylender and the trader, still reigned 'supreme in the field of rural credit, supplying 70 per cent or more of the total requirements'. The findings of the Committee also revealed 'the magnitude of the inadequacy of the Governments and the cooperatives as sources of rural credit'.[33]

---

31 The Bank of Bengal dared to return a cheque of Bentinck because his account was four annas (quarter of a rupee) short. (Rs-annas-pies was the standard currency of India before the introduction of the decimal system.) Bentinck, on being informed of the circumstance, applauded the proceeding and remarked, 'This was the bank to do business with which would not violate its rules in the smallest particular for the Governor General himself'. See *Allen's Indian Mail*, vol. VIII, 17 June 1850 (London), p. 350.

32 Even as early as in 1873, the Government of Madras had appointed a former acting Accountant General to investigate and submit a full report on the financial position and prospects of the Bank of Madras to enable the Government to judge how far they were warranted in entrusting to it the large State balances. See Bagchi, *The Evolution of the State Bank of India, The Roots*, part II, ch. 33, pp. 401–11.

33 While moneylenders accounted for more than 70 per cent of total borrowings, the government, co-operatives and commercial banks together accounted for only 7.3 per cent. Even more disturbing was the fact that of this very little, the major part went to the bigger agriculturists and only a minor fraction percolated to the smaller cultivator. See All India

The banks were thus ill equipped to respond to the emergent needs of economic regeneration of rural areas when the Government of India launched the First Five Year Plan (1951–56) after Independence. The plan aimed to use public-sector outlays to stimulate increased savings and investment in the economy as a whole, with special emphasis on agricultural and community development. In order therefore to serve the economy in general and the rural sector in particular, the Committee recommended the creation of

> one strong, integrated, State-sponsored, State-partnered commercial banking institution with an effective machinery of branches spread over the whole country, which, ... can be put in a position to take over cash work from non-banking treasuries and sub-treasuries, provide vastly extended remittance facilities for co-operative and other banks, thus stimulating the further establishment of such banks, and, generally, in their loan operations, in so far as they have a bearing on rural credit, follow a policy which, while not deviating from the canons of sound business will be in effective consonance with national policies as expressed through the Central Government and the Reserve Bank ... .[34]

The new bank was to be created by taking over the Imperial Bank of India and integrating with it the former state-owned or state-associated banks. It was realized that the venerable Imperial Bank, the 'most important joint-stock bank in the country', with its vast network of offices, its long and intimate connection with the government and its efficient organization, would be able to address best the needs for developing the rural economy. Having steadfastly held on to the sound principles of banking all along, the bank had earned the compliment of the then Indian Finance Minister as a 'very fine instrument of banking' forming the 'backbone of the Indian banking system'.[35] It was this tradition of banking excellence which eventually led the Government of India to transform the bank originally founded for financing the wartime needs of a belligerent Governor General into a major initiator of modern India's economy and society.[36]

On 1 July 1955 by an Act of Parliament the State Bank of India was constituted as successor to the Imperial Bank of India. More than a quarter of the resources of the Indian banking system thus passed under the direct control of the state. Four years later the State Bank of India (Subsidiary Banks) Act was passed, enabling the State Bank to take over eight former state-associated banks as its subsidiaries (later renamed Associates).

The State Bank was born with a new sense of social purpose, aided by 480 offices comprising branches, sub offices and three local head offices inherited from the Imperial Bank. The concept of banking underwent a sea-change as the new bank, unlike its predecessors, was no longer to be a mere repository of the community's

---

Rural Credit Survey: Report of the Committee of Direction, Vol. II, The General Report: Summary (Bombay, 1955), ch. III, p. 5.

34 Ibid., p. 404.

35 C.D. Deshmukh, Indian Finance Minister in Lok Sabha on 21 November 1950 quoted in Ray, *The Evolution of the State Bank of India*, vol. 3, ch. 9, p. 611.

36 For the story of the nationalization of the Imperial Bank of India see Ray, *The Evolution of the State Bank of India*, vol. 3, ch. 9.

savings and lender to creditworthy parties. There came about a distinct shift in the focus – from security-oriented to need-based lendings, from urban to rural banking, from class to mass banking and also from activities that contributed essentially to the bank's commercial objectives to those that largely served a social purpose. This transition from a primarily profit-seeking commercial bank to a great national institution with public responsibilities was however by no means an easy task. It became necessary for the Bank to reshape its organization and reset its tradition to make them sufficiently dynamic to suit the altered conditions. It also involved a re-orientation of the Bank's policies, a modification of its business methods and practices and a change of outlook on the part of its staff engaged at every level.

From its inception the State Bank began to play a dual role with due 'regard being had to public interest'.[37] As a commercial bank it continued, as hitherto, to provide finance to industry and trade. As a nationalized institution, it undertook several promotional and developmental activities by way of opening branches all over the country,[38] evolving and implementing a special scheme for financing small-scale industries, extending financial accommodation to marketing and processing cooperative societies and fostering India's foreign trade. The bank tried to align itself with the planned economic development of the country and allocate credit according to the needs of the economy. Even before the Government had initiated measures under the scheme of social control in 1968 to secure a better alignment of banking policy to the needs of economic planning, the State Bank had evolved schemes for all agricultural operations up to the marketing of agricultural produce as also for mechanization and modernization of farms, provision of irrigation facilities and development of land. Innovative and well-planned strategies were also evolved as the bank's response to the main thrust of the government on removing poverty and creating employment opportunities through accelerated economic development of the rural sector, with special emphasis on agricultural production, cottage industries, small industries, arts and crafts. By 1980, loans to agriculture, small-scale industries, small business and exports, categorized as priority-sector advances, constituted about 36.2 per cent of its total advances. Financial assistance to rural poor apart, an integrated view of the composite needs of the rural people covering economic, social and cultural areas was also evolved. The bank also extended assistance in meeting social needs such as removal of illiteracy, improvement of sanitation, provision of medical facilities, library and sports facilities, street lighting, supply of drinking water and building of roads and other infrastructure, including developing local leadership and enterprise.

In order to secure a larger share of the foreign-exchange business, the bank not only stepped up exports but also, through a coordinated plan for overseas expansion, opened offices in many important centres in the Middle East, South and Southeast Asia, Far East, Africa, Europe, North and Latin America. Financing foreign trade

---

37 Section 17(2) of the State Bank of India Act.

38 As with the Imperial Bank of India in 1921, the State Bank too was charged with the task of opening 400 offices during its first five years, which it succeeded in achieving. See Abhik Ray, *The Evolution of the State Bank of India*, vol. 4, *The Era of the State Bank of India, 1955–1980* (forthcoming), ch. 12.

THE EVOLUTION OF MODERN BANKING IN INDIA

apart, the bank also performed complex other functions such as raising foreign currency loans and meeting the banking needs under bilateral trade agreements with other countries.[39]

Assuming a multi-dimensional role, the State Bank pursued its strategies to achieve the objective of 'Profit with Growth'. The strategy involved improved customer service to its corporate (including mid-corporate), small industrial and agricultural customers and high-value retail customers through specialized branches.

Since 1955 the State Bank has to its credit several first initiatives in the Indian banking sector, like varieties of business handled including merchant banking, focusing on national priorities, overseas presence, human resources and organizational interventions. Several restructuring measures undertaken in 1971, 1979 and 1995 have ensured the bank's response to change and helped sharpen its competitive edge in key areas.[40]

The State Bank's strategic resources and marketing interventions with the changing economic scenario are perhaps unparalleled. In 1991, it mobilized a sum of US $1.6 billion by issuing India Development Bonds to help bolster India's foreign exchange reserves. In 1994, it became the first public-sector bank in India to access the domestic capital market. Two years later, in the first-ever Global Depository Receipt issue by any Indian commercial bank, the State Bank raised US $369.95 million to augment its capital resources. The 'World Equity' journal adjudged it as the 'Asian Equity Issue of the Year'. In August 1998, it launched the Resurgent India Bonds Scheme to tap the deposit potential of Non-Resident Indians and Overseas Corporate Bodies. As the most preferred vehicle for raising funds abroad, it mobilized Rs.203 billion (then US $4.23 billion), more than twice the targeted amount – an outstanding achievement coming in the wake of India's nuclear test. The bank followed this with Rs. 264 billion (then US $5.5 billion) through the India Millennium Deposit programme launched in October 2000 to raise long-term resources to increase India's foreign-exchange reserves and meet the needs of infrastructure projects.

Today the State Bank with its non-banking subsidiaries has emerged as a financial services supermarket offering the entire gamut of financial services including factoring, stockbroking, leasing, mortgage, project finance services, credit card,[41] insurance, etc.

An aggressive Information Technology policy is also in place as a strategic initiative to meet the growing competition for business and market share, achieve efficiency in internal operations and meet customer expectations.[42]

---

39 As at the end of March 2006, the bank handled approximately 27.80 per cent of the country's foreign trade.

40 The first two exercises were undertaken under the aegis of the Indian Institute of Management (IIM), Ahmedabad and the last one drawing upon the expertise of McKinsey & Co. with the objective of positioning itself as a world-class bank. The 1971 exercise was incidentally the first of its kind in the Indian banking industry.

41 The bank entered the credit-card segment in collaboration with GE Capital in 1999 and today has more than 2.64 million cards in force.

42 The bank has launched the BPR Project for redesigning business processes to leverage the Core Banking Solution (CBS) platform for improving its performance in key business

The State Bank Group (State Bank and its Associates) today has a network of 13,908 fully computerized branches including 4731 branches of its Associate Banks, with more than 3900 branches enabled for Internet Banking actively being used by one million retail and corporate customers, 5571 ATMs, 70 overseas offices spread over 30 countries covering all time zones and correspondent relationships with 539 international banks in 124 countries. Backed by state-of-the-art technology and communications, dedicated human resources and a vibrant organizational structure, the State Bank Group will soon emerge as a global bank.

As the largest Indian bank in terms of profits, assets, deposits, branches and employees and playing a crucial role in the nation's development, the State Bank of India with an asset base of over US $126 billion and profits in excess of US $1 billion is the only Indian bank to be ranked among the top 100 banks in the world in terms of Tier 1 capital and also among the top 20 banks in Asia.[43]

The journey of two centuries has been long and eventful, with the Bank maintaining its unbroken record of continuous profits and adapting itself to the changing times. As an instrument of public policy, the State Bank has discharged its role efficiently – be it while servicing a colonial power or later as an instrument of social and economic change in independent India. All through this period, it has functioned as the flagship of Indian banking and been in the forefront of all areas of banking – traditional, developmental as well as innovative. Today, while the focus of the bank is on remaining competitive in all fields – quality of service, pricing of products, use of technology and range of products and services, it has not lost sight of its primary role as an instrument of national policy. One would recall in this regard the words of R.K. Talwar, perhaps the most illustrious among State Bank's past Chairmen

> The State Bank is conscious of its obligations to society and the long journey yet to be traversed. It is a dedicated national instrument striving hard to blend itself with the mainstream of national life. It derives inspiration from our past heritage and moves onward to its destiny with sincerity faith and devotion.[44]

The leitmotif of the State Bank of India is to reach out to the people and their aspirations.

---

areas and improve the quality of service. As in March 2006, as many as 2741 branches of the State Bank were on the CBS platform across the country at 612 centres.

43 It was ranked 93rd by *The Banker* (London, July 2005).

44 State Bank Archives, Kolkata, letter dated 30 March 1976 from R.K. Talwar to Indira Gandhi, Prime Minister of India.

Closing Remarks

Alice Teichova

The chapters presented in this volume cover a wide range of approaches to the history of banking in the nineteenth and twentieth centuries, and the authors endeavour to assess developments under the motto of *finance and modernization*. In various ways the place of banks and bankers in modern and contemporary history and their reactions to the up- and downswings of capitalism are investigated in this volume. Seeking to appraise 'the bankers' view' of economic and political development is the main concern of Dieter Stiefel's introductory piece, which provides a frame for the content of the volume by a sweeping overview concentrating on the eventful Austrian history from the multinational Habsburg Monarchy in the mid-nineteenth century to the small neutral modern state of Austria at the end of the twentieth century. Throughout this period the bankers' place tended to be among the social elites. The remarkable adaptability of bankers to changing political and socio-economic systems emerges from the author's survey – the only dramatic exception was the economic and physical extinction of Jewish bankers under National Socialism. Concurrently in the field of business the author traces modernization from individual to mass banking.

In general, the contributors pursue success and failure of banking drawing upon their research by applying tools of historical, economic, mathematical, socio-political, legal and comparative techniques. In short, their deliberations are based on research results employing interdisciplinary methods.

The question asked in this summing up is what do authors tell us – to quote Eric Hobsbawm, 'why things happened as they happen'. Beginning with some general remarks applying to the content as a whole certain questions arising from the individual contributions will be discussed.

Chronologically the papers cover a long and varied sequence of time. They pay attention to the economic environment of expanding capitalism in Europe of the 'long' nineteenth century – if we include the pre-First World War years – then closely examine the failing capitalist market economy during the crisis-ridden decades between the wars, which ended in fascist dictatorships, war and destruction. The post-Second World War period was characterized by planning both in capitalist market economies in their attempts at building welfare states and in fully planned economies. The latter get attention in papers on Central and Southeast Europe and also on India. Additionally, some papers – more in passing – mention the return to liberalization, i.e. the unhampered free capitalist market economy enhanced by the collapse of the socialist planned economies. This contemporary period is not dealt with in detail by the papers; however, the underlying criterion for economic success or failure seems, in general, to be judged through the eyes of the authors by the business performance of banks within the capitalist market economy.

Geographically the contributions encompass Europe and Asia. Appropriate to the event of the 150th anniversary of the Creditanstalt, the celebration of which was the impulse to this international conference, the geographical weight of the presentations rests on central, particularly central east and southeast Europe (Germany and the Habsburg Monarchy, Austria and Greece) with an excursion to northern Europe, into Holland and Sweden. The centre of attention, in the context of this conference rightly so, is Vienna. Universal banking was practised throughout the European countries, which are the subject of the papers, but the vast areas of China and India which mainly British and French bankers and speculators attempted to open up produced a different type of financing, with the emphasis on trade, only later shifting to industry. This wide geographical reach provides a basis for comparing the history of universal banking in Continental Europe and imperial banking in China and India.

Looking at the main content of the papers – almost half of them deal with central Europe – we are confronted with the rise and fall of Vienna as a financial centre, dramatically described by Peter Eigner and Fritz Weber. Their analysis is supported by Aurel Schubert's appreciation of the role of the Oesterreichische Nationalbank in turbulent times as crisis manager driven by political decisions of the Austrian government, and finally as 'lender of last resort'. The author cites historical examples of the interplay of finance, the economy and politics in describing the Austrian central bank's attempt to secure financial stability in 1931, which led to the destruction of monetary stability.

Step by step we are able, with Peter Eigner's analysis, to follow the path which led to Viennese banks representing the *purest form of universal banking* between the mid-nineteenth century and 1931, with the attendant phenomenon of the largely weak and ineffectual position of the stock market. While economic historians long thought that Germany was the leader in universal banking because of the weakness of the Börse, Hartmut Kiehling documents in his statistical evidence that the early stock market in Germany was financially stronger and more effective and could especially have played a more important role in financing early German industrialization than was hitherto believed. These are interesting and provocative findings which would need to be backed up by a critical analysis of historical evidence. In addition, applying Kiehling's mathematical methods to the later periods of the nineteenth century could test the question whether stock exchanges in Germany, particularly in Prussia after unification, did indeed play a greater part in financing Germany's more rapid pace in industrial development in comparison with financing industry by banks – and whether market efficiency was enhanced.

Coming now to Austria, there is no doubt that with the crash of the big Viennese banks after 1931, which produced a domino effect, the demise of Vienna was sealed. These events beg the question of the character and aftermath of the famous financial crises of 1871 and 1931. While both Peter Eigner and Fritz Weber, agree in their assessment of the nature and impact of these crises on international financial relations and on the economic development in the region, Fritz Weber makes the comparison of the two crises the subject of his paper. Importantly, he corrects the previously held view of the crisis of 1873 as the 'great depression' by putting forward evidence that the so-called 'great depression' was, in the Austro-Hungarian case, a mere 'breathing space' in the ascent from an agrarian to an industrial society. Indeed, economic growth continued after a temporary weakening – he calls it a 'cleansing thunderstorm' – which prepared the ground for financing industry by the banks rather than the stock exchange. In comparison, by 1931, there was no recovery from the recurring crises and accelerating bank mergers of the interwar period. Indeed, what took place was in Fritz Weber's words 'a process of contraction rather than concentration'. Both authors document the universal banks' path from the zenith of power (1890s to 1913), with Vienna as the financial centre of central and southeast Europe and mediator between western and eastern capital, to their crash into insignificance after 1931.

One of the leading questions asked, also investigated in the papers, is for instance whether bank-oriented systems – not only in the case of Vienna but also in Sweden or Greece – have been more efficient than stock-market-oriented systems in channelling funds to industry. It appears, not surprisingly, that large enterprises benefited, while medium and particularly small businesses were starved of funding and thus had to go under in times of recurring economic crises. However, this seems according to Peter Eigner to have been not altogether the case in the less-developed parts of the Habsburg Monarchy, although no significant economic growth seems to have accompanied this type of financing. This is an area which needs to be investigated more closely. In Greece too, in the second half of the twentieth century, the successful rise of a commercial bank emanated from its policy and ethical image directed, as Margarita Dritsas shows, to the middle class and small borrowers. However, in the long run, this bank similarly could not withstand competition from the large universal banks, which did not favour medium and small borrowers.

Considering the problem of finance and modernization the question arises whether modernization is to be seen as the process of concentration, internationalization and, finally, globalization. In the papers analysing and assessing universal banking in central and northern Europe modernization is not the central theme but seems to be embedded in the measure of economic growth, and tends to be seen as the role of banks in financing industrialization. This begs the question how the expansion of banking affected the banks' business practices, their organization and techniques.

While there is no special attempt at a definition of the meaning of the concept of modernization, several authors address modernization in different ways, at different periods, and in different areas. The modernizing role of banks is seen by Peter Hertner in financing projects in transport, mainly railways, bridge building and canals, that is, in their role in expanding capitalism into economically backward regions. A further striking feature of modernization in banking practices, commented on by Peter Hertner, was the innovation of including small investors in new financial schemes. Methods such as the sale of small denominations of bonds or securities, or the sale of lottery tickets, spread from Brussels eastwards. In the case of the Balkans, one could say that such ventures played a role in opening up semi-feudal systems to capitalist finance and enterprise. Indeed, as Hertner remarks, this linked West to East. The question whether modernization through the expansion of capitalism into southeast Europe, that is through the involvement of Western European banks, brought about economic development, if not in the short run then perhaps in the long run, needs to be more closely examined.

Rainer Liedtke traces modernization through the history of the Rothschilds' growing network of information gathering, i.e. internationalization of information gathering within the widespread Rothschild financial interests. In the process he questions the general misconception about the Rothschild banks' seemingly perfect command of information, and he regards the network as rather more dependent on family ties and especially appointed employees than on technological progress. Indeed, their suspicious attitude to the electric telegraph does not seem to suggest that the Rothschilds were enthusiastic modernizers in this field.

Oskar Broberg finds modernization in Sweden through the progress of incorporation peaking by 1919 rather than at the turn of the century as hitherto assumed, which slightly changes the chronological picture of growth. He emphasizes the positive role of the stock exchange in Sweden, which afforded banks the opportunity to lend against shares. Interestingly, what brought progress in Sweden ended with disastrous consequences for the Vienna banks. Thus modernization, Broberg argues, is achieved by the growth of impersonal property relations in the rapidly growing numbers of joint-stock companies. Broberg backs this up by constructing a database, including industry, transport and trade, which shows the long historical development from a few chartered companies annually (1607 until 1842) to a steadily rising, until virtually exploding, number of incorporated companies since 1848. In his paper he is not measuring overall business activity but exclusively the incorporation process as such. In this development, the banks played a vital role as lenders against the security of shares.

In a different way this kind of modernization by incorporation is forced on the family bank, the Twentsche Bank, in Van der Werf's personalized company history: this story provides an example of the trend by which pressures of changing business conditions were leading to family firms either going out of business or changing into limited-liability enterprises.

Differences in approach to modernization appear in the papers on imperial banking in China and India. Frank King finds little modernization but rather frustration in the competitive struggle between – to quote him – 'ill-formed imperialists' who were involved in French and British banking in China. The result in the case of China was that neither did France's role enhance modernization, nor was modernization advanced by British bankers. Thus the author regards this as a story of failure of modernization.

In contradistinction Abhik Ray's case study on India is a success story of modernization furthering economic development. It follows the path from the mainly British imperial banking from the eighteenth to the mid-twentieth century, which aided the commercialization process, to Indian state banking after 1955 which underpinned and supported economic growth and national development.

Finally, the chapters reviewed here touch upon aspects of the general questions posed in the beginning of these closing remarks. They analyse and contrast phenomena, each forming part of the process of modernization which in the case of the history of banks relates to their fundamental role as provider of finance in the development of capitalism.

Bibliography

A. Ableitinger, 'Österreichische Versuche um Zugang zum Pariser Finanzmarkt vor 1914', in F. Kreissler (ed.), *Relations franco-autrichiennes 1870–1970*. Actes du Colloque de Rouen 29 février–2 mars 1984 (Rouen, 1986).

F. Adanir, *Die makedonische Frage. Ihre Entstehung und Entwicklung bis 1908* (Wiesbaden, 1979).

F. Ahmad, *The Young Turks. The Committee of Union and Progress in Turkish Politics 1908–1914* (Oxford, 1969).

G. Alogoskoufis, 'Greece, the two faces of Janus: Institutions, Policy Regimes and Macroeconomic Performance', in *Economic Policy*, April 1995, pp. 149–91.

B.W. Ambrose et al., 'Fractal Structure in the Capital Markets Revisited', in *Financial Analysts' Journal*, vol. 3, 1993.

M. Anastassiadou, *Salonique, 1830–1912. Une ville ottomane à l'âge des Réformes* (Leiden New York Cologne, 1997).

L. Andersson-Skog, 'Omvandlingens sekel' in L. Andersson-Skog and O. Krantz (eds), *Omvandlingens sekel. Perspektiv på ekonomi och samhälle i 1900-talets Sverige* (Lund, 2002).

W. Antonowicz and B. Mussak, 'Torn between monetary and financial stability – What Do the Archives of the Oesterreichische Nationalbank Reveal?', Paper presented at the EABH Conference *Finance and Modernization* (Vienna, 2005).

S.O. Arlebäck, *Från ägarmakt under ansvar till företagsledarmakt u p a* (Lund, 1995).

K. Ausch, *Als die Banken fielen. Zur Soziologie der politischen Korruption* (Vienna Frankfurt Zurich, 1968), pp. 312–13 and pp. 344–6.

D.L. Augustine, 'The Banking Families in Berlin and Vienna around 1900', in H. Diederiks and D. Reeder (eds), *Cities of Finance* (Amsterdam, 1996), p. 230.

A. Autheman, *La Banque impériale ottomane* (Paris, 1996).

K. Bachinger et al. (eds), *Abschied vom Schilling. Eine österreichische Wirtschaftsgeschichte* (Graz, 2001).

K. Bachinger, *Umbruch und Desintegration nach dem 1. Weltkrieg. Österreichs wirtschaftliche und soziale Ausgangssituation in ihren Folgewirkungen auf die Erste Republik*, unpubl. habilitation, Wirtschaftsuniversität Vienna, 1981.

K. Baedeker, *Konstantinopel, Balkanstaaten, Kleinasien, Archipel, Cypern. Handbuch für Reisende*, 2nd ed. (Leipzig, 1914).

J.M. Baernreither, *Fragmente eines politischen Tagebuches. Die südslawische Frage und Österreich-Ungarn vor dem Weltkrieg*, ed. by J. Redlich (Berlin, 1928).

A.K. Bagchi, 'Introduction: Money, Banking and Finance in India since Early Medieval Times', in A.K. Bagchi (ed.), *Money & Credit in Indian History: From Early Medieval Times* (Indian History Congress, 2002).

A.K. Bagchi, *Perilous Passage: Mankind and the Global Ascendancy of Capital* (Delhi, 2006).

A.K. Bagchi, *The Evolution of the State Bank of India, The Roots, 1806–1876*, part I, *The Early Years, 1806–1860* (Oxford University Press, 1987).

A.K. Bagchi, *The Evolution of the State Bank of India, vol. 2, The Era of the Presidency Banks, 1876–1920* (New Delhi, 1997).

A.K. Bagchi, *The Presidency Banks and the Indian Economy, 1876–1914* (Calcutta, 1989).

W. Bagehot, *Lombard Street* (1873; reprinted Homewood, Ill., 1962).

T. Balderston, 'German Banking between the Wars: The Crisis of the Credit Banks', in *Business History Review*, vol. 65, 1991, pp. 588–96.

F. Baltzarek, *Die Geschichte der Wiener Börse* (Vienna, 1973).

F. Baltzarek, 'Finanzplatz Wien – die innerstaatliche und internationale Stellung in historischer Perspektive', *Quartalshefte der Girozentrale*, vol. 15, 1980.

B. Barth, *Die deutsche Hochfinanz und die Imperialismen. Banken und Außenpolitik vor 1914* (Stuttgart, 1995).

B. Barth, 'The financial history of the Anatolian and Baghdad railways, 1889–1914', in *Financial History Review*, vol. 5, 1998.

F. Bartsch, *Statistische Daten über die Zahlungsbilanz Österreich-Ungarns vor Ausbruch des Krieges* (= Mitteilungen des k.k. Finanzministeriums, XXII) (Vienna, 1917).

H. Bauer, *Schweizerischer Bankverein 1872–1972* (Basel, 1972).

E. Bergelmer, *Redogörelse för det viktigaste af den utländska lagstiftningen om aktiebolag* (Stockholm, 1907).

A.A. Berle and G. Means, *The Modern Corporation and Private Property* (New York, 1932).

G. Bischof and D. Stiefel, *80 Dollar. 50 Jahre ERP-Fonds und Marshall-Plan in Österreich 1948–1998* (Vienna, 1999).

D.C. Blaisdell, 'European financial control in the Ottoman Empire. A study of the establishment, activities, and significance of the Administration of the Ottoman Public Debt', Ph.D. thesis, Columbia University (New York, 1929).

O. Blumtritt, *Nachrichtentechnik* (Munich, 1988).

J.A. Boot, *De Twentsche Katoennijverheid 1830–1873* (Amsterdam, 1935).

M.D. Bordo and D. Wheelock, 'Price Stability and Financial Stability: The Historical Record', *Review, Federal Reserve Bank of St. Louis*, September/October, 1998.

K.E. Born, 'Die Deutsche Bank in der Inflation nach dem Ersten Weltkrieg', *Beiträge zu Wirtschafts- und Währungsfragen und zur Bankengeschichte*, vol. 17, 1979.

J. Bosmans, 'Alfred Rudolph Zimmerman', in J. Charité (ed.), *Biografisch woordenboek van Nederland*, vol. 1 (The Hague, 1979).

K. Bösselmann, *Die Entwicklung der deutschen Aktiengesellschaft im 19. Jahrhundert* (Berlin, 1939).

J. Bouvier, *Le Crédit Lyonnais de 1863 à 1882. Les années de formation d'une banque de depôts*, vol. 2 (Paris, 1961).

J. Bouvier, *Le krach de l'Union Générale (1878–1885)* (Paris, 1960).

K. Braun-Wiesbaden, *Reise-Eindrücke aus dem Südosten*, vol. 3 (Stuttgart, 1878).

U. Brunnbauer and K. Kaser (eds), Vom Nutzen der Verwandten. Soziale Netzwerke in Bulgarien (19. und 20. Jahrhundert) (Vienna Cologne Weimar, 2001).

J.B. Brunyate, *An Account of the Presidency Banks* (Calcutta, 1900).

E. Bussière, *Paribas 1872–1992. L'Europe et le monde* (Antwerp, 1992).

F. Butschek, *Statistische Reihen zur österreichischen Wirtschaftsgeschichte. Die Österreichische Wirtschaft seit der Industriellen Revolution* (WIFO, Vienna, 1996).

Th. Buzug, *Analyse chaotischer Systeme* (Mannheim, 1994).

R.E. Cameron (ed.), *Banking in the Early Stages of Industrialization* (New York, 1967).

R.E. Cameron, *France and the economic development of Europe, 1800–1914* (New York, 1975, 1st ed. Princeton, N.J. 1961).

F. Capie, C. Goodhart and N. Schnadt, *The Development of Central Banking. Monograph prepared for the Tercentenary of the Bank of England* (London, 1994).

A.M. Carlos and N. Stephen, 'Agency Problems in Early Chartered Companies. The Case of the Hudson's Bay Company', in *Journal of Economic History*, vol. 50, 1990, pp. 853–75.

G. Chaloupek, 'Industriestadt Wien', in G. Chaloupek et. al, *Wien. Wirtschaftsgeschichte 1740–1938, Teil 1: Industrie* (= Geschichte der Stadt Wien, vol. 4) (Vienna, 1991).

D.N. Chorafas, *Chaos Theory in the Financial Markets* (Chicago, 1994).

C. Clay, *Gold for the Sultan. Western bankers and Ottoman finance 1856–1881: a contribution to Ottoman and international financial history* (London and New York, 2000).

R. Coase, 'The Nature of the Firm', in *Economica*, vol. 4, 1937.

T. Coelli, *An introduction to efficiency and productivity analysis* (Dordrecht, 1998).

C.N. Cooke, *The Rise, Progress and Present Condition of Banking in India* (Calcutta, 1863).

P.L. Cottrell, 'Aspects of Commercial Banking in Northern and Central Europe, 1880–1931', in S. Kinsey and L. Newton (eds.), *International Banking in an Age of Transition. Globalisation, Automation, Banks and their Archives* (Aldershot, 1998).

P.L. Cottrell, 'Aspects of Western Equity Investment in the Banking Systems of East Central Europe', in A. Teichova and P.L. Cottrell (eds), *International Business in Central Europe, 1918–1939* (Leicester, 1983).

P. Cottrell, *Industrial Finance 1830–1914* (London, 1980).

P.L. Cottrell, 'London financiers and Austria 1863–1875: the Anglo-Austrian Bank', in *Business History*, vol. 11, 1969.

P.L. Cottrell with C.J. Stone, 'Credits, and Deposits to Finance Credits', in P.L. Cottrell et al. (eds), *European Industry and Banking, 1920–1939: A Review of Bank Industry Relations* (Leicester, 1992).

R.J. Crampton, *A concise history of Bulgaria*, 2nd ed. (Cambridge, 2005).

A. Crockett, 'The Theory and Practice of Financial Stability', *GEI Newsletter* Issue No. 6, U.K., 1997.

E. Dahmén, *Svensk industriell företagarverksamhet. Kausalanalys av den industriella utvecklingen 1919–1939* (Stockholm, 1950).

F.A. Dankers, 'Emile David van Walree, consul en bankdirecteur', in J. Charité (ed.), *Biografisch Woordenboek voor Nederland*, vol. 3 (The Hague, 1989).

M.J. Daunton, 'Finance and Politics: Comments', in Y. Cassis (ed.), *Finance and Financiers in European History, 1880–1960* (Cambridge, 1992).

P. Dehn, 'Deutschland und die Orientbahnen' in *Jahrbuch für Gesetzgebung, Verwaltung und Volkswirthschaft im Deutschen Reich*, vol. 9, 1885, n° 2.

J.B. De Long and M. Becht, '"Excess Volatility" and the German Stock Market, 1876–1990', EUI Working Paper ECO 92, 1982.

O.K. Deutelmoser, *Kilian Steiner und die Württembergische Vereinsbank* (Ostfildern, 2003).

J. de Vries, *Herinneringen en dagboek van Ernst Heldring (1871–1954)* (Groningen, 1970).

J. de Vries, W. Vroom and T. de Graaf (eds), *Wereldwijd bankieren ABN AMRO 1824–1999* (Amsterdam, 1999).

'Die Erwerbung der Orientalischen Eisenbahnaktien', in *Der Oesterreichische Volkswirt*, no. 31, 3 May 1913.

R.M. Dimtschoff, *Das Eisenbahnwesen auf der Balkan-Halbinsel. Eine politisch-volkswirtschaftliche Studie* (Bamberg, 1894).

F. Edelmayer, *Söldner und Pensionäre: Das Netzwerk Philipps II. im Heiligen Römischen Reich* (Munich, 2002).

E.W. Edwards, 'British Policy in China 1913–1914. Rivalry with France in the Yangtze Valley', in *Journal of Oriental Studies*, vol. 40, 1977, pp. 20–36.

E.W. Edwards, 'The Origins of British Financial Co-operation with France in China, 1903–6', in *English Historical* Review, vol. 86, 1971, pp. 286–317.

T. Eggertsson, *Economic behavior and institutions* (Cambridge, 1990).

W. Ehrlicher, 'Strukturwandlungen des Kapitalmarktes', in *Aktuelle Beiträge zum Geld- undBankenwesen*, Österreichisches Forschungsinstitut für Sparkassenwesen, vol. 4, 1980.

P. Eigner, 'Die Konzentration der Entscheidungsmacht. Personelle Verflechtungen zwischen den Wiener Großbanken und Industrieaktiengesellschaften, 1895–1940', unpublished diss., 2 vols. (Vienna, 1997).

P. Eigner, 'Interlocking Directorships between Commercial Banks and Industry in Interwar Vienna', in A. Teichova et al. (eds.), *Universal Banking in the Twentieth Century. Finance, Industry and the State in North and Central Europe* (Aldershot, 1994).

E. Eldem, 'The Imperial Ottoman Bank: actor or instrument of Ottoman modernization?', in K.P. Kostis (ed.), *Modern banking in the Balkans and West-European capital in the nineteenth and twentieth centuries* (Aldershot, 1999).

H.S. Ellis, *Exchange Control in Central Europe* (Cambridge, Mass., 1941).

A. Elon, *Founder. Meyer Amschel Rothschild and his Times* (New York, 1996).

P.H. Emden, *Money powers of Europe in the nineteenth and twentieth centuries* (London, 1936).

S. Eube, *Der Aktienmarkt in Deutschland vor dem Ersten Weltkrieg: Eine Indexanalyse* (Frankfurt, 1998).

E.F. Fama, 'Efficient Capital Markets: A Review of Theory and Empirical Work', in *Journal of Finance*, vol. 25, 1970.

W. Federn, 'Die österreichischen Banken', in special issue: *Der österreichische Volkswirt (10 Jahre Nachfolgestaaten)*, 1928.

W. Federn, 'Der Zusammenbruch der Österreichischen Kreditanstalt', in *Archiv für Sozialwissenschaft und Sozialpolitik*, vol. 29, 1932, pp. 403–35.

H. Feis, *Europe, the World's Banker, 1870–1914* (New Haven, 1930, Clifton, 1974).

G.D. Feldman et al., *Österreichische Banken und Sparkassen im Nationalsozialismus und in der Nachkriegszeit*, 2 vols (Munich, 2006).

N. Ferguson, *The World's Banker. The History of the House of Rothschild* (London, 1998).

W. Fischer, J. Krengel and J. Wietog (eds), *Sozialgeschichtliches Arbeitsbuch I* (Munich, 1982).

M. Flandreau, *The Bank, The States, and the Market: An Austro-Hungarian Tale for Euroland, 1867–1914*, Working Paper 43, Oesterreichische Nationalbank (Vienna, 2001).

C. Fohlin, 'Universal Banking in Pre-World War I Germany: Model or Myth?', in *Explorations in Economic History*, vol. 36, 1999, pp. 305–43.

C.E. Freedeman, *Joint-Stock Enterprise in France 1807–1867* (Chapel Hill, 1979).

R. Fremdling, 'European railways 1825–2001. An overview', in *Jahrbuch für Wirtschaftsgeschichte*, 2003.

A.F. Freris, *The Greek Economy in the Twentieth Century* (London 1986).

H. Furber, *John Company at Work* (Cambridge, 1951).

H. Fürstenberg (ed.), *Carl Fürstenberg. Die Lebensgeschichte eines deutschen Bankiers, 1870–1914* (Berlin, 1931).

T. Gårdlund, *Industrialismens Samhälle* (Stockholm, 1942).

A. Giannitsis*, Accession into the EEC and the Effects on Industry and Trade*, Foundation of Mediterranean Studies (Athens, 1988) (in Greek).

B. Gille, *Histoire de la maison Rothschild*, vol. 2 (Geneva, 1967).

J. Glete, *Ägande och industriell omvandling* (Stockholm, 1987).

H. Gollwitzer*, Ludwig I. von Bayern* (1986, reprinted Munich, 1987).

R. Gömmel, 'Entstehung und Entwicklung der Effektenbörsen im 19. Jahrhundert bis 1914', in H. Pohl (ed.), *Deutsche Börsengeschichte* (Frankfurt, 1992).

Y. Gonjo, 'La banque coloniale et l'Etat: la Banque de l'Indochine devant l'interventionnisme (1917–1931)', in *Le Mouvement social*, vol. 142, 1988, pp. 45–74.

D.F. Good, Modern Growth in the Habsburg Monarchy, in H. Matis (ed.), *The Economic Development of Austria since 1870. An Elgar Reference Collection* (Aldershot, 1994).

M. Goodfriend and J.M. *Lacker, Limited Commitment and Central Bank Lending*, Federal Reserve Bank of Richmond Working Paper 99–2.

C. Goodhart and H. Huang, 'The lender of last resort', in *Journal of Banking and Finance*, vol. 29, 2005.

B.C. Gounaris, *Steam over Macedonia, 1870–1912. Socio-economic change and the railway factor* (Boulder, Colorado, 1993).

N. Götz, 'Stadt und "Verstädterung" seit der Mitte des 19. Jahrhunderts', in G. Bott (ed.), *Leben und Arbeiten im Industriezeitalter* (Stuttgart, 1985).

M. Granovetter, 'The Strength of Weak Ties', in *American Journal of Sociology*, vol. 78, 1973, pp. 1360–80.

K. Grunwald, *Türkenhirsch. A study of Baron Maurice de Hirsch, entrepreneur and philanthropist* (Jerusalem, 1966).

J. Günther and D.Jajesniak-Quast (eds), *Wilkommene Investoren oder nationaler Ausverkauf? Ausländische Direktinvestitionen in Ostmitteleuropa im 20. Jahrhundert* (Berlin, 2006).

B. Gustafsson, 'The industrial revolution in Sweden', in M. Teich, B. Gustafsson and R. Porter (eds), *The industrial revolution in national context: Europe and the USA*, (New York, 1996).

W. Gutsche, *Monopole, Staat und Expansion vor 1914. Zum Funktionsmechanismus zwischen Industriemonopolen, Großbanken und Staatsorganen in der Außenpolitik des Deutschen Reiches 1897 bis Sommer 1914* (Ost-Berlin, 1986).

W. Gutsche, 'Serbien in den Mitteleuropaplänen des deutschen Imperialismus am Vorabend des ersten Weltkrieges', in *Zeitschrift für Geschichtswissenschaft*, vol. 23, 1975.

A. von Gwinner, *Lebenserinnerungen*, 2nd ed., ed. by M. Pohl (Frankfurt, 1992).

K. Hafner, *Die schweizerischen Finanzierungsgesellschaften für elektrische Unternehmungen*, Ph.D. thesis Université de Fribourg (Geneva, 1912).

J. Hagströmer, *Om aktiebolag enligt svensk rätt* (Stockholm, 1872).

P.R. Haiss, 'Central European Strategies of Austrian Banks', in *Österreichisches Bankarchiv*, no. 5, 1991.

P.R. Haiss, 'Internationale Aktivitäten österreichischer Banken', in *Zeitschrift für das gesamte Kreditwesen*, Sep. 1991.

G.W.F. Hallgarten, *Imperialismus vor 1914. Die soziologischen Grundlagen der Aussenpolitik europäischer Grossmächte vor dem Ersten Weltkrieg*, 2nd ed., vol. 1 (Munich, 1963).

O. Handlin and M.F. Handlin, 'Origins of the American Business Corporation', in *Journal of Economic History*, vol. 5, 1945.

E. Heckscher, *Svenskt arbete och liv* (Stockholm, 1941).

K. Helfferich, *Georg von Siemens. Ein Lebensbild aus Deutschlands großer Zeit*, 2nd ed., vol. 3 (Berlin, 1923).

R. Hentsch, *Hentsch. Banquiers à Genève et à Paris au XIXe siècle* (Brussels, 1996).

J. Herres and M. Neuhaus, *Politische Netzwerke durch Briefkommunikation. Briefkultur der politischen Oppositionsbewegungen und frühen Arbeiterbewegungen im 19. Jahrhundert* (Berlin, 2002).

P. Hertner, 'Les sociétés financières suisses et le développement de l'industrie électrique jusqu'à la Première Guerre Mondiale', in F. Cardot (ed.), *Un siècle d'électricité dans le monde* (Paris, 1987).

R. Hilferding, *Das Finanzkapital. Eine Studie über die jüngste Entwicklung des Kapitalismus* (Vienna, 1910).

R. Hilferding, *Finance Capital. A Study of the Latest Phase of Capitalist Development* (London, 1981).

W.G. Hoffmann, *Das Wachstum der deutschen Wirtschaft seit der Mitte des 19. Jahrhunderts* (Berlin, 1965).

A. Houben, J. Kakes and G. Schinasi, *Towards a framework for financial stability*, De Nederlandsche Bank, Occasional Studies, vol.2, 1, 2004.

R.W. Huenemann, *The Dragon and the Iron Horse, the Economics of Railroads in China, 1876–1937* (Cambridge, Mass, 1984).

G. Jacquemyns, *Langrand-Dumonceau. Promoteur d'une puissance financière catholique*, vol. 4 and 5 (Brussels, 1964, 1965).

S. Janas, 'Die Konzentration im österreichischen Bankwesen', in *Bankarchiv*, vol. 10, 1968.

J.-N. Jeanneney, 'L'affaire de la Banque industrielle de Chine', in *Revue Historique*, vol. 253, 1975, pp.377–416, esp. pp. 382–3.

M.C. Jensen and W.H. Meckling, 'Theory of the Firm: Managerial Behavior, Agency Costs and Ownership Structure', in *Journal of Financial Economics*, vol. 3, 1976.

J. Joham, 'Geld- und Kreditwesen in Österreich', in *Österreichische Zeitschrift für Bankwesen*, vol. 2, 3, 1937.

W.A. Jöhr, *Schweizerische Kreditanstalt 1856–1956. Hundert Jahre im Dienste der schweizerischen Volkswirtschaft* (Zurich, 1956).

C. Jobst, *How to Join the Gold Club: The Credibility of Austria-Hungary's Commitment to the Gold Standard 1892–1913* (thesis, University of Vienna, 2001).

J. Jonker, *Merchants, Bankers, Middlemen, The Amsterdam money market during the first half of the 19th century* (Amsterdam, 1996).

L. Jörberg, *Growth and Fluctuations* (Stockholm, 1961).

P. Jordan, ´Die Entwicklung des Eisenbahnnetzes auf dem Gebiet des heutigen Jugoslawien (bis 1918)', in R. Plaschka, A.M. Drabek and B. Zaar (eds), *Eisenbahnbau und Kapitalinteressen in den Beziehungen der österreichischen mit den südslawischen Ländern* (Vienna, 1993).

M. Jörgens, *Finanzielle Trustgesellschaften*, Ph.D. thesis Universität München (Stuttgart, 1902).

J. Jörnmark, *Skogen, staten och kapitalisterna* (Lund, 2004).

Jüttner, 'Die orientalischen Eisenbahnen', in *Archiv für Eisenbahnwesen*, vol. 5, 1882, pp. 209–11.

A. Kanitz-Wiesenburg, Wiener Bankverein, typescript preserved in the Historical Archives of BankAustria-Creditanstalt, Vienna [ca. 1936], part 3, pp. 123–4.

H.H. Kaplan, *Nathan Mayer Rothschild And The Creation Of A Dynasty: The Critical Years 1806–1816* (Stanford, 2006).

S. Kapsaskis, *Anamniseis 15 chronon syn-Ergasias* (Cooperation souvenirs of the past 15 years) (Athens, 1991).

Y.N. Karkar, *Railway development in the Ottoman Empire, 1856–1914* (New York, Washington, Hollywood, 1972).

L. Katseli, 'Structural Adjustment of the Greek Economy', in C. Bliss and J. de Macedo (eds) *Unity with Diversity in the European Economy: The Community's Southern Frontier* (Cambridge, 1990).

I. Katz, *August Belmont. A Political Biography* (New York London, 1968).

A. Kausel, 'Österreichs Volkseinkommen 1830 bis 1913', in *Geschichte und Ergebnisse der amtlichen Statistik in Österreich 1829 bis 1979* (Vienna, 1979).

B. Kautsky, 'Die Bankbilanzen des Jahres 1925', in *Arbeit und Wirtschaft*, vol. 1, 1926, pp. 16–9.

J.W. Kaye, *The Life and Correspondence of Henry St. George Tucker* (London, 1854).

P. Kazakos, *Anamesa se Kratos kai Agora. Oikonomia kai oikonomiki politiki sti metapolemiki Hellada 1944–2000* (Between State and Market. Economy and Economic Policy in post-war Greece 1944–2000) (Athens, 2001).

H. Kernbauer, *Währungspolitik in der Zwischenkriegszeit* (Vienna, 1991).

H. Kernbauer and E. März, 'Das Wirtschaftswachstum in Deutschland und Österreich von der Mitte des 19. Jahrhunderts bis zum Ersten Weltkrieg – eine vergleichende Darstellung', in W.H. Schröder and R. Spree (eds), *Historische Konjunkturforschung* (Stuttgart, 1980).

H. Kernbauer and F. Weber, 'Die Wiener Großbanken in der Zeit der Kriegs- und Nachkriegsinflation 1914–1922', in G.D. Feldman et al. (eds), *Die Erfahrung der Inflation im internationalen Zusammenhang und Vergleich* (Berlin New York, 1984).

H. Kernbauer and F. Weber, 'Multinational Banking im Donauraum? Die Geschäftspolitik der Wiener Großbanken 1918–1929', in *Österreichische Zeitschrift für Geschichtswissenschaften*, vol. 4, 1994, pp. 585–616.

H. Kernbauer and F. Weber, 'Multinational Banking in the Danube Basin', in A. Teichova et al. (eds), *Multinational Enterprise in Historical Perspective* (Cambridge, 1986).

J.M. Keynes, 'Indian Currency and Finance', reprinted in *The Collected Writings of John Maynard Keynes*, vol. I (London, 1971).

C.P. Kindleberger, *A Financial History of Western Europe* (London, 1984).

C.P. Kindleberger, *Manias, Panics and Crashes. A History of Financial Crisis*, 2nd edition (London, 1989).

F.H.H. King, 'Angelo Luzzatti and Early Mining Concessions in Siam, 1885–1891', in *Proceedings of the 4th International Conference on Thai Studies* (Institute of Southeast Asian Studies, Kunming, China, 1990), vol. 1, revised and updated version in [New Mexico Military Institute], *Faculty Symposia Lecture Series, 1989–1990* (Roswell, New Mexico, 1991).

F.H.H. King, 'Joint Venture in China: the Experience of the Pekin Syndicate, 1897–1961, in *Business and Economic History*, second series, vol. 19, 1990, pp. 113–22.

F.H.H. King, 'Nothing but bad', in *Modern Asian Studies*, vol. 40, 3, July 2006, pp. 663–90.

F.H.H. King, *Survey our Empire! Robert Montgomery Martin, 1801(?)–1868: a Bio-bibliography* (Hong Kong, 1979).

F.H.H. King, 'The Founding of the Pekin Syndicate, 1897–1900: I. the Anglo-Italian Syndicate', presented at the Association for Asian Studies, Western/Southwestern Conference, Austin, Texas, Oct. 12–13, 1990.

F.H.H. King , *The History of the Hongkong and Shanghai Banking Corporation, Vol. I, The Hongkong Bank in Late Imperial China, 1864–1902: On an Even Keel* (Cambridge, 1954).

F.H.H. King, *The Hongkong Bank in the Period of Imperialism and War, 1895–1918* (= The History of the Hongkong and Shanghai Banking Corporation, vol. 2) (Cambridge, 1988).

O. Klambauer, 'Zur Frage des deutsches Eigentums in Österreich', in *Jahrbuch für Zeitgeschichte*, 1978.

B. Kling, *Partner in Empire: Dwarkanath Tagore and the Age of Enterprise in Eastern India* (Berkeley, 1976).

B. Koehler, *Ludwig Bamberger. Revolutionär und Bankier* (Stuttgart, 1999).

A. Koersner, *Om aktiebok, inregistrering av aktier och aktieförvärvsrätt* (Stockholm, 1929).

E. Kolm, *Die Ambitionen Österreich-Ungarns im Zeitalter des Hochimperialismus* (Frankfurt, 2001).

K. Kostis, *Collaboration and Competition: Seventy Years of the Union of Greek Banks* (Athens, 1997).

G. Köver, 'The Austro-Hungarian Banking System', in R. Cameron and V.I. Bovykin (eds), *International Banking 1870–1914* (New York Oxford, 1991).

S. Kumpf-Korfes, 'Die ökonomische Expansion des deutschen Finanzkapitals in Bulgarien vom Ende des 19. Jahrhunderts bis zum Ausbruch des ersten Weltkrieges', in *Zeitschrift für Geschichtswissenschaft*, vol. 17, 1969.

J. Lampe and M. Jackson, *Balkan Economic History, 1550–1950: From Imperial Borderlands to Developing Nations* (Bloomington, 1982).

D.S. Landes, *Bankers and pashas. International finance and economic imperialism in Egypt* (London, 1958).

E. Laspeyres, 'Die Rentabilität der industriellen Unternehmungen, namentlich der Actien-Gesellschaften', *Neue Freie Presse* (Vienna), 27 Nov. 1873.

W. Layton and C. Rist, *The Economic Situation of Austria.* Report presented to the Council of the League of Nations (Geneva, 1925).

B. LeBaron, 'A Fast Algorithm for the BDS Statistic', in *Studies in Nonlinear Dynamics and Econometrics*, vol. 2, 1997.

R. Lee, *France and the Exploitation of China, 1885–1901* (Hong Kong London, 1989).

R. Lee, 'Railways, space and imperialism', in G. Dinhobel, *Eisenbahn/Kultur. Railway/culture* (= Mitteilungen des Österreichischen Staatsarchivs, Sonderband 7) (Vienna, 2004).

E. Lichtenberger, *Wien – Prag: ein Städtevergleich* (Vienna, 1993).

L. Lieb, *Die Entwicklung der Augsburger Effektenbörse (1816–1896)* (Augsburg, 1930).

A.J. Liebl, *Aufgeh'n wird die Erde in Rauch. Geschichte der ersten Privaten Eisenbahnen in Bayern* (Munich, 1985).

R. Liedtke, *N M Rothschild & Sons: Die Kommunikation im Bankenwesen im Europa des 19. Jahrhunderts* (Cologne, 2006).

R. Liefmann, *Beteiligungs- und Finanzierungsgesellschaften. Eine Studie über den modernen Kapitalismus und das Effektenwesen*, 2nd ed. (Jena, 1913).

J.H. Little, *The House of Jagat Seth* (Calcutta, 1967).

D. Löding, 'Deutschlands und Österreich-Ungarns Balkanpolitik unter besonderer Berücksichtigung ihrer Wirtschaftsinteressen', Ph.D. thesis Universität Hamburg (Hamburg, 1969).

O. Loistl and I. Betz, *Chaostheorie: Zur Theorie nichtlinearer dynamischer Systeme* (1993, reprinted Munich and Vienna, 1996).

Rev. James Long, *Selections from unpublished records of Government for the years 1748 to 1767*, vol. I (Calcutta, 1886).

E. Lopuszánski, 'Einige Streiflichter auf das österreichische Bankwesen', in: *Volkswirtschaftliche Wochenschrift von Alexander Dorn*, 31 Dec. 1908, no. 1305.

J. Luiten van Zanden and A. van Riel, *Nederland 1780–1914, staat, instituties en economische ontwikkeling* (The Hague, 2000).

J. Macey, *Svensk aktiebolagsrätt i omvandling – en rättsekonomisk analys* (Stockholm, 1993).

C. Mackenzie, *Realms of Silver: One hundred years of Banking in the East* (London, 1954).

J.V.A. MacMurray (ed.), *Treaties and Agreements with and concerning China, 1894–1919* (New York, 1921), vol. 1.

A. Maddison, *Monitoring the World Economy 1820–1992* (OECD, Paris, 1995).

L. Magnusson, *Sveriges ekonomiska historia* (Stockholm, 1997).

E. März, 'Besonderheiten in der Entwicklung des österreichischen Bankwesens', in *Schmollers Jahrbuch*, vol. 77, 2, pp. 61–71.

E. März, *Österreichische Bankpolitik in der Zeit der großen Wende 1913–1923. Am Beispiel der Creditanstalt für Handel und Gewerbe* (Vienna, 1981).

E. März, *Österreichische Industrie- und Bankpolitik in der Zeit Franz Josephs I* (Vienna Frankfurt Zurich, 1968).

E. März and K. Socher, 'Währung und Banken in Cisleithanien', in A. Brusatti (ed.), *Die wirtschaftliche Entwicklung der Habsburgermonarchie* (Vienna, 1973).

E. Marx, *Die Entwicklung der deutschen Provinzbörsen* (Vienna, 1913).

H. Matis and F. Weber, 'Kaisertum Österreich – Donaumonarchie', in H. Pohl (ed.), *Europäische Bankengeschichte* (Frankfurt, 1993).

W.N. Medlicott, *The Congress of Berlin and after. A diplomatic history of the Near Eastern settlement 1878–1880*, 2nd ed. (London 1963).

F. Meinhard, ´Die Entwicklung der Balkanbahnen vom Jahre 1892 bis zum Jahre 1904´, in *Archiv für Eisenbahnwesen*, vol. 28, 1905, pp. 1352–3.

P. Mentzel, 'Accidents, sabotage, and terrorism: Work hazards on Ottoman railways', in C. Imber, K. Kiyotaki and R. Murphy (eds), *Frontiers of Ottoman Studies: State, province, and the West* (London, New York, 2005).

M. Meuleau, *Des pionniers en Extrême-Orient. Histoire de la Banque de l'Inochine (1875–1975)* (Paris, 1990),

B. Michel, *Banques et Banquiers en Autriche au Debut du 20e Siècle* (Paris, 1976).

W. Miller, *Travels and politics in the Near East* (London, 1898).

A. Montgomery, *Industrialismens genombrott i Sverige* (Stockholm, 1947).

C. Morawitz, *Die Türkei im Spiegel ihrer Finanzen. Nach dem französischen Original 'Les finances de la Turquie'* (Berlin, 1903).

A. Mosser, *Die Industrieaktiengesellschaft in Österreich, 1880–1913* (Vienna, 1980).

A. Mosser, 'Financing Industrial Companies in Interwar Austria: Working Capital and Liquidity', in A. Teichova et al. (eds), *Universal Banking in the Twentieth Century. Finance, Industry and the State in North and Central Europe* (Aldershot, 1994).

A. Mosser and A. Teichova, 'Investment Behaviour of Industrial Joint-Stock Companies and Industrial Shareholding by the Österreichische Credit-Anstalt: Inducement or Obstacle to Renewal and Change in Industry in Interwar Austria', in H. James et al. (eds), *The Role of Banks in the Interwar Economy* (Cambridge, 1991).

N. Mouzelis, *Modern Greece, Facets of Underdevelopment* (London, 1978).

J. Müller, *Der deutsche Rentenmarkt vor dem Ersten Weltkrieg: eine Indexanalyse* (Frankfurt, 1992).

C. Natmeßnig, *Britische Finanzinteressen in Österreich. Die Anglo-Oesterreichische Bank* (Vienna Cologne Weimar, 1998).

C. Natmeßnig, 'Die österreichische Bankenkrise und ihre Auswirkungen auf die niederösterreichische Industrie', in A. Kusternig (ed.), *Beiträge über die Krise der Industrie Niederösterreichs zwischen den beiden Weltkriegen* (Vienna, 1985).

C. Natmeßnig, 'Die österreichischen Großbanken in der Zwischenkriegszeit', in *Christliche Demokratie*, vol. 4, 1985, pp. 346–7.

J. Neuwirth, *Die Spekulationskrisis von 1873* (Leipzig, 1874).

C.-A. Nilsson, 'Business incorporations in Sweden 1849–1896', in *Economy and History*, vol. 2, 1959.

A. Ögren, *Empirical Studies in Money, Credit and Banking. The Swedish Credit Market in Transition under the Silver and Gold Standards 1834–1913* (Stockholm, 2003).

J.F. Padgett and C.K. Ansell (eds), 'Robust Action and the Rise of the Medici, 1400–1434', in *American Journal of Sociology*, vol. 98, 1993, pp. 1259–1319.

M. Palairet, *The Balkan economies, c. 1800–1914. Evolution without development* (Cambridge, 1997).

S. Pamuk, *The Ottoman Empire and European capitalism, 1820–1913. Trade, investment and production* (Cambridge, 1987).

U. Parlitz, 'Identification of True and Spurious Lyapunov Exponents from Time Series', in *International Journal of Bifurcation and Chaos*, vol. 2, 1992.

V. Paskaleva, 'Die Anfänge des deutschen wirtschaftlichen Einflusses auf dem Balkan und in der Türkei in den 60er und 70er Jahren des 19. Jahrhunderts', in R. Melville and H.-J. Schröder (eds), *Der Berliner Kongreß von 1878. Die Politik der Großmächte und die Probleme der Modernisierung in Südosteuropa in der zweiten Hälfte des 19. Jahrhunderts* (Wiesbaden, 1982).

A.-J. Pernotte, *Pourquoi et comment fut fondée la Banque industrielle de Chine* (Paris, 1922).

E.E. Peters, *Chaos and Order in the Capital Markets* (New York, 1991).

J.-H. Pirenne, 'Bauer (Raphaël, chevalier de)', in *Biographie Nationale, publiée par l'Académie Royale des Sciences, des Lettres et des Beaux-Arts de Belgique*, vol. 39 (Brussels, 1976).

M. Pohl with A. Raab-Rebentisch, *Von Stambul nach Bagdad. Die Geschichte einer berühmten Eisenbahn* (Munich, Zürich, 1999).

R. Poidevin, *Les relations économiques et financières entre la France et l'Allemagne de 1898 à 1914* (Paris, 1969).

K. Polányi, 'Das Ausmaß der Wirtschaftskrise', in *Der österreichische Volkswirt*, 20 May 1933.

H.T. Prinsep, 'Note on the principle of banking in its application to the condition of things in India' in Papers presented for the use of the proprietors of the Bank of Bengal agreeably to a resolution at their special general meeting held on 25 February 1837 (Calcutta, 1837), p. 46.

S. Pressburger, *Das österreichische Noteninstitut 1816–1916* (Vienna, 1962).

S. Pressburger, *Oesterreichische Nationalbank 1816–1966* (Vienna, 1966).

H. Pugach, 'Keeping an Idea Alive: the Establishment of a Sino-American Bank', in *Business History* Review, vol. 56, Summer 1982, pp. 267–93.

H. Pugach, *Same bed, different dreams, a history of the Chinese American Bank of Commerce, 1919–1937* (Centre of Asian Studies, University of Hong Kong, 1997).

D. Quataert, *The Ottoman Empire, 1700–1922*, 2nd ed. (Cambridge, 2005).

A. Ray, *The Evolution of the State Bank of India, vol. 3, The Era of the Imperial Bank of India, 1921–1955* (New Delhi, 2003).

D. Read, *The History of Reuters* (Oxford, second ed. 1999).

W. Rechberger, 'Zur Geschichte der Orientbahnen. Ein Beitrag zur österreichisch-ungarischen Eisenbahnpolitik auf dem Balkan in den Jahren von 1852–1888', unpublished Ph.D. thesis (Universität Wien, 1958).

W. Reibel, 'Die Gründung ausländischer Eisenbahn-Unternehmungen durch deutsche Banken', Ph.D. thesis Universität Köln (Düsseldorf, 1934).

W. Reik, *Die Beziehungen der österreichischen Großbanken zur Industrie* (Vienna, 1932).

J. Rendboe, 'De to forste danske aktieselskabslove af 1917 og 1930 – var de påvirket af intressegrupper?', in *Erhvervshistorisk Årbog 1998–98* (Århus, 1999).

G. Rhode, 'Der Berliner Kongress und Südosteuropa', in K.O. Frhr. v. Aretin (ed.), *Bismarcks Außenpolitik und der Berliner Kongreß* (Wiesbaden, 1978).

H.V. Roberts, 'Statistical versus Clinical Prediction on the Stock Market', unpublished paper (University of Chicago, 1967).

R. Roberts, 'The Economics of Cities of Finance', in H. Diederiks and D. Reeder (eds.), *Cities of Finance* (Amsterdam, 1996).

M.B. Rose, *Firms, Networks and Business Values. The British and American Cotton Industries since 1750* (Cambridge, 2000).

H. Rosovsky, 'Alexander Gerschenkron: A Personal and Fond Recollection', in *Journal of Economic History*, vol. 39, 1970, pp. 1009–13.

K.W. Rothschild, 'Wurzeln und Triebkräfte der Entwicklung der österreichischen Wirtschaftsstuktur', in W. Weber (ed.), *Österreichs Wirtschaftsstruktur gestern-heute-morgen*, vol. 1 (West Berlin, 1961), pp. 79–90.

R.L. Rudolph, *Banking and Industrialization in Austria-Hungary. The Role of Banks in the Industrialization of the Czech Crownlands, 1873–1914* (Cambridge, 1976).

R. Rudolph, 'The Pattern of Austrian Industrial Growth from the Eighteenth to the Early Twentieth Century', in H. Matis (ed.), *The Economic Development of Austria since 1870. An Elgar Reference Collection* (Aldershot, 1994).

G. Russel and C. Tuite (eds), *Romantic Sociability. Social Networks and Literary Culture in Britain 1770–1840* (Cambridge, 2002).

Salomon Smith Barney, Global Equity Research, Greece, 19 August 1999, p. 5.

A. Schäffle, 'Der "große Börsenkrach" des Jahres 1873', in *Gesammelte Aufsätze* (Tübingen, 1885).

D. Schell, 'Beiträge zur Geschichte der ehemaligen Handelsbörse zu Elberfeld', in *Zeitschrift des Bergischen Geschichtsvereins*, vol. 40, 1907.

E. Schick, *Handbuch des deutschen Staatspapier- und Actienhandels* (Leipzig, 1849).

G. Schinasi, *Defining Financial Stability, International Monetary Fund*, Working paper WP/04/187, 2004.

G. Schöllgen, *Imperialismus und Gleichgewicht. Deutschland, England und die orientalische Frage, 1871–1914*, 3rd ed. (München, 2000).

L. Schön, *En modern svensk ekonomisk historia. Tillväxt och omvandling under två sekel* (Stockholm, 2000).

A. Schubert, 'The Causes of the Austrian Currency Crisis of 1931', in J. Komlos (ed.), *Economic Development in the Habsburg Monarchy and in the Successor States* (New York, 1990).

A. Schubert, *The Credit-Anstalt Crisis of 1931* (New York, 1991).

J. Schumpeter, *The theory of economic development* (1911, reprinted Cambridge, 1934).

O. Schwarzer et al., 'Das System des internationalen Zahlungsverkehrs', in J. Schneider, O. Schwarzer and F. Zellfelder (eds), Währungen der Welt, vol. I, 1 (Stuttgart, 1991).

T. Schweizer, 'Einführung', in T. Schweizer (ed.), *Netzwerkanalyse. Ethnologische Perspektiven* (Berlin, 1988).

R.E. Seavoy, *The Origins of the American Business Corporation 1784–1855* (London, 1982).

H. Seidel, *Österreichs Wirtschaft und Wirtschaftspolitik nach dem Zweiten Weltkrieg* (Vienna, 2005).

F. Seidenzahl, 'Bank für Orientalische Eisenbahnen (Eine Finanzholding und ihr Portefeuille)', in Deutsche Bank (ed.), Beiträge zu Wirtschafts- und Währungsfragen und zur Bankgeschichte, nos. 1–20 (Mainz, 1984), pp. 15–16.

F. Seidenzahl, *100 Jahre Deutsche Bank* (Frankfurt, 1970).

N. Shinonaga, 'La Formation de la Banque industrielle de Chine et son ecroulement – un defi des frères Berthelot', doctoral thesis, University of Paris VIII (May 1988).

R. Sieghart, *Die letzten Jahrzehnte einer Großmacht. Menschen, Völker, Probleme des Habsburger-Reichs* (Berlin, 1932).

I. Simeonoff, 'Die Eisenbahnen und Eisenbahnpolitik in Bulgarien', Ph.D. thesis Universität Erlangen (Halle/Saale, 1909).

S. Skarstedt, *Allmänna aktiebolagslagen* (Stockholm, 1930).

M. Sokal and O. Rosenberg, 'The Banking System of Austria', in H.P. Willis and B.H. Beckhart (eds), *Foreign Banking Systems* (New York, 1929).

F. Somary, *Erinnerungen aus meinem Leben* (Zurich, 1959).

A. Spitzmüller, *... und hat auch Ursach' es zu lieben* (Vienna, 1955).

W.-H. Steeb, *A Handbook of Terms Used in Chaos and Quantum Chaos* (Mannheim, 1991).

J. Steen, *Die zweite industrielle Revolution, Frankfurt und die Elektrizität 1800–1914* (Frankfurt, 1981).

F.G. Steiner, *Die Entwicklung des Mobil-Bankwesens in Österreich* (Vienna, 1913).

F. Stern, *Gold and iron. Bismarck, Bleichröder, and the building of the German Empire* (London, 1977).

D. Stiefel, *Arbeitslosigkeit. Soziale, politische und wirtschaftliche Auswirkungen – am Beispiel Österreichs 1918–1938* (Berlin, 1979).

D. Stiefel, 'Austrian Banks at the Zenith of Power and Influence', in H. Matis (ed.), *The Economic Development of Austria since 1870. An Elgar Reference Collection* (Aldershot, 1994), reprinted in *German Yearbook on Business History* (Cologne, 1986).

D. Stiefel, *Die große Krise in einem kleinen Land. Österreichische Finanz- und Wirtschaftspolitik 1929–1938* (Vienna, 1988).

D. Stiefel, '50 Years State-Owned Industries in Austria 1946–1996', in F. Amatori (ed.), *The Rise and Fall of State-Owned Enterprises in Western Countries* (London, 2000).

D. Stiefel, *Finanzdiplomatie und Weltwirtschaftskrise. Die Krise der Credit-Anstalt für Handel und Gewerbe 1931* (Frankfurt, 1989).

D. Stiefel, 'For better, for worse: the Credit-Anstalt and its Customers in 1931', in A. Teichova et al. (eds), *Universal Banking in the Twentieth Century. Finance, Industry and the State in North and Central Europe* (London, 1994).

D. Stiefel, 'Has the course of Denazification been determined by Economic Necessities?', in S.U. Larsen (ed.), Modern Europe after Fascism 1943–1980s (New York, 1998).

D. Stiefel, 'The Reconstruction of the Credit-Anstalt', in A. Teichova et al. (eds), *International Business & Central Europe, 1918–1939* (Leicester, New York, 1983).

F. Stieve, *Der diplomatische Schriftwechsel Iswolskis 1911–1914. Aus den Geheimakten der Russischen Staatsarchive*, vol. 3 (Berlin, 1926).

F. Stix, 'Zur Geschichte und Organisation der Wiener Geheimen Ziffernkanzlei. Von ihren Anfängen bis zum Jahre 1848', in *Mitteilungen des Österreichischen Instituts für Geschichtsforschung*, vol. 51, 1937, pp. 131–60.

H. Strach, 'Geschichte der Eisenbahnen Österreich-Ungarns von den Anfängen bis zum Jahre 1867', in *Geschichte des Eisenbahnwesens des österreichisch-ungarischen Monarchie*, vol. 1, I (Teschen, 1898).

L.A. Stroink, *Stad en land van Twente* (Amsterdam, 1974).

P.F. Sugar, 'Railroad construction and the development of the Balkan village in the last quarter of the 19th century', in R. Melville and H.-J. Schröder (eds), *Der*

Berliner Kongreß von 1878. Die Politik der Großmächte und die Probleme der Modernisierung in Südosteuropa in der zweiten Hälfte des 19. Jahrhunderts (Wiesbaden, 1982).

A. Surminski, *Versicherung unterm Hakenkreuz* (Berlin, 1999).

J. B. Tavernier, *Travels in India*, trans. V. Ball, ed. W. Crooke (Oxford, 1925).

A. Teichova, *An Economic Background to Munich. International Business and Czechoslovakia 1918–1938* (Cambridge, 1974).

A. Teichova, 'Banking and Industry in Central Europe, Nineteenth to Twentieth Century', in A. Teichova et al. (eds.), *Banking, Trade and Industry. Europe, America and Asia from the Thirteenth to the Twentieth Century* (Cambridge, 1997).

A. Teichova, 'Commercial (Universal) Banking in Central Europe – from Cisleithania to the Successor States', in M. Fase et al. (eds), *How to Write the History of A Bank* (Aldershot, Brookfield, 1995).

A. Teichova, 'East-Central and South-East Europe, 1919–1939', in P. Mathias and S. Pollard (eds), *The Cambridge Economic History of Europe* (Cambridge, 1989).

A. Teichova, 'Peripetien des Finanzzentrums Wien', in K. Bachinger and D. Stiefel (eds), *Auf Heller und Cent. Beiträge zur Finanz- und Währungsgeschichte* (Frankfurt Vienna, 2001).

A. Teichova, 'Versailles and the Expansion of the Bank of England into Central Europe', in N. Horn and J. Kocka (eds), *Recht und Entwicklung der Großunternehmen im 19. und 20. Jahrhundert* (Göttingen, 1979).

A. Teichova, 'Wiens wechselhafte Rolle als Finanzzentrum in Europa während des 20. Jahrhunderts', in *Geld und Kapital. Jahrbuch der Gesellschaft für mitteleuropäische Banken- und Sparkassengeschichte*, vol. 1997, pp. 24–5.

P. Thane, 'Financiers and the British state: the case of Sir Ernest Cassel', in *Business History*, vol. 28, 1986, pp. 80–99.

'The Laws of Manu', trans. G. Buhler, in *Sacred Books of the East* (1886).

The Russo-Chinese Bank, Birmingham Slavonic Monographs no. 2 (Birmingham, 1977).

J. Thobie, *Intérêts et impérialisme français dans l'empire ottoman (1895–1914)* (Paris, 1977).

J. Thobie, 'Les choix financiers de l'"Ottomane" en Méditerranée orientale de 1856 à 1939', in *Banque et investissements en Méditerranée à l'époque contemporaine.* Actes du Colloque de Marseille, 4–5 Feb. 1982 (Marseille, 1985).

G. Tichy, 'Drei Phasen des Strukturwandels im österreichischen Kreditapparat', in *Bankarchiv*, no. 8, 1977, pp. 307–19.

G. Tichy, 'Strukturwandel im Kreditapparat und die auf uns zukommenden Finanzierungsprobleme', in *Aktuelle Beiträge zum Geld- und Bankwesen*, Österreichisches Forschungsinstitut für Sparkassenwesen, no. 4, 1980, pp. 55–86.

G. Tichy, 'Zu einigen wichtigen Strukturmerkmalen des österreichischen Kreditapparates', in *Bankarchiv*, no. 9, 1977, pp. 322–40.

R. Tilly, 'German Banking. Development Assistance for the Strong', in *Journal of European Economic History*, vol. 15, 1986, pp. 113–52.

R. Tilly, 'International Aspects of the Development of German Banking', in R. Cameron and V.I. Bovykin (eds.), *International Banking 1870–1914* (New York Oxford, 1991).

R.H. Tilly, 'The Berlin Securities Exchange in National Context: Actors, Rules, and Reforms to 1914', 1955 *ASSA Abstracts, Newsletter of The Cliometric Society* 9, 1995.

E.G.J. Tilman, *Over commanditaire vennootschappen bij wijze van aandelen* (Leiden, 1860).

G. Todd, 'Some Aspects of Joint Stock Companies 1844–1900', in *Economic History Review*, vol. 4, 1932.

Trapeza Hellados, Ta prota Peninta Chronia (Bank of Greece, The first fifty years) (Athens, 1977),

D. Tripathi, *The Oxford History of Indian Business* (New Delhi, 2004).

A. Tripathi, *Trade and Finance in the Bengal Presidency, 1793–1833* (Calcutta, 1956).

G. Tyson, *100 years of Banking in Asia and Africa* (London, 1963).

'Über den Bau und Betrieb der Serbischen Eisenbahn (Belgrade – Nisch – Wranja)', in *Archiv für Eisenbahnwesen*, vol. 4, 1881, p. 173.

A.L. Van der Hagen and S. Cederschiöld, *Svenska Aktiebolag med begränsad ansvarighet 1848–1881* (Stockholm, 1882).

D.C.J. van der Werf, 'The two Dutch bank mergers of 1964: the creations of Algemene Bank Nederland and Amsterdam-Rotterdam Bank', in *Financial History Review*, vol. 6, 1999, pp. 67–84.

J.G. van Maarseveen, *Briefwisseling van Nicolaas Gerard Pierson 1839–1909* (Amsterdam, 1993).

C.A. van Manen, *De Nederlandsche Overzee Trustmaatschappij*, vol. 3 (Amsterdam, 1935).

G. Wärmer, *Das österreichische Kreditwesen* (Vienna, 1936).

F. Weber, 'Central European Banking Between 1850 and 1950', in M. Fase et al. (eds), *How to Write the History of A Bank* (Aldershot, Brookfield, 1995).

F. Weber, Vor dem großen Krach. Die Krise des österreichischen Bankwesens in den zwanziger Jahren, unpubl. habilitation, University of Salzburg, 1991.

F. Weber, 'Universal Banking in Interwar Central Europe', in H. James et al. (eds), *The Role of Banks in the Interwar Economy* (Cambridge, 1991).

W.K. Weiß-Bartenstein, 'Bulgariens Verkehrspolitik und Verkehrswesen', in *Archiv für Eisenbahnwesen*, vol. 38, 1915.

V. Wellhöner, *Großbanken und Großindustrie im Kaiserreich* (Göttingen, 1989).

C. Wetzel, *Die Auswirkungen des Reichsbörsengesetzes von 1896 auf die Effektenbörsen im Deutschen Reich, insbesondere auf die Berliner Fondsbörse* (Münster, 1996).

V. Wheeler-Holohan, *The History of the King's Messengers* (London, 1935).

M. Wirth, *Geschichte der Handelskrisen* (Frankfurt, 1883).

H. Wixforth, *Banken und Schwerindustrie in der Weimarer Republik* (Cologne, Weimar, 1995).

H. Wixforth and D. Ziegler, 'Bankenmacht: Universal Banking and German Industry in Historical Perspective', in Y. Cassis et al. (eds), *The Evolution of Financial Institutions and Markets in Twentieth-century Europe* (Aldershot, 1995), p. 250.

O. Wormser, *Die Frankfurter Börse* (Tübingen, 1919).

H. Yule and A.C. Burnell, *Hobson-Jobson: A Glossary of Colloquial Anglo-Indian Words and Phrases, and of Kindred Terms, Etymological, Historical, Geographical and Discursive* (Calcutta, 1903).

D. Ziegler, 'The Influence of Banking on the Rise and Expansion of Industrial Capitalism in Germany', in A. Teichova et al. (eds.), *Banking, Trade and Industry. Europe, America and Asia from the Thirteenth to the Twentieth Century* (Cambridge, 1997).

A. Zitridis, *The Banking System in Greece* (Athens, 1973).

Index